A LIFE OF JOHN CALVIN

A Life of John Calvin

A Study in the Shaping of Western Culture

ALISTER E. McGRATH

Oxford UK & Cambridge USA

First published 1990

Reprinted 1991

First published in paperback 1993

Blackwell Publishers
108 Cowley Road, Oxford OX4 1JF, UK

238 Main Street,
Cambridge, Massachusetts 02142, USA

British Library Cataloguing in Publication Data

A CIP catalogue record for this book is available from the British Library.

Library of Congress Cataloging in Publication Data

McGrath, Alister E., 1953–
A life of John Calvin : a study in the shaping of Western culture/Alister E. McGrath.
p. cm.
Includes bibliographic references.
ISBN 0-631-18947-5 (pbk)
I. Calvin, John, 1509–1564. 2. Reformation—Biography. 3. Calvin, John, 1509–1564—Influence. 4. Calvinism. 5. Reformed Church—Doctrines. I. Title
BX9418.M29 1990
284'.2'092—dc20 90-31240
[B] CIP

Typeset in Baskerville on 11/12 point
by Photo·graphics, Honiton, Devon
Printed in Great Britain by T. J. Press, Padstow, Cornwall

Contents

List of Illustrations

Plates between 144 and 145

Preface

NO APOLOGY is needed for attempting another general survey of the life and times of John Calvin. The religious, social, economic and cultural issues which focus upon this remarkable individual remain both profound and inexhaustible. Calvin proved to be a seminal figure in European history, changing the outlook of individuals and institutions at the dawn of the modern period, as western civilization began to assume its characteristic form. In addition, our knowledge and understanding of the European Reformation in general, and Calvin in particular, have been considerably deepened during recent years, allowing fresh insights into Calvin's world and his role within it.

It is no longer regarded as appropriate to think of history as the 'biographies of great men'. Nevertheless, certain individuals – such as Calvin, Marx and Lenin – do appear to have exercised sufficient influence over the historical process to lend a certain credibility to the notion. The ideas, outlook and structures developed by Calvin proved capable of generating and sustaining a movement which transcended the limitations of his historical location and personal characteristics. His importance lies primarily, but by no means exclusively, in his being a religious thinker. To describe him as a 'theologian' is proper but misleading, given the modern associations of the term. A theologian is now one who is generally seen to be marginalized as an irrelevance by church and academy alike, whose public is limited to a severely restricted circle of fellow theologians, and whose ideas and methods are generally derived from other intellectual disciplines. The originality, power and influence of Calvin's religious ideas forbid us to speak of him merely as a 'theologian' – though that he certainly was – in much the same way as it is inadequate to refer to Lenin as a mere political theorist. Through his remarkable ability to master languages, media and ideas, his insights into the importance of organization and social structures, and his intuitive grasp of the religious needs and possibilities of his era, Calvin was able to forge an alliance between religious thought and action which made Calvinism a wonder of its age.

To understand at least some of the religious, political, social and economic history of western Europe and North America in the sixteenth and seventeenth centuries, it is arguably necessary to come to terms with the ideas of this thinker, and their creative reinterpretation and diffusion in the writings of his early followers. Through the extraordinary dynamism and brilliance of his colleagues, agents and successors, Calvin's ideas were fashioned into one of the most potent intellectual forces history has known, directly comparable in its influence and pervasiveness to the more recent rise of Marxism. The German sociologist of religion Ernst Troeltsch suggested that it has been at two points only that Christianity has been able to decisively transform human culture and civilisation: during the Middle Ages, through the scholastic synthesis of Thomas Aquinas, and in the early modern period, through Calvinism. To engage with Calvin and his legacy is thus to wrestle with one of the rare moments in modern history when Christianity moulded, rather than accommodated itself to, society.

Although Calvinism possesses a distinctively religious core, it must be stressed that it is not a purely religious movement: like a snowball rolling down an alpine piste, it accumulated additional material and incorporated it into its substance, perhaps obscuring some of the original core material, and thus changing its shape and form as a consequence. Even today, these ideas in some shape or form still exercise a largely unrecognized influence over western culture. In that western capitalism may ultimately rest, at least in part, upon Calvinist foundations, it may reasonably be argued that even Marxism itself may be obliged to enter into dialogue with the Genevan legacy of the west.

To speak of Calvin is to speak of Geneva. While the phrase 'Calvin's Geneva' is laden with potentially misleading implications, perhaps amounting to misunderstandings of the reformer's status and scope for free action within Geneva, it is helpful in that it highlights the close interaction of the man and the city. The impact of Calvin upon the fame and fortune of Geneva, even to the point of creating a mythology with that city at its centre,[1] is a commonplace of history. If Calvin shaped Geneva, however, it is also true that Geneva shaped Calvin. The influence of the city upon the man is delicate and nuanced, and is arguably slight in comparison with the impact of the man upon the city: nevertheless, that influence exists, and is open to historical investigation and theological evaluation. Calvin's insistence that Christianity is not concerned with abstract theorizing, but engages directly with social and political realities, inevitably raises the question of whether the Genevan situation may have assumed a normative status for Calvin's theorizing. In certain limited but significant respects, Geneva may have become Calvin's paradigm for the city of God. Given the importance of this possibility, the present work aims to trace the subtle influence of existing Genevan economic and political concerns and assumptions upon the thought of its leading reformer. Certain central aspects of Calvin's thought may ultimately be a reflection of existing contemporary Genevan policies, practices and assumptions.

It is a pleasure to be able to write such a book in the knowledge that the demonology of the past is in what may fervently be hoped to be terminal decline. The great stereotypes of the past, portraying Calvin as a bloodthirsty dictator and Calvinism as mindless moral rigorism, are – despite their occasional resuscitation in polemical writings – behind us. It is perhaps inevitable that a work of this nature is obliged to engage with a series of myths, some doubtless cherished by those who entertain them, concerning Calvin and his heritage. Thus Stephan Zweig's influential portrayal of Calvin as the great dictator of Geneva, *un homme sans coeur et sans entrailles*, ruling that unfortunate city with a rod of iron, must be judged largely to lack any substantial historical foundation, being generally inconsistent with the brute facts of history and based upon an inadequate understanding of Genevan power structures and decision-making procedures.

Equally, the dismissal of Calvinism or its English manifestation in Puritanism as a religious killjoy, intellectually sterile and devoid of any serious importance for western civilisation, is largely due to the polemical strategies of its contemporary opponents, who were understandably anxious to discredit the movement. The English high church Tory portrayal of Calvinism in these aggressively negative terms is little more than a defensive response to a movement which was perceived – rightly, as the English Civil War, culminating in a Calvinist military victory, demonstrated – as a major threat to the political and religious status quo. Calvinism, with its credible political vision of the City of God, proved to be a major challenge to the vested interests of English church and state in the seventeenth century. The Tory and high Anglican stereotype of the movement, resting upon somewhat flimsy historical foundations, still exercises an unmerited influence over its later critics. As Edmund Morgan points out in his masterly study of the Puritan family

> Contrary to popular impression, the Puritan was no ascetic. If he continually warned against the vanity of the creatures as misused by fallen man, he never praised hair shirts or dry crusts. He liked good food, good drink and homely comforts; and while he laughed at mosquitoes, he found it a real hardship to drink water when the beer ran out. [2]

Nor was Calvinism the enemy of intellectual progress. For the last hundred years, Calvin's attitude to Copernicus' heliocentric theory of the solar system has been the subject of ridicule. In his vigorously polemical *History of the Warfare of Science with Theology* (1896), Andrew Dickson White wrote:

> Calvin took the lead, in his *Commentary on Genesis*, by condemning all who asserted that the earth is not at the centre of the universe. He clinched the matter by the usual reference to the first verse of the ninety-third Psalm, and asked, 'Who will venture to place the authority of Copernicus above that of the Holy Spirit?'

This assertion is slavishly repeated by virtually every subsequent writer on the theme of 'religion and science', such as Bertrand Russell, in his *History of Western Philosophy*. Yet it may be stated categorically that Calvin wrote no such words and expressed no such sentiments in any of his known writings. The assertion that he did is first to be found, characteristically unsubstantiated, in the writings of the nineteenth-century Anglican dean of Canterbury, Frederick William Farrar (1831–1903).[3] Modern treatments of the theme 'Calvin and Science' have, however, been dominated by this fiction. It remains to be seen how many more such myths have become a fixed feature of our perception of Calvin. It is a sad fact of life that he has been grossly misrepresented, and that there still persists a widespread belief that Calvin, and subsequently Calvinism, were woodenly hostile towards the 'new learning' of the natural sciences.

This book is not concerned with praising or condemning Calvin or his cultural legacy, but with establishing the nature and extent of that legacy in the first place. It is an attempt to bring out the vitality of this remarkable character, and to trace the genesis and structure of his ideas and their influence upon western culture. The book has been written in the conviction, not that Calvin is a saint or a rogue, but simply that he is profoundly worthy of study by anyone concerned with the shaping of the modern world in general and western culture in particular. To aid such study, a glossary of technical and historical terms, the frequent use of which is inevitable in a work of this nature, has been provided. It is often impossible to explain these terms in the body of the text, and so the reader is referred to the glossary.

This work owes much to many. My thanks are due to the British Academy for a generous research award to permit me to study the early Swiss Reformation in some depth; to Oxford University for the award of the Denyer and Johnson Travelling Fellowship, allowing me to undertake research on the late Renaissance and early Reformation at a number of European centres; and to Wycliffe Hall, Oxford, for a period of leave from academic responsibilities, during which this research was brought to a close. I am particularly grateful to the following institutions for their hospitality and the free use of their enviable resources: the Biblioteca Nazionale Centrale, the Biblioteca della Facoltà di Lettere e Filosofia, and the Biblioteca Medicea Laurenziana (Florence); the Archives d'Etat, Bibliothèque Publique et Universitaire, and the Institut d'Histoire de la Réformation (Geneva); the Institute of Historical Research (London); the Bodleian Library (Oxford); the Archives Nationales, the Archives de l'Université, the Bibliothèque Nationale, and the Musée de l'Histoire de France (Paris); the Stadtsbibliothek Vadiana (St Gallen); the Archive et Bibliothèque de la Ville and the Bibliothèque Nationale et Universitaire (Strasbourg); the Österreichische Nationalbibliothek and the Universitätsbibliothek (Vienna); the Institut für schweizerische Reformationsgeschichte, the Staatsarchiv, and the Zentralbibliothek (Zurich). I would also like to express particular thanks to Professor Francis Higman, director of the Institut d'Histoire de la Réformation at Geneva, for invaluable criticisms of an earlier draft of this text. What errors of fact and interpretation remain are entirely my own responsibility.

I

Introduction

HIGH IN the Swiss alps, a torrent pours out from the base of the Rhône glacier, eventually to form one of Europe's greatest rivers. Before the Rhône turns south to flow to the Mediterranean, it passes through a lake, at whose western extremity a commercial centre was established in Roman times. Roman settlers, moving northwards into Germany, named the lake *lacus lemannus*, and the trading centre *Genava*. Genava initially had the status of a town (*vicus*), dependent upon the city of Vienne, capital of the immense sprawling territory of the Allobroges.[1] Under the Diocletian administrative reforms of the late second century, Genava was elevated to the status of a city (*civitas*) in Gallia Narbonensis, and lent its name – by then altered to Geneva – to a great medieval diocese. The coveted status of Imperial City was eventually gained through the efforts of one of its bishops, Ardutus, in 1153. In more recent times, too, Geneva has assumed a position of importance in world affairs. The International Committee of the Red Cross was established there in 1864, deriving its familiar symbol by inverting the colours of the Swiss national flag. The Geneva Convention introduced a humanitarian element into modern warfare. Many international organizations have their headquarters in the city. Such is its modern international reputation that Geneva is now widely regarded as the natural setting for disarmament conferences. The hopes of modern international stability, so often dashed and so often revived, tend to centre upon this city.

Yet in the sixteenth century, Geneva was the centre of an international movement which threatened to disrupt and destabilize the established order of western Europe, and which later seemed set to create a radically new social order in North America.

The city became an icon of religious and political subversion. The ideas emanating from Geneva proved to exercise a strange fascination over generations of Europeans, and still retain some of their force today. Just as mention of the word 'Moscow' during the years of the Cold War evoked powerful images of a social, political and economic order which threatened to destroy or overwhelm western civilization, so the word 'Geneva' once evoked the image of a man and his movement, who together conspired to change the face of sixteenth-century Europe, and exercise a powerful influence over times and territories far beyond. That man was John Calvin, and that movement was international Calvinism.

Our story begins in the Europe of the sixteenth century. This Europe must not, however, be confused with the Europe of today. The emergence of modern Europe is to be dated from the eighteenth century, with the establishment of independent political entities, based on mutually exclusive and markedly different nationalities. Nation states then came to be regarded as distinct and totally independent structures, which claimed loyalty from their inhabitants on the basis of a common national identity.[2] The Europe of the sixteenth century was very different. National boundaries were vague, and were supplemented by more tangible and relevant barriers of language, culture and class. A sense of national identity was generally absent: individuals tended to define themselves in relation to a town or region, rather than the greater nation of which they were part. Movement across these ill defined national frontiers was frequent and uncomplicated. Students migrated from one university to another without the need of passport or visa; merchants traversed the great transnational trade routes with the minimum of formalities. Certain twentieth-century institutions, too, like the great multinational corporations, have paid scant regard to the existence of national boundaries. By far the most important institution of this kind during the Middle Ages was the western church, whose organization and influence covered the entire region. This institution was to undergo profound changes in the sixteenth century – and in those changes may be seen mirrored the transformation of Europe itself. Probably by accident rather than design – or perhaps through sheer exhaustion after the Hundred Years War – an equilibrium of power had gradually been established in late medieval Europe, with the church assuming a pivotal role in its maintenance. It was, however, an unstable equilibrium: any disruption of the delicate interplay of its constituent parts could cause it to shudder, perhaps even to crumble. To reform the western church, with all that this would bring in its wake, was thus potentially to restructure western Europe.

As the fifteenth century warily gave way to the sixteenth, the need for reform and renewal of that church was everywhere evident. The western church gave the appearance of being exhausted by the demands of the Middle Ages, which had seen the political power of the church, and especially the papacy, reach previously unknown heights. The church's administrative, legal, financial and diplomatic machinery was well oiled and in good working order. It was certainly true that the Renaissance popes were presiding over a period of moral degeneration, financial intrigue and spectacularly unsuccessful power politics, which seriously challenged the credibility of the church as a spiritual and moral guide. Yet as an institution, the church in western Europe gave every impression of solidity and permanence. Nevertheless, the signs of weariness, of decay, were there. Many in western Europe were convinced that the church had lost its sense of direction. What, it was increasingly asked, had the splendours of the Renaissance papacy to do with the lowly figure of Jesus of Nazareth?

Study after study of the church in western Europe in the closing period of the Middle Ages confirms its gentle descent into a state of degeneration.[3] There was widespread popular dissatisfaction with the absence of clergy and bishops from their parishes and dioceses, with the questionable morality of clerical life, with the low standards of clerical education, with the seeming indifference of the church to the economic and social conditions of the early sixteenth century, and with the apparent absence of spiritual direction within the church. There was a hardening of ecclesiastical arteries through what was widely regarded as overinvolvement in secular affairs. Although proclaiming itself the steward of the values of the City of God, the church demonstrated itself to be firmly enmeshed in the needs, ambitions, desires, pleasures and possessions of the worldly order.

The Pressure for Reform

A number of factors, culminating in the early sixteenth century, led to the growing dissatisfaction with the church in the later Middle Ages. It must be stressed that these factors are not simply religious, but embrace social, political and economic matters. To understand the Reformation, and especially the crucial role played within its drama by John Calvin, it is necessary to appreciate the multifaceted character of its appeal to the people of western Europe in the early sixteenth century, particularly in France.

The Growth in Adult Literacy

By the dawn of the sixteenth century adult literacy was increasingly common, made possible by the development of printing, the growth of the paper industry, and the growing appeal of the humanist movement. In the early Middle Ages, the charmed circle of the literate was virtually exclusively clerical. Written material took the form of manuscripts which had to be painstakingly copied out by hand, and were generally confined to the libraries of monasteries on account of their scarcity. In order to save precious parchment, words were abbreviated, making manuscripts difficult to decipher. Humanism, however, made adult literacy a social achievement, a skill which opened the way to social refinement and advancement. The Renaissance style of handwriting was both elegant and legible, contrasting sharply with the crabbed scrawl of the Gothic script favoured by the scholastics. With the advent of printing and the development of new paper-making industries, it became possible for an educated lay person to obtain and understand works which hitherto had been the exclusive preserve of the clergy. As the newly emerging professional classes began to gain power in the cities, gradually wresting control from the old patrician families, they brought to their practice and interpretation of the Christian faith much the same critical acumen and professionalism they employed in their secular careers. The clerical monopoly on literacy was thus decisively broken.[4] This development opened the way for an increasingly critical lay assessment of the abilities of the clergy, and growing lay confidence in religious matters.

An examination of the personal libraries of sixteenth-century French bourgeois demonstrates the importance of the new lay awareness in matters religious as much as it does a growth in literacy, and suggests the dependence of the former on the latter. Most patrician families in fifteenth-century Florence owned copies of the New Testament. Lefèvre's French New Testament of 1523, addressed 'à tous les chrestiens et chrestiennes', along with his French Psalter of 1524, were widely read throughout France, and were even distributed free of charge within the diocese of Meaux.[5] Copies of these works, along with the New Testament commentaries of Erasmus, Philip Melanchthon and Lefèvre himself, are frequently to be found jostling for space in bourgeois libraries.[6]

The growth of this new lay confidence may be seen reflected in the attention paid to Erasmus' *Enchiridion*, or 'Handbook of the Christian Soldier', which appeared in 1503.[7] This work was reprinted in 1509, and entered its third edition in 1515. From that moment onwards, it became a cult work, apparently going through twenty-three editions in the next six years. It was devoured by educated laity throughout western Europe. The work developed the radical and – to lay minds – attractive idea that the church could be reformed and renewed by its laity. The clergy may assist the laity in their understanding of their faith, but do not have any superior status. Religion is an inner spiritual affair, in which the individual believer seeks to deepen his or her knowledge of God by the reading of scripture. Significantly, the *Enchiridion* plays down the role of the institutional church, in order to emphasize the importance of the individual believer.

It is now known that the fifteenth century, far from witnessing a decline in religious belief, actually saw a remarkable growth in popular religion. The growing literature in the late fifteenth and early sixteenth centuries listing complaints about the church[8] – once thought to point to a decline in the influence of religion in the period – is now thought to point to a growing ability and willingness on the part of the laity to criticize the church, with a view to reforming it. For example, the period 1450–1520 saw a considerable increase in popular religion in Germany. Just about every conceivable objective criterion – the number of masses endowed, the fashion for forming religious brotherhoods, the donations to religious charities, the building of new churches, the number of pilgrimages made, and the growth in popular religious literature – points to a remarkable growth in popular interest in religion.[9]

A renewed interest in the Christian faith on the part of more academic individuals, linked with a perception of the need to refashion and renew it if it was to regain its vitality, is also evident from the final decade of the fifteenth century onwards. The dynamism unleashed by the remarkably sudden (and still largely unexplained) development of Spanish mysticism in the 1490s was harnessed through the reforms instigated by the Spanish catholic church under Cardinal Ximénez de Cisneros, leading to a new concern for religious education and a revival of religious vocations in Spain. The University of Alcalá and the Complutensian Polyglot (a multilingual version of the Bible) were perhaps the most tangible results of these reforms. There was renewed interest in the writings of St Paul and Augustine in Italian humanist circles, reflecting the great humanist desire to return *ad fontes* – back to the original sources of the Christian faith – in order to drink from the spring of the Christian tradition freshly at its source, rather than have to tolerate the polluted and stagnant waters of the later Middle Ages. A river was purest at its source: why should anyone be obliged to read the New Testament through a filter of obscurantist medieval commentators, when it could be read directly, in its original language?

The Phenomenon of Personal Religion

The rise of individual consciousness, perhaps one of the most significant contributions of the Italian Renaissance to western European self-perceptions at the dawn of the sixteenth century, was the occasion of a new concern to relate Christianity to the needs of the individual. A purely institutional Christianity, which defined itself in external and institutional terms (attendance at church, formal acceptance of ecclesiastical teachings, and so forth) was inadequate for this new period. One of the most subtle and significant developments in the self-understanding of Christianity began to take place, as a religion which had grown used to expressing and defining itself in external forms began to rediscover its appeal to the inward consciousness. The Christian writers of the Renaissance recognized the need to implant the gospel firmly in the experiential world of the individual, as something which could and should be personally and inwardly appropriated. The age-old appeal of both Paul and Augustine to the introspective conscience of the individual[10] led to these writers being reappropriated with fresh interest, whether in the sonnets of Petrarch or the new religious writings of Renaissance theologians, preachers and biblical commentators.[11]

A generation of thinkers subsequently rose to the challenge on the eve of the Reformation. In Paris, Lefèvre d'Etaples explored the relevance of Paul's understanding of faith for the individual. At Oxford, John Colet stressed the importance of a personal encounter with the risen Christ in the Christian life. In the Low Countries, Erasmus won the hearts and minds of the educated elite of Europe with the reforming programme outlined in the *Enchiridion*, with its stress on a personally assimilated and inward faith, which Erasmus contrasted unfavourably with the concern for external matters characteristic of the institutional church. In Italy, the movement often known as 'catholic evangelicalism' or 'evangelism', with its stress on the question of personal salvation, became firmly established within the church, even penetrating deeply within its hierarchy, without being regarded as in any way heretical.

The origins of these movements, it must be stressed, owed nothing to Luther. While Luther was still an obscure monk, patiently lecturing to small audiences in one of the most insignificant universities of Europe, the famous and the great were breathing the fresh air of the New Testament once more. A new and widespread emphasis upon personally assimilated religion and a new interest in the writings of Paul and Augustine appear to be characteristic of many influential groups and individuals in the first two decades of the sixteenth century. Such was the odium which subsequently became attached to the name of Martin Luther that similarities between the ideas of these groups and individuals and those of Luther came to be treated as evidence of heresy on the part of the former, rather than orthodoxy on the part of the latter. Lefèvre at Paris, Guillaume Briçonnet at Meaux, and the *alumbrados* (a group of mystical writers) in Spain, only came under suspicion of heresy once Luther's views became known. However positively Luther's contribution to the Reformation is to be evaluated, it must be conceded that he had the universally negative effect of causing authentically catholic and orthodox views, potentially capable of injecting new vitality into a tired church, to be regarded as heretical. By generating a climate of suspicion, Luther rendered a grave disservice to his age.

This renewal in both popular and intellectual religion owed little to the ecclesiastical establishment, which increasingly came to be seen as exploiting the phenomenon of lay religion without contributing to it. Popular religion, for example, centred on the affairs of rural communities, reflecting their rhythms and seasons. The agrarian needs of these rural communities – such as haymaking and harvesting – were firmly enmeshed in popular religious cults. Thus in the French diocese of Meaux, we find religious cults invoking the saints in order to ward off animal and infant diseases, the plague and eye trouble, or to ensure that young women find appropriate husbands.[12] Perhaps the most important element of late medieval popular religion was a cluster of beliefs and practices concerning death, in which participation by a priest was indispensable.[13] The expenses attending such cults of the dead were considerable, a fact reflected in the rise of religious fraternities dedicated to the provision of the appropriate rites of passage for their members. In times of economic hardship, anti-clerical sentiment was an inevitability: the clergy came to be seen as profiting from the anxiety of the impoverished living concerning their dead kinsfolk.

In Germany, the indulgence traffic was viewed by Luther as a morally outrageous, and theologically questionable, exploitation of the natural affections of the common people for their dead. His Ninety-Five Theses (31 October 1517) were a direct criticism of those who asserted that a dead soul might be freed instantly from purgatory on payment of an appropriate amount to an authorized ecclesiastical tradesman. Insult was added to injury: the fees paid by Germans eventually found their way to Italy, to finance the extravagances of the Renaissance papacy. Luther took particular exception to the advertising copy of Johann Tetzel, promoting indulgences:

> As soon as the coin in the coffer rings
> The soul from purgatory springs!

Luther's doctrine of justification by faith alone obviated the need for purgatory and indulgences: the dead could rest in peace on account of their faith, which made them right with God, and not on account of the payment of a sweetener to the church.[14] In France, an indulgence campaign had also been arranged by Leo X and Francis I in 1515, with a view to financing a crusade; in 1518 the Parisian faculty of theology, however, protested against some of the superstitious ideas to which this campaign gave rise. It condemned as 'false and scandalous' the teaching that 'whoever puts into the collection for the crusade one teston or the value of one soul in purgatory sets that soul free immediately, and it goes unfailingly to paradise.'[15]

Equally, the rise of evangelical views – whether of Erasmian or monastic origins – led to the ecclesiastical establishment being viewed as reactionary, hostile to the new learning and threatened by both its progress and its emphasis upon the personal appropriation of faith. Literature began to appear in the 1520s, suggesting that clergy had a vested interest in retaining the old and lax ways, which made little demands on them as teachers, as spiritual guides, or as moral examples or agents. Rabelais was not alone in exposing and deriding monastic abuses, nor was Erasmus in criticizing the aridness of scholasticism and the inadequacies of the clergy.

The Growth of Anti-Clericalism

Among the more significant elements in our understanding of the background to the Reformation is the new contempt with which clergy were viewed by an increasingly literate and articulate laity. The phenomenon of anti-clericalism was widespread, and not specifically linked to any part of Europe. In part, the phenomenon reflects the low quality of the rank and file clergy. In Renaissance Italy, it was common for parish priests to have had virtually no training; what little they knew, they gleaned from watching, helping and imitating. Diocesan visitations regularly revealed priests who were illiterate, or had apparently permanently mislaid their breviaries. The poor calibre of the parish clergy reflected their low social status: in early sixteenth-century Milan, chaplains had incomes lower than those of unskilled labourers. Many resorted to horse and cattle trading to make ends meet.[16] In rural France during the same period, the lower clergy enjoyed roughly the same social status as vagabonds: their exemption from taxation, prosecution in civil courts and compulsory military service apart, they were virtually indistinguishable from other itinerant beggars of the period.[17]

The fiscal privileges enjoyed by clergy were a source of particular irritation, especially in times of economic difficulty. In the French diocese of Meaux, which would become a centre for reforming activists in the years 1521–46, the clergy were exempted from all forms of taxation, including charges relating to the provisioning and garrisoning of troops – which provoked considerable local resentment. In the diocese of Rouen, there was popular outcry over the windfall profits made by the church by selling grain at a period of severe shortage.[18] Clerical immunity from prosecution in civil courts further isolated the clergy from the people. In France, the subsistence crises of the 1520s played a major role in the consolidation of anti-clerical attitudes. In his celebrated study of Languedoc, Le Roy Ladurie pointed out that the 1520s witnessed a reversal of the process of expansion and recovery which had been characteristic of the two generations since the ending of the Hundred Years War.[19] From that point onwards, a crisis began to develop, taking the form of plague, famine, and migration of the rural poor to the cities in search of food and employment.

A similar pattern has now been identified for the period in most of France north of the Loire.[20] This subsistence crisis focused popular attention on the gross disparity between the fate of the lower classes and the nobles and ecclesiastical establishment.

The vast majority of late Renaissance bishops in France were drawn from the nobility,[21] a trend illustrated by diocese after diocese. In Meaux, the higher echelons of the ecclesiastical establishment were drawn from the urban patriciate, as were the senior clergy throughout the Brie.[22] A similar pattern can be established at Rouen,[23] as it can at John Calvin's birthplace, Noyon, where the de Hangest family monopolized ecclesiastical affairs, exercising substantial powers of patronage as well as providing most of the bishops of the diocese for more than a quarter of a century.[24] In the province of Languedoc, the senior clergy were generally outsiders, often nobility imposed upon the dioceses by royal patronage. Rarely resident within their dioceses, these clergy regarded their spiritual and temporal charges as little more than sources of unearned income, useful for furthering political ambitions elsewhere. The noble background and status of the episcopacy and senior clergy served to distance them from the artisans and peasants, and to insulate them from the economic subsistence crisis of the 1520s. It is this growing tension during the 1520s in the relationship between the upper clergy – largely based in the towns and cities – and the rural population which constitutes the backdrop to the origins of the Reformation in France.[25]

A Crisis in Authority within the Church

To speak of a 'crisis of authority' within the late medieval church[26] appears to indicate a falling victim to the tendency to resort to tired and outworn clichés. Nevertheless, it is used advisedly: the phrase conveys neatly an aspect of society in general and religious life in particular in the later Middle Ages which did much initially to promote the development of, and subsequently to inhibit effective measures against, the Reformation. Two elements may be discerned within this crisis. In the first place, it was far from clear who had authority to speak on behalf of the church; in the second, through an unfortunate amalgam of theological incomprehension, political confusion and military impotence, the church found itself increasingly unable to enforce orthodoxy (assuming that agreement could ever be reached on what 'orthodoxy' designated. If a novel theological opinion developed, who was to determine whether it was consistent with the teachings of the church?)

The rapid expansion of the university sector throughout western Europe in the late fourteenth and fifteenth centuries led to an increased number of theology faculties, with a corresponding increase in the number of theological treatises produced. Then, as now, theologians had to do something to justify their existence. These works frequently explored new ideas. But what was the status of these ideas? The general failure to draw a clear distinction between theological opinions and church teaching, between private opinion and communal doctrine, caused considerable confusion. It is quite possible that Martin Luther may have confused one theological opinion with the official teaching of the church, and initiated his programme of reform on the basis of this misunderstanding. The historian may chide him for this lapse in comprehension; yet the Saxon reformer appears to have been typical of the many who were bewildered and confused by the vastness of the late medieval theological panorama. And who would distinguish between opinion and doctrine? The pope? an ecumenical council? a professor of theology? Failure to clarify such crucial questions contributed in no small manner to the crisis of authority in the late medieval church. In France, as elsewhere in Europe, a 'long period of magnificent religious anarchy' (Lucien Febvre) set in.

Confusion over the official teaching of the church contributed considerably to the origins of Luther's programme of reform in Germany. Of central importance to Luther was the doctrine of justification – the question of how an individual enters into a relationship with God.[27] The most recent known authoritative pronouncement on the part of a recognized ecclesiastical body relating to this doctrine dated from 418, more than a millennium before the Reformation – and its confused and outdated statements did little to clarify the position of the church on the matter in 1518. It seemed to Luther that the church of his day had lapsed into Pelagianism, an unacceptable understanding of how an individual entered into fellowship with God. The church, he believed, taught that individuals could gain favour and acceptance in the sight of God on account of their personal achievements and status, thus negating the whole idea of grace. Luther may well have been mistaken in this apprehension – but there was such confusion within the church of his day that none was able to enlighten him on its authoritative position on the matter. Even within the papal sovereign enclave at Avignon, an anarchy of ideas prevailed.

'Everyone has his own opinion,' wrote Boniface Amerbach, who added further to the chaos during the 1520s by promoting the ideas of the 'excellent doctor Martin' within this papal stronghold.

More significant, however, in relation to the Reformation as it concerns John Calvin was the growing inability of the church to enforce orthodoxy. In Germany, the complex network of diocesan and provincial synods – charged with the identification and suppression of heresy – failed to meet, let alone take decisive action, in the period during which Luther's views were beginning to attract attention. The attempt by the French authorities to suppress the Waldensians (*Vaudois*) in the spring of 1487 was not particularly successful, dispersing this allegedly heretical group rather than eliminating it.

Most threatening of all was the printing press. The traditional medieval boundaries were impotent against the printed word. It was one thing to legislate against the circulation of unorthodox books; it was quite another to detect them, and prevent them being read. As the French authorities devised increasingly comprehensive measures to prevent the importation of seditious printed material from abroad, publishers became increasingly adept at disguising the origins of their wares. Books printed at Geneva (and hence eventually banned completely in France) disguised their origins with false addresses of their printers, or even by mimicking typefaces known to be used by French printers.[28]

The dramatic victory of Francis I over the combined papal and Swiss forces at Marignano in September 1515 established him as a force to be reckoned with in Italian affairs, and enhanced his authority over the French church. The ensuing Concordat of Bologna (1516) gave Francis the right to appoint all the senior clergy of the French church, effectively weakening the direct papal control over it. Francis' gradual move towards absolutism, although temporarily interrupted by his defeat at the battle of Pavia (1525) and subsequent imprisonment at Madrid, led to a corresponding decrease in papal influence over French affairs, whether state or ecclesiastical. As a result, reforming movements within France were treated as a matter concerning Francis I rather than the pope. Had the pope wished to intervene in the affairs of the French church, a formidable series of diplomatic and legal obstacles awaited him. Having just defeated the pope in battle, Francis showed relatively little interest in defending papal interests in France, save when they happened to coincide with those of the French monarchy.

The Concordat of Bologna points to a fundamental difference between the German and French ecclesiastical situations on the eve of the Reformation. As the German ecclesiastical grievance literature makes clear, intense resentment was felt against the pope. In part, this reflected an incipient German nationalism, marked by a resentment of all things Italian. It also reflected popular irritation at the fact that ecclesiastical revenues (including the proceeds of indulgence sales) were destined for Rome, and the maintenance of the somewhat extravagant lifestyles, building programmes and political adventures of the Renaissance popes. The ruling classes of Germany resented the manner in which their local political authority was compromised through papal interference in ecclesiastical and political affairs. In many ways, Luther's reforming programme made an appeal to (perhaps even to the point of a crude exploitation of) German nationalism and anti-papalism, allowing the Reformation to ride on the crest of a wave of popular anti-papal sentiment. The Concordat of Bologna, however, largely defused anti-papal sentiment in France. The centralization of political and ecclesiastical authority in the person of the French monarch – so fundamental a programme of the absolutist monarchial policy pursued by Francis I and his immediate successors – created a power structure in which the pope was conspicuous by his absence. If anti-papalism fuelled the German Reformation, its French equivalent had to draw on other sources for its growth.

These, then, are some of the forces at work within the western European church and society at the dawn of the sixteenth century. In retrospect, historians have characterized the period as 'Europe on the eve of the Reformation'. In fact, of course, this insight was largely denied to those living at the time, who did not even think of themselves as European, let alone as living on the eve of some imminent Reformation. Indeed, contemporary writings give little hint of any real awareness of the social, political and religious upheaval which lay ahead, despite the routine prophetic intimations of some.

It was into this world that the second son of Gérard Cauvin was born on 10 July 1509. He would have been baptized Jehan at the church of Sainte-Godeberte a few days later, although we possess no record of this ceremony. The English-speaking world remembers Jehan Cauvin by its version of his Latinized name – Johannes Calvinus – John Calvin. Of his childhood, we know virtually nothing with any degree of certainty, despite the diligence of his early seventeenth-century biographers, who scoured the Noyon cathedral and chapter registers for mention of his name and interviewed local *noyonnais* in the hope that they would recollect something of Gérard Cauvin's son from the mists of a distant past. The genuine historical substance of those memories probably amounts to little more than platitudes – 'a clever boy, that Jehan Cauvin'.[29] Here, as throughout his career, a curious silence resonates through history concerning the personality of Calvin. Of the intellectual stimulus he injected into the history of ideas we know much, yet of the historical person who generated them we know tantalizingly little. As a human being, Calvin remains an enigma.

The Genesis of an Enigma

To suggest that Calvin represents something of an historical enigma may initially appear absurd. Do we not know more concerning him than of many figures of the sixteenth century? Before beginning historical analysis and reconstruction of Calvin's remarkable career, however, it is only proper to draw attention to the fact that we know considerably less about him, especially his early period, than we would like. His greatest bequest to western civilization was his ideas and the literary forms in which they were expounded. Indeed, more than one historian has suggested parallels between Calvin and Lenin, in that both were possessed of a remarkable degree of theoretical vision and organizing genius.[30] Both provided theoretical foundations for revolutionary movements which depended upon precisely such a foundation for their organization, direction and ultimate success. Calvin himself, however, as the human figure of flesh and blood behind these ideas, remains elusive. The reasons for this are not difficult to discern, and are perhaps best appreciated by comparing Calvin with the great Saxon reformer, Martin Luther.

In the first place, we possess an abundance of material from Luther's prolific pen, dating from the period prior to his emergence as a major reformer. His career as a reformer may be dated with reference to his Ninety-Five Theses concerning indulgences (31 October 1517), the Leipzig Disputation of June–July 1519, and the three reforming treatises of 1520. By 1520, Luther was firmly established as a popular charismatic reformer. Underlying this vocation, however, was a set of religious ideas which had evolved prior to his public activity. In the years 1513–17, Luther had been engaged in theological teaching at the University of Wittenberg, during the course of which he wrestled with the ideas which were destined to exercise so great an influence over subsequent events. We possess most of his writings, in one form or another, for those formative years, enabling us to trace the development of these foundational religious ideas.

In the case of Calvin, however, we are confronted with a near-total absence of material from his own pen relating to his formative period. The origins of his career as a reformer may be dated from some point in late 1533 or early 1534; it is not at all clear precisely when. His commentary on Seneca's *De clementia*, which appeared in April 1532, gives away little concerning its author, save for his erudition and possible youthful ambitions as a humanist scholar. The reason for this dearth of material is not difficult to discern. Relations between the French crown and evangelical activists had been steadily deteriorating during the early 1530s. In the early morning of Sunday 18 October 1534, the thundercloud which had been gathering for some time finally broke, with the 'Affair of the Placards'.[31] Placards vigorously denouncing catholic religious practices, composed by the pamphleteer Antoine Marcourt, were posted in prominent places throughout the kingdom of France, including the antechamber to the king's bedchamber at Amboise.

Stung by these events, Francis I was moved to instigate a long-threatened series of repressive measures against evangelicals within France,[32] making it inadvisable for those with reforming views to draw attention to the fact. This conclusion had already been drawn in November 1533 by John Calvin, who fled Paris for the relative safety of Angoulême the day after Nicolas Cop – newly installed as rector – delivered an inflammatory All Saints' Day oration at the University of Paris. As we shall indicate, Cop's address, which seemed to advocate evangelical views, aroused considerable opposition from more conservative elements. Calvin, possibly suspected of writing the address (see pp. 64–6), deemed it wise to get out of Paris as quickly as possible, a course of action amply justified by subsequent events. As his biographers emphasize, it was a close escape:[33] within hours, the police had searched his rooms and confiscated his personal papers. Those personal papers, which would have unquestionably shed invaluable light upon the development of Calvin's thought at this important phase, have never been traced. We are thus forced to treat his formative period as an enigma. Reluctant to be constrained by this lack of evidence, however, some accounts of his early years appear to have fallen victim to the temptation to present historical inference as historical fact. Even Doumergue, who rightly notes that at least part of Calvin's career must be conceded to represent 'une énigme chronologique',[34] is prone to accept the inferences of his historical authorities rather than attempt their critical reconstruction.

In the second place, Luther is exceptionally generous with autobiographical references, which may be found scattered throughout his writings. Perhaps the most famous of these is the 'autobiographical fragment' of 1545, written in the year before his death. This piece of writing serves as an introduction to the first edition of Luther's collected Latin works, in which he introduces himself to his readers. In the course of this preface, he describes in some detail his personal background, the development of his religious ideas, and the manner in which the crisis leading to the genesis of the Lutheran Reformation unfolded. While the personal reminiscences of old men are notoriously unreliable, Luther's historical recollection appears accurate, in so far as it may be verified. The manner in which he suggests his religious ideas (upon which his programme of reform would be based) evolved may also be checked against his writings from the formative period of his development.[35] Calvin, however, appears to have been reticent to introduce any self-reference in his writings. It is possible that a passage in the *Reply to Sadoleto* (1539), in which an evangelical spokesman describes his break with the medieval church, may be autobiographical;[36] no such claim, however, is actually made by Calvin. The explicitly autobiographical section of the preface to the 1557 *Commentary on the Psalms*[37] is tantalizingly brief, and at points difficult to interpret. In his sermons, Calvin often speaks in the first person – but cannot necessarily be concluded to disclose much about himself in so doing.[38] His personal modesty inhibited him from the reflections and reminiscences upon which so much historical reconstruction depends.

The historical reconstruction of Calvin's complex personality has been considerably hindered by the perseverance of the intensely hostile portrait of the reformer due to Jerome Bolsec, with whom Calvin crossed swords in 1551. Disgruntled over the episode, Bolsec published his *Vie de Calvin* at Lyons in June 1577. Calvin, according to Bolsec, was irredeemably tedious and malicious, bloodthirsty and frustrated. He treated his own words as if they were the word of God, and allowed himself to be worshipped as God. In addition to frequently falling victim to his homosexual tendencies, he had a habit of indulging himself sexually with any female within walking distance. According to Bolsec, Calvin resigned his benefices at Noyon on account of the public exposure of his homosexual activities. Bolsec's biography makes much more interesting reading than those of Théodore de Bèze or Nicolas Colladon; nevertheless, his work rests largely upon unsubstantiated anonymous oral reports deriving from 'trustworthy individuals' (*personnes digne de foy*), which modern scholarship has found of questionable merit. Despite this, Bolsec's reconstruction of Calvin has found its way into many less sympathetic modern portrayals of the reformer's life and actions, with an increasingly hazy dividing line being drawn between fact and fiction. The Bolsec myth, like so many other myths concerning Calvin, lives on as a sacred tradition through uncritical repetition,[39] despite its evident lack of historical foundation.

Nevertheless, it is probably fair to suggest that Calvin was not a particularly attractive person, lacking the wit, humour and warmth which made Luther so entertaining at dinner parties. Calvin's persona, as it emerges from his writings, is that of a somewhat cold and detached individual, increasingly inclined towards tetchiness and irritability as his health declined, and prone to launch into abusive personal attacks on those with whom he disagreed, rather than dealing primarily with their ideas. In the year of his death, he wrote to the physicians of Montpellier, describing the presenting symptoms of the illnesses which were taking their toll of his health. Significantly, some of these are consistent with migraine headaches and an irritable bowel condition – both recognized symptoms of stress. It is impossible to determine whether the exceptionally stressful situations which Calvin had to face, especially during the early 1550s, contributed to this condition, or whether he was endemically vulnerable to stress on account of some personality trait. Nevertheless, despite his reluctance to speak of himself, it is clear that he was an unhappy man, with whom it is difficult for the modern reader to feel any great bond of sympathy. It is very easy to be predisposed to a hostile attitude towards him.

Why should Calvin have been so reluctant to project himself? The key to his complex personality lies in his understanding of his calling. In a rare moment of personal disclosure, he made clear his passionate belief that he had been set aside by God for a specific purpose. Reflecting upon his career, he could discern the hidden hand of God, he believed, directing his life at crucial moments. He considered that, despite his personal worthlessness, God had called him, changed the course of his life, directed him to Geneva, and conferred upon him the office of pastor and preacher of the gospel.[40] Whatever authority Calvin possessed he understood to derive from God rather than his own innate talents and abilities. He was but an instrument in the hand of God. It must be stressed that Calvin shares the common Reformation emphasis, given expression in the Lutheran doctrine of justification by faith and the Reformed doctrine of election without reference to foreseen merit (*ante praevisa merita*), on the sinfulness and worthlessness of fallen humanity. That God should choose Calvin was an expression of God's mercy and generosity, rather than of any merit or personal qualities that Calvin might possess. To suggest that his sense of divine calling reflects his personal arrogance indicates a singular lack of familiarity with the spirituality of the Reformation.

It is this understanding of his calling which underpins the apparent tensions in our knowledge of Calvin's personality. A timid and withdrawn character, he was nonetheless capable of a courage bordering on intransigence, a refusal to compromise, when he believed the will of God to be at stake. Willing to be mocked as a person (although often deeply wounded as a result), Calvin was not prepared to allow that ridicule to be transferred from himself as an individual to the cause and the God he believed he was serving. Above all, he appears to have been convinced that he was but an instrument through which God could work; a mouthpiece through which God might speak. He viewed his personality as a potential obstacle to these divine actions, and appears to have cultivated personal modesty in response.

The reader must therefore be alerted from the outset to the difficulties attending any historical reconstruction of Calvin's career and personality, and the natural – and thoroughly understandable – tendency to adopt a hostile attitude towards him. In what follows, we shall attempt to use the resources now at the disposal of historians of the late Renaissance to build up as plausible a picture as possible of the religious, social, political and intellectual forces which shaped some of the worlds that Calvin inhabited, and subsequently changed. There are, however, significant gaps in our knowledge. Calvin was a remarkably private individual, who chose to deny the historian material which would have illuminated the shadows of his history.[41] It is thus inevitable that he emerges as something of a colourless figure, a man whose innermost thoughts, attitudes and ambitions are largely denied to us. Unsatisfied with the resulting monochrome sketch, some historians have fallen to the perennial temptation to expand the brevities of history. While such an attitude is understandable, its dangers must immediately be recognized: the portrait may reflect hidden presuppositions on the part of the precommitted historian, whose tinted spectacles may even deny us access to the historical Calvin.[42]

Calvin's place in human history rests largely upon his ideas. It is therefore essential, not merely to indicate what those ideas might be, but to allow the reader access to the intellectual traditions which may have played a part in shaping them. The two chapters which follow are concerned with identifying those intellectual traditions – the texts, the methods, and the ideas which Calvin may have drawn upon to forge his new outlook upon the world. We must thus tell the tale of three cities and their universities: Paris, Orléans and Bourges.

2

Paris: The Formation of a Mind

Paris is curiously modest about its connections with Calvin, perhaps reflecting a certain degree of ambivalence over the merits of his impact on French history. Among the few tangible acknowledgements of that connection is an inscription on the façade of the Bibliothèque Sainte-Geneviève, facing the Panthéon. There, inscribed among a list of leading intellectual and cultural figures which includes both Erasmus and Rabelais, may be found the name of the French reformer. The library stands on the site of the medieval Collège de Montaigu, an institution suppressed at the time of the French Revolution, and demolished shortly afterwards. It is the memory of this long-vanished college, and its distinguished alumni, which is preserved amidst the dense traffic of modern Paris.

Uncertainties concerning Calvin's Paris Period

It has become part of the received tradition of Calvin scholarship that Calvin went up to the University of Paris for the first time in 1523 at the age of fourteen, initially attending the Collège de La Marche, before moving on to the Collège de Montaigu.[1] The third-century writer Cyprian of Carthage, however, warns us that ancient traditions may simply be old mistakes; unfortunately, it seems highly likely that this confident assertion of Calvin biographers – which borders on a sacred tradition – concerning the date of his arrival at Paris and the college he first attended may have to be questioned as a considerable overinterpretation of the evidence.

The unqualified assertions of the vast majority of Calvin's biographers that he went to Paris aged fourteen are ultimately based upon a short paper, first published in 1621 by the local historian Jacques Desmay. Desmay noted an entry in the Noyon chapter registers for 5 August 1523, to the effect that Gérard Cauvin had been given permission to send his son Jean – we shall now use the modern version of his name – away from Noyon until 1 October of that same year.[2] No mention is made of either the city or the university of Paris. Cauvin's reasons for wishing Jean to leave Noyon are explicitly stated as a desire that his son might escape an outbreak of plague then afflicting the town. Desmay's inference is that this was a convenient moment for Calvin to begin his studies at Paris; no such conclusion is, however, warranted on the basis of the register entry itself. Indeed, if Calvin possessed anything even approaching the precocious intelligence with which his biographers credit him, he would probably have been capable of the university curriculum by the age of twelve, if his Latin was good enough: by the standards of the period, fourteen could possibly have been considered a late age to begin such an education.[3] In 1598 the faculty of arts at Paris, presumably responding to an unwelcome spate of precocious young students, was obliged to lay down that the minimum age at which formal studies might be begun was ten years. The fact, however, is that we simply do not know with any degree of certainty when Calvin went up to Paris.

Other possibilities certainly exist. On 19 May 1521 Jacques Regnard, secretary to the bishop of Noyon, reported to the cathedral chapter that, following the resignation of Michel Courtin, Calvin had been given a chaplaincy at La Gésine.[4] He would hold this chaplaincy until 1529, when he resigned it, only to take it up again in 1531. He finally resigned from the post in May 1534. Pierre Imbart de la Tour suggested that the award of this chaplaincy was the essential prerequisite to a university education – effectively functioning as an educational grant – and thus that Calvin went up to Paris later that same year, aged eleven or twelve. Once more, it is possible that this may represent an overinterpretation of the evidence. It does, however, serve to indicate how slender is the documentary evidence for our knowledge of Calvin's early period.

There is no compelling evidence, either, that Calvin was ever a member of the Collège de La Marche before moving on to the Collège de Montaigu. In the first edition of his *Vie de Calvin* (1564), Théodore de Bèze omits any reference to La Marche in his very brief account of Calvin's Paris period. However, in a reference in this same biography to the celebrated pedagogue Mathurin Cordier, whose educational skills Calvin admired enormously, de Bèze speaks of Cordier as 'his regent at the Collège de Sainte-Barbe at Paris in his youth'.[5] Although this does not necessarily imply that Calvin attended the Collège de Sainte-Barbe before moving on to Montaigu, it points to the existence of an early tradition within Calvin's circle which omits reference to the Collège de La Marche in favour of Sainte-Barbe. De Bèze's statement could be taken to imply simply that Calvin attended Mathurin's classes during the period in which Mathurin was a regent at Sainte-Barbe (that is to say, it is Cordier, not Calvin, who is associated with Sainte-Barbe). It must be remembered, however, that de Bèze wrote this biography of Calvin in some haste,[6] fearing the circulation of less respectful versions of events from other quarters unless he acted with expedition: nevertheless, it gives every indication of being at least partly based upon his recollection of Calvin's personal reminiscences.

A year later, a second biography of Calvin appeared, written by the lawyer Nicolas Colladon. This biography provided considerably more detail concerning Calvin's Paris period, enlarging de Bèze's somewhat scanty narrative. It is here that we encounter for the first time the suggestion that Calvin initially attended the Collège de La Marche.[7] It is, however, difficult to establish the identity and reliability of Colladon's sources. Whatever his considerable merits may have been, they are perhaps not best judged from his skills as Calvin's biographer, particularly in relation to the enigma of Calvin's life prior to 1534. Colladon informs us, to note but one example, that Calvin wrote his commentary on Seneca's *De clementia* 'when he was only about twenty-four':[8] the work actually appeared in April 1532, when Calvin was twenty-two. Nevertheless, Colladon's account of Calvin's Paris years became accepted as normative, for reasons which are ultimately impossible to establish. When de Bèze revised his biography of Calvin a decade later, he omitted his earlier reference to Sainte-Barbe, harmonizing his account of the Paris period with Colladon's statements concerning La Marche.[9] The definitive and official version of Calvin's Paris university affiliations was thus created.

We possess no statement whatsoever from Calvin himself concerning which Paris college he attended prior to Montaigu – if, indeed, he ever attended one. The early biographies clearly imply that his primary affiliation at Paris was Montaigu. The reference to a period at Sainte-Barbe or La Marche, followed by a move to Montaigu, is difficult to explain within the conventions of the University of Paris as we know them. Calvin does, however, explicitly refer to Cordier as his teacher during his time in Paris, without specifically linking him with any college. We know that Cordier was employed as a pedagogue by half a dozen or so *collèges de plein exercice*; in his personal recollections of his Paris period, published on 6 February 1564 (in other words, before Calvin's death and the subsequent biographies of de Bèze and Colladon), Cordier listed those colleges as including Reims, Lisieux and Navarre, as well as both La Marche and Sainte-Barbe.[10] Such multiple affiliation of members of the teaching faculty was not out of the ordinary at Paris in the early sixteenth century: for example, in 1512 Alexis de Rantilly was a *bursarius* in theology at the Collège de Navarre, a regent in arts at the Collège de Bourgogne, and resident at the Collège de Tréguier. It is thus considerably more difficult than might be anticipated to refute those who suggest that Calvin began his Parisian period with a spell at Sainte-Barbe.[11] In fact, as we shall suggest below, it is much more probable that confusion over his reference to Cordier may have led to the origins of the puzzling belief that Calvin attended another college before Montaigu.

The formal transference of students between colleges at Paris was a not uncommon occurrence in the early sixteenth century. As far as can be established, this invariably happened for one of two reasons. In the first place, a student at one college might be awarded a bursary (or similar academic award or promotion) at another. About twenty colleges are known to have awarded bursaries to those studying theology, including Montaigu. The Collège de la Sorbonne allowed students to attend for an initial probationary period on a paying basis as *hospites*; if it approved of their progress, they might be elected as fellows (*socii*) and given board and lodging free of charge. A student at a smaller college (such as La Marche) might move to a larger college (such as the Sorbonne, Navarre, or Harcourt) to take up a bursary there.[12] Calvin might thus have begun at La Marche or Sainte-Barbe, only to be offered a bursary at Montaigu. Sainte-Barbe, a relatively new college, was unable to offer bursaries of any kind until 1525, when its rector, Diogo de Gouevia, managed to persuade the king of Portugal to provide bursaries for Portuguese students. Unfortunately, we do not possess reliable information concerning the financial arrangements for Calvin's studies at Paris; it is reasonable to infer that

Calvin's father, with diocesan support, was responsible for his son's education. As we shall see, there are reasons for supposing that Calvin was a *camériste* (see p. 28) at Montaigu, which points to access to independent financial means. Had he been a *boursier* (or *bursarius*, to use the Latin term), he would have been entitled to lodging in college. There is, however, no suggestion in the early biographies that he was awarded a bursary (or that he needed financial support), or that he was ever made a *socius*, at Montaigu – both of which would have merited mention on the part of his sympathetic early biographers to enhance Calvin's intellectual credentials, in addition to explaining his alleged change of college.

The second ground for moving college concerned the transition from the faculty of arts ('arts' was generally understood to mean 'philosophy') to one of the three higher faculties, such as theology (the others being medicine and law), for which the four- or five-year course of studies within the faculty of arts was preparation (see p. 33). A student might graduate in arts from one college, and then move college to study theology. The modern convention of studying theology as a first degree immediately on entering university was unknown at sixteenth-century Paris: Calvin could not have begun the study of theology without completing the required four or five years of preliminary studies within the faculty of arts. A survey of sixteenth-century college records suggests that the move from arts to a higher faculty was often regarded as a convenient moment at which to alter college affiliation. Noël Bédier was unusual, in that he studied both arts and theology at the same college (Montaigu); more typical was John Mair, who studied arts at Sainte-Barbe and theology at Navarre, or Jean Gillain (arts at Montaigu, theology at Harcourt).

Most recent Calvin biographies slavishly repeat Rashdall's statement that theology was taught – apart from at the houses of the various religious orders – solely at the Sorbonne and the Collège de Navarre. This assertion rests upon an unreliable seventeenth-century source – the notebook of Philippe Bouvot.[13] While this document provides much useful material, mainly copied from lost sixteenth-century sources, concerning these two colleges during the sixteenth century, it is, though, quite unreliable as a source for the teaching activities of other colleges at the time. Material relating to the graduates and lectures of other colleges is conspicuously absent, simply because Bouvot had no interest in them: the long-standing rivalry between the Sorbonne and Navarre dominated his editorial horizons, and acted as a filter in relation to the material present in his original sources. However, extant sixteenth-century sources indicate that theology was being taught and studied at a range of colleges, including Montaigu: in the years 1512–15, for example, lectures on theology were given at Montaigu by several doctors, including John Mair.[14] A student might thus have studied arts at La Marche, and transferred to Montaigu in order to study theology.

However, the evidence available does not permit us to conclude that Calvin actually began to study theology while at Paris. If he were to have gone up to Paris in 1523, he could have completed the quinquennium by 1527 or 1528. At this point, he would have been able to begin studies in one of the superior faculties – theology,[15] law or medicine. Yet it is at this point that Calvin's father appears to have directed his son to the study of law, rather than theology, and that the move to Orléans took place. This suggests that Calvin had graduated in arts by this point, in order to enter the superior faculty of civil law at Orléans. It is therefore necessary to stress that we have no evidence that Calvin ever *began* formal study within the Parisian faculty of theology, although we have ample evidence that he *initially intended* to do so, probably on account of the direction of his father.[16]

It would therefore seem that there are difficulties associated with Colladon's statement that Calvin attended the Collège de La Marche prior to Montaigu: the evidence for this foundational statement of Calvin biography is slight. But the merits, however slight, of de Bèze's statement concerning Sainte-Barbe cannot be overlooked. The alleged transference from La Marche to Montaigu cannot be accommodated adequately within our understanding of internal Parisian university routines in the early sixteenth century. We therefore suggest that Colladon's statement concerning La Marche may rest upon a misunderstanding, and quite possibly represents an unconscious historical inference being perceived and represented as an historical fact. It is, for example, quite possible that Calvin may have been taught Latin grammar by Mathurin Cordier during the period when Cordier was associated with La Marche (or, perhaps, Sainte-Barbe), without implying that *Calvin* had any formal association with either of those colleges. A student beginning the study of arts would probably have registered with a 'Nation' (see p. 33) – in Calvin's case, the Nation of France – and would associate himself with an individual master who would prepare him for his preliminary examinations. Calvin's association with Cordier unquestionably conforms to this general pattern.

College affiliation, however, was established *after* the successful completion of the Latin grammar course, the evidence being strongly in favour of Calvin then establishing an affiliation with Montaigu which he would maintain throughout his quinquennium. We therefore suggest that the most reliable approach to the evidence available concerning Calvin's Paris period may be summarized as follows:

1. Calvin was taught Latin grammar by Mathurin Cordier.
2. He was then formally affiliated with the Collège de Montaigu.
3. He studied arts, probably with a view to studying theology subsequent to successful graduation.
4. References to Sainte-Barbe and La Marche in the early biographies may ultimately rest upon mistaken inferences or misunderstandings on the part of his earliest biographers. Calvin probably attended Latin classes under the supervision of Cordier at either La Marche or Sainte-Barbe, without the young Frenchman having any formal association with either or any college at this initial stage.

The Collège de Montaigu

The Collège de Montaigu was founded in the early fourteenth century by a philanthropic archbishop of Rouen,[17] who was spared the distress of witnessing its dramatic decline in fortunes during the fifteenth century. The reversal of this deterioration in the final years of the century is to be credited virtually entirely to the enormous energy and dedication of a single figure, Jan Standonck.[18] Standonck had studied under the Brethren of the Common Life, a monastic movement centring on the Low Countries with a particular vocation for the reformation of monastic life as an end, and sound educational methods as a means thereto. The stern discipline which he introduced has traditionally been attributed to the influence of this movement,[19] although the reliability of this judgement is questionable.[20] There are indications that towards the end of the fifteenth century, strong associations began to develop between the Brethren of the Common Life and the *via moderna*. For example, Gabriel Biel and Wendelin Steinbach, leading proponents of the *via moderna* in Germany, were members of the Tübingen house of the order. In the case of Montaigu, the links with the *via moderna* were strengthened under Noël Bédier, who appears to have established the college as the chief stronghold of the *via moderna* at Paris by the second decade of the sixteenth century.[21]

Erasmus had the misfortune to spend some time at Montaigu in the 1490s. Under Jan Standonck, the college had opened its doors to those who did not possess sufficient means to pay for their studies. Erasmus was obliged to enlist in this *collegium pauperum*, which carried with it obligations to assist with domestic chores. He recorded his impressions of the place and its personalities in the *Colloquies*. Montaigu emerges as lice-ridden, decrepit and brutal, stinking of open latrines and populated by tyrants.

FIRST SPEAKER:	From what coop or cave did you come?
SECOND:	From the Collège de Montaigu.
FIRST:	Then I suppose you are full of learning?
SECOND:	No, just lice.

The reader with a sense of historical empathy may care to wander within the precincts of the modern Bibliothèque Sainte-Geneviève, and attempt to imagine a lice-ridden Erasmus shivering, five centuries ago, in his rotting cubicle next to the latrines.

A passing remark of Colladon suggests that Calvin had a somewhat better time of it at Montaigu. Students were divided into five categories: *boursiers*, who were provided with lodgings; *portionnistes*, who paid for room and board; *caméristes*, who rented rooms for themselves and paid for their support; *martinets*, who lived in houses, and paid only for lectures; and *pauvres*, who earned their keep through domestic chores and attended what lectures they could. Whereas Erasmus was among *les pauvres*, Calvin appears to have been among *les riches*, more specifically a *camériste*, living out of college in rooms.[22] Montaigu was situated in the city's Latin Quarter, a maze of dirty narrow streets criss-crossing each other with, at intersections, colleges, monasteries, churches, chapels, inns and various other establishments concerned with catering for the needs of students (including both bookshops and brothels: as a result, theology students were obliged to go around in pairs, to minimize risks of intellectual and physical contamination by the outside world). The town plan of Truschet and Hoyau (1552) (see Plate 1) allows an appreciation of the ramshackle nature of the district, but fails to convey the narrowness of the streets. Estimates of student numbers vary somewhat: between 4,000 and 5,000 would seem reasonable, out of a total city population of some 300,000.[23] At the time, all students seem to have been obliged to wear cassocks of some sort, irrespective of their ecclesiastical status.[24] Montaigu's students were nicknamed *Capettes*, on account of their grey college gowns.

The Latin Quarter has been almost totally redeveloped, making it difficult to envisage the daily sights familiar to Calvin. However, archival material allows us to attempt a partial reconstruction of main features of the region.[25] The main entrance to Montaigu was on the east side of its main quadrangle, leading into the Rue des Sept Voies, at the south end of which was the gateway of the abbey church of Sainte-Geneviève, and the smaller church of Saint-Etienne-du-Mont, with its cemetery. Had Calvin turned left, he would have walked past the infamous Rue des Chiens separating Montaigu from the neighbouring Collège de Sainte-Barbe. Later maps, dating from the seventeenth century, refer to the street as the Rue Saint-Symphorien, after the church at its western end. This chapel had been derelict for some time, but served as the site of an annual fair on 22 August, its patronal festival. This street appears to have been little more than a human and canine latrine. Although it was usually referred to as the Rue des Chiens (on account of the animals), it was popularly known as the Rue des Chiers (on account of what the dogs deposited, lent extra credibility on account of Montaigu's use of the street as an open sewer). When darkness fell, the street became the haunt of libidinous characters and other undesirables. It posed a particular difficulty for Montaigu, which owned property on both sides.

At some point in 1500,[26] Montaigu finally obtained permission to build a small raised covered walk across the road, to allow access to its *jardin des pauvres* without obliging college members to risk entering the Rue des Chiens. This gallery over the street was completed on 26 November 1500. A second improvement was completed a week or so later; on 4 December, a barrier was erected across the Montaigu end of the street, where it adjoined the Rue des Sept Voies. This barrier was locked at nights, in the hope of preventing the street remaining a haunt of footpads. The street was paved in 1522, and Montaigu's sewage, instead of being discharged directly into it, was later conducted by an underground channel into a cesspit on the Sainte-Barbe side.

Directly opposite the Rue des Chiens was the Collège de Fortet, where, according to Colladon, Calvin took rooms in the period immediately before Cop's fateful All Saints' Day oration of October

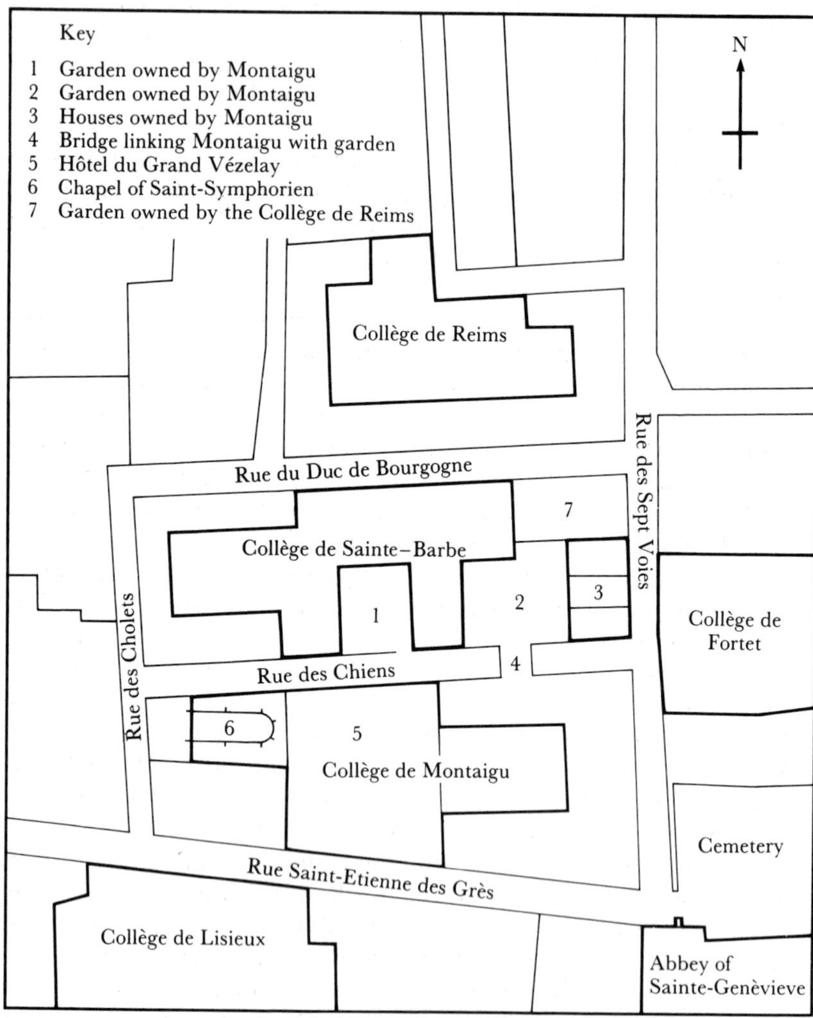

FIGURE 2.1 Plan of the Collège de Montaigu and its vicinity, c. 1510

1533 (see p. 65). Further down the Rue des Sept Voies was the Collège de Reims. Had Calvin turned right on leaving Montaigu, he would have followed the Rue des Sept Voies, passing a cemetery before turning right to enter the Rue Saint-Etienne des Grès. He would then pass the Collège de Lisieux on his left and the Rue des Cholets on his right, before joining the Grande Rue Saint-Jacques. This great street, whose course is followed by the modern road of the same name, linked the Petit Pont of the Ile de la Cité with the Porte Saint-Jacques on the south side of the city, and was flanked on both sides by tall, gabled houses. One side of this street was dominated by the rear of the Collège de la Sorbonne, although its main façade was located on the Rue de la Sorbonne, running parallel to and west of the Rue Saint-Jacques. Beside the Sorbonne was the Collège de Calvin, often referred to as 'la petite Sorbonne' (the two colleges shared a common benefactor, without any apparent relation to the reformer who would later share his name).

Montaigu itself consisted of a quadrangle bounded by the Rue des Chiens to the north, the Rue des Sept Voies to the east, the Rue des Cholets and the church of Saint-Symphorien to the west, and the Rue Saint-Etienne des Grès to the south. Most colleges of the period consisted of a group of adjoining houses, both large (*hôtels*) and small (*maisons*). Montaigu followed this pattern, although its largest building, the Hôtel du Grand Vézelay, was only acquired from the abbey of the same name in 1517.[27] On the west side was the Hôtel du Petit Vézelay, while on the upper floor of the north side were a small chapel and a study hall. The *logis des pauvres*, once lent dignity by the presence of Erasmus, were situated on the ground floor of the portion of the main building bordering the Rue Saint-Etienne des Grès. The college also owned two gardens adjoining the Collège de Sainte-Barbe. The smaller of the two gardens, reserved for theologians, included a cesspit (whose malfunctions and diversions were the cause of some friction between Sainte-Barbe and Montaigu), while the larger garden, for the use of Latin and arts students, adjoined two houses owned by Montaigu. It was this larger garden which could be reached by the covered walk.

Calvin's Course of Studies at Paris

Why did Calvin's father send him to university? On the basis of the fifteenth-century matriculation lists for the University of Avignon, Jacques Verger was able to show that the great majority of students during this period came from aristocratic or rising bourgeois families.[28] The motivation underlying university education was varied: while some undoubtedly wished to acquire a professional training in law, many saw a university education as a means of fulfilling social expectations and ensuring their social advancement. Education was rarely envisaged as a means of achieving personal fulfilment, except in the somewhat restricted and material sense of enhancement of career prospects. We do not possess comprehensive matriculation lists for the University of Paris in the early sixteenth century. Where such records exist, however, it is evident that a substantial majority of students matriculating at Paris during the first quarter of the century came from a background which could reasonably be designated *grande bourgeoisie* (though sixteenth-century categories of social distinction are notoriously imprecise). Although French universities were in a state of general decline in the late medieval period, especially as centres of professional training,[29] it seems clear that Calvin's father regarded a university education as an excellent and obvious means of social advancement for his son, consolidating the important advances made by the family in the last generation.

According to Calvin, his father initially intended him to study theology at Paris.[30] The motivation for this intention is clear: Gérard Cauvin was in good standing with both the bishop and chapter of Noyon, opening the way for rapid ecclesiastical advancement for his son; Cauvin himself had achieved a considerable advancement in the status of his family since the days of his father (who was either a boatman or a cooper at Pont-l'Evêque), and may well have hoped that his son would further enhance its fortunes. Furthermore, the development of personal links with the powerful Montmor (and hence indirectly with the de Hangest) family – both prominent in the affairs of Noyon – seemed certain to enhance Calvin's career prospects. What might have happened if he had pursued theology at Paris, and avoided associating with those of evangelical sympathies, may be surmised from the fact that in 1532 Jean de Hangest – a cousin of the Montmor brothers – would become bishop of Noyon, with considerable powers of patronage within the diocese and beyond, even if these were sullied somewhat by a protracted and undignified squabble with the cathedral chapter. The evidence available does not allow us to infer that Calvin did, in fact, even begin the study of theology. It is virtually certain that he never progressed beyond the study of arts (in other words, philosophy).[31] In the event, his father withdrew Calvin from Paris at some point in 1527 or 1528, in order that he should study civil law at Orléans. The motivation which Calvin attributes to his father for this change of subject and university was purely financial: there was more money to be had from the practice of law. (Civil law, it should be noted, was not taught at Paris: the faculty of law was devoted to the study of canon – that is, ecclesiastical – law.) The dark hints of the discovery of financial irregularities involving Gérard Cauvin at Noyon at this point would, of course, have made an ecclesiastical career for Calvin a little problematical. We possess ample evidence concerning the normal course of study followed by potential theologians at Paris, allowing us to infer what Calvin might have experienced during his time at the university.

As we have noted, the University of Paris was organized on a collegiate basis, similar to that then (and now) associated with the Universities of Oxford and Cambridge.[32] In the early sixteenth century, more than fifty colleges were brought together under its collective umbrella.[33] It consisted of four faculties: theology, law, medicine and arts. A student was required to become a graduate before he would be permitted to undertake studies in the first three, which were designated 'superior'. A student who was a member of a religious order would be obliged to be taught within its religious houses, due to a centuries-old hostility between the university and the religious orders: the university was determined to avoid being swamped by mendicant friars. Other students, such as Calvin, could begin the arts course as soon as they were able to read and write, and cope with Latin, the language in which they would be taught and examined. In his second biography of Calvin (1575), de Bèze states that Calvin was so proficient at Latin that he was able to move on to the study of the arts ahead of schedule.[34]

No formal matriculation of any kind was required of students at this stage. They were obliged to register with one of the 'Nations' of the university.[35] At Paris there were four such 'Nations': France, Picardy, Normandy and Germany. A similar pattern existed at other medieval universities: Prague recognized Bohemia, Bavaria, Saxony and Poland; while at Vienna, the four recognized Nations were Austria, the Rhineland, Hungary and Saxony. Such was the size of the *honoranda natio gallicana* at Paris that it was subdivided into five provinces: Bourges, Paris, Reims, Sens and Tours. Each of the 'Nations' was once responsible for maintaining schools for its students at the heart of the city's Latin Quarter; but by the early sixteenth century this practice had lapsed, with teaching responsibilities having devolved to the forty-odd colleges of the university. Of those colleges, the Collège de Montaigu appears to have possessed a particular attraction for potential theologians: during the period 1500–24, more than one quarter (25.4 per cent) of theological students who did not belong to religious orders received their training in arts at this college.[36] Montaigu's nearest rival was the Collège de Sainte-Barbe (14.6 per cent), followed by the Collège de Navarre (9.1 per cent). Of the remaining colleges preparing students for theological study in this period, none attracted more than 7 per cent of the student population. Furthermore, Montaigu drew heavily on the province of Reims (which included the diocese of Noyon) for its theological students: during the years 1490–1512, the college gained 35 per cent of its students from this province. Interestingly, none of the seven theological students to graduate at Montaigu from the diocese of Noyon at this time belonged to a religious order. Calvin's association with Montaigu certainly points to an informed intention to study theology at this stage.

What would Calvin have studied during his Paris period? We possess detailed accounts of the arts course and its recommended texts at Paris in the first decades of the sixteenth century, allowing us to infer what he would probably have studied then. Of particular importance is Robert Goulet's *Compendium*, a document dating from 1517, giving details of Parisian university life a few years before Calvin's arrival.[37] Arts students were divided into three groups, according to year: summulists, logicians and physicists.[38] The first two years of the arts course were thus devoted to logic. In his first year, as a summulist, Calvin would have been obliged to study the *Summulae logicales* of Peter of Spain, a somewhat tedious work which went through more than one hundred and seventy editions in its time. It was usually read in conjunction with commentaries. Goulet singles out three such commentaries as being especially esteemed: those of George of Brussels, Jacques Lefèvre d'Etaples and John Mair.[39]

Once this elementary grounding in logic had been completed, the students were ready to move on to the study of Aristotle's *Logic* in its entirety.[40] Once more, the set texts were read in conjunction with commentaries. Just as John Mair's commentary on the *Summulae* was highly esteemed, his commentary on Aristotle's *Logic* was regarded as the best available.[41] Both of Mair's commentaries adopted a terminist standpoint. In his final year, Calvin would have moved on to study Aristotle's *Physics*, perhaps drawing on more recent works dealing with the natural sciences, such as Pierre d'Ailly's *de sphaera*.

That the faculty of arts at Paris adopted a positive and conservative attitude to Aristotle, even in the field of the sciences, will be evident. Elsewhere in Europe, Aristotle was increasingly becoming the subject of criticism and scepticism.[42] Pietro Pomponazzi, perhaps the most distinguished Aristotelian of the later Italian Renaissance, had little hesitation in abandoning Aristotle's views where these were called into question by the wave of geographical and physical discoveries which so entertained that age. In his lectures at Bologna during the academic year 1522–3, Pomponazzi challenged Aristotle's views concerning the uninhabitability of the southern tropical zones:

> Let me tell you that I had some letters from a friend of mine, who tells me that the King of Spain sent three ships to go south beyond 25 degrees. They passed through the tropical zones, and found them to be inhabited, and discovered many islands. After passing the Pillars of Hercules [Gibraltar], they sailed for three months, with a favourable wind. So everything proved on the basis of Aristotle is wrong.[43]

Such advanced views had yet to reach Paris, which remained firmly committed to Aristotelianism. The progressive and radical cast of mind which characterizes Calvin as a reformer does not appear to have its origins in Paris.

Further, it seems that Calvin retained much of the Aristotelian natural philosophy which he absorbed at Paris, despite his later distaste for medieval scholasticism in general. There are occasional references to Aristotelian meteorology in his commentary on Seneca's *de clementia* (1532) and the first edition of the *Institutes* (1536), while his works dating from the 1550s are often peppered with discussion of Aristotelian cosmology.[44] In particular, it seems that he knew and accepted the basic principles of Aristotle's natural philosophy, particularly his physics, astronomy and meteorology. The reference to such views as early as 1532 certainly suggests that he became acquainted with them during his period of prescribed study at Paris. (Incidentally, Calvin's later commitment to humanism, with its characteristic stress upon a return to original sources, would deny him access to later medieval refinements and criticisms of Aristotelian natural philosophy.)

What hours would Calvin have studied? Goulet, anticipating this question, writes thus: 'It is pointless to talk about hours of study for the dialecticians. The day is scarcely long enough! There are constant disputations, vigorous defences of sophisms on Sundays and feast days, and general repetitions three times a week, and reviews and debates on Saturdays.'[45] In keeping with the rigid discipline imposed upon students by their colleges, it was expected that they would engage in logical and philosophical disputations, publicly and privately; before, during and after meals; at all times and in all places. Every account we possess of student life at Paris stresses the demands made of the young students at this stage in their careers. In the end, however, we do not know with any certainty precisely what Calvin studied while at Montaigu; we do not know under whom he studied (with the obvious exception of Cordier), or what lectures he attended; we do not even know what books he read. We may identify the main primary texts he would have studied – but these were merely points of departure, to be interpreted and supplemented by the views of commentators. Which, if any, of the three great contemporary commentaries on the *Summulae* did he use? And which commentary on Aristotle's *Logic*? It is possible that several confused mentions of Spaniards in early biographies[46] may be interpreted as references to the celebrated dialectician Antonio Coronel, whose *Rosarium logices* was published at Paris in 1510, and who was associated with Montaigu in the 1520s.

Most attention, however, has centred on the figure of John Mair (or Major), who studied arts at Sainte-Barbe and theology at Navarre before becoming regent master at Montaigu in the years 1525–31. In an important study of 1963, Karl Reuter claimed that Calvin was taught by Mair during his time at Paris, and that this distinguished Scottish theologian exercised a decisive influence over the young man's intellectual development.[47] In particular, Reuter claimed that Mair introduced Calvin to a 'new conception of anti-Pelagian and Scotist theology, and a renewed Augustinianism,' and that Calvin's positivism in regard to scripture was also due to Mair's influence. Torrance also pointed to certain similarities between Mair and Calvin in connection with their theories of knowledge.[48] Reuter's position represented a significant development of earlier understandings of Mair's relation to Calvin. Wendel suggested that Mair introduced Calvin to the seminal medieval theologian Peter Lombard's *Four Books of the Sentences*, and taught him to read them in an Ockhamist manner.[49] W. F. Dankbaar regarded Mair as having done little more than initiate Calvin's theological thinking, without necessarily shaping its subsequent form, and possibly also introducing him to a series of patristic writers.[50]

There are a number of difficulties attending Reuter's theory. For example, it is far from clear that Calvin studied under Mair in the first place. We do not know whether the two men overlapped during their periods at Montaigu (Mair was regent at Montaigu in the period 1525–31), because of doubts concerning the precise chronology of Calvin's Paris period. Two major criticisms of the Reuter thesis were made by Alexandre Ganoczy:

1 Although Ganoczy concedes that Calvin may have read Mair's *Commentary on the Sentences* during 1540–59, and that ideas similar to those associated (although not exclusively) with Mair may be found in the 1559 edition of the *Institutes*, there is no textual evidence in the first edition of the *Institutes* (1536) to warrant the conclusion that he had read the work prior to 1536. Ganoczy makes the proper observation that the influence of Mair ought to be demonstrated at the level of continuity of sources in Calvin's earlier works, rather than similarity of ideas in his later works.
2 In the first edition of the *Institutes*, Calvin tends to identify scholastic theology with Gratian and Peter Lombard.[51] For example, there are some thirty-five references to the latter in this edition, and no references whatsoever to *any* theologians of the later medieval period, let alone Mair.

In response to Ganoczy, however, it must be pointed out that Reuter's hypothesis cannot be dismissed with such ease, and on the basis of the evidence offered. Reuter lists six aspects of Calvin's theology which may reasonably be considered to reflect currents of thought prevalent at Montaigu in the 1520s,[52] while Goumaz earlier demonstrated the manner in which Calvin is familiar with, and occasionally even uses, the extraordinarily technical theological jargon of the later medieval period.[53] It is clear that Calvin has been influenced in some manner and to some extent by currents of thought associated with Montaigu: Reuter may be guilty of gross overinterpretation of the evidence in specifically linking that influence to John Mair, but some such influence remains, however it is to be explained. The absence of explicit reference to writers such as Gregory of Rimini, John Mair and William of Ockham in Calvin's 1536 *Institutes* cannot be taken as demonstrating that their ideas – whether encountered directly or indirectly – have not found their way into Calvin's thinking.

A more serious objection to Ganoczy's critique of Reuter concerns the nature of the 1536 *Institutes*, and particularly Calvin's polemical strategy. This point may be illustrated by considering the different situations faced by Luther and Calvin. Luther, writing some twenty years earlier during the first phase of the Reformation, was obliged to mount a direct attack on the ideas which he considered to be opposed to the reforming movement. For Luther, those ideas were the religious teachings of the scholastic theologians prevalent in the university circles which he knew at first hand. Thus the 1517 *Disputation against Scholastic Theology* identifies the ideas of one school of scholastic theology (the *via moderna*) as opposed to the gospel. Luther's programme of reform (at any rate, as far as he himself understood it) thus demanded that he engage with the personalities and ideas of scholastic theology. His reforming programme is initially academic, directed towards the reformation of the theological curriculum of a minor German university; subsequently, from 1520 onwards, that programme becomes essentially popular in character, directed towards the reformation of the life and doctrine of contemporary church and society.

Calvin, however, faced a totally different situation as he wrote the 1536 edition of the *Institutes* and subsequently revised it over the next quarter of a century. In the first place, scholastic theology was an utter irrelevance to his situation: Calvin was not concerned with the reformation of a university theological curriculum – in the great free cities of Strasbourg and Geneva, the chief enemies were indifference and ignorance, demanding a systematic presentation of reforming ideas rather than an engagement with the intricacies of scholastic theology. Calvin's educational strategy involved the complete marginalization of scholastic theology, rather than engaging in critical dialogue with it – in this respect, Calvin employs tactics already used with considerable success by Erasmus and Zwingli. Calvin's decision not to engage with medieval theologians (such as Ockham, Mair or Scotus) cannot be taken to imply that he was unfamiliar with their ideas, nor that he had not absorbed them, to however limited an extent. It was his polemical strategy, rather than his personal theological obligations, which dictated his attitude to medieval writers in 1536.

In the second place, the battleground had shifted between 1517 and 1536. For the Lutheran Reformation at Wittenberg, the battlefront with Roman Catholicism concerned the question of how an individual enters into fellowship with God – the celebrated doctrine of justification by faith alone. This question would continue to preoccupy the Lutheran faction for some time. Further south, the Reformation concerned a different question. Zwingli had little interest in the doctrine of justification, concentrating instead on the reformation of both church and society according to scriptural paradigms. Increasingly, the ecclesiological question came to dominate the soteriological one, as the question of the identity and character of the true church came to be seen as being even more urgent and significant than the question of how one entered into fellowship with God.

By the 1530s – and increasingly in the years which followed – the doctrine of the church assumed new significance. Recognizing the importance of this question, Calvin addresses it directly in the 1536 *Institutes*. In order to discredit Roman Catholic theories of the church, he mounts a direct attack on the origins of those theories, which he discerns to lie with the medieval writers Gratian and Peter Lombard. There is no need for Calvin to enter into critical dialogue with later medieval theologians on this question: his strategy is to discredit medieval ecclesiologies by attacking their *fons et origo*. Calvin's references to Peter Lombard's *Four Books of the Sentences* in the 1536 *Institutes* are, without exception, taken from the fourth book, which deals with the doctrine of the church and sacraments.

In the third place, especially in his later period, Calvin's more explicitly polemical concerns tended to relate to matters which were the subject of controversy within the Protestant churches, rather than the subject of controversy with the Roman Catholic church. The Osiandrist controversy (see p. 164) is an excellent example of this tendency, although the growing threat posed by the Radical Reformation and increased tension with Lutheranism are significant components in shaping Calvin's later writings. It was more important that Calvin engage with his living and active Protestant opponents, rather than with the long-dead voices of scholasticism, whose distant echoes found no resonance at Strasbourg or Geneva.

On the basis of these considerations, it will be clear that Calvin has no need to engage with later medieval writers in the 1536 – or any other – edition of the *Institutes*. Absence of explicit reference to writers such as Gregory of Rimini, William of Ockham or John Mair reflects Calvin's apologetic and polemical strategy, and has no immediate bearing upon his direct or indirect knowledge of their ideas. A more reliable manner of assessing the influence of Montaigu upon Calvin's intellectual formation would be to identify currents of thought prevalent at Montaigu in the 1520s, and ask to what extent such ideas are reflected in his writings.

Intellectual Currents at Paris

Scholasticism is probably one of the most despised intellectual movements in human history. Thus the English word 'dunce' derives from the name of one of the greatest scholastic writers, Duns Scotus. Scholasticism is best regarded as the medieval movement, flourishing between 1250 and 1500, which placed great emphasis upon the rational justification of religious belief. It is the demonstration of the inherent rationality of Christian theology by an appeal to philosophy, and the demonstration of the complete harmony of that theology by the minute examination of the relationship of its various elements. Scholastic writings tended to be long and argumentative, frequently relying upon closely argued distinctions. But what philosophical system was best suited to the rational defence of Christianity? By about 1270, Aristotle had become established as 'the Philosopher'. His ideas came to dominate theological thinking, especially at Paris, despite fierce opposition from more conservative quarters. By the dawn of the sixteenth century, a thorough immersion in Aristotelian logic and physics was regarded as essential for the study of Christian theology at Paris. Although other universities were breaking free from the baleful influence of Aristotle at this time, Paris remained firmly wedded to his ideas and methods.

Scholastic thinkers – the 'schoolmen' – are often represented as debating earnestly, if pointlessly, over how many angels could dance on the head of a pin. Although this particular debate never actually took place, intriguing though its outcome would unquestionably have been, it summarizes precisely the way in which scholasticism was regarded by humanists at the beginning of the sixteenth century: it was pointless, arid intellectual speculation over trivia.[54] The University of Paris possessed an international reputation as a centre for this much despised movement.

In addition to his memories of Parisian student life, Erasmus also passed down to us his recollections of the theological debates which excited the *théologastres* at Montaigu. Could God have become a cucumber instead of a man? Or could God undo the past, for example by making a prostitute into a virgin?[55] If there was a serious side to these questions,[56] Erasmus' waspish wit allowed it to be overlooked. Could circles be made square? Surely Jesus had not debated such matters with the doctors in the temple? Why bother with them?

Such questions, however, reflected accurately the philosophical and theological interests of a movement which gained increasing influence during the fourteenth century, often referred to as 'nominalism' in the older literature, but also known as 'terminism' or the *via moderna*.[57] John Mair may be regarded as one of its many representatives at Paris in the early sixteenth century, even to the point of debating whether God could have become an ass instead of a man. The success of nominalism at Paris reflected a general trend in the faculties of arts throughout northern European universities in the fifteenth century. The statutes of the University of Basle, founded in April 1460, initially laid down that instruction should be according to the *via moderna*. Heidelberg and Erfurt are examples of universities whose faculties of arts came to be affected in this way; interestingly, Luther's University of Wittenberg remained committed to the *via antiqua* until the surprisingly late date of 1508, reflecting the stolid and unimaginative traditionalism for which it apparently gained a reputation at a remarkably early stage.

It may be helpful to clarify the difference between realism and nominalism.[58] Consider two white stones. Realism affirms that there is a universal concept of 'whiteness' which these two stones embody. These particular white stones possess the universal characteristic of 'whiteness'. While the white stones exist in time and space, the universal of 'whiteness' does not. Nominalism, however, asserts that the universal concept of 'whiteness' is unnecessary, and instead argues that we should concentrate on particulars. There are these two white stones – and there is no need to appeal to some 'universal concept of whiteness'.

During the second third of the fourteenth century the *via antiqua*, associated with thinkers such as Thomas Aquinas and Duns Scotus and characterized by its realism, found itself coming under increased pressure from the rival nominalism or terminism of the *via moderna*, associated with writers such as William of Ockham, Jean Buridan, Gregory of Rimini and Marsilius of Inghen. The faculty of arts at Paris felt itself threatened by this movement, and attempted to suppress it. On 29 December 1340, a statute condemning the *errores Ockhanicorum* took effect. Henceforth, any candidate who wished to supplicate for the degree of Master of Arts at Paris would have to swear that he would observe the statutes of the faculty of arts *contra scientiam Okamicam*, and refrain from teaching such ideas to his pupils. The general ineffectiveness of this measure may be seen by considering the brilliant career of

Pierre d'Ailly, a noted supporter of the *via moderna*. In 1384, he was appointed rector of the Collège de Navarre – one of his first actions was to ensure the college's theologians had ample supplies of wine. This appointment was shortly followed by his election to the chancellorship of the university itself (1389). The University of Cologne, defending its teaching of the *via moderna* to sceptical princes in 1425, was able to declare that nominalism was now well regarded at Paris.

In the later fifteenth century, however, hostility towards the *via moderna* at Paris intensified. On 1 March 1474, a further decree was issued by the king of France against the nominalists, in an attempt to stem the growing influence of *Guilelmus Okam et consimiles*. The chief effect of the decree was to persuade many Paris students and masters sympathetic to the movement to transfer with immediate effect to German universities, where their ideas were more welcome.[59] Its futility and small-mindedness being evident, the decree was eventually rescinded in 1481, leaving the way open for the re-establishment of the *via moderna* at Paris. The Collège de Montaigu appears to have been in the forefront of this nominalist revival in the first decades of the sixteenth century. Calvin thus attended a college at which the influence of the *via moderna* appears to have been unquestioned.

The rigorous instruction in terminist logic and dialectic which Calvin would have received at Paris appears to have left its mark on his mind, although the precise extent of this influence, as well as its general nature, remain controversial.[60] For example, Calvin's dialectic between God and humanity – brilliantly exploited as a leading principle in the 1559 *Institutes* – probably rests upon terminist foundations. It is also clear that the central epistemological issue addressed by terminism – namely, the relation between the mental conception of an object, and that object itself – would dominate Calvin's later thought concerning God. How can human conceptions of God be related to God himself? In what way may the term 'God' be correlated with the external reality which it designates? Underlying much of Calvin's more mature thought is the question of how human concepts are constructed – a question of crucial theological importance when the concept at issue is that of God. Nevertheless, many of the aspects of Calvin's thought which allegedly result from the influence of his terminist teachers at Paris may also be explained through influences encountered later in his career, particularly that of humanism.

More intriguing is the possible influence of another school of thought upon the young Calvin's development.[61] Many older textbooks dealing with the Reformation refer to a confrontation between 'nominalism' and 'Augustinianism' on the eve of the Reformation, and interpret the Reformation as the victory of the latter over the former. In recent years, however, considerable progress has been made in understanding the nature of late medieval scholasticism. It now seems that there were *two* different nominalist schools of thought, whose sole common feature was anti-realism. These schools are now known as the 'modern way' (*via moderna*) and the 'modern Augustinian school' (*schola Augustiniana moderna*). Both schools adopted a nominalist position in matters of logic and the theory of knowledge – but their theological positions on the question of how salvation comes about differed radically. Strictly speaking, the term 'nominalism' referred to the question of universals, and did not designate any particular theological position. Both schools rejected the necessity of universals – but adopted radically different approaches to the question of how humanity could be redeemed. One was profoundly optimistic concerning human abilities, the other considerably more pessimistic.

The doctrine of justification, which assumed particular importance within the Lutheran Reformation, concerns, as we noted earlier, the question of how an individual enters into a relationship with God. How can a sinner be accepted by a righteous God? What must the individual do, in order to be acceptable to God? This same question had earlier been debated with some intensity during the early fifth-century controversy between Augustine and Pelagius, known as the 'Pelagian controversy'.[62] In many ways, this debate was replayed in the medieval period, with the *via moderna* tending towards the position of Pelagius, and the *schola Augustiniana moderna* towards that of Augustine.

For Augustine, humanity was trapped in its situation, and could not redeem itself. Left to its own devices and resources, it was impossible for humanity ever to enter into a relationship with God. Nothing that a man or woman could do was sufficient to break the stranglehold of sin. To use an image which Augustine was fortunate enough never to have encountered, it is like a narcotic addict trying to break free from the grip of heroin or cocaine. The situation cannot be transformed from within – and so, if transformation is to take place, it must come from outside the human situation. According to Augustine, God intervenes in the human dilemma. He need not have done so, but out of his love for fallen humanity, he enters into the human situation in the person of Jesus Christ in order to redeem it.

Augustine lays such emphasis upon 'grace' that he is often designated *doctor gratiae*, 'the doctor of grace'. 'Grace' is the unmerited or undeserved gift of God, by which God voluntarily breaks the hold of sin upon humanity. Redemption is possible only as a divine gift. It is not something which we can achieve ourselves, but which has to be done for us. Augustine thus emphasizes that the resources of salvation are located outside of humanity, in God himself. It is God who initiates the process of salvation, not men or women. For Pelagius, however, the necessary resources for salvation are located within humanity. Individual human beings have the capacity to save themselves. They are not trapped by sin, but have the ability to do all that is necessary to be saved. Salvation is something which is earned through good works, which place God under an obligation to humanity. Pelagius marginalizes the idea of grace, understanding it in terms of demands made of humanity – such as the Ten Commandments – in order that salvation may be achieved. The ethos of Pelagianism could be summed up as 'salvation by personal achievement', whereas Augustine taught 'salvation by divine grace'.

It will be obvious that the two theologies have very different understandings of human nature. For Augustine, human nature is weak, fallen and impotent; for Pelagius, it is autonomous and self-sufficient. For Augustine, it is necessary to depend upon God for salvation; for Pelagius, God merely indicates what has to be done if salvation is to be attained, and then leaves men and women to meet the conditions unaided. For Augustine, salvation is an unmerited gift; for Pelagius, salvation is a justly earned reward.

In the ensuing controversy within the western church, Augustine's position was recognized as authentically Christian, and Pelagius' views were censured as heretical. Two important councils established Augustine's views as normative: the Council of Carthage (418), and the Second Council of Orange (529). The term 'Pelagian' hence came to be pejorative as well as descriptive, meaning 'placing excessive reliance upon human abilities, and insufficient trust in the grace of God'. At the time of the Reformation, Luther was convinced that most of the western church had fallen into Pelagianism, by losing sight of the idea of the 'grace of God', and had come to rely upon human self-sufficiency.

The 'modern Augustinian school' combined a philosophical nominalism with a theological Augustinianism. In common with the *via moderna*, the school had no sympathy with the realism of

Thomas Aquinas or Duns Scotus. Yet it developed a doctrine of salvation, reflecting the influence of Augustine, which is diametrically opposed to that of the 'modern way'. There is a radical emphasis upon the absolute need for grace, upon the fallenness and sinfulness of humanity, upon the divine initiative in justification, and upon divine predestination. Salvation is understood to be *totally* a work of God, from its beginning to its end. Where the *via moderna* held that humans could inaugurate their justification by 'doing their best', the *schola Augustiniana moderna* insisted that only God could initiate justification. Where the *via moderna* held that all necessary soteriological resources were located *within* human nature, the modern Augustinian school argued that these resources were located exclusively *outside* human nature. It is obvious that these are two totally different ways of understanding the human and divine roles in justification.

The leading characteristics of the epistemology and theology of the *schola Augustiniana moderna*, exemplified by Gregory of Rimini, may be summarized as follows (with apologies for the intrusion of unavoidable theological jargon):

1 A strict epistemological 'nominalism' or 'terminism'.
2 A voluntarist, as opposed to intellectualist, understanding of the grounds of human merit, and also of the merit of Jesus Christ.
3 The extensive use of the writings of Augustine, particularly his anti-Pelagian works, which concentrate upon the doctrine of grace.
4 A strongly pessimistic view of original sin, with the Fall being identified as a watershed in the history of human salvation.
5 A strong emphasis upon the priority of God in the salvation of humanity.
6 A radical doctrine of absolute double predestination.
7 A rejection of the role of created habits of grace in justification or merit (these were seen as necessary intermediates by earlier medieval writers).

All seven of these foundational features of the modern Augustinian school are faithfully echoed in the writings of Calvin. The second point may be singled out for further discussion at this stage.

Reuter's thesis that Calvin learned a 'new conception of anti-Pelagian and Scotist theology, and a renewed Augustinianism' at Paris may be restated in terms of the influence of a general late medieval theological current, rather than of any specific individual (such as John Mair). The later medieval tradition as a whole (including both *via moderna* and *schola Augustiniana moderna*) adopted a strongly voluntarist approach to the basis of merit.[63] That is to say, the meritorious value of a human action does not rest upon its inherent value, but is grounded solely in the worth which God chooses to impose upon it. This principle is summarized in the maxim of Duns Scotus (usually, though not entirely correctly, regarded as the originator of the trend towards voluntarism in later medieval thought), to the effect that the value of an offering is determined solely by the divine will, rather than its inherent goodness.[64] In the *Institutes*, Calvin adopts an identical position in relation to the merit of Christ. Although this is implicit in earlier editions of the work, it is only explicitly stated in the 1559 edition, in the aftermath of Calvin's correspondence with Laelius Socinus on the subject.[65]

In 1555, Calvin responded to questions raised by Socinus concerning the merit of Christ and the assurance of faith, and appears to have incorporated these replies into the 1559 edition of the *Institutes* without significantly modifying them. In the course of this correspondence, the strongly voluntarist approach which Calvin adopts to the *ratio meriti Christi* – the grounds of the merit of Christ – becomes obvious. He makes clear that the basis of Christ's merit is not located in Christ's offering of himself (which would correspond to an intellectualist approach to the *ratio meriti Christi*), but in the divine decision to accept such an offering as of sufficient merit for the redemption of mankind (which corresponds to the voluntarist approach). For Calvin, 'apart from God's good pleasure, Christ could not merit anything' (*nam Christus nonnisi ex Dei beneplacito quidquam mereri potuit*).[66] The continuity between Calvin and the late medieval voluntarist tradition will be evident.

In the past, this similarity between Calvin and Scotus has been taken to imply the direct influence of Scotus on Calvin, or perhaps an indirect influence mediated via Socinus: thus Alexander Gordon argued that Calvin adopted a Scotist approach to the *ratio meriti Christi*, and on the basis of his presupposition that Scotism constituted the basis of Socinianism, traced the continuous development of that movement from Scotus through Calvin.[67] In fact, however, Calvin's continuity appears to be with the late medieval voluntarist tradition, deriving from William of Ockham and Gregory of Rimini, in relation to which Scotus marks a point of transition. No reason may be given for the meritorious nature of Christ's sacrifice, save that God benevolently ordained to accept it as such. The continuity of Calvin with this later tradition is evident, whatever its explanation may be.

The seven features of the *schola Augustiniana moderna* noted above clearly include those aspects of Calvin's thought attributed by Reuter to the influence of John Mair.[68] It is perhaps significant that, in the preface to the first book of his *Commentary on the Sentences*, Mair explicitly acknowledges his debt to three theologians: Scotus, William of Ockham and Gregory of Rimini.[69] It is certainly therefore a remarkable coincidence, to say the least, that Calvin should reproduce the leading features of an academic Augustinianism which developed at the university that he himself attended, if he had not been familiar with such theological currents. Nor need he have encountered these views through attending theological lectures: Gregory's *Commentary* went through three editions at Paris (1482, 1487, 1520), the last appearing shortly before Calvin's arrival.[70] If Calvin read as widely as we are led to believe by his contemporaries, it is not improbable that this work – a standard of both logic and theology by one of the two recognized doctors of the *via nominalium* at Paris[71] – would have attracted his attention. Indeed, the suggestion has been made that Calvin's theological education may derive partly from personal study or reading during his Paris period.[72] Reuter, of course, put forward his thesis before the *schola Augustiniana moderna* had been identified and characterized, and his theory is considerably weakened through unnecessary subsidiary hypotheses (such as personal contact with Mair). It is therefore interesting to note the possibility that the major themes of Calvin's theology of salvation may reflect currents of thought he encountered at Paris. This possibility, it must be stressed, cannot be investigated with the rigour necessary to confirm it, given the fragmentary character of our knowledge of Calvin's Paris period. It is, though, intriguing, and serves to remind us that Calvin, far from breaking totally with the medieval tradition, actually adopts many theological and philosophical positions of an impeccable medieval pedigree.

The Parisian Preoccupation with Lutheranism

During 1523, the faculty of theology had been obliged to meet 101 times, far in excess of the thirty or so meetings usually held. The cause for these additional meetings was a distant and largely unknown figure – Martin Luther – whose ideas threatened to take city, university and church by storm. Lutheranism did indeed come to dominate the affairs of both city and university, making it difficult for any informed person within the city to avoid at least some familiarity with its ideas. As contemporary witnesses make abundantly clear, the works of Martin Luther found a substantial and enthusiastic readership within the intellectual elite of Paris as early as 1519; second-hand versions of those ideas, frequently distorted and exaggerated by well-meaning but sensationalist religious gossips, circulated even more widely.

Event after event in city and university alike pointed to popular fascination with the new ideas soon to be branded as heresy. By far the best-attended meeting of the faculty of theology for years assembled on 14 July 1523 to hear Pierre Lizet denounce the evils of Lutheranism on behalf of the king.[73] Three weeks later, the Augustinian monk Jean Vallière was burned alive for having read and commented on Lutheran works. On 4 December 1526, seven men dressed as devils paraded around Paris leading a horse mounted by a woman, surrounded by men dressed as doctors of theology with the words 'Lutherans' prominently displayed at front and rear.[74]

The origins of this concern with Lutheranism may be traced to 1519, in the aftermath of the Leipzig Disputation between Luther and Johann Eck, at which Luther called key aspects of catholic teaching into question. Both had agreed that their respective positions should be placed before the universities of Erfurt and Paris for evaluation. Erfurt indicated that it was not willing to take part in the proceedings. At Paris, no response was initially forthcoming, leading some to suspect that it would eventually decline to be involved. Paris was a centre of Gallicanism – a movement which asserted the more or less complete freedom of the French church from the ecclesiastical authority of the pope. The Concordat of Bologna (1516) was widely seen as enhancing the position of both the French king and the papacy, at the expense of the treasured *libertés de l'église gallicane* (liberties of the French Church), while simultaneously threatening the independence of both the university and *parlement* of Paris. The university refused to permit the printing or distribution of copies of the Concordat for circulation. As a result, the question of papal authority became contentious within university circles by 1518. As one of the chief issues debated at Leipzig was the nature of papal authority, the University of Paris found itself in a difficult position. If they censured Luther for questioning the papal authority, they might be thought to compromise the centuries-old Gallican tradition of the university.[75] Contemporary records suggest a difficult series of faculty meetings in 1520.[76] The internal problems faced by the university were unwittingly removed by Luther himself, through the publication of the three reforming treatises of 1520, which the university had no difficulty in finding unacceptable.

On 15 April 1521, final approval was given to a detailed condemnation of 104 propositions attributed to Luther, now generally known as the Parisian *Determinatio*.[77] This document alleged that Luther had joined the ranks of heretics such as Marcion, Arius and Wycliffe; not content with resurrecting their older heresies, however, he had also had the impudence to invent new ones. The polemical strategy adopted by the faculty of theology was to associate Luther with older heresies wherever possible, thus demonstrating his historical and theological continuity with already discredited positions.[78] It is, however, highly significant (and perfectly understandable) that the *Determinatio* failed to address the question of papal primacy – a matter which the Leipzig Disputation had raised as central.

The *Determinatio* received wide attention, having been reprinted nine times in Latin by 1524, and also translated into Dutch and German. As a result of this condemnation, Luther's views began to receive increasing attention at Paris. During Calvin's time there, the Lutheran question dominated the agenda of the theological faculty, forcing it to hold extended meetings. These often appear to have been tedious and vitriolic, with suspicion of heresy being openly directed towards at least fifteen faculty members (who never numbered more than eighty). Nevertheless, the faculty was able to maintain at least the appearance of unity in the face of the threat posed by Luther, even if the nature and significance of this threat was poorly understood. Such was the odium which came to be attached to Luther's name in conservative ecclesiastical circles that similarities between his ideas and those of humanists or reform-minded French clergy were increasingly seen as a sign of heresy on the part of the latter, rather than orthodoxy on the part of the former.[79] Francis I, initially inclined to defend humanism against its critics, gradually came to regard Lutheranism as a threat to the stability of his realm. Although this attitude would only express itself in action in the aftermath of the *Affair of the Placards* (October 1534), its origins may be traced to the period during which Calvin studied in Paris.

Nevertheless, Luther's ideas appear to have gained a wide hearing in university circles at Paris, however hostile a reaction they would provoke within the faculty of theology. It would have been difficult for the young Calvin to avoid hearing of Lutheranism while a student at Paris, and encountering speculation and rumours concerning the mysterious Saxon figure who had given rise to it. Public processions of penitence or protest (see Plate 3), public executions for heresy, and anti-Lutheran polemic within the University of Paris (by no means restricted to the faculty of theology) make it probable that the young Picard would have encountered at least some of the constitutive ideas of this foreign heresy, in however distorted a form, and perhaps have gained an impression of both the popular interest in and the hostility building up towards it within conservative Parisian university circles. Once more, however, we must acknowledge that we do not know when, or in what form, Calvin first encountered Lutheran ideas.

'Uncertainty', then, is a word which recurs throughout our discussion of Calvin's Paris period, regarding both its chronology and its significance for our understanding of the development of his career and ideas. Time and time again the historian is forced to take refuge in the dangerous practice of generalization, in the hope that Calvin will fit a common pattern. Fortunately, however, there are reasons for supposing that his period at the University of Paris was not of decisive importance in shaping his mature ideas. If Calvin's later – admittedly sparse – reminiscences are anything to go by, he appears to have regarded Paris as little more than the place at which he mastered Latin. A more plausible analysis would suggest that Calvin's powers of reasoning and analysis may be traced to his rigorous training under the influence of his terminist masters. It is certainly true that he may also have absorbed certain quite definite logical and philosophical ideas current at Paris; nevertheless, these were little more than the common coinage of much conventional contemporary academic wisdom, and lack the radical character associated with the later Calvin. Our attention now turns to Orléans and Bourges, at which Calvin probably entered a different intellectual world. It is during this period that many historians suspect that he may have encountered individuals, methods and ideas which finally shaped and set his mind towards the idea of reform.

3

The Years of Wandering: Orléans and the Encounter with Humanism

AT SOME point in the later 1520s, possibly within the years 1526–8, Calvin left Paris as a young *licencié en arts* to begin the study of civil law at Orléans under Pierre de l'Estoile, 'the prince of French lawyers'.[1] It is not entirely clear why Calvin chose to study law. His early biographers cite several possible grounds for this radical new course: the influence of his father or of the future reformer Pierre Olivétan, a growing disillusionment with theology, or the dawning of an awareness of the nature of 'true religion'.[2] However little we may understand Calvin's motivation for moving to Orléans, the new intellectual world which he entered is relatively well documented and understood. At Orléans and subsequently at Bourges, he encountered a form of humanism which captured his imagination, and which he would later adapt for his own particular purposes.

Orléans differed from Paris in a number of important respects: it was not a collegiate university, it had been reformed radically in 1512, and it possessed only one faculty – that of law, with civil law predominating over canon law. Erasmus had studied at Orléans for six months in 1500, and recalled the experience with a certain degree of distaste. His life, he remarked, had been made miserable by Accursius and Bartholus. Instead of being able to study the classic text of Roman law, the Justinian *Institutes*, he had been obliged to immerse himself in the tedious intricacies of later commentators. The medieval commentators took their work seriously, scribbling comments prolifically in the margins and between the lines of their text. Glossators such as Accursius and Bartholus developed the art of marginal and interlinear glossing to the point at which the glosses became of greater importance than the text to which they originally referred.

This development paralleled a similar move in the field of theology. There was never a shortage of medieval biblical commentators, prepared to add their own interpretations and explanations to the text of scripture. From its origins in the late Dark Ages, the art of glossing scripture became increasingly systematized, as the accumulated comments, annotations and digressions of generations of glossators began to assume an authority of their own, virtually independent of the biblical text upon which they were originally based.[3] Gloss was added to gloss as if they were coats of paint. Biblical commentaries often did little more than reproduce the contents of traditional glosses. With the rise of humanism, however, all this was set to change.

The Nature of Humanism

In the twentieth century the term 'humanism' has come to mean a philosophy or outlook on life which affirms the dignity of humanity without any reference to God. 'Humanism' has acquired very strongly secularist, perhaps even atheist, overtones. To speak of the 'rise of humanism' at the time of the Reformation might therefore seem to suggest a confrontation of religion and atheism. Yet that confrontation, with all that it would have entailed, never materialized. The Renaissance was not the Enlightenment. Remarkably few – if any – humanists of the fourteenth, fifteenth or sixteenth centuries correspond to our modern understanding of 'humanism'. Indeed, they were generally remarkably religious, if anything concerned with the *renewal* rather than the *abolition* of the Christian faith and church.[4]

The term 'humanism' was coined by the German educationalist F. J. Niethammer in 1808 to refer to a form of education which placed emphasis upon the Greek and Latin classics. Niethammer was alarmed at the growing stress upon the natural sciences and technology in German secondary education, and believed that the potentially dehumanizing consequences of this emphasis could be reduced only through immersion in the study of the humanities.

Interestingly, the term was not used at the time of the Renaissance itself, although the Italian word *umanista* is frequently encountered. This word refers to a university teacher of *studia humanitatis* – 'the study of humanity' or 'liberal arts', such as poetry, grammar and rhetoric. Study after study of prominent humanist writers of the Italian Renaissance has revealed a common underlying concern for eloquence. If there is any common theme to humanist writings, it is the need to promote spoken and written eloquence, with Greek and Latin classics serving as models and resources for this ambitious aesthetic programme.

The rise of classical scholarship, which is so characteristic a feature of the Italian Renaissance, reflects this new interest in rediscovering the cultural values and norms of antiquity. Classic culture and civilization were seen as contemporary resources. Greek and Latin works were widely studied in their original languages as *a means to an end*, rather than *an end in themselves*. The humanists studied the classics as models of written eloquence, in order to gain inspiration and instruction. Classical learning and philological competence were simply the tools used to exploit the resources of antiquity. As has often been pointed out, the writings of the humanists devoted to the promotion of eloquence, written or spoken, far exceed in quality and quantity those devoted to classical scholarship or philology.

The recognition that humanists shared a common view on how ideas were to be arrived at, rather than sharing common ideas in themselves, allows us to understand and accommodate the otherwise disquieting and disruptive fact that 'humanism' was remarkably heterogeneous. For example, many humanist writers were Platonists – but others favoured Aristotelianism. The stubborn persistence of Aristotelianism (for example, at the University of Padua) throughout the Renaissance is a serious difficulty for those who regard humanism as philosophically homogeneous.[5] Some Italian humanists displayed what seem to be anti-religious attitudes – but other Italian humanists were profoundly pious. Some humanists were republicans – but others were strongly monarchical. Recent studies have also drawn attention to a less attractive side of humanism – the obsession of some humanists with magic and superstition – which is perhaps difficult to harmonize with the conventional view of the movement. 'Humanism' appears to have lacked any coherent or distinctive philosophy. No single religious, philosophical or political idea dominated or characterized the movement. Designating a writer as a 'humanist' thus threatens to convey no essential information concerning his philosophical, political or religious views; rather, it points in the first place to an engagement with the resources of the classical period as a means of generating modern ideas, and in the second to a recognition of the classical norms of style in expressing those ideas.

In short: humanism was concerned with *how ideas were obtained and expressed*, rather than with the precise nature of the ideas themselves. A humanist might be a Platonist or an Aristotelian – but in both cases, the ideas involved derived from antiquity. A humanist might be a sceptic or a believer – but both attitudes could be defended from antiquity. The diversity of *ideas* which is so characteristic of Renaissance humanism is based upon a general consensus concerning *how those ideas are to be derived and expressed.*

Although humanism had its origins in Renaissance Italy, it proved to be remarkably mobile. It is becoming increasingly clear that northern European humanism was decisively influenced by Italian humanism at every stage of its development. If there were indigenous humanist movements in northern Europe which originated independently of their Italian counterpart (which, it has to be stressed, is very much open to doubt), the evidence unambiguously points to those movements having subsequently been decisively influenced by Italian humanism. Three main channels for the northern European diffusion of the methods and ideals of the Italian Renaissance have now been identified.[6] First, through northern European scholars moving south to Italy, perhaps to study at an Italian university or as part of a diplomatic mission. On returning to their homeland, they brought the spirit of the Renaissance back with them. Second, through the foreign correspondence of the Italian humanists, the full extent of which was considerable, extending to most parts of northern Europe. Humanism was concerned with the promotion of written eloquence, and the writing of letters was seen as a means of embodying and spreading the ideals of the Renaissance. Third, through printed books, originating from sources such as the Aldine Press in Venice. These works were often reprinted by northern European presses, particularly those at Basle in Switzerland.[7] Italian humanists often dedicated their works to northern European patrons, thus ensuring that they were noted and circulated in the right quarters.

The general principle underlying Renaissance humanism can be summarized in the slogan *ad fontes*, 'back to the sources'. By returning to the original sources, the intellectual stagnation and squalor of the Middle Ages could be bypassed, in order to engage directly with the cultural glories of antiquity. Instead of wrestling with the conceptual confusion and literary inelegance of medieval commentaries on the Bible, it was necessary to return to the biblical texts themselves, and recover their freshness and vitality. The realization of this dream seemed increasingly within the grasp of the late Renaissance, as humanist scholarship began to make available the resources necessary in its pursuit. Of particular importance in this respect is Erasmus of Rotterdam's *Enchiridion*, or 'Handbook of the Christian Soldier'.[8] Although the work was first published in 1503 and then reprinted in 1509, its real impact dates from the third printing in 1515. From that moment onwards, it became a cult work, apparently going through twenty-three editions in the next six years. Its appeal was to educated lay men and women, whom Erasmus regarded as the true treasure of the church. Its amazing popularity in the years after 1515 suggests that a radical alteration in the expectations and confidence of the educated laity resulted – and it can hardly be overlooked that the reforming rumbles at Zurich (1519) and Wittenberg (1517) date from so soon after the *Enchiridion* became a best-seller. Erasmus' success also highlighted the importance of printing as a means of disseminating radical new ideas – a point which Calvin did not overlook, when his turn came to propagate such ideas.

Erasmus' *Enchiridion* developed the enormously attractive thesis that the church could and should be reformed by a collective return to the writings of the fathers and scripture. The regular reading of scripture is put forward as the key to the renewal and reform of the church. Erasmus conceived his work as a lay person's guide to scripture, providing a simple yet learned exposition of the 'philosophy of Christ'. Through his efforts the stagnant waters of the medieval commentators could be set to one side, as individuals were enabled to drink deeply and directly of the fresh water of original sources. This demanded a knowledge of languages – Latin and Greek in the case of the classics, supplemented by Hebrew for the study of the Old Testament – as well as access to the foundational writings of the Christian faith in their original languages.

In response to this market force, a minor industry developed among humanist educationalists, who produced manuals of grammar and lexicons, often combined in a single volume, to meet the developing appetite for classical wisdom. Calvin was among the many who would avail themselves of such tools, as he studied

Greek at Orléans in private under the supervision of his friend Melchior Wolmar. Erasmus of Rotterdam was responsible for a remarkable feat of editorial work, producing a series of patristic editions which were the marvel of the age. Although his edition of the writings of Augustine compares unfavourably with the great eleven-volume Amerbach edition of 1506, his edition of the works of Jerome was widely regarded as an intellectual wonder of the world. Most important of all, however, was Erasmus' publication of the New Testament in its original Greek in 1516.[9] For the first time, theologians had the opportunity of comparing the original Greek text of the New Testament with the later Vulgate translation into Latin. One major result of this comparison was a general loss of confidence in the reliability of the Vulgate, the 'official' Latin translation of the Bible.

When a medieval theologian refers to 'scripture', he almost invariably means the *textus vulgatus*, 'the common text'. The standard edition of this text was the upshot of a joint speculative venture by some Paris theologians and stationers in 1226, resulting in the 'Paris version' of the Vulgate. By then, Paris was recognized as the leading centre of theology in Europe, with the inevitable result that – despite attempts to correct its obvious errors and imperfections – the 'Paris version' of the Vulgate became established as normative. This version, it must be emphasized, was not commissioned or sponsored by any ecclesiastical figure: it appears to have been a purely commercial venture. Medieval theologians, attempting to base their theology upon scripture, were thus obliged to identify 'scripture' with a rather bad commercial edition of an already faulty Latin translation of the Bible. The rise of humanist textual and linguistic techniques showed up the alarming discrepancies between the Vulgate and the texts it was supposed to translate – and thus opened the way to doctrinal reformation. No longer could 'scripture' and 'the Vulgate text' be regarded as one and the same thing.

Erasmus demonstrated that the Vulgate was seriously inaccurate at many points of major theological importance in its translation of the Greek text of the New Testament. As a number of medieval church practices and beliefs were based upon these texts, his allegations were viewed with consternation by many conservative catholics (who wanted to retain these practices and beliefs) and with equally great delight by the Reformers (who wanted to eliminate them). Two examples will indicate the relevance of Erasmus' humanist biblical scholarship to the Reformation.

The Vulgate translated the opening words of Jesus' ministry (Matthew 4:17) as '*do penance*, for the Kingdom of heaven is at hand', with a clear reference to the sacrament of penance. Erasmus pointed out that the Greek should be translated as '*repent*, for the Kingdom of heaven is at hand.' Where the Vulgate seemed to refer to the ecclesiastical rite of penance, Erasmus insisted that the reference was to an inward individual attitude – that of 'being repentant'. A significant challenge was thus posed to the necessity and relevance of existing ecclesiastical ceremonies.

Another area of theology which medieval theologians had developed far beyond the modest views of the early church relates to Mary, the mother of Jesus. For many later medieval theologians, Mary was to be treated rather like a reservoir of grace, which could be tapped when needed. In part, this view rested upon the Vulgate translation of the angel Gabriel's words to Mary (Luke 1:28). According to the Vulgate, Gabriel greeted Mary as 'the one who is full of grace' (*gratia plena*), thus suggesting the image of a reservoir. But, as Erasmus pointed out, the original Greek text simply meant 'favoured one', or 'one who has found favour'. Once more, an important development in medieval theology seemed to be contradicted by humanist New Testament scholarship.

Calvin would later demonstrate himself to be a master of humanist linguistic and textual techniques for interpreting scripture. Our concern at this stage, however, relates to the particular form of humanism which he encountered at Orléans and Bourges. One result of the humanist programme of proceeding directly *ad fontes* was a marked impatience with glosses and commentaries. Far from being viewed as useful study tools, these became increasingly regarded as obstacles to engagement with the original text. They were like distorting filters, placed between the reader and the text. They were like layers of dust obscuring a mosaic, or coats of paint covering a mural: they denied or hindered access to a precious original. Unlike the Victorian architects who destroyed medieval Oxford by 'restoring' it, however, the glossators merely interposed themselves between the original text and the modern reader. They could be set to one side, and the original – whether this was the New Testament or the Justinian legal codes – read directly, unsullied by their glosses. As the new scholarship became more confident in its assertions, the reliability of Accursius and others was increasingly called into question by legal humanists. The great Spanish scholar Antonio Nebrija published a detailed account of errors he had detected in Accursius' glosses, while Rabelais wrote scornfully of 'the inept opinions of Accursius'. The foundations of French legal humanism had been well and truly laid.

French Legal Humanism

In sixteenth-century France, the study of law was in the process of radical revision. Whereas the southern regions had never entirely lost touch with the finer points of Roman law, the northern provinces had become little more than *pays de coutume*, where 'law' was virtually to be equated with unwritten or uncoded customs. The absolutist French monarchy under Francis I, with its increasing trend towards administrative centralization, regarded such legal diversity as outdated. In order to speed up the process of legal reform, eventually leading to the formulation of a legal system universally valid throughout France, it lent judicious support to those who were engaged on the theoretical aspects of general codes of law founded on universal principles.[10] A pioneer among these latter was Guillaume Budé, who argued for a direct return to Roman law as a means of meeting the new legal needs of France which was both eloquent and economic. In contrast with the Italian custom (*mos italicus*) of reading classical legal texts in the light of the glosses and commentaries of the medieval jurists, the French developed the procedure (*mos gallicus*) of appealing directly to the original classical legal sources in their original languages.[11] Although the *légistes* of Orléans and Bourges had no authority to enforce a revived Roman law, the quality of their engagement with the theoretical problems attending the interpretation of a classic text and its transposition to meet current needs established men such as Budé as foremost among the intellects of his age.

Calvin probably arrived at Orléans in 1528, although we possess no documentary evidence to this effect. The following year, he was attracted to Bourges by the reputation of a newly arrived Italian professor of law, the noted jurist Andrea Alciati.[12] As part of a series of reforms pushed through in 1527, Bourges began to poach established scholars from other institutions, its high salaries compensating for any lack of prestige on the part of the university. Alciati was enticed from Avignon by an attractive financial arrangement. After a while, however, Calvin found Alciati's appeal to be distinctly on the wane; he appears to have returned to Orléans in October 1530.

In studying civil law at Orléans and Bourges, Calvin thus came into first-hand contact with a major constituent element of the humanist movement. To suggest that he merely gained insights into the theoretical foundations of law and the practicalities of legal codification is to underestimate the importance of this encounter. It is certainly true that when Calvin was subsequently called upon to assist with the codification of the 'laws and edicts' of Geneva, he was able to draw on his knowledge of the body of classical Roman civil law (*Corpus Iuris Civilis*) for models of contracts, property law, and judicial procedure;[13] like Andrea Alciati, attracted to Bourges at enormous expense, Calvin was both humanist thinker and practical lawyer. Budé's literary output points to a conviction that the classical heritage in general, and not only its legal institutions and codes, was laden with importance for the present. The link between law and letters (*bonae litterae*), established in the person of Budé, appears to have introduced Calvin to the world of humanist values, methods and sources. In addition to his *De asse et partibus eius* (1514) and *Commentarii graecae linguae* (1529), and *Annotationes in quatuor et viginti Pandectarum libros* (1508), Budé produced writings on the New Testament and the remarkable *De transitu hellenismi ad Christianismum*, tracing the development from Greek wisdom to Christian faith. This last-mentioned work sets out a comprehensive justification of the basic principles of Christian humanism, arguing that the study of antiquity is a proper preparation for the gospel of Jesus Christ. Calvin would adopt a similar approach in the great 1559 edition of the *Institutes of the Christian Religion*, allowing Cicero to guide the reader from the natural religion of antiquity towards the superior gospel of Jesus Christ.[14]

The origins of Calvin's methods as perhaps the greatest biblical commentator of his age lie in his study of law in the advanced atmosphere of Orléans and Bourges. There is every indication that he learned from Budé the need to be a competent philologist, to approach a foundational text directly, to interpret it within the linguistic and historical parameters of its context, and to apply it to the needs of the present day. Yet Calvin would first publicly apply those methods, not to scripture, but to a minor work of Seneca.

The Seneca Commentary

Early in 1531, Calvin graduated as *licencié ès lois* from the University of Orléans. The Calvin whom we find emerging from the study of law gives little indication of any ambition to become a *légiste* (that he should study law in the first place appears to have been his father's decision, as we noted earlier); rather, his aspirations appear firmly directed towards the pursuit of eloquence and good letters, along with whatever fame their possession might bring. After returning to Paris in June 1531, he brought to completion a major scholarly work begun while he was still a law student at Orléans in 1530. The study of law had led Calvin on to a love of letters. Presumably in an attempt to gain a reputation as a humanist scholar, he dedicated two years of his life to writing a commentary on Seneca's *De clementia*, which he published at his own expense in April 1532. A stranger to the world of vanity publishing, Calvin soon discovered its hazards: the lack of interest in the book left him financially embarrassed, and obliged to borrow money from friends such as Nicolas Cop (son of the distinguished Paris physician and scholar, Guillaume Cop) and Nicolas du Chemin.[15] Attempting to exploit the fact that he was a known name at Orléans, Calvin tried to persuade lecturers to mention the work and Philip Loré, the book agent, to stock no fewer than one hundred copies.[16]

The particular treatise which Calvin chose to expound had been included by Erasmus of Rotterdam in his 1515 edition of Seneca. At that time, Erasmus had been preoccupied with his work on Jerome and the New Testament, and it is not impossible that he may have devoted less time and care to Seneca than the work demanded; unsatisfied with his efforts, he published an improved edition in January 1529. It was this second edition which attracted Calvin's attention, perhaps on account of its preface. Erasmus cordially invited anyone of greater ability and leisure to improve upon his work; it was an obvious invitation to nemesis. It is perhaps an indication of his immaturity that Calvin, with an eye to the approbation of the commonwealth of letters, picked up the gauntlet,[17] where others had been wise enough to leave it untouched.

It was a poisoned chalice. Calvin's career as a professional man of letters may be said to have begun and ended with this work. If fortune eluded him through the Seneca commentary, then it must also be said that his fame does not rest upon it either. It is probably fair to suggest that, had Calvin continued in this vein for the remainder of his career, he would have done little more than merit a footnote in some history of classical scholarship, eventually to retire in fully merited obscurity. The work demonstrates a thorough grounding in the history, literature and culture of antiquity; fifty-five Latin and twenty-two Greek authors are cited.[18] These statistics are perhaps less impressive when it is appreciated that most of the quotations derive from existing compilations, such as Aulus Gellius' *Attic Nights* or Budé's *Commentarii graecae linguae*, suggesting a literary accomplishment perhaps comparable to one who has dipped into the *Oxford Dictionary of Quotations*.[19] Nevertheless, if Calvin's material is borrowed rather than original, he still shows considerable dexterity and creativity in handling it.

Perhaps more significantly, however, the commentary also shows Calvin as a man concerned with the gentle art of persuasion through words. The future rhetorician, who mastered human words in order that the word of God might be channelled through them, stands revealed in this early work. Time after time Calvin shows himself to relish a particularly apt illustration, a well turned phrase, an elegant expression, or the carefully weighed *bon mot* (he even criticizes Seneca on occasion for his rambling style). His passionate concern for ease of communication, for the ability to bridge the gulf between speaker and hearer, between writer and reader, is evident throughout the work. Anglo-Saxons may eschew the term 'rhetoric', where they find acceptable the more cumbersome 'communication theory and skills'; nevertheless, the two terms designate the same discipline, which Calvin demonstrated himself to have mastered while still in his early twenties. It was a discipline which became a weapon which he would deploy with considerable success in the Reformation struggles which lay ahead.

Although some commentators have suggested that the Seneca commentary is the tiny mustard seed which contains *in nuce* the mighty tree of the Reformation, this judgement may only be allowed to stand in relation to the methods Calvin employed, rather than the results gained through their application. In this work, he appears to have been concerned primarily with expression rather than substance, this preoccupation being perhaps the most original and creative element in a work whose content is generally dull and derivative. In the commentary we find Calvin establishing the meaning of phrases or words by providing a philological explanation, followed by an appeal to grammar and rhetoric in order to explain the manner in which the words are related. Final refinements of interpretation are provided by illustrating parallel uses of terms or phrases from other sources of antiquity, as well as from additional writings by Seneca. Learned explanations of Latin terms and phrases abound, interspersed with impressive etymologies of Greek words. The overall impression gained is that this is a work written by a man who cares about words and language, even if the ideas which they convey often appear, at this stage, to be relegated to the background. If Calvin seems to display a lack of interest in the outcome of this rigorous process of approaching his text, it is perhaps on account of his overriding concern with method, rather than substance, at this point. The same patient concern for the literary and historical contextualization of his text undergirds his mature preaching and work as a biblical commentator; on these later occasions, however, Calvin appears to be enthralled and captivated, even entranced, by the substance of his texts. There is a distinct mark of commitment, of existential concern, for scripture, which is conspicuously absent from the pedestrian inquiry of the Seneca commentary.

During the second half of May 1532, Calvin left Paris for Orléans. His intention was presumably to complete his legal studies. He is known to have served as *substitut annuel du procureur* of the Picard Nation at Orléans in the months of May and June 1533;[20] although the precise nature of this office is unclear (it seems to have been honorary and administrative), it would appear to have been conferred for the full academic year of 1532–3. After that year ended, Calvin appears to have returned to his native Noyon: he is known to have attended a meeting of the cathedral chapter on 23 August 1533.[21] Two months later, he was in Paris.

Paris in 1533

In many ways, the situation at Paris then mirrored that which existed while Calvin had first studied there. There was intense hostility towards any views which could be considered Lutheran, or of questionable orthodoxy.[22] On 30 April 1530, the faculty of theology condemned as scandalous the suggestion that 'Holy Scripture cannot be understood correctly without Greek, Hebrew or other similar languages.'[23] This decision is generally regarded as an attempt to undermine the authority of the readers of the Collège Royal (Guillaume Budé, Nicolas Cop, Pierre Danès and

François Vatable), later to become the Collège de France, a bastion of humanism within a university still clinging to the familiar old ways of scholasticism. On 1 February 1532, the faculty issued its condemnation of a series of subversive doctrines propounded by Etienne Le Court, including the radical suggestion that 'now that God has willed that the Bible should be in French, women will take over the office of bishops, and bishops the office of women. Women will preach the gospel, while bishops will gossip [*broderont*] with young girls.'[24] The faculty found this too advanced for their understanding of orthodoxy.

Nevertheless, the period 1528–35 was fraught with difficulty for the faculty of theology. In 1532 Jean du Bellay, a long-standing and outspoken critic of the faculty, was appointed bishop of Paris. A certain coolness developed around this time between the faculty and the Parisian *parlement*. Relations between the king and the faculty were also strained. The faculty had been defeated by Francis I over the divorce of Henry VIII, and had noted with alarm the growing influence of the evangelically minded Marguerite of Navarre over Francis following the death of the queen mother. Under the patronage of Marguerite, the evangelical Gérard Roussel began to draw large crowds with his preaching during Lent 1533. It was not long before other preachers began to imitate his style and ideas. Seriously worried over the impact of Roussel, on 29 March 1533 the faculty instructed six of its number to preach against the 'errors and perverse doctrines of the Lutherans'.[25] The strictly limited success of this move prompted the faculty to mount an intelligence-gathering operation, authorized by the vicar of Paris, in order to lay the foundations of a prosecution for heresy against Roussel. Roussel's sermons met with unusually acute attention on the part of some of their hearers in April of that year. The king, however, was alarmed at the potential implications of such a heresy trial for Roussel's patron, Marguerite of Navarre (who was pregnant at the time): on 13 May 1533, the king ordered Noël Bédier (the faculty syndic) and certain of Roussel's critics to be banished from Paris. (The post of syndic was created on 5 May 1520, in response to dissatisfaction with the effectiveness of the holders of the existing senior faculty positions of dean and vice-dean. Bédier was invited to become syndic, and effectively take charge of the faculty. He held this position virtually continually until 1533.)

This was widely interpreted as a decisive blow against the faculty of theology. The faculty, however, promptly elected a new syndic, and seemed to retaliate against the king in October by allowing Marguerite's poem *Miroir de l'âme pécheresse*, to be censured (the printer, they argued, had failed to submit the work for faculty approval, as laid down by *parlement*).[26] This impression gained credibility on account of a recent attempt to perform a student play on 1 October at the Collège de Navarre (a noted stronghold of the faculty of theology), in which Marguerite of Navarre was portrayed as a housewife who became demented on reading the Bible. Calvin related these events with some amusement in a letter to his 'brother and good friend, Monsieur [François] Daniel, lawyer of Orléans'.[27] A heavily veiled, conspiratorial and appreciative reference to 'M.G.' in this letter suggests that Calvin was sympathetic to the evangelical opinions of 'Monsieur Gérard [Roussel]',[28] thus pointing to at least some degree of alignment on Calvin's part with the moderate reforming programme with which Roussel was associated.

As October 1533 drew to a close, there were thus conflicting signals to be observed concerning the climate for reform at Paris. The faculty of theology retained its former hostility, whether to Lutheranism or humanism; its power, however, seemed temporarily to have been reduced. The king, on the other hand, perhaps increasingly inclined to take account of the pro-evangelical views of Marguerite of Navarre, seemed well disposed towards the moderate reformist views associated with Lefèvre d'Etaples and his disciples, such as Roussel. These men, although clearly passionately concerned for the spiritual state of the catholic church, saw themselves as called to renew it from within; they are not 'reformers' as that word would later be understood.[29] It was perhaps easy for those sympathetic to the cause of reform to be seduced by such positive signs, and overlook more ominous indicators suggesting the climate was hardening against the *évangéliques*. Nicolas Cop, newly elected as rector of the University of Paris in the autumn of 1533,[30] chose to devote his inaugural address to the need for reform and renewal within the church. It was to prove a catastrophic error of judgement.

The All Saints' Day Oration

On 1 November 1533, Cop delivered the customary oration to mark the beginning of the new academic year. Since the publication in 1580 of the definitive *Histoire ecclésiastique des églises réformées au royaume de France*, compiled at Geneva under the direction of Théodore de Bèze, it has become part of the fixed tradition concerning Calvin's Paris period to assert that this address was delivered at the 'church of the Mathurins'.[31] Although the oration was indeed traditionally given in the chapel of the Trinitarian convent of Saint-Mathurin, the regular meeting place of the faculty of theology, the venue for 1533 was actually the chapel of the Franciscan Observantines, known locally as the 'Cordeliers' on account of the knotted cord they wore around their waists. (This is made clear in a letter from Roderigo Manrique to Luis Vivés, dated 9 December 1533;[32] it also explains an otherwise puzzling matter – why it was the Cordeliers who were the first to condemn Cop's address.)

The address caused a sensation.[33] Although it was modest in its proposals (reflecting Fabrisian attitudes similar to those of Gerard Roussel) and derivative in its theology (drawing slightly on Erasmus and Luther, yet retaining much traditional catholic material, such as an invocation of the Virgin Mary), the address was regarded as offensive and intemperate by those who heard it. The violence of this reaction is a matter of history; it is, however, difficult to understand its intensity, in that the address bears no trace of being composed by one committed to the principles of the Reformation, as those were then understood. Writing within a month of the event, Manrique described the outrage it provoked at every level of Parisian society.[34] Marguerite of Navarre intervened in vain on Cop's behalf.[35] On 19 November he was replaced as rector by his immediate predecessor, the Portuguese academic Andreas de Gouveia. The following day, the former rector was obliged to appear before *parlement*; although Cop is known to have been in Paris at that point, he failed to appear.[36] On 13 December, Francis I wrote in anger from Lyons, ordering the arrest of the incompetent *parlementaire* who had allowed Cop to escape from Paris.[37]

Two copies of this inaugural address still exist: the first, in Calvin's own hand, appears to have several pages missing; the second, in a sixteenth-century hand, contains the full text of the address, but with a number of grammatical infelicities which suggest it is a poor copy of an unknown original.[38] A comparison of the handwriting of the latter with that of a letter from Cop to Martin Bucer, to be dated 5 April 1534, suggests that this complete text was written by Cop himself. It is, however, highly unlikely that this is the original copy of the address. In the first place, it is written on paper which appears to originate in the upper Rhineland, possibly Basle itself (suggesting that Cop wrote it while in exile in that city in 1534); the Strasbourg archivist Jean Rott discovered a letter written from Basle by the German humanist Myconius to colleagues at Strasbourg, dated 9 November 1539, the paper of which bears the same distinctive watermark as that found on folios 3 and 4 of the Strasbourg document. In the second, a study of the textual variations between the two extant versions of the text suggests that both are copies of a lost original, with the Genevan document being the better of the two.

Calvin also chose to leave Paris for an unknown destination during the final two weeks of November 1533.[39] By the beginning of December, he felt able to return.[40] But why should Calvin have felt obliged to flee Paris in the aftermath of the Cop affair? No contemporary source suggested that he was the author of, or that he was in any way implicated in the writing of, Cop's inflammatory address. (The first hint that Calvin himself wrote the work is to be found, characteristically unsubstantiated, in de Bèze's revised 1575 biography of Calvin.) At one level, the question may be answered without difficulty: in the aftermath of the Cop affair, the authorities took action against at least fifty individuals thought to be sympathetic to 'Lutheran' ideas; Calvin would unquestionably have been among their number, had he remained. Nevertheless, that more intriguing possibility remains: that Calvin did indeed *write* Cop's address. The evidence in relation to this possibility, although suggestive, is far from unambiguous. If the work is by Calvin, he has still to develop his later style. To attribute the address to Calvin is to do him no literary or theological honour. It also points to certain theological attitudes which are not characteristic of the later reformer; there is, however, no particular reason to exclude his holding these positions at this earlier stage, when he appears to have been aligned with a more moderate Fabrisian conception of reform. All the same, the question remains: why should Calvin have copied out the address in his own hand? What associations did it possess for him that merited such an action on his part? The existence of the document suggests that, at least in Calvin's mind, the address was decisively associated with, perhaps even to the point of reflecting, his own religious formation.

The central question concerning Calvin's religious formation, however, concerns his transition from humanist to reformer. At what point did he move away from the moderate Fabrisian programme of reform, and adopt the more radical agenda now associated with his name? What considerations led him to this decision? To deal with such questions is to turn to the matter of Calvin's 'sudden conversion' – an apparently catastrophic (in the sense of an abrupt and far-reaching) decision to commit himself irrevocably to the cause of the Reformation.

4

From Humanist to Reformer: The Conversion

A CENTRAL THEME of Christian spirituality is the notion that great sinners may be redeemed from their waywardness through a single, often dramatic, moment of conversion. Paul and Augustine, the two fountainheads of western Christianity, both underwent conversion experiences which later generations took as models.[1] To speak of 'conversion', however, is not merely to draw attention to a sudden change of mind or heart; it is to suggest, discreetly yet definitely, that behind this volte-face there is to be discerned the hand of God. Conversion is something directed towards and accomplished by God. Paul's experience on the road to Damascus (Acts 9:1–19) points to a distinct perception on his part, and subsequently within early Christian circles, of the influence of God on apparently unpromising and unyielding material. Paul – or Saul of Tarsus, as we must call him at this stage – regarded himself as irredeemably set in his ways, irreconcilably opposed to Christianity; his subsequent about-turn was of such a magnitude and intensity that he could only attribute it to divine intervention.

As the Reformation gained momentum, there was a growing tendency to regard the medieval catholic church as resembling the worst aspects of post-exilic Judaism. Did it not teach justification by works of the law, according to Paul the chief theological error of Judaism?[2] A certain parallel was noted between medieval catholicism and Judaism on the one hand, and evangelicalism and New Testament Christianity on the other. Just as Paul symbolized the momentous transition between Judaism and Christianity, so his conversion might be paralleled in the sixteenth century by one who broke with his catholic background, in order to assume, deliberately and decisively, an attachment to the Reformation. No one was born an evangelical in the 1520s or 1530s; to become one involved a conscious decision to break with the past, paralleling that experienced by Jewish converts to Christianity in its first period. The decisive conversion experience narrated by Augustine was also assimilated by the image-makers of the Reformation. Were there not parallels between Augustine's gradual disillusionment with pagan superstition (as they saw it), culminating in a decisive change of course and an open embracing of the gospel, and their own spiritual pilgrimages from the religious superstitions of the medieval church to the rediscovered religion of the gospel?

The term 'conversion' was thus heavily loaded with overtones and implicit appeals to pivotal events of, and normative patterns within, Christian history. As one who deplored the cult of personality, Calvin provides few clues to his own religious development. There is only one passage in his writings which may realistically be taken as an authentic account of his decision to break with his past: the preface to the *Commentary on the Psalms* (1557).[3] In describing this break with the medieval church as a 'sudden conversion' (*subita conversio*), Calvin was unquestionably aligning himself with these powerful associations. 'Conversion' did not designate merely a private and interior religious experience; it embraced an outward, observable and radical shift in institutional allegiance. In describing how his vocation as a reformer developed, he asserts that he was 'so strongly devoted to the superstitions of the papacy' that nothing less than an act of God could extricate him from his situation.[4] He was a 'stick-in-the-mud', unable to wade to freedom, possibly even content to wallow in the comforting and familiar mire of catholic spirituality. In a series of terse images, Calvin portrays his situation as that of one who is trapped in his ways, unable and perhaps even unwilling to break free. Intervention from outside was necessary if he was ever to be liberated from the matrix of late medieval religion. Deploying an equestrian image, he compares God's dealings with him at this stage to a rider who directs his horse through its reins. 'At last, God turned my course in a different direction by the hidden bridle [*frenum*] of his providence. . . By a sudden conversion [*subita conversione*] to docility, he tamed a mind too stubborn for its years.'[5]

Calvin's grammar here illuminates both his theology and his understanding of his personal religious experiences. Throughout the narrative, it is God who is presented as the active party; Calvin is passive. God acts; Calvin is acted upon. A similar attitude is struck by the Zurich reformer Huldrych Zwingli in a poem dating from 1519, in which he reflected upon his experience of coming close to death as a result of the plague then ravaging the city. Whether he lived or died lay in the lap of God. Zwingli records his perception of total powerlessness; he was no longer captain of his own soul, but a divine plaything, a piece of clay to be moulded, a vessel to be broken.[6] As a result, the notions of divine providence and omnipotence come to assume a central role in Zwingli's thought, invested with existential importance. His near-fatal illness lent vitality and relevance to the idea of God's providence. Providence was no longer some abstract notion, but a force to be reckoned with, something which affected Zwingli's very survival.

Calvin's brief and dense account of his conversion is both revealing and enigmatic. It clearly indicates that he regarded himself as having been singled out by God; he considered himself to have been called to serve God in some quite definite, if as yet undefined, capacity and location.[7] In no way, it must be stressed, can this consciousness of a divine vocation be taken as a mark of arrogance on Calvin's part: his understanding of the conditions upon which humans relate to God precludes any such attitude. Those insights central to Luther's doctrine of justification by faith are echoed by the young Calvin: God calls the unrighteous, the outcasts and the downcasts, those who are foolish and weak in the eyes of the world. To be called by God is almost a mark of total failure, by human standards. There are important parallels between Calvin's account of his own conversion and his comments on that of Paul,[8] suggesting that he recognized an historical and religious affinity between the two events.

Yet enigmas remain – indeed, Calvin's account of his own conversion generates as many riddles as it resolves. What historical and human agencies were employed by the 'providence of God'? And how are his sense of vocation and his conversion related? Did Calvin become conscious of a call to serve God as a minister of the gospel before, during or after his conversion? The intensely compressed account in the preface of 1557 suggests that they may have been simultaneous – but is there not the possibility that Calvin, in his old age, has telescoped into an instant developments which took place over a sustained period of time? Martin Luther, recalling in his dotage his great moment of religious insight some thirty years after the event, appears to have compressed history substantially; insights which may be shown to have taken place over a period of years are presented as if they took place in a moment of devastating illumination.[9] Is there not a real possibility that Calvin may have done the same, with memory being influenced by theory, or by the patterns of Augustine or Paul?

Ganoczy has suggested, with some justification, that Calvin's references to a 'sudden conversion' are not intended to be understood as an historical account of, but rather as a theological commentary upon, his early career.[10] There are excellent reasons for suggesting that Calvin wishes to identify in his own life an example of the general phenomenon of the momentary yet decisive divine invasion of the realm of humanity. No particular chronological references are implied, still less explicitly stated. The term *subita* resonates with overtones of the unexpected, the unpredictable, the uncontrollable – all essential aspects of the manner in which God acts, according to the later Calvin. By speaking of his conversion, he does not intend to inform us historically, but wishes to signal his alignment with the great 'twice-born' figures of Christendom – men and women whom God turned about in their tracks, in order that they might perform a great service to him.

Despite this, it is perhaps inevitable that an appeal to history must be made in an attempt, however limited in its potential success, to unravel the enigma of Calvin's 'sudden conversion'. In spite of his apparent unwillingness to locate this experience on the map of human history (his distinct preference being to discuss the matter *sub specie aeternitatis*), it is appropriate to inquire whether any episode in his career appears to correspond with the pattern of changes suggested by this tantalizing autobiographical reflection.

Calvin was, as we have seen, obliged to leave Paris – apparently still a moderate Fabrisian reformer – in the aftermath of the Cop affair of November 1533. It is not clear where he sought refuge; indeed, he returned to Paris at some point in December. Nevertheless, the deterioration of the situation in that city was obvious, and Calvin deemed it wise to lie low. By the beginning of 1534, he had settled at Saintonge, home of Louis du Tillet, then canon of Angoulême and rector of Claix. The reception du Tillet accorded his friend was cautious, and apparently based upon Calvin's humanist love of letters, rather than his religious views. According to a near-contemporary source, the du Tillet family owned a library of several thousand volumes at Angoulême:[11] Calvin's *Psychopannychia* – a work written (but not published) at this time to refute the Anabaptist teaching that the soul passes into a state of sleep on death – shows a fine, apparently first-hand, knowledge of early Christian writers, suggesting that he had access to an excellent working library at this point. Other documents suggest that Calvin came into contact with reform-minded individuals while at Angoulême. Pierre de la Place – later to be numbered among the victims of the Saint Bartholomew's Day Massacres (1572) – wrote to Calvin around 1550, recalling with evident affection their relationship at Angoulême.[12]

Nevertheless, the evidence does not point to any fundamental break at this point with what Calvin would later refer to as 'the superstitions of the papacy'. He was reform-minded at this juncture, sharing an outlook already associated with many within the French church; there is, however, no hint of a break with that church. Calvin 'still wore the mask of a catholic', as Florimond de Raemond has it, and 'did not preach, pray or worship in any way contrary to catholic custom'.[13] Furthermore, the *Psychopannychia* contains no anti-catholic polemic. It is difficult to find even a hint that the work was written by a young man recently persuaded of the errors of his former catholic ways.

All the same, a laconic entry in the Noyon chapter archives may point to a watershed in Calvin's career. On 4 May 1534, he resigned the chaplaincy of La Gésine, which passed to a new beneficiary.[14] This could be seen as marking a break with the catholic church. Perhaps Calvin had decided that, with his new insights into the nature of true religion, he could no longer allow himself to profit from what he now recognized to be a corrupt and unevangelical church. There may be some truth in this suggestion; regrettably, however, he and his early biographers pass over the incident in silence. If it possessed so great a significance for them, signalling publicly Calvin's break with the catholic church, this curious and resonating silence remains to be explained. However, it is certainly plausible to assume that he had determined to break his remaining institutional links with the church at this point, thus suggesting that a 'conversion' may have occurred shortly beforehand. Sadly, however, this remains but a conjecture.

It is possible that the weighty interpretation placed upon the Noyon resignation by some of Calvin's more recent biographers may rest upon a misreading of an event which took place three weeks later. The Noyon archives for 26 May record that one 'Iean Cauvin' was imprisoned for causing a disturbance in church on Trinity Sunday.[15] Perhaps this was a public demonstration of Calvin's dissatisfaction with the contemporary church? Released on 3 June, this person was promptly reimprisoned two days later. This interpretation of events, however, seems to rest upon a false identification; the Noyon edicts scrupulously record that the

'Calvin' who was imprisoned possessed an alias – Mudit.[16] In other words, the *Iean Cauvin dict Mudit* was carefully distinguished from the individual of the same name who had featured in the chronicles of that city only a few weeks earlier. It is worth noting in this respect that in 1545 Calvin wrote to a colleague, praising God that he had never been imprisoned;[17] had he ever been seriously in trouble with the authorities for an offence of this unseemly nature, it is unlikely that his *noyonnais* opponents would have allowed it to pass without comment.

What followed this Noyon spell is far from clear. Colladon alludes to periods spent at the court of Marguerite of Navarre, and subsequently in Paris and Orléans.[18] According to Colladon, Calvin attempted to meet Michael Servetus – who will figure prominently in our account of Calvin's later Genevan period – while in Paris. An agreed safe meeting place in the Rue Saint-Antoine had been agreed in advance, on account of the danger Calvin faced through his presence in the city; Servetus, regrettably, failed to turn up.[19] They would meet again, however, in Geneva, some twenty years later.

The situation of the *évangéliques* deteriorated still further in the late autumn of that year, on account of the Affair of the Placards. Antoine Marcourt, the noted reforming pamphleteer of Neuchâtel, achieved the propaganda triumph of his career. Early in the morning of Sunday 18 October, anonymous placards vigorously denouncing the catholic mass were displayed in prominent locations throughout France.[20] Loyal catholics on their way to mass in Paris and some provincial towns were affronted with tabloid-size posters proclaiming the 'horrible, great and insufferable [*importable*] abuses of the papal mass'. Those who paused to read their four vitriolic paragraphs could hardly have failed to notice thinly veiled threats to the established church. Evangelicalism suddenly became perceived as a 'religion of rebels',[21] threatening to destabilize French society and endanger the status quo. Catholic orthodoxy, hitherto defended with a perceptible lack of enthusiasm by the political establishment, now came to be seen as linked with the preservation of political and social stability. New allies were found, and new alliances forged: suddenly, it became decidedly less than prudent to be an evangelical in Paris, and draw attention to the fact. To be an evangelical was perceived to be a subversive, perhaps even a traitor.

It is possible that among the outraged readers of the placards was Francis I himself, who awoke that Sunday morning at the château of Amboise to discover a specimen outside his bedchamber. Probably affronted as much by the lapse in security as by the religious content of the offending broadsheet, Francis returned to Paris to begin the vigorous prosecution of all who were suspected of evangelical sympathies. Even before he arrived there, however, the burnings had begun.

Underlying these events and Calvin's recollections of his religious reorientation may be discerned a characteristic pattern – the transition from a 'consensual' to a 'committed' understanding of religion.[22] Events brought home to Calvin the importance of his developing religious views. These were not ideas conceived and debated in ivory towers; they were ideas which threatened to destabilize a city and a kingdom, and which identified Calvin as a marked man. His existence came to be linked inextricably with his religious beliefs. Who he was as a person was shaped by his ideas – in his own mind, as well as in the perception of others. The integration of life and thought, of person and ideas, unquestionably dates from his year of wandering, during which the alliance of personal identity, theology and action was forged.

In the light of the events of October 1534, Calvin deemed it wise to leave France. Nicolas Cop had already sought and found refuge in the Swiss city of Basle, by then distinguished as a centre of letters as much as a safe haven for those with evangelical sympathies.[23] The expense of this trip would have been considerable; Calvin made the journey in the company of his friend du Tillet, who seems to have borne its costs without complaint. Travelling by way of Strasbourg, they probably arrived in Basle in January 1535. Calvin was now safe: but where would he go next? And what would he do during his enforced exile?

Adopting the pseudonym of Martinus Lucianus (an anagram of 'Caluinus'), he adapted himself to life in exile. Basle, like Strasbourg, was a German-speaking city; Calvin, who knew virtually no German, was limited in his social and literary contacts to those who spoke Latin or French. The University of Basle, once a major centre for humanist learning, had virtually become extinct; there was no community of scholars to whom Calvin could easily relate. Among those whom he is known or thought to have had contact with during this period were Elie Couraud, Pierre Caroli, Claude de Feray, Guillaume Farel, Pierre Toussaint and Pierre Viret.[24] Erasmus of Rotterdam, once a force to be reckoned with in the cosmopolitan world of letters, returned to Basle in May of that year, housebound and ill, having spent five years in Freiburg im Breisgau. There is no hint of any personal meeting between the two men; Erasmus died in June 1536.

Nevertheless, despite the restrictions placed upon him by life in Basle, Calvin made the most of his time in the northern Swiss city. His place of exile became an observatory, from which he could keep watch over happenings elsewhere. He would learn of dramatic events in the city of Geneva: the poisoning of the reformer Pierre Viret; the public disputation in which evangelical speakers gained an easy victory over their catholic opponents; the abolition of the catholic mass by the Council of Two Hundred on 10 August. Here he would learn of disastrous events in France, such as the execution of his friend Etienne de la Forge, burned alive on 16 February 1535.[25] He would see the *évangéliques* described as seditious and rebellious Anabaptists, not worthy to be compared with their distinguished German Protestant counterparts.[26] This was an extremely sensitive charge at the time: the Peasants' War (1525) had brought home to the German Protestant establishment how dangerous Anabaptism was as a radical social force; the impression had been reinforced through the recent Anabaptist takeover of the city of Münster under Jan van Leyden (1533–5), which eventually had to be ended forcibly by siege. Just as the German princes had felt justified in executing Anabaptists, so Francis had every right to execute the seditious elements of his population masquerading as religious reformers.

It was a powerful argument, deftly deployed on the advice of Francis' ambassador Guillaume du Bellay, brother of the bishop of Paris. Calvin was outraged by such suggestions, particularly since he had just written a treatise against the Anabaptists himself. He was deeply wounded by the implication that the *évangéliques* owed their inspiration to political, rather than religious, motives:[27] 'Et ce fut la cause qui m'incita à publier mon Institution de la religion Chrestienne.' Characteristically, as time would show, Calvin decided on action of the only type available to his politically naive yet literary and adept mind: he took up his pen, and wrote a book.

By 23 August 1535, the work was complete,[28] although not in time to permit the book to appear at the Frankfurt book fair that same autumn. The intended readership for the first edition of the *Institutes* is often thought to have been French evangelicals, anxious to consolidate their understanding of their faith. It is possible that some such intention may lie behind an early conception of the work, although it must be conceded that it is unclear when Calvin began to compose it. In fact, however, it seems that, when all the diplomatic conventions and niceties of the prefatory letter are discounted, the specific readership envisaged by Calvin for the work in its final form was rather different: the book is primarily intended to prove the utter stupidity of the allegation that the persecution of the *évangéliques* could be justified by comparing them with German Anabaptists. Incensed and stung by the statements emanating from the French court, now receiving wide circulation in Germany, Calvin wrote vigorously against those who portrayed the *évangéliques* as 'Anabaptists and seditious men'. His presentation of 'almost the whole sum of piety and whatever it is necessary to know in the doctrine of salvation' is intended to demonstrate the orthodoxy of the views of those working for reform, and thus to discredit those who, for political purposes (Francis I needed the support of the German princes against the Holy Roman Emperor Charles V), sought to portray them as heretical and radical.

In fact, however, the work had an effect perhaps rather different from that intended by Calvin, although not necessarily from that which he hoped for it. We shall consider the *Institutes* in some detail in chapters 7 and 8; at this stage, it is necessary only to point out that Calvin's considerable reputation as a religious writer and thinker may be justified on its basis alone.

Presumably after correcting the proofs of the *Institutes*, Calvin set off for the Italian city of Ferrara, probably attracted there by the evangelical views of the then Duchess of Ferrara, a cousin of Marguerite of Navarre. A number of French *évangéliques* appear to have regarded her court as a safe haven in the aftermath of the Affair of the Placards. Among these was the poet Clément Marot, accompanied by an individual named Jehannet. This person was at the centre of an incident on Good Friday (14 April), which threatened to trigger a wave of anti-evangelical sentiment within the court at Ferrara, compromising the position of the numerous *évangéliques* who had taken refuge there.

The entire court and its entourage – including Jehannet, and possibly also Calvin – had assembled for the traditional Good Friday ceremony of the veneration of the cross. At the climax of the ceremony, Jehannet strode out of the chapel, apparently drawing as much attention to his departure as was possible. Upon questioning over his extraordinary and offensive conduct, Jehannet declared his evangelical sympathies, and apparently made it clear that, unknown to the rest of the court, the duchess was sheltering numerous other individuals with the same inclinations. Convinced that his position was fatally compromised, Calvin returned to Basle, before (according to Colladon) proceeding to France.[29] The Edict of Coucy (16 July 1535) allowed religious fugitives to return there, provided they renounced their views within six months.[30] Taking advantage of this, Calvin journeyed to France, to settle remaining family affairs. A notice of power of attorney still exists, dated 2 June 1536, in which 'John Calvin, *licencié ès lois*, resident in Paris', gave his brother Antoine authority to wind up family affairs in Noyon.[31] On 15 July, he set off for Strasbourg, leaving behind the perils of France.

Unfortunately, the direct road to Strasbourg was threatened by movements of troops accompanying the war between Francis I and the Emperor. Calvin had to take an indirect route, heading south. He paused for the night in a city. That city was Geneva.

5

Geneva: The First Period

To speak of Calvin is to speak of Geneva. Calvin would shape, and be shaped by, Geneva. The interaction of this man and his adopted city is one of the great symbiotic relationships of history. Calvin himself was occasionally irritated by the closeness of this relationship, which he frequently found embarrassing: all too often, he complained, ill-informed individuals attributed the actions of the Genevan city council to him personally.[1] Although his first period of ministry in the city was short and, in many ways, disastrous, his subsequent return in something approaching triumph marked the opening of a new and momentous period in its history. But Geneva, curiously, is marginalized by many of Calvin's biographers. It is not that it is totally ignored, but rather that it tends to be treated in much the same way as Edwardian biographies of the great British empire-builders and pioneers refer to the wives of those same individuals – as minor, non-formative influences, worthy of brief and honourable mention, yet possessing no decisive relevance to their theme. Geneva cannot be treated in this manner. To understand Calvin as a man of action, rather than a builder of ahistorical cathedrals of the mind, it is necessary to come to terms with the city which occasioned and modified so much of his thought. Certain of Calvin's ideas appear to have been developed with the Genevan situation in mind. If this chapter seems to suggest that Geneva is, temporarily, more important than Calvin, it is partly to correct a fatal imbalance of much existing Calvin biography.

An example may illustrate the points we have in mind. In several ways, Calvin's ordering of the Genevan church in the *Ordonnances ecclésiastiques* of 1541 (see p. 111) represents a judicious, considered, and thoroughly pragmatic response to existing Genevan structures. The fourth order of ministry recognized by the *Ordonnances* is the diaconate. By the end of the medieval period, the diaconate had been seen as little more than an apprenticeship for the priesthood, allowing a decent interval to pass before an individual was finally consecrated priest. Calvin insisted that deacons should be a separate lay ministry, with a particular set of functions and responsibilities in its own right. In part, this insistence upon the distinctive role of the diaconate is founded upon he reading of the New Testament: in commenting on Acts 6:1–6, he links the diaconate with *cura pauperum*, the apostolic responsibility of caring for the poor.[2]

The idea may indeed be biblical; the manner in which it was to be implemented was thoroughly Genevan.[3] Calvin laid down that there should be five deacons, four of whom were to be *procureurs* and one a *hospitallier*. In effect, Calvin was doing little more than lending religious sanction to the work of the Genevan Hôpital-Général, founded before the Reformation, and charged with a programme of social welfare.[4] This institution brought together under a single authority (and eventually within a single building, the former convent of Sainte-Claire) the various relief agencies within the city. Six individuals were appointed to administer poor relief within the city; five were to be *procureurs*, responsible for the general administration of the social welfare programme; the sixth was designated *hospitallier*, charged specifically with the supervision of the Hôpital itself. Calvin's conception of the ecclesiastical office of deacon merely lent religious authority to an existing secular Genevan institution. It illustrates neatly the way in which Geneva influenced Calvin, as much as Calvin influenced Geneva.

The Reformation as a City Phenomenon

One of the most outstanding features of the European Reformation is that it was largely an urban phenomenon. In Germany, more than fifty of the sixty-five imperial free cities responded positively to the Reformation, with only five choosing to ignore it altogether. In Switzerland, the Reformation originated in an urban context (Zurich), and spread through a process of public debate within confederate cities such as Berne and Basle, and other centres – such as Geneva and St Gallen – linked to these cities by treaty obligations. French Protestantism began as a predominantly urban movement, with its roots in the major cities such as Lyons, Orléans, Paris, Poitiers and Rouen. Why, it has often been asked, was the Reformation so attractive to sixteenth-century urban communities?

A number of theories have been advanced to explain this phenomenon. Berndt Moeller argued that the urban sense of community had been disrupted in the fifteenth century through growing social tension within the cities, and an increasing tendency to rely upon external political bodies, such as the imperial government or the papal curia.[5] By adopting the Lutheran Reformation, Moeller suggested, such cities were able to restore a sense of communal identity, including the notion of a common religious community binding inhabitants together in a shared religious life. Significantly, Moeller drew attention to the social implications of Luther's doctrine of the priesthood of all believers, which broke down certain traditional distinctions within urban society and encouraged a sense of communal unity. Moeller argued that Luther's thinking was the inevitable product of the less culturally developed north-eastern part of Germany, lacking the sophistication of the more developed communities of south-western Germany. Coming from a small town that lacked the corporate structures of guilds and the communal impulses of the great cities, Luther could hardly avoid producing a theology which was inward-looking, provincial rather than urban, failing to engage with communal discipline and corporate urban structures. It was only to be expected that Luther's lack of familiarity with contemporary urban ideologies would lead to the formulation of a theology which was as profound and subjective, orientated towards the introspective individual, as it was unconcerned for communal regeneration and discipline. The theologies of Bucer and Zwingli were, in marked contrast, orientated towards the realities of urban existence. Bucer and Zwingli based their ecclesiologies upon the historical correlation of the urban and ecclesial communities, whereas Luther was obliged to construct his ecclesiology on the basis of the abstract notion of grace, which threatened to rupture civic unity.

A second explanation, based largely upon his analysis of the city of Strasbourg, was advanced by Thomas Brady.[6] Brady argued that the decision to adopt Protestantism at Strasbourg was the outcome of a class struggle, in which a ruling coalition of patricians and merchants believed that the only means by which their social position could be maintained was through alignment with the

Reformation. The urban oligarchs introduced the Reformation as a subtle means of preserving their vested interests, which were threatened by a popular protest movement. A similar situation, Brady suggested, existed in many other cities.

A third explanation of the appeal of the Reformation to sixteenth-century urban communities centres on the doctrine of justification by faith. In a study published in 1975, Steven Ozment argued that the popular appeal of Protestantism derived from this doctrine, which offered relief from the psychological pressure of the late medieval catholic penitential system and an associated 'semi-Pelagian' doctrine of justification.[7] As the weight of this psychological burden was greatest and most evident in urban communities, he argued, it was within such communities that Protestantism found its greatest popular support. Ozment argued that Moeller had vastly exaggerated the differences between Luther and the theologians of the south-west. The early reformers shared a common message, which could be summarized as the liberation of individual believers from the pyschological burdens imposed by late medieval religion. Whatever their differences, the magisterial reformers – such as Bucer, Zwingli and Luther – shared a common concern to proclaim the doctrine of justification by faith through grace, thereby eliminating the theological necessity of, and diminishing the popular concern for, indulgences, purgatory, invocation of the saints, and so forth.

Each of these theories is significant, and they have provided an important stimulus to the more detailed study of the development of urban Protestantism in the first phase of the Reformation.[8] Equally, each has been shown to have obvious weaknesses, as one might expect from ambitious global theories. For example, in the case of Geneva, as we shall see, the social tensions which eventually resulted in alignment with the Protestant city of Berne and adoption of the Zwinglian Reformation did not arise from class differences, but from division within a common social class over whether to support Savoy or the Swiss Confederacy (Helvetic Confederation). The pro-Savoyard Mammelukes and the pro-Bernese Eiguenots were both drawn from a common social group, characterized by a range of identifiable shared economic, familial and social interests. Similarly, Ozment's suggestion of a universal concern for the doctrine of justification finds little support in the case of many cities within, or linked with, the Swiss Confederacy – such as Zurich, St Gallen and Geneva – and overlooks the obvious hesitations concerning the doctrine on the part of many Swiss reformers.[9]

Nevertheless, some common features emerge from a study of the origins and development of the Reformation in cities such as Augsburg, Basle, Berne, Colmar, Constance, Erfurt, Frankfurt, Hamburg, Lübeck, Memmingen, Ulm and Zurich. It is helpful to identify these factors, and note how they bear upon the genesis of the Reformation at Geneva itself.

In the first place, the Reformation in the cities appears to have been a response to some form of popular pressure for change. Nuremberg is a rare instance of a city council imposing a reformation without significant preceding popular protest or demand. Dissatisfaction among urban populations of the early sixteenth century was not necessarily purely religious in character; social, economic and political grievances are unquestionably present, to varying extents, within the agglomerate of unrest evident at the time. City councils generally reacted in response to this popular pressure, often channelling it in directions appropriate to their own needs and purposes. This subtle manipulation of such pressure was an obvious way of co-opting and controlling a potentially dangerous popular protest movement. One of the more significant observations which may be made concerning the city Reformation is that existing urban regimes were often relatively unchanged by the introduction of new religious ideas and practices,[10] suggesting that city councils were able to respond to popular pressure without radical changes in the existing social orders.

In the case of Geneva, there was considerable internal popular pressure for the development of links with the Swiss Confederacy during the 1520s. This pressure developed as a result of a number of factors, none of which can conceivably be thought of as religious. If any consideration may be identified as predominant, it was a desire on the part of a number of leading citizens to be freed from the baleful influence of the duchy of Savoy. Like many cities of the period, Geneva craved for total independence, after the model of the Swiss cities.[11] (Geneva, it will be recalled, did not enter the Swiss Confederacy until 1815.) It was political freedom which was the lodestar of much Genevan unrest in the 1520s, rather than any specifically religious concerns.

In the early 1530s, however, a major religious element entered the picture, eventually to dominate it. The city's alliance with Berne led to growing popular sympathy with the evangelical views of that city. The city council was obliged to respond to this pressure, while avoiding a potentially disastrous military confrontation with Savoy. Through a series of diplomatic moves in 1534–5, the city council was able to outmanoeuvre the representatives of Savoy, enhancing its own authority and subtly promoting evangelicalism without provoking a showdown with the duchy. It was only in January 1536 that Savoy lost patience with diplomacy, and turned to military intervention.

Second, the success of the Reformation within a city was dependent upon a number of historical contingencies. To adopt the Reformation was to risk a disastrous change in alignment, in that existing treaties or relationships – military, political and commercial – with territories or cities which chose to remain catholic were usually deemed to be broken as a result. A city's trading relationships – upon which her economic existence might depend – might thus be compromised fatally. So the success of the Reformation in St Gallen was partly due to the fact that the city's linen industry was not adversely affected to any significant degree by the decision to adopt the Reformation.[12] Equally, a city (such as Erfurt) in close proximity to a catholic city (Mainz) and a Lutheran territory (Saxony) could not risk becoming embroiled in military conflict with one or other of these interested parties, with potentially lethal results for the independence of that city.[13] Furthermore, serious internal disunity as a result of a decision to introduce the Reformation could render the city vulnerable to outside influence – a major consideration in Erfurt city council's decision to halt reforming activities in the 1520s.

In the case of Geneva, a paramount historical contingency was the presence of the catholic duchy of Savoy and its allies on the very doorstep of the city. If the Reformation was to succeed, the major political and military threat posed to its progress by this duchy had to be neutralized. The growing movement within Geneva towards alignment with evangelical forms of Christianity in the years 1532–5 eventually provoked a military response from Savoy in January 1536. Geneva would have been totally overwhelmed by this, had it not been for a military alliance with the city of Berne, itself committed to evangelicalism from the late 1520s. This would be complemented by financial support from evangelical banking sources, particularly within Basle, once Geneva was firmly committed to the Reformation. As a result, the external pressure to retain catholicism was more than counterbalanced. A Reformation could proceed. However, a further historical contingency now complicated the situation: Berne, having lent Geneva its support at a crucial stage in its history, now demanded its pound of flesh. Geneva was not free to choose its own road to reformation: it must adopt the religious beliefs and practices already associated with Berne itself.

Third, the romantic and idealized vision of a reformer arriving in a city to preach the gospel with an immediately ensuing decision to adopt the principles of the Reformation must be abandoned as quite unrealistic. Throughout the process of Reformation, from the initial decision to implement a process of reform to subsequent decisions concerning the nature and the pace of reforming proposals, it was the city council who remained in control. Zwingli's Reformation in Zurich proceeded considerably more slowly than he would have liked on account of the cautious approach adopted by the council at crucial moments.[14] Bucer's freedom of action in Strasbourg was similarly limited. As Calvin would discover, city councils were perfectly able to evict reformers from their precincts if they stepped out of line with publicly stated council policy or decisions.

In practice, the relationship between city council and reformer was generally symbiotic. The reformer, by presenting a coherent vision of the Christian gospel and its implications for the religious, social and political structures and practices of a city, was able to prevent a potentially revolutionary situation from degenerating into chaos. The constant threat of reversion to catholicism or subversion by radical Anabaptist movements rendered the need for a reformer inevitable. Someone had to give religious direction to a movement which, unchecked and lacking direction, might fall into disorder, with momentous and unacceptable consequences for the existing power structures of the city, and the individuals who controlled them. Equally, the reformer was a man under authority, one whose freedom of action was limited by political masters, jealous for their authority and with a reforming agenda which generally extended beyond that of the reformer to include consolidation of their economic and social influence. The relation between reformer and city council was thus sensitive and easily prone to disruption, with real power permanently in the hands of the latter.

In the case of Geneva, a delicate relationship developed between the city's council and its reformers (initially Guillaume Farel and Calvin, subsequently Calvin alone). Conscious and jealous of its hard-won authority and liberty, the council was determined not to substitute the tyranny of a reformer for that of a catholic bishop.

In 1536, Geneva had just gained its independence from Savoy, and had largely retained that independence, despite the attempts of Berne to colonize the city. Geneva was in no mood to be dictated to by anyone, unless they were in a position to bring massive economic and military pressure to bear. As a result, severe restrictions were placed upon Calvin's actions. His expulsion from Geneva in 1538 demonstrates that political power remained firmly in the hands of the city council. The notion that Calvin was the 'dictator of Geneva' is, as we shall show, totally devoid of historical foundation. Nevertheless, the city council found itself unable to cope with a deteriorating religious situation in Calvin's absence. In a remarkable act of social pragmatism and religious realism, the council recalled their reformer, and allowed him to continue his work of reform. Geneva needed Calvin, just as Calvin needed Geneva.

With these general observations in mind, we may turn to consider the first phase of the Reformation in Geneva. Even before Calvin's accidental arrival in the city, a programme of reform was under way. How this happened is a fascinating story in its own right. Although we have touched upon some of its aspects already, the story demands to be told in detail.

Geneva before Calvin

Before the Reformation Geneva was an episcopal city in decline. Its prosperity was largely due to four annual international trade fairs, dating back to 1262, which took place at Epiphany, Easter, Petertide and All Saints' Day. These attracted considerable numbers of merchants from the Rhine and Danube valleys, from northern Italy, Burgundy and the Swiss Confederacy.[15] So important were these fairs that the Medici bank even deemed it worth their while to open a branch at Geneva.[16] The situation changed radically, however, at the end of the Hundred Years War. Louis XI established privileged trade fairs at nearby Lyons, carefully selecting their dates to overlap exactly with those of their only rival in the region, Geneva. Decline soon set in; the Medicis, sensing the way the wind was blowing, moved their activities from Geneva to Lyons.

The affairs of the pre-Reformation city were governed by the neighbouring duchy of Savoy.[17] This domination can be traced back to the thirteenth century, when the bishop of Geneva granted the house of Savoy the office of *vidomne* in 1265, giving Savoy the right to select the individual responsible for maintaining civil and criminal justice for laymen within the city. From 1287, the *vidomne* resided in the former episcopal castle on the island in the Rhône. As the power of Savoy grew in the fifteenth century, so did its influence over the affairs of the city. Many of the rural areas and villages around Geneva belonged to Savoy or its nominees. Most important of all, in 1449 the house of Savoy effectively gained control of the diocese of Geneva, when the anti-pope Felix V (formerly the first Duke of Savoy, Amadeus VIII) relinquished his papal title, while retaining many of its privileges. From that point onwards, the bishop of Geneva was virtually a Savoyard puppet, with no obvious religious abilities required of him: in 1451, the newly appointed bishop (Amadeus VIII's grandson) was a mere eight years of age.

The temporal and spiritual ruler of Geneva was thus virtually permanently absent from the city. His powers, though considerable, were generally exercised by his nominees in his absence, chiefly by the episcopal council and the cathedral chapter of thirty-two canons. The bishop, however, permitted the lay population of the city to elect certain officers to share in the work of local government. Perhaps the most important such officers were the syndics, four laymen elected annually by a plenary assembly of all male adult citizens. In addition to the right to act as judges in certain criminal cases, the syndics also chose a *Petit Conseil* (Little Council) of between twelve and twenty-five citizens with responsibility for routine maintenance of the city.

As the sixteenth century dawned, Geneva was simply one of many minor planets orbiting the Savoyard sun. If the Genevan population thoroughly disapproved of this state of affairs, their protests were discreet and virtually inaudible. Nevertheless, the winds of change were blowing. Within Geneva itself, Savoyard influence was crumbling; outside Geneva, the political and military influence of the Swiss Confederacy was becoming increasingly apparent.

The first traces of a movement within Geneva for independence from Savoy may be discerned in the period 1482–90. An episcopal interregnum allowed the cathedral chapter to extend its powers and heighten a sense of civic identity. The city's merchants, conscious that the financial viability of the annual trade fairs was now largely dependent upon Swiss and German traders, advocated closer links with the Swiss Confederacy. A tension began to emerge

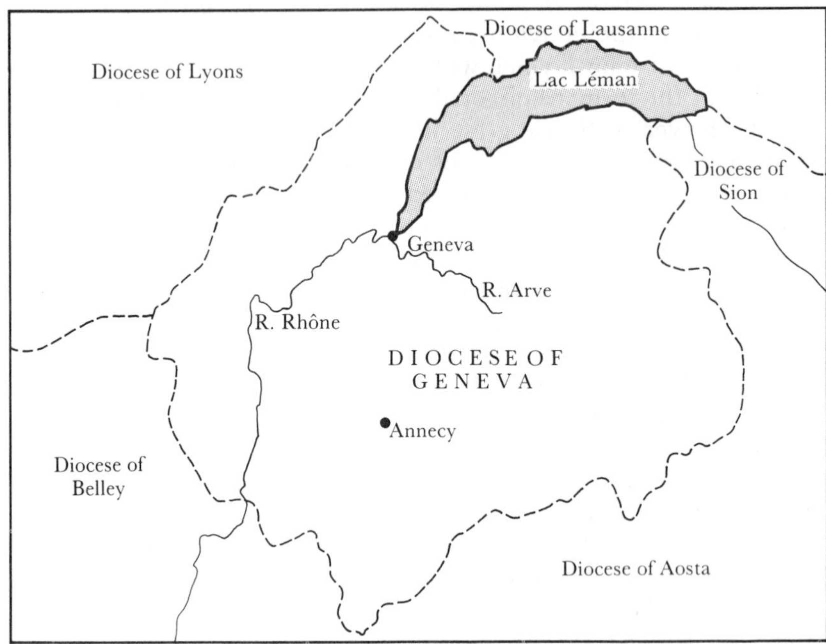

FIGURE 5.1 The diocese of Geneva, 1530

within the city, as factions developed. Eighty-six Genevans, headed by François Bonivard, travelled to the Swiss city of Fribourg, where they were made citizens on 7 January 1519. The following month, the city of Geneva, acting without Savoyard authority, entered into an alliance with Fribourg. Savoyard pressure resulted in this *combourgeoisie* being annulled that April; four months later, the chief Genevan instigator of the *combourgeoisie* was publicly executed. Although physically suppressed, however, the pro-Swiss party was not long in regrouping. The city council minutes for 1519 record the name given to this party as *aguynos*; those of 1520 identify it as *eyguenots*.

The introduction of this term merits attention. At the time, the Swiss were not referred to as such, but as 'the confederates'. The Swiss–German word for 'confederate', *Eidgnoss*, proved virtually impossible to pronounce in the Genevan patois (which was much closer to Savoyard than French; French remained a language alien to most Genevans during the sixteenth century). The term *eiguenot* or *eyguenot* represents the Genevan attempt to reproduce the term for 'confederate'. It is the later history of the term which has proved of particular interest, in that the French *huguenot* may well derive from it, perhaps through the intermediate Savoyard term *enguenô*, or the later Genevan *enguenot*.[18]

On 4 December, the independent city of Lausanne entered into a *combourgeoisie* with the Swiss cities of Berne and Fribourg. Like Geneva, Lausanne was an episcopal city in the Savoyard-controlled Pays de Vaud. News of this pact reached Geneva, and attracted considerable interest. Moving quickly, some pro-Swiss merchants travelled to Fribourg and Berne, to negotiate a similar pact with the cities. Despite an attempt by the then bishop of Geneva, Pierre de la Baume, to veto the pact, Berne agreed to the arrangement on 7 February 1526. The Savoyard party – the Mammelukes, who wore holly as the Welsh wear leeks – were furious with their Eiguenot fellow citizens (who had taken to wearing cock feathers, as a token of their rival allegiances). The bishop, however, realizing that his position in relation to the duchy of Savoy had been compromised by his failure to prevent the pact, decided to hedge his bets, and attempted to gain the sympathy of the Eiguenots by lending his support to the *combourgeoisie* with Berne. It was the first of a disastrous series of moves, in which the bishop, more by accident than design, ceded authority to the Genevan city council in one matter after another. By 1530, the council was virtually judicial master of the city.

Up to this point, religious matters had not figured at all in Geneva's flirtations with the Swiss. That situation now changed. The origins of this important development lie mainly in Zwingli's reformation at Zurich. Although his reforming activities at Zurich began in 1519, they entered a new phase with the Great Disputation of 29 January 1523. Some six hundred people assembled to hear Zwingli present and defend his reforming ideas and practices before his catholic opponents, selected by the bishop of Constance. After hearing the arguments, the city council voted to adopt the 'key principles' of Zwingli's reformation. It was a milestone in the course of the Swiss Reformation, in that it established a crucial principle: independent cities would decide whether to adopt the Reformation by hearing the arguments for and against it, and proceeding to a vote.

Five years later, a similar disputation (or *Gemeinschwörung*) took place in Berne. Zwingli, Bucer, and the Strasbourg humanist Wolfgang Capito and others represented the evangelical standpoint with such skill that the city council voted to accept the Zwinglian Reformation. The importance of this decision for Geneva cannot

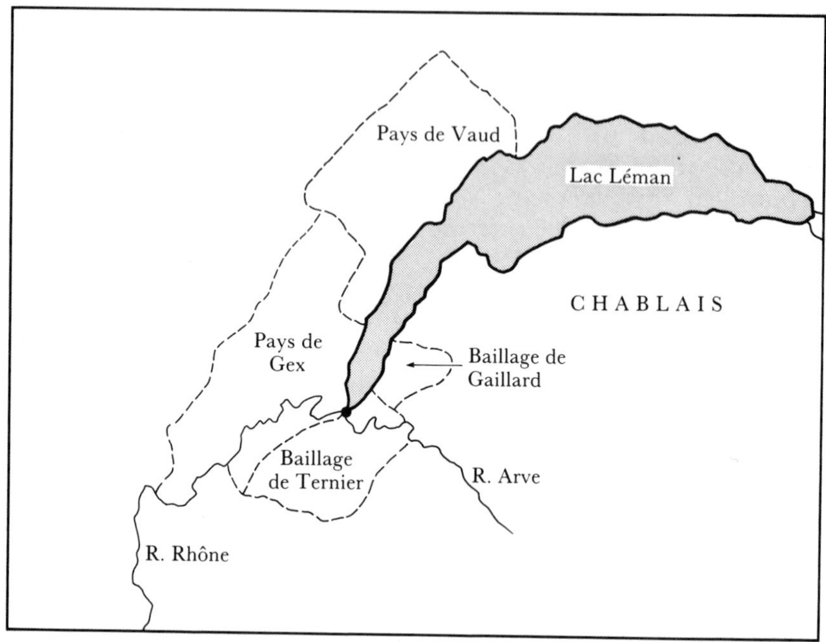

FIGURE 5.2 Geneva and its environs, 1500–35

be stressed sufficiently: the Berne allied with Geneva in 1526 was catholic; from January 1528, it was evangelical. Significantly, Fribourg – Geneva's other *combourgeois* – remained catholic, causing tensions which would reach a climax in 1534. Berne, already a major military power in the region of the Pays de Vaud, was now also engaged in a crusade directed towards the propagation of the Zwinglian Reformation.

Events began to move apace in Geneva during 1532. German merchants visiting the city brought with them Lutheran publications, which found a ready market there.[19] Lutheran placards began to be circulated in local churches. The Reformed theologian Guillaume Farel arrived, with a Bernese safe-conduct pass, and began to propagate evangelical views within the city. His preaching met with considerable success. Fribourg protested over the growing influence of evangelicalism within the city, and threatened to terminate its alliance with Geneva unless its growth was checked. On 10 April 1533 Garin Muète publicly celebrated a service of holy communion according to the reformed rite of Farel. The service, which took place in the garden of Etienne Dada in the

Faubourg du Temple, was subsequently repeated several times daily.[20] Religious riots broke out within Geneva that May, further alarming Fribourg. The catholic city demanded that Farel be expelled. Conscious of its obligations to evangelical Berne, the city council hesitated. Aware of the opportunities the situation offered, on 31 December 1533 Berne city council ordered Pierre Viret to proceed to Geneva in haste, in order that he might assist Farel.[21] He arrived there on 4 January 1534.

Following a model adopted by Zurich and Berne, the council decided to pit Farel against a catholic opponent in a public disputation, in order to ascertain the relative merits of evangelical and catholic forms of Christianity. Guy Furbity, a Dominican doctor of theology with strong links with the Parisian faculty of theology, was invited to present the catholic case. The disputation began on 27 January 1534, and centred on the question of papal authority; however, it degenerated into chaos when the catholic representative suggested that Farel was merely a puppet of the Swiss Confederacy. The outcome of the debate itself is unclear, except that it was widely perceived to be a victory by default for the reforming party. A contemporary account of these events, mingling the dramatic with the ironic, may be found in *Le levain du Calvinisme*, the memoirs of Jeanne de Jussy, a novice in the Genevan convent of Sainte-Claire at the time of the debate. This convent, situated on the Rue Verdaine as it entered the Bourg-de-Four in the centre of Geneva, subsequently became, as we noted earlier, the Hôpital-Général, charged with the administration of the reformed city's social welfare programme. In exasperation at the course of events, Fribourg washed its hands of the entire matter: on 15 May, it withdrew from its alliance with Geneva. Suddenly, Geneva had but one protector – Protestant Berne. And Berne was known to offer aid on a cash-only basis. Under the terms of the *combourgeoisie*, Geneva was obliged to pay for any assistance which Berne might render. A financial as much as a political crisis seemed inevitable.

In the middle of this growing crisis, Farel and Viret, both living under Bernese protection, brought increasing pressure on the city council to adopt the Reformation in its totality, rather than in a partial and piecemeal manner. The council yielded slightly; in the early summer of 1535, they announced the abolition of the catholic mass. The bishop of Geneva retaliated on 22 August by excommunicating the entire population of the city. There was an immediate exodus of catholic clergy and religious from the city, to seek safety in Savoyard Annecy. The council took over church land and

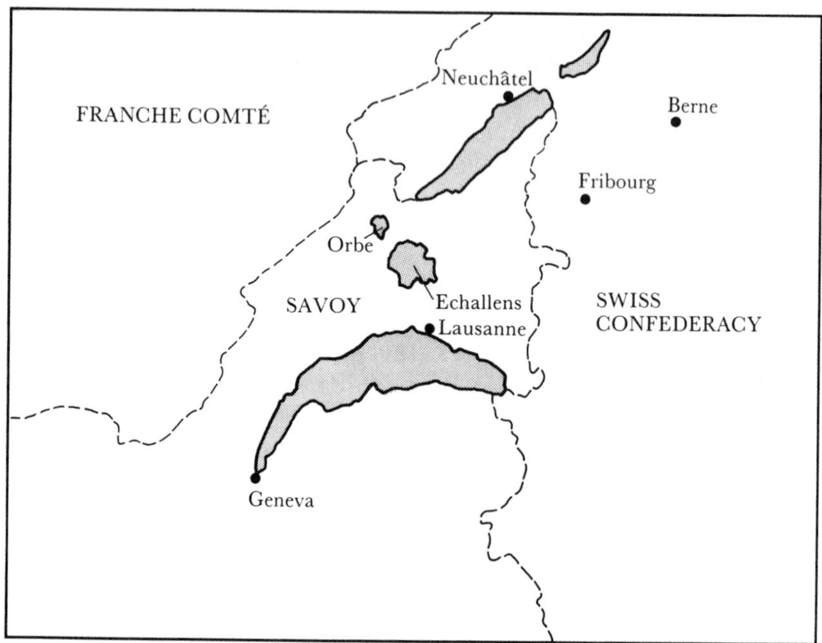

FIGURE 5.3 The boundaries of Swiss Confederate and Savoyard territories, 1535

property, dismantling the traditional seigneurial and ecclesiastical establishment. In a remarkable act of defiance, they even opened their own public mint on 26 November. The new coins of the city bore a slogan which would resonate throughout the Reformation: *post tenebras lux* – 'after the shadows, light!'

Savoy was now thoroughly alarmed by these developments. It responded in a Machiavellian manner: where diplomacy failed, military intervention could be relied upon to deliver results. Geneva was effectively under permanent siege by January 1536, with all her links with the outside world severed. The city had no choice but to make an appeal to Berne. Berne intervened, not overlooking the obvious possibilities which the situation afforded for expansion of her sphere of political influence. After the defeat of Charles the Bold and the Burgundians in 1477, the Swiss Confederacy had long coveted the idea of expanding its influence westward at the expense of Savoy. During the Burgundian wars, Berne and Fribourg had annexed, individually and jointly, considerable tracts of Savoyard territory.[22] Berne had seized Erlach,

Les Ormonts, Aigle and Bex; Fribourg had taken Illens. Acting jointly, the two cantons had taken possession of Morat, Grandson, Orbe and Echallens. Le Valais, taking advantage of Savoyard weakness, seized the Rhône valley between Vétroz and Massongez, to the south-east of Lac Léman.

The capture of Orbe and Echallens was particularly important. Although insignificant in terms of their territory, they were situated deep within Savoyard territory. Ever since 1477, the Bernese had marked the Pays de Vaud as ripe for annexation. By the early 1530s, Orbe was a centre for Protestant agitation within the region;[23] Pierre Viret, a native of the town, would subsequently become a central figure in the Reformation struggle in the area. Geneva's appeal seemed to offer a plausible legitimation for appropriation of this Savoyard territory – and more besides. Berne, Fribourg and Le Valais moved to exploit the situation.

Bernese armies moved westwards, annexing Lausanne – which had entered into a *combourgeoisie* with Berne and Fribourg in 1525 – as a Bernese possession. The whole of the Pays de Vaud was occupied, and the entire area around Geneva – including the Pays de Gex and the *baillages* (bailiwicks) of Ternier and Gaillard – was seized, thus placing a Bernese cordon sanitaire between Geneva and its erstwhile owners, Savoy. Finally, the Bernese occupied the western region of Chablais, on the southern shores of Lac Léman. In the meantime, Fribourg had seized Estavayer, Roment-Châtel-Saint-Denis, Surpierre, Vuissens and Saint-Aubin, while Le Valais extended its territory to include the eastern region of Chablais.

On 2 February, the Bernese entered Geneva. As became clear three days later, their object was not so much freeing the city from Savoy, as making it a dependency of Berne. The Bernese occupation force demanded the same rights over Geneva as those formerly enjoyed by Savoy. By 17 February, the situation had altered. The Bernese backed down. For some reason, Geneva was not to share the fate of hapless Lausanne, and was allowed to retain her independence, subject to certain treaty requirements. It is possible that the Bernese were wary of the ambitions of a French army in the neighbourhood, and were consequently anxious not to over-extend themselves.

And so the republic of Geneva was inaugurated. It inherited a financial crisis: during the war of independence, considerable expenses had been incurred: the city's neglected fortifications had been rebuilt, the faubourgs had been razed to the ground and their inhabitants relocated, and large numbers of soldiers had to

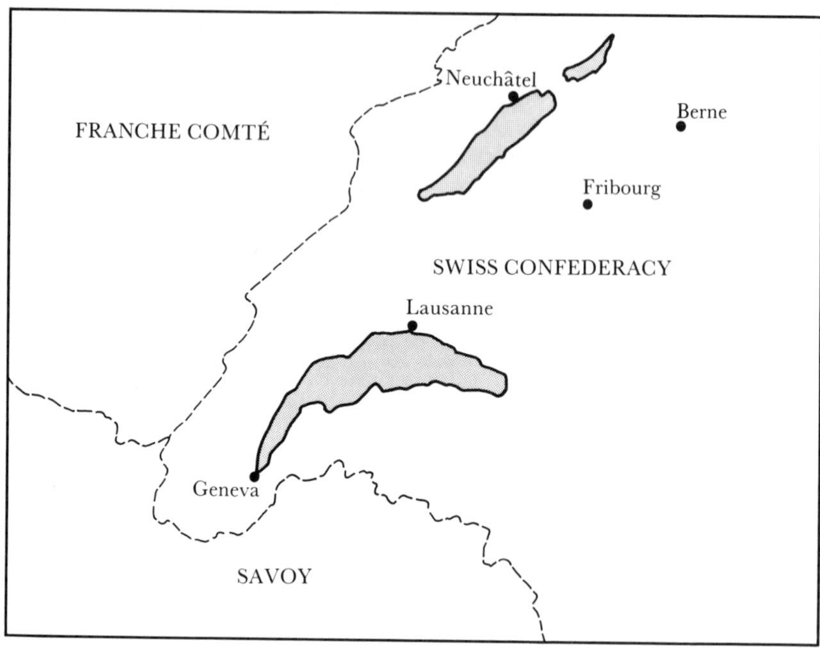

FIGURE 5.4 The boundaries of Swiss Confederate and Savoyard territories, 1536

be hired. In addition, Bernese aid had to be paid for. The city treasurer, Claude Pertemps, met the expenses through a vigorous programme of secularization, by which the city council confiscated all ecclesiastical properties and sources of revenue within Geneva. Extensive support from the evangelical financial sources would also be forthcoming, once Geneva had firmly committed herself to the Reformation.[24] Also, fines were imposed upon Genevan citizens who had fled the city during the period 1534–6, and who now wished to return.[25] In effect, it was the losers who paid the price of Geneva's war of independence.

Farel now pressed the city council to adopt the Reformation explicitly, with positive results: on 19 May, the Little Council decided to summon 'a great general council to ask if the people want to live according to the new reformation of the faith'.[26] Less than a week later, on 25 May, a public assembly of the citizens of Geneva voted to bring the first phase of the Reformation within the city to a close, by vowing to 'live henceforth according to the law of the gospel and the word of God, and to abolish all papal abuses'. The republic would retain its independence for a quarter of a millennium, until invading French Revolutionary armies finally seized the city in the last decade of the eighteenth century.

The declaration of the citizens of Geneva might seem to have created a Reformed church. In fact, it did little more than create a reform-minded vacuum, with intentions taking precedence over action. To reject catholicism was one thing; to build a new system of church government and order was another. Without some definite religious ideology, no positive steps of this nature could be taken. A degeneration into chaos was a distinct possibility. With the arrival of John Calvin, Farel believed that he had found just the man he and Geneva needed. But how did Calvin come to be in Geneva?

Calvin's Arrival in Geneva

Calvin's *Institutes* were slow to bring him fame. As he journeyed from France to Strasbourg in the summer of 1536, he made a point of making no mention of the work:

> Nobody there knew that I was its author. Here, as everywhere, I made no mention of the fact, and intended to continue doing the same until finally Guillaume Farel kept me at Geneva, not so much by advice and argument, as by a dreadful curse, as if God had laid his hand upon me from heaven to stop me. I had intended to go on to Strasbourg; the most direct road, however, was closed by the wars. I decided to pass through Geneva briefly, without spending more than one night in the town. A little while previously, popery [*la Papauté*] had been driven out by the good man I have mentioned, and by Pierre Viret. Things, however, were still far from settled, and there were divisions and serious and dangerous factions among the inhabitants of the town. Then someone, who has now wickedly rebelled and returned to the papists, discovered me and made it known to others. Upon this Farel (who burned with a marvellous zeal to advance the gospel) went out of his way to keep me. And after having heard that I had several private studies for which I wished to keep myself free, and finding that he got nowhere with his requests, he gave vent to an imprecation, that it might please God to curse my leisure and the peace for study that I was looking for, if I went away and refused to give them support and help in a situation of such great need. These words so shocked and moved me, that I gave up the journey I had intended to make. However,

> conscious of my shame and timidity, I did not want myself to be obliged to carry out any particular duties. [27]

Thus it was that in August 1536 Calvin found himself persuaded to remain in Geneva. Precisely what Farel saw in him we shall never know.

Initially, Calvin appeared ill suited to some of the challenges confronting the evangelical movement in Geneva. Withdrawn in personality and intellectual in inclination, he gave little indication of being of potential value in the cut-and-thrust world of Genevan politics of the 1530s. He totally lacked pastoral experience, and was virtually innocent of the realities of urban political and economic life. Calvin may have been at home in the cosmopolitan republic of letters; the needs of the republic of Geneva were something rather different. His initial responsibilities at Geneva suited his temperament very well: he was not required to exercise any pastoral ministry, nor to liaise with the city council, nor even to preach; his obligation was simply to act as a teacher, or a public lecturer on the Bible.[28]

Calvin's first weeks at Geneva were thus uneventful. Nevertheless, he was soon propelled to prominence. The Bernese, having occupied Lausanne earlier that year, now wished to consolidate their hold on their new acquisition by converting its population to evangelicalism. The tried and tested means of doing this was by organizing a public disputation in the vernacular. Wasting little time, the Bernese organized such a disputation for the first two weeks of October 1536.[29] Lausanne, however, was French-speaking, thus making it difficult for the German-speaking Bernese to present their case with total conviction. The Bernese city council – Messieurs de Berne, as they will be known in the Geneva council minutes – invited Farel and Viret to present the case for reform. They decided to bring Calvin with them.

Ten articles were presented for disputation.[30] *Les conclusions qui doibvent estre disputées a Lausanne nouvelle province de Berne* on 1 October 1536 broadly define the main points of the Reformation. Even though pitted against representatives of the local catholic clergy, Farel and Viret found the debate hard going. On 5 October Calvin finally intervened.[31] He turned the tide of the debate. A catholic speaker suggested that the evangelicals despised the fathers (that is, the Christian writers of the first five centuries), regarding them as possessing no authority in matters of doctrine. It seems that Calvin's immersion in the study of the fathers at Saintonge left an indelible impression upon him. Rising, he declared that this was simply not true: not merely did the evangelicals respect the fathers more than their catholic opponents; they also knew them better. Reeling off a remarkable chain of references to their writings, including their location – apparently totally from memory – Calvin virtually destroyed the credibility of his opponent. Cyprian is quoted to the letter ('in the second book of his letters, the third letter'), Chrysostom even more precisely ('the twenty-first homily, about half-way through').[32] The dramatic effect of this intervention was considerable, and gave the evangelical side an even greater advantage than that which they already enjoyed.

If we look into Calvin's quotations more closely, a more sanguine estimation of his scholarship results. The fathers are quoted out of context, often omitting material which points to a different interpretation from that which Calvin suggested. Nevertheless, his catholic opponents at Lausanne (and, indeed, as time would prove, elsewhere) lacked the ability to refute him.[33] Calvin emerged from the Lausanne Disputation with a new-found (and, it must be said, a fully merited) reputation as an orator and religious controversialist. Perhaps more importantly, his success at Lausanne appears to have persuaded him that he possessed more abilities than he had hitherto suspected. The *Confession de la Foy*, presented to the syndics and the rest of the Little Council on 10 November, reflects this confidence. The new respect with which he was treated by Farel and Viret also suggests a new attitude on their part towards their younger colleague; by the end of 1536, Calvin had been appointed a preacher and pastor of the church of Geneva.[34]

At this point, it is necessary to stress that the evangelical ministers of Geneva in 1536 were little more than civil servants (indeed, it is highly likely Calvin was never 'ordained' in any ecclesiastical sense of the term; he was probably simply licensed as a pastor by the city council). Unlike their catholic predecessors, they were devoid of power and wealth within the city; indeed, they were not even citizens of Geneva, with access to decision-making bodies. After the Reformation, the Genevan ministers were generally French émigrés, rather than local Genevans – a situation which gave rise to some tension within the city. Pierre Viret was a native of the region around Geneva now known as the Suisse Romande; nevertheless, he was not a Genevan citizen. It is true that after the second revolution of 1555, the evangelical ministers of Geneva assumed a commanding position in the domestic and international affairs of the republic of Geneva; not a hint of these future roles and status, however, is evident in the final six months of 1536.[35] Calvin was little more than a minor civil servant, living in the city under suffrance. It was the city council – not Calvin, Farel or Viret – who controlled the religious affairs of the new republic.

The position of the ministers was thus exceptionally vulnerable to shifts in political alliances within the city. So it was unfortunate, to say the least, that Farel himself should have become the centre of divisions within the city, which may be traced back to 1535. By 1537, pro- and anti-Farel factions were well established. The former (known as Guillermins or Farets) were led by Michael Sept, the latter (later to be known as the Articulants or Artichauds) by the militia commander Jean Philippe.

The situation boded well for the reformers early in 1537. The four new syndics were all Guillermins, personal friends of Farel. Indeed, one had even been elected without being on the preliminary list of eight candidates. Taking full advantage of the reforming mood of Messieurs (as the syndics and Little Council were collectively known), a series of reforming measures was proposed. On 16 January, the pastors, apparently acting on their own initiative, placed before Messieurs an informal draft of ecclesiastical ordinances, designed to produce 'a well ordered and regulated church'.[36] These *Articles sur le Gouvernement de l'Eglise* proceeded to lay down five features which the pastors regarded as desirable. Communion was to be celebrated frequently, in a reverent and godly manner; however, on account of the 'infirmity of the people', the pastors were prepared to compromise their ideals, and accept monthly celebration as the norm. The 'corrective and discipline of excommunication' (in other words, exclusion from communion services, but *not* from hearing sermons) was commended as necessary for the maintenance of reverence.[37] The ministers argued for setting up an ecclesiastical disciplinary tribunal, independent of the usual civil tribunals, to judge such cases. Psalms were to be sung, the young were to be instructed and publicly examined on their grasp of the Reformed faith, and new regulations concerning marriage were proposed. A *Catéchisme* (originally entitled *Instruction et confession de la foy*) was prepared with the fourth desideratum in mind in November of the same year. However, in November of the previous year, Calvin had requested that Messieurs de Genève require every resident (*habitant* – that is, a legal resident alien, p. 107) of Geneva to subscribe to each and every one of the twenty-one articles of his Confession of Faith. It is not quite clear why he should have restricted his demand for subscription to *habitants* (such as himself and Farel), who were denied both the right to vote in Genevan elections and the right to stand for public office; the most likely explanation is that it provided a means of removing from the city foreigners sympathetic to the old religion. The articles of January 1537, however, required that 'all citizens and inhabitants of Geneva and subjects of the area' should affirm their allegiance to such a confession.

It might thus seem that by the end of 1537 much had been achieved in constructing the New Jerusalem of which Calvin and Farel dreamed. In fact, however, a backlash had been precipitated. The Reformation at Geneva might have altered civil and ecclesiastical structures and practices; it did not, and could not, alter human nature. The anti-Farel faction found that its hand had been enormously strengthened through the unpopularity of Calvin's and Farel's measures. Genevans did not like being forced to attend sermons, any more than they liked the threat of excommunication. Even the pro-Farel party was hesitant over the latter: in January 1537, the magistrates demanded that all who wished to present themselves for communion might be admitted. Messieurs rejected the setting-up of any tribunal which might seem to threaten the powers of the magistrates, and – mindful of their treaty obligations to Berne, which laid down that communion should be celebrated four times a year – refused to accept the idea of monthly communion. The Genevans also resented the imposition of what they saw as harsh and legalistic measures, which seemed inconsistent with the new freedom claimed by the city in 1536. The result was perhaps inevitable: all four syndics elected on 3 February 1538 were hostile to Farel and Calvin, adopting a pro-Bernese line on matters of religious belief and practice. Immediately afterwards, six Guillermins were suspended from the Little Council, accused of political intrigue.

Tension grew still further in March. A series of events undermined Calvin's authority within the city. The ministers were forbidden to become involved in any kind of political matters.[38] As if to emphasize who was in control of Geneva, the council added insult to injury by simultaneously laying down how the religious affairs of the city would henceforth be conducted: the Bernese pattern, rather than that laid down by Calvin and Farel, would be adopted.[39] When in Geneva, one would now do as the Bernese did. Mindful of Geneva's vulnerable position, and aware of the fate of the hitherto independent city of Lausanne, the city council had little stomach for religious arguments with their 'liberators'.

A month later, a letter from Messieurs de Berne to Calvin and Farel demanded that they conform to the Bernese pattern.[40] After a period of equivocation and defiance, culminating on Easter Day (21 April), the council finally lost patience. Calvin and Farel were expelled from Geneva.

Exile in Strasbourg, 1538–41

It seems that it took Calvin some time to accept that he had, in fact, been irrevocably expelled from Geneva. His initial temptation was to return to the obscurity of private life, taking up the scholarly pursuits he had been obliged to abandon in 1536. His return to Basle certainly suggests this line of thought. More fundamentally, however, his belief in his own vocation to ministry appears to have been shaken. Had God *really* called him to minister in the church? His expulsion from Geneva seemed to call his earlier sense – indeed, *certainty* – of such a calling into question.[41] This doubt was unquestionably aggravated through a letter from du Tillet, suggesting that Calvin had no divine call of any kind to ministry.[42]

Part of Calvin's difficulty, as he himself realized, was that he had been exposed as inexperienced and naive by his Genevan experience. While positively refusing to accept that he had done anything that was wrong while at Geneva, he clearly recognized that certain things could and should have been done differently.[43] His personal crisis appears soon to have resolved itself. On 20 October, Calvin wrote to du Tillet, stating firmly that he no longer doubted his divine calling to be a minister: 'the Lord has given me firmer reasons to convince me of its validity.'[44] It seems that this new confidence in his calling is to be attributed to the new sphere of ministry and literary activity to which he had been called – Strasbourg.

Where Geneva was a byway of Europe, Strasbourg was one of its great centres. Under Johann Sturm, Strasbourg had gained an international prestige totally denied to minor cities such as Geneva. The Reformation had been established there for some time;[45] it thus offered the young Calvin the possibility of a settled, rather than a pioneering, ministry. Above all, it promised him something he hitherto lacked – pastoral and political experience. Its leading reformer, Martin Bucer, had gathered around him a galaxy of minor stars, such as Wolfgang Capito. The possibility of moving to Strasbourg had been mooted in July; only in September did

Calvin finally accept. Although Strasbourg, like Basle, was a German-speaking city, there was a substantial colony of French-speakers resident within its bounds. Calvin was to become pastor to the French Reformed congregation within the city. It is evident that the positive response to his preaching and ministry restored his confidence in his abilities.[46]

If Calvin had any misgivings about moving to Strasbourg, these were soon allayed. Every aspect of his life, save one, proved rewarding. He was able to gain experience of ecclesiastical diplomacy at the highest level, accompanying Bucer and his colleagues to international colloquies at Worms and Ratisbon. From the safety of his observatory at Strasbourg, he was able to discern the totally unsatisfactory nature of the church–state relationship in the German territories, perhaps Luther's most baleful bequest to the Reformation; noting how the state dominated the churches, Calvin devised other models. He was able to develop his gifts as a teacher in Johann Sturm's newly founded academy. He was also able to begin to put into practice the measures he had demanded for the Genevan church earlier, then without success, and learn from the experience of doing so. Bucer had already adopted, independently, many of the measures then suggested by Calvin: the psalms were sung, instruction in catechisms was compulsory for the young, and only the faithful were admitted to the communion service.

His one difficulty related to his financial situation. Calvin was living in reduced circumstances. It seems that he was obliged to sell some of his own library during his period at Strasbourg.[47] Writing in 1543, Calvin felt obliged to apologize for the lack of detailed quotations in the 1539 edition of his *Institutes* (completed at Strasbourg around October 1538): he had, he explained, been obliged to quote from memory, having only a single volume of Augustine to hand.[48]

Despite being destitute of books, however, Calvin's literary output while at Strasbourg was impressive: the new edition of the *Institutes*, which appeared in August 1539, was soon complemented with the ground-breaking French translation of 1541. The *Reply to Sadoleto*, in which Calvin defended the basic notions of the Reformation at Geneva against the criticisms and enticements of this distinguished curial diplomat, was published in October 1539. (Sadoleto's letter to the Genevans also revealed a potential threat to that city from a reversion to catholicism, which Calvin's opponents at Geneva were not able to counter.) The first of

Calvin's major commentaries – on Paul's letter to the Romans – was completed at the same time, and published the following year. The *Short Treatise of the Lord's Supper* appeared in print in 1541. Even a casual inspection of these works – for example, the new edition of the *Institutes* – points to a new clarity of expression and breadth of vision, which can only be attributed to the broadening of his intellectual and institutional horizons achieved through first-hand experience of running a church in Strasbourg. The vague generalities of 1536 give way to the precision of detail, clarity of direction and thoroughgoing realism which are the hallmarks of thinkers who have cut their teeth on the real world of human society and institutions. By 1541, Calvin had gained considerable practical experience of church management and had given much thought to the theory of church and civil polity and discipline (in which he was considerably influenced by Bucer). The Reformed church and community which had existed only in his mind at Geneva in 1538 were now concrete realities. Abstract theory and pure day-dreaming had given way to practical and concrete experience.

Calvin gave no indication of wishing to leave his place of exile. In July 1540 he had taken *strasbourgeois* citizenship, and the following month had followed Bucer's advice and married a local widow, Idelette de Bure. He was under no pressure whatsoever to leave Strasbourg; indeed, his intellectual and social prestige were in the ascendancy. But in Geneva, the situation had changed. As early as October 1540, feelers were extended to Strasbourg: would Calvin return to Geneva?

The Return to Geneva

The Genevan elections of 1539 were inconclusive, failing to remove totally the opponents of Farel and Calvin from positions of influence, while still denying power to their supporters. Relations between Berne and Geneva began to deteriorate, particularly over some obscurities within the 1536 agreement between the cities which ended the Bernese occupation of Geneva. Jean Lullin, a noted opponent of Farel and Calvin and supporter of Philippe, led a delegation of three Genevan representatives to Berne to sort things out. The Bernese insisted on negotiating in Swiss German, a language which Lullin declared himself to understand perfectly well. A series of articles was agreed. The Articulants (named after the articles which they had negotiated) seemed to have secured their ascendancy.

Two months later, however, the Bernese thoughtfully provided a French translation of the agreed articles for the benefit of their allies. The Genevans were horrified: Lullin's knowledge of Swiss German was less than anyone had expected. The articles were immediately repudiated, and Lullin ordered back to Berne to renegotiate the 1536 treaty. He refused. In April 1540, Berne became insistent: the 1536 treaty, as 'clarified' in 1539, must be fully implemented. A riot followed, with demands for the arrest of the Articulants, who were now widely regarded as little more than Bernese agents within the city. Berne's appeal for clemency simply confirmed this impression: all three were condemned to death *in absentia*. After further rioting, Jean Philippe and one of his supporters were arrested and executed. The anti-Farel faction ceased to be a significant force in Genevan politics, having been fatally compromised by its Bernese sympathies.

By October 1540, the pro-Farel faction had gained control of the city. Events in the absence of Farel and Calvin had demonstrated the close interdependence of reformation and autonomy, of morals and morale. Although the city council was concerned primarily with the independence and morale of the city, the fact that Farel's religious agenda could not be evaded gradually dawned.[49] The pro-Farel party probably had little enthusiasm for religious reformation or the enforcement of public morals; nevertheless, it seemed that the survival of the Genevan republic hinged upon them. One of their first actions was thus to recall Farel and Calvin, with a view to restoring Farel's reforms of 1536. Their enemies had been neutralized; it was safe to return. The invitation, it seems, was primarily addressed to Farel. Farel, however, was now resident in Neuchâtel, and employed by the Bernese. Even if he was prepared to return to Geneva (and it seems he had no inclination to do so), his Bernese employers were not prepared to allow him to, lest relations between Berne and Geneva deteriorated further. Calvin also initially showed no inclination to go back. In February 1541, however, Farel was able to persuade a reluctant and hesitant Calvin to do so. On 13 September of that same year, Calvin re-entered Geneva. The inexperienced and impetuous young man who had left in 1538 was now replaced by an experienced and skilful ecclesiastical organizer, alert to the ways of the world. The second Geneva period would eventually see a decisive shift in the balance of power within the city in his favour. But that, it proved, was still some distance in the future. A false dawn lay ahead, as Calvin made preparations to return.

6

Geneva: The Consolidation of Power

As Byron remarks in *Hints from Horace*, it is difficult to 'lend fresh interest to a twice-told tale'. The story of Calvin's miseries at Geneva during his second period have been told so often and so well that it will serve little purpose to repeat them. Myths concerning the period abound, reflecting the intense distaste with which Calvin has been viewed by many in the nineteenth and twentieth centuries.[1] It may be of interest to note some, to indicate how deeply the myth of 'the great dictator of Geneva' is embedded in popular religious and historical writing. As we shall stress throughout this work, where this myth is not a total invention, it is a serious distortion of the historical facts.

In *La Comédie humaine*, Honoré de Balzac informs us that, immediately upon Calvin's return to Geneva in 1541, 'executions began, and Calvin organized his religious terror.' Perhaps Balzac, in exercising his considerable poetic licence, has confused Calvin and Robespierre; at any rate, there was no reign of terror at Geneva, and Calvin was never in any position to instigate, let alone control or direct, such a campaign. From his return to his death, there was but one execution in Geneva for a religious offence; Calvin's involvement in that affair was, as we shall see, somewhat peripheral. In seeking to discredit Calvin more recently, Aldous Huxley asserts, without documentation, that 'during the great Calvin's theocratic rule of Geneva a child was publicly decapitated for having ventured to strike its parents.'[2] In the first place, there is no record of any such incident in the Genevan archives (which are as comprehensive as one could wish); in the second, there is no basis in the Genevan criminal or civil codes which could conceivably justify such a prosecution, let alone such a draconian penalty; in the third place, the substance and execution of the Genevan civil and criminal codes owed nothing to Calvin. As a professional lawyer, he was occasionally involved in drafting Genevan legislation; for example, at some point around 1543, he was invited to draft laws concerning such matters as the city watchmen. They were not, however, *his* laws, but the city's.

Fourthly, Huxley may be challenged on his uninformed use of the phrase 'theocratic rule'. It has indeed often been suggested that Calvin's political thought is profoundly theocratic.[3] It is nevertheless important to clarify what this nuanced term might mean. It is popularly taken to imply a political regime in which the civil authority is dominated by the clergy, or some other ecclesiastical instrument of power; in this sense, it is easily demonstrated that Calvin never succeeded in establishing, and anyway never intended to establish, a theocracy at Geneva, despite Huxley's rhetorical assertions to the contrary. The term has a second meaning, though, which is perhaps more justifiable at the theological and etymological levels: a regime in which all authority is recognized to derive from God.[4] Calvin's understanding of civil government, particularly as it bears upon the situation within Geneva, may be considered radically theocratic in this latter, less threatening, sense of the word. In both senses, however, God is understood to be involved indirectly in matters of order and government, either through the clergy as his alleged agents, or through the notion of civil authority itself, which ultimately derives from him.

It is possible that Calvin may have thought he was returning in triumph to take charge of the reformation of Geneva. If he was ever possessed of such an illusion (and the documentary evidence suggests he was not), it would have been rudely shattered within a matter of months. There may indeed have been a honeymoon period, during which the council seemed to allow him sufficient freedom to reform the structures of the Genevan church. This, however was relatively short-lived. Time after time Calvin was thwarted in his designs by a shrewd council, anxious to preserve or enhance its own control over the city. In the late 1540s it became increasingly obvious that Calvin simply did not have the political status necessary to attain his objectives. The city council became increasingly hostile towards him, as the 'Libertins' (the party associated with Ami Perrin, otherwise known as 'Perrinists') gained the ascendancy. In effect, it behaved as an inverted Mr Micawber, always looking for something to turn down. Calvin's professional difficulties were compounded by personal tragedy. As we noted earlier, he had married a widow, Idelette de Bure, while at Strasbourg. Their only child, a son, died shortly after birth.[5] His wife herself became seriously ill in 1545, and, after much intermittent suffering, died in March 1549, leaving Calvin to care for her two children by her first marriage. It seems that Calvin had many supporters, but few friends; he was desolated by his bereavement.[6] Until 1555, he seemed largely bereft of support within the power structures of this city. To understand how this situation arose, it is necessary to consider the organization of Geneva at the time.

Calvin and the Government of Geneva

If any political entity of the sixteenth century may be compared to a Greek city-state, it is the city of Geneva. François Bonivard dedicated his French-language edition of Guillaume Postel's study of the classical Athenian magistrates to the Genevan *Petit Conseil*, suggesting that certain parallels were perceived to exist between the two city-states, ancient and modern. Geneva's territory was strictly limited by considerations of physical geography, military prudence and political ambition – considerations which occasionally pulled in opposite directions. In practice, sixteenth-century Geneva was a small fortified city, enclosed within walls of questionable reliability (their fortification was a constant drain on the local economy). Government of the city followed a pattern well established in the larger French cities.[7] From the time of the Second Bourgeoisie onwards, the basic structure of Genevan government took the following form.[8]

From 1526, the inhabitants of Geneva were divided into three categories. Citizens (*citoyens*) were those who were born (and subsequently baptized) within the city to *citoyen* parents. The ruling body – the *Petit Conseil* – was entirely composed of citizens. Those born outside the city limits fell into two categories. Those inhabitants of the city who possessed (or were able to purchase or otherwise negotiate) the privileged position of *bourgeois* were entitled to meet annually to elect the governing officials, and to be elected to the Council of Sixty (the *Conseil des Soixante*) or the Council of Two Hundred (the *Conseil des Deux Cents*). Strictly speaking, no *bourgeois* was eligible for membership of the *Petit Conseil*. The remainder (*habitants*) effectively possessed the status of legal resident aliens, with no right to vote, to carry weapons or to hold any public position within the city. One exception was made: an *habitant* might become a pastor, or lecture at the *haute école* – but only on account of a virtually total absence of Genevan-born persons qualified to discharge such duties. It was into this final category that Calvin himself fell until 1559.

It is far from clear what function the *Conseil des Soixante* served; it appears to have been little more than a vestige of fourteenth-century structures, and achieved nothing which can be said to be of any significance during the period of Calvin's association with the city. The Council of Two Hundred was established in 1527, in the light of difficulties experienced with the General Council: the *Conseil Général* had proved itself a crude and clumsy instrument, obviously dating from a period when Geneva's population was sufficiently small to permit the summoning of its entire native-born population for decision-making purposes. By Calvin's time, it was ordinarily summoned twice a year, for strictly limited and predetermined purposes: the election of syndics in February, and the fixing of corn and wine prices in November. Following a model already adopted by such cities as Berne and Zurich, the *Conseil des Deux Cents* was brought into existence as a compromise, allowing the broadly representative character of the *Conseil Général* to be maintained, without the inconvenience attending large assemblies of individuals.

The central organ of Genevan government, as we noted earlier, was the *Petit Conseil*, also known as the *Senatus*, *Conseil Ordinaire*, *Conseil Estroicte* – or simply as the *Conseil*. An unqualified reference to the 'Genevan city council' should invariably be understood to refer to this council. Its members are variously referred to as 'Messieurs de Genève' or the *Seigneurie*. This council consisted of twenty-four male citizens of the city, including the four syndics. Virtually every area of public activity was subject to the scrutiny of Messieurs de Genève, who had no intention of allowing any aspect of the life of the city to slip out of their control. For a small city such as Geneva to maintain its independence of powerful neighbours seemed a virtual impossibility at the time; it is a tribute to the jealousy and shrewdness with which the city council preserved and exercised its authority that it retained its hard-won independence for a quarter of a millennium. It would retain its sovereignty until French Revolutionary armies, in search of new spheres of influence, invaded the city in the 1790s (an event, it may be added, which played no small part in Geneva's decision to join the Helvetic Confederation in 1815). The rigid restrictions on voting rights in sixteenth-century Geneva reflected widespread anxieties within the city over the possible influence of foreigners upon its affairs. By restricting citizenship, with its full rights to vote and hold office, to certain native-born residents, the council had effectively forestalled the ambitions of any foreigner to exercise political influence within the city.

Calvin was thus denied access to the city's decision-making machinery. He could not vote; he could not stand for office. From 1541 to 1559, his status within the city was that of *habitant*. Unlike Geneva's later luminary, Jean-Jacques Rousseau, Calvin was never in a position to emblazon the title pages of his published works with the coveted words *citoyen de Genève*. On 25 December 1559, his name was finally entered in the *Livre des bourgeois de l'ancienne république de Genève*;[9] although belatedly granted the status of *bourgeois*, Calvin was permanently excluded from becoming a citizen of the city which had become so closely associated with his name. His influence over Geneva was exercised indirectly, through preaching, consultation and other forms of legitimate suasion. Despite his ability to influence through his moral authority, he had no civic jurisdiction, no *right*, to coerce others to act as he wished. Calvin could and did urge, cajole and plead; he could not, however, command.

The image of Calvin as the 'dictator of Geneva' bears no relation to the known facts of history. Stephan Zweig's image of him as the authoritarian leader who ruled the unfortunate inhabitants of Geneva with a rod of iron perhaps owes more to Zweig's imagination and his anti-authoritarian agenda, informed by and tempered with images of Robespierre, Hitler and Stalin, than to realities of life in sixteenth-century Geneva. The city council had no intention of surrendering its hard-won rights and privileges to anyone, let alone one of its employees – a foreigner devoid of voting rights, whom they could dismiss and expel from the city as they pleased. No part of Genevan law or civil ordering – with the exceptions of the Consistory and the Venerable Company of Pastors – owed its existence, its form or its agreed sphere of activity to Calvin. Throughout, the city council retained its authority in religious matters. That Calvin's authority in civic matters was purely personal and moral in character was demonstrated by the difficulties his successors faced after his death.

By March 1553, Calvin's position had become untenable. An anti-Calvin coalition had gained control of the major offices within the city. In the February elections of 1552, his long-standing opponent Ami Perrin was elected as first syndic, with his sympathizers taking two of the remaining three positions as syndics. Perrin's brother-in-law, Pierre Tissot, became the city's lieutenant. By 1553, the Perrinist party – usually known as the Libertins – had gained control of the *Petit Conseil*. They now felt able to challenge Calvin on his home territory – the matter of ecclesiastical discipline, which, under the *Ordonnances* of 1541, was the agreed sphere of authority of the ministers, exercised through the Consistory. The Genevan church, following the Bernese model, had four red-letter days on which communion was celebrated, spread evenly over the ecclesiastical year – Christmas, Easter, Pentecost and September – prompting one French cynic to remark that they seemed to be modelled on the four annual trade fairs at Lyons.[10] With the Easter communions of 1553 drawing near, the council requested that the Consistory provide them with a list of all those currently excommunicated, along with justification of the bans in each case. The implication was clear: the council regarded itself as having the right to review all verdicts relating to ecclesiastical discipline. This amounted to a rejection – or, at best, a perverse interpretation – of the *Ordonnances* of 1541, by which Calvin thought he had settled the question of who had authority to exercise ecclesiastical discipline.

A few months later, a new decision further weakened Calvin's position within Geneva: ministers, even if citizens of Geneva, were forbidden to be members of the General Council, the body which elected the syndics. A significant section of Calvin's supporters was thus effectively disenfranchised. Shortly afterwards, the council intervened in an ecclesiastical matter, thus encroaching still further upon Calvin's steadily diminishing sphere of authority: François Bourgoin, minister of the village of Jussy, was moved to a post in Geneva, and replaced by the council's nominee. On 24 July 1553, Calvin offered to resign; his request was refused.[11] Shortly afterwards, however, the attention of both Calvin and the city council was diverted from their power struggle as a new threat emerged – the Servetus affair. To understand Calvin's role within this affair, it is necessary to consider the role of the Consistory, before turning to the city council's monopolization of the judiciary.

The Consistory

If the *Institutes of the Christian Religion* were the muscles of Calvin's reformation, his ecclesiastical organization was its backbone. The *Ecclesiastical Ordinances* (1541), which gave the Genevan church its characteristic shape and identity, were drawn up by Calvin almost immediately on his return to Geneva from his period of exile in Strasbourg. Convinced of the need for a disciplined, well-ordered and structured church, he proceeded to lay down detailed guidelines governing every aspect of its existence.[12] The establishment of an ecclesiastical apparatus appropriate to Calvin's goals must be regarded as one of the most significant aspects of his ministry, and lends added weight to the case for comparing him to Lenin; both were admirably aware of the importance of institutions for the propagation of their respective revolutions,[13] and lost no time in organizing what was required.

The importance of church structures to the international development of Calvinism can perhaps be appreciated best by comparing the very different situations within which Lutheranism and Calvinism came to be established in western Europe and North America. Lutheranism generally advanced through the sympathy of monarchs and princes, perhaps not totally unaware of the important ecclesiastical role allotted to them by Luther's doctrine of the 'Two Kingdoms'. Although Calvin was aware of the potential of winning over monarchs to his ideas (his particular ambition being to gain a sympathetic hearing within the French court), Calvinism generally had to survive and advance in distinctly hostile situations (such as France in the 1550s), in which both monarch and the existing church establishment were opposed to its development. Under such conditions, the very survival of Calvinist groups was dependent upon a strong and well-disciplined church, capable of surviving the hostility of its milieu. The more sophisticated Calvinist church structures proved capable of withstanding considerably more difficult situations than their Lutheran equivalents, providing Calvinism with a vital resource for gaining ground in what might at first sight seem thoroughly unpromising political situations.

The most distinctive and controversial aspect of Calvin's system of church government was the Consistory. This institution came into being in 1542, with twelve lay elders (selected annually by the magistrates), and all the members of the Venerable Company of Pastors (nine in 1542, nineteen in 1564). The body was intended to meet weekly on a Thursday, with the purpose of maintaining ecclesiastical discipline. The origins of this institution are unclear; it seems that existing matrimonial courts, such as Zurich's *Ehegericht*, may have served as a model,[14] and that a prototype had actually been established in Geneva during Calvin's exile in Strasbourg.[15] It is certainly significant that one of the early activities of the Consistory centred on marital problems, viewed as a pastoral, as much as a legal, difficulty; this may well reflect the role of already existing matrimonial courts (which were predominantly lay in character).

The question of ecclesiastical discipline had much exercised the authorities in the Reformed Swiss cities. If any dominant general pattern may be said to have emerged by the 1530s, it was the Zwinglian view of the subordination of ecclesiastical discipline to the secular magistrates.[16] Under Zwingli's successor, Heinrich Bullinger, the city of Zurich regarded excommunication as a civil matter, to be handled by magistrates rather than clergy.[17] Basle also had serious reservations concerning the propriety of a purely ecclesiastical tribunal being entitled to excommunicate individuals.[18] If the city of Berne is in any sense an exception to this rule, it is because it did not excommunicate members of its churches.[19]

The origins of a rival theory may be traced to Basle in 1530, when Johann Oecolampadius argued before Basle city council that there was a fundamental difference between civil and ecclesiastical authority. It was necessary to introduce an ecclesiastical court, whose brief was to deal with sin, while secular magistrates would continue to deal with criminal offences.[20] The former should have the right to excommunicate offenders, in order to encourage them to mend their ways and avoid disrupting the unity and life of the church. The Basle city council disagreed, and there the matter rested.

Nevertheless, the idea of a specifically ecclesiastical court gained support during the 1530s. Although Martin Bucer wrote to Zwingli on 19 October 1530 indicating his hostility towards the idea of such a court,[21] he appears to have shifted ground shortly afterwards. It is not impossible that this reflects Bucer's alienation from Zwingli, as a result of the latter's letter of 12 February 1531 in which he accused Bucer of betraying evangelical truth in the interests of political expediency.[22] In 1531, Bucer supported the suggestion that the city of Ulm should have an ecclesiastical court, composed of both laity and pastors, to deal with matters of church discipline. The seizing of Münster by the radicals in February

1534 brought home to Strasbourg city council the need to enforce church discipline and orthodoxy, if Strasbourg – by then with an established reputation as a haven for radicals – was to avoid the fate of Münster. However, the council rejected Bucer's preference for a specifically ecclesiastical court; control of church discipline was to remain firmly in the hands of the civil authorities.[23] It was Bucer's ideas, rather than Strasbourg's practice, which appear to have fired the imagination of Calvin during his sojourn in the city.[24] The articles for the organization of the church at Geneva, drawn up by Farel and Calvin in January 1537, anticipate virtually every aspect of the *Ordonnances ecclésiastiques* of 1541 – with the notable exception of the Consistory.[25] This suggests that it was during his Strasbourg period that Calvin developed the notion.

Calvin conceived of the Consistory primarily as an instrument for the 'policing' of religious orthodoxy. It was the guarantor of the discipline which Calvin's experience at Strasbourg had led him to recognize as essential to the survival of Reformed Christendom. Its primary function was to deal with those whose religious views were sufficiently devious to pose a threat to the established religious order at Geneva. Persons whose behaviour was regarded as unacceptable for other reasons, pastoral or moral, were to be treated in the same way. Such individuals were, in the first instance, to be shown the error of their ways; should this fail, the penalty of excommunication was available as a deterrent. This, however, was an ecclesiastical rather than a civil penalty; the miscreant might be denied access to one of the four annual communion services at Geneva, but he could not be subjected to any civil penalty by the Consistory itself. The city council, perennially jealous of its authority, had insisted that 'all this is to take place in such a manner that the ministers have no civil jurisdiction, nor use anything but the spiritual sword of the Word of God . . . nor is the Consistory to detract from the authority of the *Seigneurie* or ordinary justice. Civil power is to remain unimpeded.'

After Calvin's death, the Consistory appears to have lost its sense of direction, and degenerated into little more than a crude instrument of social control, verging on the hysterical. In 1568 two men and a woman were excommunicated for 'scandal and disrespect for the institution of marriage': they had been present at a post-wedding breakfast at which the groom had cut a loaf of bread into pieces, this visual aid being intended to convey the number of times he had enjoyed sexual intercourse with his bride. During the years 1564–9, 1,906 excommunication orders were made.[26] In 1568, for example, one individual achieved the dubious distinction of being excommunicated four times, thus being obliged to miss each and every communion service held that year. The reasons for excommunication make fascinating reading: wife-beating and quarrels, domestic or otherwise, resulting in violence account for much of the Consistory's routine business. Gambling, drunkenness and fornication are all to be found amongst the Consistory's diet; they are, however, less common than might have been expected. Nevertheless, it is clear that the distinctively *religious* role assigned to the Consistory by Calvin had become eroded; with his passing, the institution he had brought into existence lost much of its sense of direction.

The controversy which surrounded the role of the Consistory in the early 1550s centred on the question of whether Messieurs de Genève or the Consistory had the right to impose the penalty of excommunication. Under the *Ordonnances ecclésiastiques*, it seemed to Calvin that this right was unequivocally vested in the Consistory. His opponents, led by Ami Perrin, held that only the city council could impose such a penalty. A major contributing cause to the friction which developed between Calvin and the Perrinists concerned the issue of ecclesiastical discipline.[27] Although Perrin and his suppporters were not hostile to the Reformation, they objected intensely to Calvin's system of discipline. (It is for this reason that they are usually referred to as 'Libertins', although the modern term 'liberal' perhaps conveys their position more aptly.) The matter came to a head with the Servetus affair.

The Servetus Affair

If there was one area of civic life which the city council was determined to keep totally within its control, it was the administration of justice. The Genevan magistracy had seized the right to administer civil and criminal justice during their revolt against the bishop of Geneva and his patrons, the duchy of Savoy. We noted earlier that, prior to Geneva's moves towards independence, the symbol of episcopal authority within the city had been the *vidomne*. This official, who, along with his staff, had occupied the castle on the island in the middle of the river Rhône, had served as a visible reminder of the sovereignty of the bishop over his city. In 1527, the right of the bishop to try civil cases was ceded to the city. Over the years which followed, full judicial authority was gradually ceded to Messieurs de Genève: the right to execute criminal sentences was transferred to the syndics, and appeals from within the city to external superior courts were blocked. By 1530, the city had gained total control of the judiciary. The right to dispense high justice was, in effect, seen as a public demonstration of the city's independence. To allow any foreign power or individual to influence Genevan justice was to erode the city's hard-won sovereignty.[28] There was no way in which Messieurs de Genève were prepared to allow a foreigner any influence over this central feature of the Genevan civic administration. Calvin might be allowed authority within the Consistory to discipline wayward members of his congregations by temporarily barring them from communion services; as a mere *habitant* he was, however, rigorously excluded from the dispensation of civil and criminal justice. It is with this consideration in mind that we may turn to consider the event which eventually led to the consolidation of Calvin's power within Geneva on the one hand, and his vilification as a bloodthirsty tyrant on the other.[29]

The trial and execution of Michael Servetus as a heretic have, more than any other event, coloured Calvin's posthumous reputation.[30] It is not entirely clear why scholars have singled out the execution of Servetus as somehow more notable or significant than the mass executions carried out within Germany after the abortive Peasants' War (1525) and after the ending of the siege of Münster (1534), or the ruthless policy of execution of Roman Catholic priests in Elizabethan England. Even as late as 1612, the English secular arm, at the behest of the bishops of London and Lichfield, publicly burned two individuals who held views like those of Servetus. In France, similar ruthless policies of execution were employed: thirty-nine individuals were ordered to be burned at Paris for heresy between May 1547 and March 1550.[31] The Edict of Chateaubriant (27 June 1551) abolished the requirement that capital punishment for heresy had to be confirmed in individual cases by *parlement*: from that moment onwards, lower courts were free to proceed against heretics as they pleased. The sixteenth century knew little, if anything, of the modern distaste for capital punishment, and regarded it as a legitimate and expedient method of eliminating undesirables and discouraging their imitation. The city of Geneva was no exception: lacking a long-term prison (short-term prisoners were held captive, at their own expense, while they awaited trial), it had only two major penalties at its disposal – banishment and execution. Nor is it entirely clear why the affair should be thought of as demonstrating anything especially monstrous concerning Calvin. His tacit support for the capital penalty for offences such as heresy which he (and his contemporaries) regarded as serious makes him little more than a child of his age, rather than an outrageous exception to its standards. Post-Enlightenment writers have every right to protest against the cruelty of earlier generations; to single out Calvin for particular criticism, however, suggests a selectivity approaching victimization. To target him in this way – when the manner of his involvement was, to say the least, oblique – and overlook the much greater claims to infamy of other individuals and institutions raises difficult questions concerning the precommitments of his critics. Servetus was the *only* individual put to death for his religious opinions in Geneva during Calvin's lifetime, at a time when executions of this nature were a commonplace elsewhere.

Furthermore, the trial, condemnation and execution (including the selection of the particular mode of execution) of Servetus were entirely the work of the city council, at a period in its history when it was particularly hostile to Calvin. The Perrinists had recently gained power, and were determined to weaken his position. Their prosecution of Servetus – paralleling that of Gentilis at Berne the following decade – was intended to demonstrate their impeccable orthodoxy, as a prelude to undermining Calvin's religious authority within the city. The Consistory – the normal instrument of ecclesiastical discipline, over which Calvin had considerable influence – was bypassed altogether by the council in its efforts to marginalize Calvin from the affair. Nevertheless, he could not be totally bypassed in such a major matter of religious controversy. He was involved in the affair initially as an indirect first preferrer of charges, and subsequently as an expert theological witness; that witness, however, could have come from any orthodox theologian of the age, whether Protestant or Roman Catholic.

This point may be pressed further. Some critics of Calvin appear to suggest that his entire religious system is discredited on account of the Servetus affair. Yet Thomas Aquinas himself had written explicitly in support of the burning of heretics, as follows: 'If the heretic still remains pertinacious the church, despairing of his conversion, provides for the salvation of others by separating him from the church by the sentence of excommunication and then leaves him to the secular judge to be exterminated from the world by death.'[32] This, and many other aspects of Aquinas' thought – for example, his defence of slavery, his attitudes towards Jews, and his belief in the natural inferiority of women[33] – are totally unacceptable, with good reason, to many in the modern world; this does not, however, render his religious and political thought unacceptable *in its totality*. The modern reader may – and generally does – exercise a degree of selectivity at such points, bearing in mind that many of Aquinas' views were historically conditioned, and continue to find in Aquinas a fertile source of religious and other ideas. The same is, and must be, true of Calvin. We are not for one moment suggesting that it is acceptable for any individual to be implicated in trials leading to capital punishment. It is not necessarily a defence of the attitudes and actions of either the Genevan city council or Calvin himself to point out that they find ample support within the writings of Thomas Aquinas. But if Calvin cannot be excused in this manner, he may and must be contextualized, in an era which, lacking many of the sensitivities of twentieth-century liberal thought, regarded the execution of heretics as routine.

The modern reader may be inclined to regard 'heresy' as the expression of an opinion at odds with the prevailing orthodoxy – and, as such, to be welcomed as an expression of creativity and personal liberty. It must be stressed that this is a modern understanding of the notion, for which the sixteenth century was not prepared. Detailed socio-political studies of the major historical Christian heresies suggest that they were not merely concerned with ideas, but with a much broader social and political agenda. For example, the Donatist controversy of the late classical period might seem merely to concern rival theories of the nature of the Christian church; the fundamental agenda, however, concerned the tensions between the indigenous Berber people of North Africa and Roman colonists. Theological issues were often the veneer imposed upon social and national movements, concerned with challenging the socio-political status quo as much as its 'official' religious standpoint.[34] The considerable popular appeal associated with heresies in the medieval period usually reflects not so much interest in their *religious* ideas, as a perception of their social or political implications. A particularly illuminating example of this is provided by Hussitism, the movement associated with Jan Huss in the early fifteenth century. Although the movement might notionally seem to centre upon such theological abstractions as the nature of the church, its primary strength lay in its potent appeal to Bohemian nationalism and its social and economic programmes. The catholic church was obliged to move quickly against the heresy on account of its potentially destabilizing tendencies. It was the power, as much as the doctrine, of the church which was under threat.

With the coming of the Reformation to the cities of western Europe, the destabilizing tendencies of heresy became increasingly obvious. From the beginning, there was a tension between those reformers (such as Luther, Zwingli, Bullinger, Bucer and Calvin) who saw reform as a symbiotic process involving reformers and magistrates acting together within the established order, and those radical reformers (such as Jakob Hutter) who regarded the true Reformation as sweeping away the existing corrupt social and political order. Zurich city council felt itself under threat from such radical elements in the 1520s, and took every step available to prevent them attaining any influence within the city. The radical wing of the Reformation, also known as Anabaptism, was primarily characterized at the religious level by its rejection of infant baptism: at the social level, however, its views were radically anti-authoritarian, often including important hints of communism. Events at Münster, which came under radical control in 1534,[35] confirmed the serious threat which that radical wing of the Reformation posed to existing social structures. Although Protestant and Roman Catholic city councils might differ on many matters, they were united in their belief that heresy threatened the stability and hence the existence of their cities. The fate of Münster – which had to be retaken by a protracted and bloody siege – brought home the fact that heresy concerned far more than mere ideas: it posed a serious menace to urban existence. No city could afford to allow such a destabilizing influence within its bounds. The drastic steps adopted after 1534 by Strasbourg city council to eliminate the radical threat illustrate graphically how seriously this threat was taken at the time.[36]

Geneva was no exception. Once it had been proven that there was a heretic in their midst with sympathies which placed him alongside the radical wing of the Reformation, the Genevan authorities had little option but to act, despite the difficulties occasioned by the fact that Servetus was not, strictly speaking, subject to Genevan justice. It is not entirely clear why Servetus should have chosen to visit Geneva; possibly he had paused in the city on his way to seek refuge in Basle, as Calvin had before him.[37] He had already been condemned as a heretic by the catholic authorities in France; he had, however, escaped from prison in Vienne, and made his way to Geneva, to be arrested on 13 August 1553.

He had recently published a book entitled *Christianismi Restitutio.* (Perhaps there was a deliberate parallel here with Calvin's *Institutio Christianae religionis?*) The work denied one central article of Christian faith (the Trinity), and one traditional practice (infant baptism). Although Calvin clearly regarded the former as infinitely the more serious, to judge by his ferocious verbal assaults upon Servetus (assaults, it must be said, the nature of which confirms the general impression of Calvin's increasing pettiness and bitterness as old age approached), it is probably the latter which holds the key to the city council's anxieties. For denial of infant baptism instantly aligned Servetus with the Anabaptists (the word literally means 're-baptizers'), the radical wing of the Reformation which had caused such problems at Zurich, Münster, Strasbourg and elsewhere. Anabaptists had abolished private property, and made all possessions a common utility; they had introduced the principle of economic equality[38] – in short, they posed a vital threat to the economic and social order upon which Geneva's fragile existence depended. The city council could have had little doubt that a real threat existed. Although it was Calvin, acting as an individual, who arranged for Servetus' accusation and arrest, it was the city council who – despite their intense hostility to Calvin – took over the case, and prosecuted Servetus with vigour.[39] (This caused some surprise to outside observers: Wolfgang Musculus wrote of his belief that Servetus evidently expected to benefit from the hostility of the city council towards Calvin.[40]) It should be noted that Calvin's role in these procedures was subsequently that of technical advisor or expert witness, rather than prosecutor. On 21 August the Genevan authorities wrote to Vienne, asking for further information concerning their captive. In particular, they requested 'duplicates of the evidence, information and arrest warrant' against Servetus.[41] The catholic authorities at Vienne immediately demanded the extradition of Servetus to face charges there. The city council then offered him a choice: he could either return to Vienne, or remain at Geneva and face the outcome of Genevan justice. It is significant that Servetus chose to remain at Geneva.[42]

As matters had progressed, it became increasingly clear that the council had two options: they could banish Servetus from the city, or execute him. Uncertain as to how to proceed, the city council consulted with Geneva's allies at Berne, Zurich, Schaffhausen and Basle. The responses were unambiguous.[43] The entry for the registry of the Venerable Company of Pastors recorded the city council's decision on 25 October 1553 as follows:[44] 'Their Lordships, having received the opinions of the churches of Basle, Berne, Zurich and Schaffhausen upon the Servetus affair, condemned the said Servetus to be led to Champey and there to be burned alive.' Perhaps with memories of the burning of certain of his friends at Paris in mind, Calvin himself attempted to alter the mode of execution to the more humane beheading;[45] he was ignored. The following day, Servetus was executed. Geneva did not have a professional executioner. Its hangman – like its jailers and all other public officers – was an amateur.[46] The burning was a botched job.

In 1903, a granite monument was erected at the site of Servetus' execution. Its inscription condemns 'an error which belonged to his century'. Yet, sadly, every major Christian body which traces its history back to the sixteenth century has blood liberally scattered over its credentials. Roman Catholic, Lutheran, Reformed and Anglican: all have condemned and executed their Servetuses, whether directly, or – as in the case of Calvin himself – indirectly. It is fair to suggest that it is improper to single out Calvin as if he were somehow the initiator of this vicious trend, or a particularly vigorous and detestable supporter of the practice, where the majority of his enlightened contemporaries wished it to be abolished. The case of Etienne Le Court, who was publicly degraded, strangled and burned by the Inquisition at Rouen on 11 December 1533, for suggesting that, among other things, 'women will preach the gospel', would seem considerably more disturbing. Perhaps historians, like everyone else, have their axes to grind.

The aftermath of the Servetus affair was considerable. Basle, with its growing sympathy for libertarian policies, was shocked by the execution.[47] Sebastian Castellio, anticipating more modern views, wrote a pamphlet at Basle, arguing forcefully for toleration in matters of religion (and, for that matter, just about everything else). It prompted Théodore de Bèze to develop an influential theory of government which accounted for and justified the behaviour of the city council.[48] The affair also served to propel Calvin still further into the forefront of Protestantism, consolidating his already considerable reputation as a religious writer and thinker: as letter after letter from admiring colleagues in Germany and elsewhere indicates, Calvin was now regarded as the defender of the true faith within Protestant circles. Within Geneva, though, he was still seriously isolated. That situation, however, began to change, and would culminate in the revolution of 1555, which established Calvin's authority within the city once and for all.

The Revolution of 1555

The diversion of the Servetus affair having ended, the city council was able to revert to its by now traditional role of opposing Calvin. Its decision to review excommunications at Easter in 1553 had been followed by a new development in September of the same year, as another civic communion service loomed on the horizon. Philibert Berthelier, who had been excommunicated by the Consistory, appealed against the decision. His appeal, however, was not directed to the Consistory itself, but to the *Petit Conseil*, now dominated by Calvin's opponents. It was a shrewd move (in that it implied that the council had authority in the matter of excommunication). The council lost no time in overturning the verdict of the Consistory, although it requested Berthelier not to communicate on this particular occasion. Calvin was nonetheless incensed at this obvious challenge to his authority. He insisted that it was the Consistory, and the Consistory alone, which had the power to excommunicate notorious and unrepentant sinners, and that it alone should have the power to review such sentences of excommunication. The matter was debated at the Council of Two Hundred on 7 November. By a large majority, it was decided that the final decisions in matters of excommunication should rest with the council.[49] It seemed that Calvin had been finally and firmly put in his place – under the thumb of the council.

In 1555, however, a dramatic realignment of power took place. To understand how this came about, it is necessary to consider shifts in the population of Geneva which were taking place at the time. The population of the city in 1550 is estimated to have been 13,100; by 1560, it was 21,400.[50] The main reason for this massive increase was the large number of Protestant refugees seeking safety there.[51] Geneva had established an international reputation as a haven for those seeking safety on account of their religious views. These refugees were mainly drawn from France. Of the 4,776 who registered in the *Livre des Habitants de Genève* for the years 1549–60, we possess details of the professions of 2,247. Of those, 1,536 (68.5 per cent) were artisans.[52] Calvin, writing in 1547, noted that many of these refugees had been obliged to leave their goods behind them, and were now living in greatly reduced circumstances.[53] However, some were wealthy, highly educated and of considerable social standing – printers such as Robert Estienne, lawyers such as Germain Colladon, and businessmen

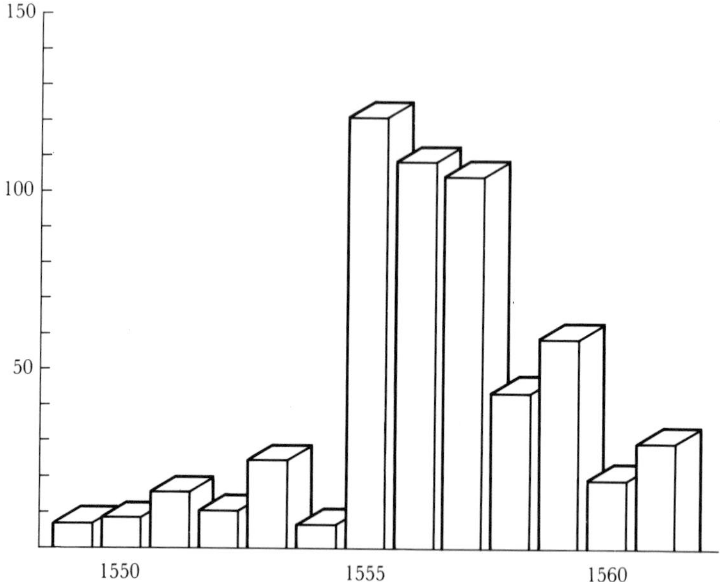

FIGURE 6.1 Numbers of new names added annually to the *Livre des Bourgeois* at Geneva, 1549–1561

such as Laurent de Normandie. They were almost invariably strong supporters of Calvin.[54]

The council had been anxious over its financial state for some time, and suddenly appears to have woken up to the possibility of tapping the considerable resources of these wealthy foreigners. The *Petit Conseil* had long possessed the right to admit individuals to the status of *bourgeois*, providing the application was possessed of sufficient wealth and social distinction. A hefty admission fee ensured that the city benefited. However, hardly any such admissions were made in the period 1540–54. For example, only six persons were granted the status of *bourgeois* in the year 1554.[55]

The floodgates were suddenly opened on 18 April 1555, as the *Petit Conseil* began to admit suitable (that is, rich and prestigious) refugees to *bourgeois* status. By 2 May of that year fifty-seven persons had been granted this coveted status,[56] with the Genevan coffers being significantly augmented as a result. A financial crisis may have been averted; a political crisis immediately followed. For the *bourgeois* were entitled to vote in Genevan elections, and promptly exercised that right. Realizing what had happened, on

16 May the Perrinists attempted to block the voting rights of the new *bourgeois*. They were not successful. The April and May sessions of the General Council – Geneva's body of electors – were packed with Calvin's supporters, who had suddenly been enfranchised. The delicate balance between Calvin's opponents and supporters within the electoral college was destroyed, and the opposition to Calvin thereby routed. This process was continued in the election of 1556. By then, Calvin's friends were in charge of the city. He could finally work in peace, and turn his thoughts to, amongst other matters, the evangelization of his native France.

Accounting for Calvin's Success

It is, perhaps, too easy for critics and supporters of Calvin's programme of reform to suggest explanations for his remarkable influence over his own and subsequent ages. The literature of the sixteenth century makes frequent reference both to divine providence (where Calvin is thought to be a good thing), and to satanic collusion (where he is viewed less appreciatively). A more historically informed approach, however, might be to compare Calvin with another reformer who, in many respects, occupied a similar position and achieved similar local success and fame, yet was denied anything even approaching the international success achieved by Calvin. We therefore propose to compare Calvin with the eastern Swiss reformer Joachim von Watt, usually known by the Latinized form of his name, Vadian (1484–1551). Vadian was based at St Gallen, a city similar in many ways to Geneva, lying slightly to the east of the frontiers of the Helvetic Confederation. While Calvin was still a student at Paris, Vadian had set his city firmly on the road to Reformation. That Reformation appears to have been achieved without bloodshed or resort to force: the statue which St Gallen has erected to Vadian shows him with Bible in hand, and sword sheathed by his side (whereas Zurich's statue of Zwingli portrays him with sword bared and ready for action). There is no monument to any Servetus at St Gallen, reflecting both the absence of a resort to deadly force in the interests of the Reformation and the unambiguously positive manner in which the city received Vadian and his Reformation.

To compare Calvin and Vadian is to identify factors which are of potential significance in accounting for the trajectory of the Reformation in Geneva and St Gallen. A preliminary examination of both cities and their reformers suggests that they were similar in many respects, with Vadian enjoying a personal reputation and institutionally legitimated authority far exceeding that associated with Calvin.

1 St Gallen and Geneva were cities of similar size, each of which was allied to cantons within the Helvetic Confederation.[57] The success of the Reformation in each city was partly due to support from Protestant cantons within the Confederation. Vadian's Reformation at St Gallen was facilitated by a significant degree of political support from Zurich, which served to undermine initial opposition to the reforms.[58] Geneva, as we noted, was assisted considerably at critical periods by political and military support from Berne. Both cities had trading networks, deriving from Geneva's status as a trading centre and St Gallen's prominence as a leading producer of high-quality linen. St Gallen's importance in this respect was much greater. Vadian's considerable personal influence was mediated in part through commercial trading contacts with, for example, Poland and Hungary,[59] as well as through an extensive family network.

2 Vadian was a humanist scholar of international status. After a brilliant career at the University of Vienna, then a centre for humanism, culminating in his election as rector of the university (and including the gaining of a doctorate in medicine and his election as professor of poetry), he returned to his native town of St Gallen to pursue his literary career (and, as it turned out, the propagation of the Reformation).[60] There were no more academic worlds for him to conquer at Vienna; St Gallen, in contrast, held the promise of access to the world of politics and statesmanship, in addition to his continued pursuit of eloquence. Calvin's reputation as a humanist was virtually non-existent, and he had held no academic posts at any of the universities he attended.

3 Vadian was a citizen of St Gallen, a member of one of its leading families,[61] a prominent member of one of its seven guilds, and in 1529 he would become its leading citizen (*Bürgermeister*) – to international acclaim[62] – while still a relatively young man. He retained this power-base within the city until his death, more than two decades later. Vadian was at the centre of power in the city and its hinterland for a long time, and was thus intimately involved in all the decisions relating to the implementation of the Reformation there. Calvin was only granted *bourgeois* status at Geneva in his old age; he never became a citizen of the city. He could not

stand for office (and, until December 1559, could not even vote in city elections); nor did he have privileged access to, or direct influence over, the city council at any point during his career.

4 Throughout the entire implementation of the Reformation at St Gallen, no major religious opposition was encountered from its citizens. This is not to say that the process was without difficulties;[63] it is to note that there was no specifically *religious* opposition to the measures implemented. At Geneva, however, there was extensive internal opposition to Calvin's religious reforms throughout his first period (1536–8), as there was during the first part of his second period in the city (1541–53). The situation which Calvin faced was considerably more difficult than that encountered by Vadian. One can only really speak of Geneva being Calvin's 'power-base' after the revolution of 1555.

On the basis of these considerations, it might therefore seem that Vadian ought to have been the more successful reformer. Indeed, if the criterion of success employed relates to the generation of a popular consensus for reform within a city, and the successful implementation of that programme of reform with the minimum of internal dissent, Vadian must be regarded as by far the more successful of the two. Yet Vadian is virtually unknown outside specialist studies in Swiss local history, whereas Calvin may reasonably be suggested to be one of the best-known names of the sixteenth century. How can this be accounted for?

A number of relevant factors may be identified.

1 Calvin and Vadian had significantly different understandings of what a 'Reformation' entailed. For Vadian, the Reformation was primarily concerned with the reform of standards of living and morality.[64] In many ways, it was a local programme of reform, tied to specific regional concerns and issues. Calvin, however, viewed the Reformation as posing a challenge to the existing structures, practices and doctrines of the church – a far more radical programme of reform, which was not bound to any local situation, but possessed the ability to transcend geographical, cultural and political divides. The rapid spread of Calvinism in France from 1555 onwards illustrates this neatly; Calvinism possessed a missionary zeal virtually absent from Vadian's understanding of the goals of the Reformation. As a result of these different understandings of the nature of the Reformation process, the two men adopted significantly different roles. Vadian was primarily concerned with changing a local situation; Calvin saw

himself initially addressing a French, and subsequently an international, audience. While political realism initially obliged Calvin to address himself to the specific situation in Geneva, his horizons were considerably broader. The moment that his position at Geneva was consolidated (April 1555), he began a major programme of evangelization – initially in secret – within the kingdom of France.

2 The two men adopted significantly different publishing programmes, reflecting these understandings of their vocation as reformers. Vadian's published works were generally of a humanist nature; with one exception,[65] his specifically theological works – such as his *Brevis indicatura symbolorum* – remained uncopied in manuscript form within the walls of St Gallen. Calvin pursued an extensive publishing programme, ensuring that his religious ideas gained as wide a hearing as possible (see chapters 7, 9).

3 Calvin's target audience was initially primarily French and Francophone; the 1536 edition of the *Institutes*, although written in Latin, appears to have the needs and difficulties of French *évangéliques* in mind. The 1541 edition, published in French, received particular attention in his homeland. Vadian's vernacular works (which remained unpublished and uncirculated in manuscript form) were written in Swiss German, and hence had a severely restricted audience – which in any case was largely already won over to the Reformation. Had Vadian's vernacular works been circulated, he would have largely been preaching to the converted. In contrast, Calvin's *Institutes* are known to have played a major role in winning converts to his understanding of the Christian faith and the reformation which it entailed – initially in France, and subsequently far beyond.

4 Calvin's career brought him into contact with a number of major printers in Basle, Strasbourg and Geneva. He had little difficulty in arranging for his material to be published. There were, however, relatively few printers in the St Gallen area; it was only in the middle of the sixteenth century that Dolfin Landolfi transferred his printing operations from either Brescia or Venice (it is not entirely clear which) to the Graubünden.[66] Vadian thus did not have easy direct access to the technological innovation which was transforming the nature of religious controversy in the early sixteenth century.

5 Presumably with the local situation at St Gallen in mind, Vadian tended to regard 'church' and 'society' as referring to more or less the same group of people. As a result, his conception of the

church lays little stress upon structure and discipline. Calvin was aware of the importance of church structures and discipline, and devised a model of the church which proved remarkably well-suited to the programme of international expansion which he instigated. To expand is one thing; to survive that expansion is quite another. Calvinism proved capable of surviving under intensely hostile conditions, virtually assuming the status of an underground movement. (There are interesting parallels between French Calvinism in the 1540s and early 1550s and the French maquis during the Nazi occupation of France in the Second World War.) The resilience of the movement owed no small amount to the structures and discipline which Calvin devised for it. His genius for organization, paralleling that of Lenin, may well have been of decisive importance in the international expansion of his movement.

6 A final impression, however subjective, should be mentioned. The reader of Vadian's writings, both Latin and Swiss-German, is perhaps more impressed by the eloquence with which he expresses his ideas than the quality of those ideas and the argumentation deployed in their generation and justification. Calvin, however, emerges from his writings (especially those of his Strasbourg period) as a first-rate mind, capable of generating and defending intrinsically interesting ideas. Vadian, like Erasmus of Rotterdam, tends to emerge as strong on expression, yet weak on substance; Calvin scores strongly on both points. As the course of the Reformation indicates, it was largely the substance of Calvin's writings which lay behind his appeal to so considerable a constituency.

These points of comparison are far from exhaustive; nevertheless, they unquestionably point to certain factors which underlie Calvin's greater influence. His perception of the possibilities afforded to his particular understanding of the Reformation by the establishment of appropriate institutions (such as the Genevan Academy) and structures (such as the Venerable Company of Pastors), and the exploitation of technology (such as printing), placed him at the forefront of a movement which was from the outset international in its orientation.

But how did that international expansion take place? How did a set of ideas associated with one man in the tiny city-state of Geneva gain such a wide hearing and evoke such a powerful response throughout Europe? Perhaps the most helpful way of understanding the remarkable impetus possessed by these ideas is to follow their impact upon the kingdom of France in Calvin's lifetime. Such was his impact that, at one point, it seemed to many that France might become the first nation to adopt a Calvinist creed. Our narrative therefore shifts to Calvin's native France (chapter 9), as we consider this extraordinary invasion of ideas.

But it is appropriate to interrupt our historical narrative briefly, in order to consider those ideas themselves. What were Calvin's religious ideas, and how were they propagated? The two chapters which follow deal with those ideas and the manner in which they were presented to his day and age. It must be stressed, however, that Calvin's ideas are not purely religious in character, and that his influence rests partly upon his political and economic thought (chapter 11). 'Christianity according to Calvin' embraces ideas, attitudes and quite definite social structures which go far beyond a mere set of abstract religious ideas. These points having been noted, we may turn to consider Calvin's highly influential presentation of the nature of Christianity.

7

Christianity according to Calvin: The Medium

'I KNEW A witty physician who found the creed in the biliary duct, and used to assert that if there was a disease in the liver, the man became a Calvinist' (Ralph Waldo Emerson). Despite the attractiveness of this thesis, those seeking an explanation of the appeal of Calvinism have generally located its attraction in the human intellect, rather than the biliary duct. The German historian Karl Holl wrote that 'a good deal of the penetrating power of Calvinism depends upon its intellectualism. The Calvinist knows *what* he believes, and *why* he believes it.'[1] An account of Calvin's religious thought must assume a place of honour in any analysis of the reformer's life and influence. But such an account must be preceded by a discussion of the media Calvin employed in developing and promoting his religious ideas. Medium and message are inextricably interwoven in his account of the Christian faith.

THE PERSUASIVE WORD OF GOD

God is able to communicate with humans through human language. This belief is fundamental, even to the point of being axiomatic, to Calvin's understanding of Christianity. Important anticipations of Karl Barth's twentieth-century battle-cry 'God has spoken! *Deus dixit! Dominus dixit!*' may be found in Calvin. Fragmentary and broken though human words may be, they nevertheless possess a capacity to function as the medium through which God is able to disclose himself, and bring about a transformational encounter of the risen Christ and the believer.

Beneath the surface of Calvin's assertions concerning the ability of human words to convey the reality of God lies a remarkably sophisticated theory of the nature and function of human language. In the modern period, the term 'rhetoric' has come to mean something like 'words elegantly phrased, yet devoid of substance'; in the sixteenth century, however, the term designated the science of communication, the investigation of what words denote and how they serve us.[2] The rise of the humanist movement brought with it a new interest in the manner in which words and texts are capable of mediating and transforming human experience and expectations; Calvin was able to draw upon such insights in formulating his views on the notion of the 'word of God' and its embodiment in the text of scripture. He wears his rhetorical learning lightly, even to the point at which it might be overlooked completely. Nevertheless, insights from the science of rhetoric resonate throughout his writings – in an exploratory manner in the Seneca commentary, in some depth in the subtle sophistication of the Romans commentary (1540),[3] and perhaps most fully of all in the later editions of the *Institutes*.

In scripture, Calvin argues, God reveals himself verbally, in the form of words. But how can words ever do justice to the majesty of God? How can words span the enormous gulf between God and sinful humanity? Calvin's discussion of this question is generally regarded as one of his most valuable contributions to Christian thought. The idea which he develops is usually referred to as the 'principle of accommodation'.[4] The word 'accommodation' here means 'adjusting or adapting to meet the needs of the situation'.

In revelation, Calvin argues, God adjusts himself to the capacities of the human mind and heart. God paints a portrait of himself which we are capable of understanding. The analogy which lies behind Calvin's thinking at this point is that of a human orator. A good speaker knows the limitations of his audience, and adjusts the way he speaks accordingly. The gulf between the speaker and the hearer must be bridged if communication is to take place. The limitations of his audience determine the language and imagery the speaker employs. The parables of Jesus illustrate this point perfectly: they use language and illustrations (such as analogies based on sheep and shepherds) perfectly suited to his audience in rural Palestine. Paul also uses ideas adapted to the situation of his hearers, drawn from the commercial and legal world of the cities in which the majority of his readers lived.[5]

In the classical period orators were highly educated and verbally skilled, whereas their audiences were generally unlearned and lacked any real ability to handle words skilfully. As a result, the orator had to come down to their level if he was to communicate with them. He had to bridge the gap between himself and his audience by understanding their difficulties in comprehending his language, imagery and ideas. Similarly, Calvin argues, God has to come down to our level if he is to reveal himself to us. God scales himself down to meet our abilities. Just as a human mother or nurse stoops down to reach her child, by using a different way of speaking than that appropriate for an adult, so God stoops down to come to our level.[6] Revelation is an act of divine condescension, by which God bridges the gulf between himself and his capacities, and sinful humanity and its much weaker abilities. Like any good speaker, God knows his audience – and adjusts his language accordingly.

An example of this accommodation is provided by the scriptural portraits of God. He is often, Calvin points out, represented as if he has a mouth, eyes, hands and feet.[7] That would seem to suggest that God is a human being. It might seem to imply that somehow the eternal and spiritual God has been reduced to a physical human being. (The question at issue is often referred to as 'anthropomorphism' – in other words, being portrayed in human form.) Calvin argues that God is obliged to reveal himself in this pictorial manner on account of our weak intellects. Images of God which represent him as having a mouth or hands are divine 'baby-talk' (*balbutire*), a way in which God comes down to our level and uses images which we can handle. More sophisticated ways of speaking about God are certainly proper – but we might not be able to understand them. Thus Calvin points out that many aspects of the story of the creation and Fall (Genesis 1–3) (such as the notion of 'six days' or 'waters above the earth') are accommodated to the mentality and received opinions of a relatively simple people.[8] To those who object that this is unsophisticated, Calvin responds that it is God's way of ensuring that no intellectual barriers are erected against the gospel; all – even the simple and uneducated – can learn of, and come to faith in, God.[9]

Calvin uses three main images to develop this idea of divine accommodation to human capacities in revelation. God is our *father*, who is prepared to use the language of children in order to communicate with us. He adapts himself to the weakness and inexperience of childhood. He is our *teacher*, who is aware of the need to come down to our level if he is to educate us concerning him. He adapts himself to our ignorance, in order to teach us. He is our *judge*, who persuades us of our sinfulness, rebelliousness and disobedience. Just as human rhetoric in a court of law is designed to secure a verdict, so God is concerned to convince and convict us of our sin; to let *his* verdict become *our* verdict, as we realize that we are indeed sinners, who are far from God. Calvin insists that true wisdom lies in the knowledge of God and of ourselves: it is through recognizing that we are sinners that we discover that God is our redeemer.[10]

The doctrine of the incarnation speaks of God coming down to our level to meet us. He comes among us as one of us. Calvin extends this principle to the language and images of revelation: God reveals himself in words and pictures we can cope with. His concern and purpose is to communicate, to bridge the great yawning gulf between himself as creator and humanity as his creation. For Calvin, God's willingness and ability to condescend, to scale himself down, to adapt himself to our abilities, is a mark of his tender mercy towards us and his care for us.[11]

It must be stressed from the outset that Calvin does not, and does not believe that it is possible to, reduce God or Christian experience to words. Christianity is not a verbal religion, but is experiential;[12] it centres upon a transformative encounter of the believer with the risen Christ. From the standpoint of Christian theology, however, that experience is posterior to the words which generate, evoke and inform it. Christianity is Christ-centred, not book-centred; if it appears to be book-centred, it is because it is through the words of scripture that the believer encounters and feeds upon Jesus Christ. Scripture is a means, not an end; a channel, rather than what is channelled. Calvin's preoccupation with human language, and supremely with the text of scripture, reflects his fundamental conviction that it is *here*, that it is through reading and meditating upon *this* text, that it is possible to encounter and experience the risen Christ. A concentration upon the means reflects the crucial importance which Calvin attaches to the end. To suggest that Calvin is a 'bibliolater', one who worships a book, is to betray a culpable lack of insight into his concerns and methods. It is precisely because Calvin attaches supreme importance to the proper worship of God, as he has revealed himself in Jesus Christ, that he considers it so important to revere and correctly interpret the only means by which full and definitive access may be had to this God – scripture.

Calvin and the French Language

It is often suggested that during the seventeenth century the French language developed abstract, denotational and analytic qualities (often described as *clarté* and *logique*). But how, it may reasonably be asked, did *la clarté française*, so characteristic of writers of the French Classical period (such as Descartes and Pascal), develop? After all, the French style of many writers of the sixteenth century (such as Montaigne, Rabelais and Ronsard) conspicuously lacks this distinctive feature. We wish to suggest that Calvin may be regarded as a precipitating factor in this important development, partly on account of his involvement in the general trend to popularize the highly intricate abstractions of Christian theology, and partly on account of his personal contribution to the shaping of the language.[13]

By the second decade of the sixteenth century, a substantial body of devotional literature existed in the French language. (French was actually the first language of a minority within France; the *langue d'oc* and Breton are examples of important regional languages.) Marguerite of Navarre's *Miroir de l'âme pécheresse*, the focus of some unpleasantness at the University of Paris (p. 64), is an excellent example of this genre of literature. An examination of these popular devotional works, however, suggests that the French style involved, while admirable for the purposes of narrative or meditation, is simply not capable of bearing the weight of detailed conceptual argumentation. Simple dialogues between the human soul and Jesus Christ may well be spiritually uplifting and capable of inspiring an appropriate religious response from their readers; but where detailed argumentation, intellectual precision and clarity, and logical sequence of presentation were required, it was necessary to revert to Latin. The French language, as it existed around the year 1500, was fundamentally unsuited to the needs of intellectual disciplines – whether political or legal theory, dogmatic theology, or philosophy. The predominance of Latin as the lingua franca of the intellectual elite of France was not simply due to their cosmopolitanism, nor their desire to distance themselves from the common people; it was largely due to the fundamental inability of the French language, as it then existed, to match the articulation and development of most intellectual disciplines.

With the advent of the Reformation, a major new development took place. The complexities of biblical exegesis, ecclesiastical polity and dogmatic theology suddenly entered the public domain.

One of the most significant moments in the history of the Reformation is Martin Luther's decision in 1520 to switch from being an academic reformer (arguing in Latin to an academic public) to a popular one (arguing in German to a broader public). The Reformation witnessed the laying down of a major challenge to existing understandings of the way that the Bible could and should be read, to the structures of the church, and to Christian doctrine. Time and time again, the reformers appealed over the heads of the clergy and theologians to the people. The people, they insisted, must decide. The practice of the Swiss Reformation, in which a public disputation between evangelicals and catholics in the vernacular was followed by a plenary vote by the assembled body of citizens on whether to accept the Reformation, reflects this basic principle.

The full complexities of Christian theology and church polity thus became a matter of public debate. In that this debate extended far beyond the narrow confines of the groves of academe, it had to be conducted in the vernacular. By 1540, it had become a commonplace to conduct theological argumentation, often of a highly abstract nature, in French. The University of Paris, in an attempt to arrest this alarming development, published a list of prohibited books which gives invaluable information concerning the extent to which religious matters were being debated in the vernacular: the *Catalogue des livres censurés* for 1543 lists forty-three titles in French; that for 1544 is extended to 121; that of 1551 (the year of the Edict of Chateaubriant) includes no fewer than 182 titles in French and that of 1556 lists 250 such titles. In the seven-year period 1560–6, no fewer than twelve printings of Calvin's *Institutes* in French-language editions are known (see table 7.1 for details), emanating chiefly from Geneva and Lyons, but also from as far north as Caen. Nor, it must be stressed, was it only evangelicals who did their theology in French. Even a cursory glance at the output of Parisian printers over the period 1550–99 suggests that some 250 works of this nature were produced by catholic opponents of the Reformation.[14] Proponent and opponent alike were obliged to argue in French, thus further refining the medium they used to express their rival ideas.

The linguistic tool of abstract argumentation – which reached its zenith in the seventeenth century – was thus forged during the French Reformation. That Reformation itself ultimately failed; nevertheless, its bequest to the French language was as decisive as it was irreversible. It was but a small step to transfer the linguistic skills first learned in religious argumentation to wider fields of polemic – the law, politics and philosophy.

In that Calvin was a major contributor to the output of French religious literature from his publishing haven of Geneva, it will be clear that he may be regarded as responsible, at least in part, for this refinement of the French language. The publication of a French edition of his *Institutes* in 1541 represents a landmark in the Reformation and the development of the French language. This work, widely regarded as 'the first monument of French eloquence',[15] triggered something approaching a panic reaction at Paris: the *Institutes* is the work specifically identified for suppression by the Parisian *parlement* on 1 July 1542. It is not difficult to see why. *La clarté française* is evident throughout its pages. Its sentences are short, with relatively few subordinate clauses. (Indeed, Calvin's sentence structure shows remarkable parallels with that later associated with Jacques du Perron, widely regarded as one of the finest French stylists of the late sixteenth century.) Each of Calvin's sentences tends to make a single point, and often begins with a conjunction, allowing the reader to gain both a sense of direction and a sense of how the present sentence relates to the previous one. A contradiction, for example, is signalled even before the reason for that contradiction is stated.[16] The work is throughout a model of clarity and concision, extending the potential of the French language as a vehicle for abstract argument. Interestingly, it is not a mere translation of the 1539 Latin edition, but a virtual reworking of the original with the limitations of both the French language and its potential public in mind. The contrast with the heavily Latinized French translations of many of his opponents (who clearly had difficulty with French) is occasionally quite spectacular.

None of the subsequent French versions of the *Institutes* (those of 1545, 1551 and 1660) is able to match that of 1541 in terms of its remarkable unity, spontaneity and lightness of touch. However superior the edition of 1560 may be as regards comprehensiveness and theological acumen, it lacks the many literary merits of the first French version. It seems that Calvin, in his old age, was more concerned to express with accuracy the theological substance of his thought than to achieve stylistic elegance.[17]

The full importance of Calvin as a French-language writer is perhaps best gauged by comparing him with two other evangelical writers that we have encountered, Guillaume Farel and Pierre Viret. In his *Sommaire* of 1542, Farel praises Calvin's *Institutes* of the previous year as an 'excellent work': his own style, however, is convoluted, at points exceptionally difficult to follow. The same, unfortunately, is true of Pierre Viret, as judged by his *Disputations chrestiennes* (1544). Farel and Viret both demonstrate a certain attachment to long sentences (on average, Viret's are twice and Farel's three times as long as those of Calvin) and large numbers of subordinate clauses (Farel can employ eleven, and Viret up to eighteen, within a single sentence). The inevitable result is a style which is difficult to read; the painful and glaring contrast with Calvin's clarity and lightness further underscores the latter's outstanding qualities as a creative writer in the French language.[18]

The *Institutes of the Christian Religion*

On March 28 1536, Marcus Bersius wrote from Basle to Vadian, burgomaster and chief reformer of the eastern Swiss city of St Gallen. After some pleasantries, Bersius gets down to the main substance of his letter: keeping Vadian up to date with the latest books to appear from the Basle presses. Among its high points are annotations on the orations of Cicero, Oecolampadius' commentary on Genesis, Chrysostom on the Pauline letters, and Bucer on Romans. The list is impressive, regarding both its quality and its quantity, reflecting Basle's growing importance as a publishing centre. Nestling in its midst we find mention of 'a catechism by some Frenchman or other, dedicated to the king of France'.[19] This brief and vague description is one of the first references known to the work which established Calvin's reputation, published by the Basle printers Thomas Platter and Balthasar Lasius earlier that same month: the *Institutio Christianae religionis*, usually known in English as the *Institutes of the Christian Religion*.

The translation of the Latin title poses some problems. The word *Institutio* immediately suggests a parallel with the *Institutes* of Justinian, a foundational legal code of the classical period, familiar to Calvin from his time at Orléans. In terms of its structure or content, however, the work bears little resemblance to a legal code. Erasmus employed the term to mean 'instruction', or perhaps even 'primer' (for example, his *Institutio principis Christiani* of 1516, which may have served as an inspiration for Calvin's title). The English word 'institution' perhaps conveys another of Calvin's concerns – to return to a more authentic form of Christianity than that encountered in the late medieval period. It is Christianity as originally instituted which concerns Calvin, not as it was developed (or deformed, in his view) in the Middle Ages. In practice, most English translations choose to render the Latin title as *Institutes of the Christian Religion*, despite the alternatives suggested by the Latin original.

It is clear that the first edition of the *Institutes* was modelled on Luther's Lesser Catechism of 1529. Both its structure and substance indicate the extent to which Calvin has drawn upon this pedagogical work of the German Reformation.[20] Its 516 small-format pages comprise six chapters, the first four of which are modelled on Luther's catechism. Calvin, however, is able to engage in more detailed discussion of questions than Luther, in that his work is not a catechism which had to be learned by rote. The first chapter is essentially an exposition of the Ten Commandments (or Decalogue), and the second an exposition of the Apostles' Creed. The influence of Bucer is immediately obvious: where Luther's discussion of the creed has three sections (the Father, the Son, and the Holy Spirit), Calvin adds a substantial fourth section on the church, recognizing both the theoretical and the practical importance of this question. After expositions of 'the law', 'faith', 'prayer' and 'the sacraments', Calvin includes two chapters of a more polemical nature on 'false sacraments' and 'the liberty of a Christian'.

The second edition of the *Institutes* dates from Calvin's Strasbourg period.[21] Published in Latin in 1539, the volume is three times as long as the first edition of 1536, with seventeen chapters instead of six. Two opening chapters now deal with the knowledge of God and the knowledge of human nature. Additional material was added on the doctrine of the Trinity, the relation of the Old and New Testaments, penitence, justification by faith, the nature and relation of providence and predestination, and the nature of the Christian life. Although the work retains much material drawn from the earlier edition, it is evident that its character and status have changed. It is no longer a primer; it is well on the way to being a definitive statement of the nature of the Christian faith, inviting comparison with the *Summa Theologiae* of Thomas Aquinas. 'My object in this work,' wrote Calvin, 'is to so prepare and train students of sacred theology for the study of the word of God that they might have an easy access into it, and be able to proceed in it without hindrance.'[22] In other words, the book is intended to be a guide to scripture, functioning as a vade-mecum and commentary to its often intricate and complex depths of meaning.

This is an important point, as Calvin himself later stressed, in that it establishes his *Institutes* as the primary resource for his religious thought. His other writings – such as biblical commentaries and sermons – are of secondary importance in this respect, whatever their merits might otherwise be. As noted above, the French edition of the *Institutes* published in 1541 is not, curiously, a direct translation of the 1539 edition; there are several points at which material from the 1536 edition, although altered in 1539, has been included, in translation, in that of 1541. This has led to speculation that Calvin may originally have intended to produce a French translation of the 1536 edition,[23] and, abandoning this project, incorporated material already translated into the 1541 edition without the modifications introduced in 1539. The work shows numerous minor alterations, all of which may be explained with reference to the projected readership. Scholarly points likely to cause difficulty are omitted (for example, all Greek words and references to Aristotle), and additional material likely to be familiar to the intended readership (for example, French proverbs and idioms) are added.

A further Latin edition appeared in 1543, with a French translation in 1545. Now expanded to twenty-one chapters, this included as its most significant addition a major section on the doctrine of the church. Minor alterations include the addition of two chapters on vows and human traditions, and the creation of a separate chapter for the material relating to angels. The impact of experience upon Calvin's religious reflections is evident in this edition, particularly in the discussion of the importance of ecclesiastical organization. Despite the obvious merits of this edition, an inherent defect, already discernible in 1539, now becomes transparently obvious: the work is poorly organized. New chapters are added, without thought being given to their overall impact upon the structure and organization of the work. Many chapters are impossibly long, without any attempt to subdivide them into sections. The Latin edition of 1550, and the subsequent French translation of 1551, attempted to remedy this deficiency by subdividing their twenty-one chapters into paragraphs. A few additions may be noted, such as new sections dealing with biblical authority and human conscience. The fundamental flaw remains, however: the edition of 1550, like that of 1543, must be regarded as a remarkably poorly organized work.

Recognizing both the need for total revision and the limited time available in which to achieve this (illness was a recurring feature of Calvin's final years), the reformer decided to recast the entire work. There are surprisingly few additions; those that were made are generally unattractive, reflecting Calvin's growing irritability and tendency to abuse and vilify his opponents. The most obvious and positive change is the total reordering of the material, which virtually restores unity to what had almost degenerated into a series of unrelated fragments. The material is now distributed among four 'books' (*libri*), arranged as follows: the knowledge of God the creator; the knowledge of God the redeemer; the manner of participation in the grace of Jesus Christ; the external means or aids which God uses to bring us to Jesus Christ. The twenty-one chapters of 1551 are now expanded to eighty, each carefully subdivided for ease of reading, and distributed over these four books. It is possible that Calvin adapted the quadripartite structure of the edition of 1543 to create the new division of material; an alternative explanation is that he noticed and adapted the fourfold division of material in the *Four Books of the Sentences* of Peter Lombard, to whom he often refers. Is Calvin setting himself up as the Protestant successor to Peter Lombard, and his *Institutes* as the successor to his great theological textbook? We shall never know. What we do know is that the *Institutes* were now firmly established as the most influential theological work of the Protestant Reformation, eclipsing in importance the rival works of Luther, Melanchthon and Zwingli.

The success of the 1559 *Institutes* reflects its superb organization. Philip Melanchthon established the definitive pattern for Lutheran works of systematic theology in 1521, through the publication of his 'Commonplaces' (*Loci Communes*).[24] In its first edition, this work simply treated a number of subjects of obvious relevance to the Lutheran Reformation. Gradually, however, polemical and pedagogical considerations obliged Melanchthon to expand the work considerably. He met this challenge in a surprisingly inadequate manner: he merely added extra material, regardless of the impression of lack of a unified structure this created. It soon became evident that this way of handling material was clumsy and disorganized, incapable of achieving the systematic analysis needed for the theological debates of the late sixteenth and seventeenth centuries. Calvin's intensely systematic and organized structure, on the other hand, proved ideally suited not merely to the needs of his own generation, but also to those of at least a century to come. Lutheranism never really recovered from the false start given to it by Melanchthon; the intellectual domination of Protestantism by theologians of the Reformed tradition is due to both the *substance* and *structure* of Calvin's final edition of the *Institutes*.

A feature of twentieth-century religious publishing has been the appearance of 'study guides' to religious best-sellers, aimed at consolidating their appeal through summarizing and illustrating their contents. The success of Calvin's 1559 *Institutes* gave rise to a similar publishing spin-off – the 'summary' or 'compendium'. Even in the sixteenth century, numerous abridgements of this massive work were in circulation, apparently enjoying considerable commercial success.[25] In 1562, Augustin Marlorat published a set of indexes to the work, facilitating the location of subjects and biblical passages within it. In 1576, Nicolas Colladon, one of Calvin's early biographers, produced an edition which included brief marginal summaries of the contents of significant passages, largely to relieve the boredom of hard-worked theological students. Thomas Vautrollier, the Huguenot refugee who became one of London's more important religious publishers, printed two study guides to the *Institutes*: Edmund Bunny's *Compendium* (1576) attempted to deal with Calvin's compressed style and subtleties of argumentation for the benefit of perplexed students. Guillaume Delaune (a Huguenot refugee who Anglicized his name as William Lawne) produced a summary (*Epitome*) of the *Institutes* in a mere 370 pages of petit octavo seven years later. In addition to summarizing Calvin, the *Epitome* provided flow charts and diagrams to allow the puzzled reader to follow the intricate structure of the work. The summary was published in English shortly afterwards, as *An Abridgement of the Institution of the Christian Religion written by M. Iohn Caluin*. Other 'study guides' were published by Caspar Olevianus (1586), Johannes Piscator (1589) and Daniel de Coulogne, also known as Colonius (1628). Through their medium, Calvin became increasingly accessible and comprehensible to an ever-widening circle of readers.

Where Calvin influenced his contemporaries, it was chiefly through the successive editions of the *Institutes*. The propagation and diffusion of his leading ideas are due almost entirely to this work. This, however, is not to suggest that Calvin's reputation or influence rests totally upon it. Such was his mastery of the written and spoken word that he was able to develop three other literary genres for his purposes. Their literary and theological importance is considerable; nevertheless, it must be stressed that their *historical* importance is somewhat less, in that they did not have anything approaching the same impact as the *Institutes* in the sixteenth

Table 7.1 Editions of Calvin's *Institutes of the Christian Religion* to 1600

Date	*Place of publication*	*Publisher*	*Language*
1536	Basle	Platter and Lasius	Latin
1539	Strasbourg	Vendelin Rihel	Latin
1541	Geneva	Michel du Bois	French
1543	Strasbourg	Vendelin Rihel	Latin
1545	Geneva	Jean Gérard	French
1550	Geneva	Jean Gérard	Latin
1551	Geneva	Jean Gérard	French
1553	Geneva	Robert Estienne	Latin
1554	Geneva	Adam and Jean Rivery	Latin
1554	Geneva	Philibert Hamelin	French
1557	Geneva	Jaquy, Davodeau and Bourgeois	French
1557	Geneva	Bourgeois, Davodeau and Jaquy	Italian
1559	Geneva	Robert Estienne	Latin
1560	Geneva	Jean Crespin	French
1560	Emden	Unknown	Dutch
1561	Geneva	Antoine Reboul	Latin
1561	London	R. Wolfe and R. Harison	English
1561	Geneva	Conrad Badius	French
1561	Geneva	Jacques Bourgeois	French
1562	London	R. Harison	English
1562	Caen	Pierre Philippe	French
1562	Unknown	Unknown	French
1562	Lyons	Louis Cloquemin	French
1562	Geneva	Jacques Bourgeois	French
1563	Lyons	Sébastien Honorati	French
1564	Geneva	Thomas Courteau	French
1565	Lyons	Jean Martin	French
1565	Lyons	Pierre Haultin	French
1566	Geneva	François Perrin	French
1568	Geneva	François Perrin	Latin
1569	Geneva	François Perrin	Latin
1572	Heidelberg	Johann Meyer	German
1574	London	Widow of R. Wolfe	English
1576	London	Thomas Vautrollier	Latin
1576	Lausanne	François le Preux	Latin
1577	Lausanne	François le Preux	Latin
1578	Dordrecht	P. Verhagen and C. Jansz	Dutch

Table 7.1 Continued

Date	*Place of publication*	*Publisher*	*Language*
1578	London	Thomas Vautrollier	English
1582	London	H. Middleton	English
1584	London	Thomas Vautrollier	Latin
1585	Edinburgh	Thomas Vautrollier	English
1585	Geneva	Eustache Vignon and Jean le Preux	Latin
1586	Herborn	Christoph Raben	German
1587	London	H. Middleton	English
1587	Edinburgh	Unknown	English
1589	Herborn	Christoph Raben	Latin
1592	Geneva	Jean le Preux	Latin
1593	Leiden	J. P. Jacobsz and J. Bouwensz	Dutch
1595	Leiden	J. P. Jacobsz and J. Bouwensz	Dutch
1596	Bremen	Jean Wessel	French
1597	London	Richard Field	Spanish
1599	London	A. Hatfield	English

This table is based upon a survey of the holdings of major European libraries, in conjunction with material assembled by M. Antal Lökkös at the Bibliothèque Publique et Universitaire, Geneva, in 1986 in commemoration of the 450th anniversary of the publication of the first edition of the work. The list provided in the McNeill/Battles translation (*Institutes*, vol. 2, 1527–9) is incomplete.

century. To recognize this fact is not to suggest that Calvin was a poor preacher or commentator; the texts available indicate that quite the reverse was the case. As a biblical commentator, for example, he is easily in the first rank of his era.[26] Rather, it is to acknowledge the astonishing success and impact of the *Institutes* upon Calvin's day and age.

Finally, mention must be made of correspondence as a vehicle for the transmission of Calvin's ideas. The importance of correspondence as a medium for the propagation of ideas and aesthetic values had long been recognized by the humanist movement. Correspondence enabled Italian humanists to transmit and illus-

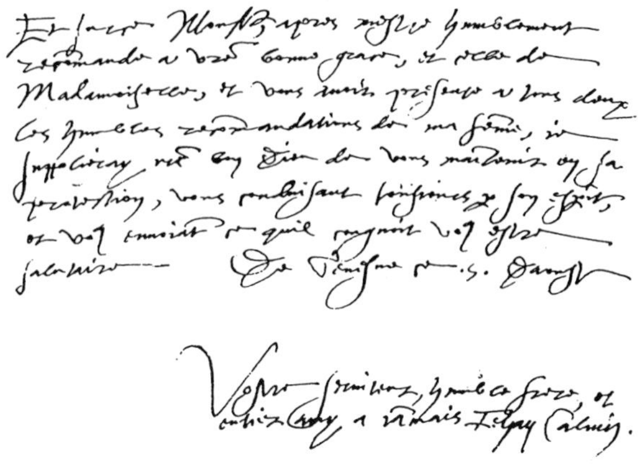

The text reads as follows:

Et sur ce, Monsieur, après m'estre humblement recommandé à vostre bonne grâce, et celle de Mademoiselle, et vous avoir présenté à tous deux les humbles recommandations de ma femme, je supplieray nostre bon Dieu de vous maintenir en sa protection, vous conduisant tousjours par son esprit, et vous envoiant ce qu'il cognoit vous estre salutaire.
De Genefve ce .5. d'aoust.

Vostre serviteur, humble frere, et entier amy à jamais, Jehan Calvin.
(Bibliothèque Publique et Universitaire de Genève, MS Fr 194, fol. 15)

FIGURE 7.1 Part of a letter, dated 5 August 1545, from Calvin to M. de Fallais (Jacques de Bourgogne)

trate their ideas on eloquence to an increasingly receptive audience north of the Alps.[27] Calvin, however, was able to develop the letter as a form of religious and political propaganda, allowing his radical ideas to enter every part of France. Though absent in person, he was able to maintain contact with his supporters in the Agenais, Angoulême, Bourges, Brie, the Champagne, Grenoble, the Languedoc, Lyons, Orléans, Paris, Poitiers, Provence, Rouen and Toulouse. Throughout the 1530s and 1540s, Calvin was closely in touch with a circle of middle-class professionals – such as lawyers, students and teachers – who kept him informed about the turbulent religious situation in his native land.[28] Through this extensive correspondence, he was able to establish and consolidate his influence over the French evangelical movement at a decisive period in its history, as his religious and economic ideas gained an increasingly attentive hearing among the disaffected bourgeoisie.

But what were those religious ideas? Having considered the medium, we must now turn to the message itself.

N

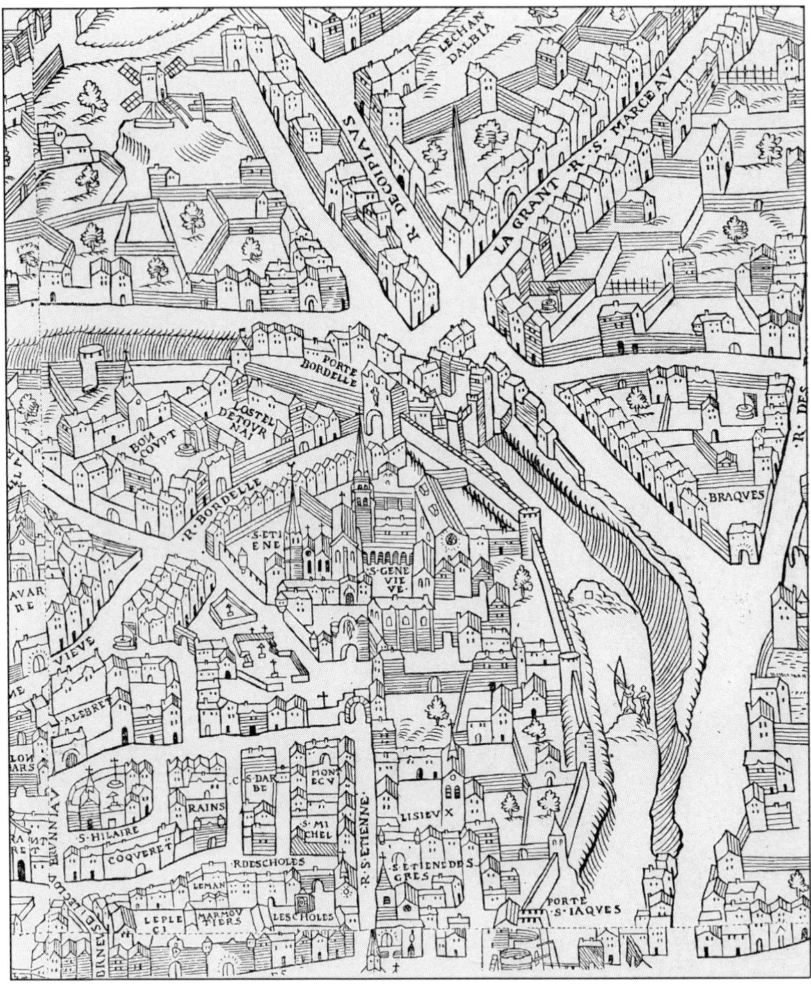

PLATE I Section of the plan of the city of Paris by Truschet and Hoyau (1552), showing the university quarter. The Collège de Montaigu (MONT ECV) is located in the lower left-hand quadrant. Note that the top of the plan indicates east, not north. (Bodleian Library, Oxford.)

PLATE 2 Portrait of Francis I, King of France, 1515–47. (Musée du Louvre, Paris. Photograph: Photographie Giraudon.)

PLATE 3 Francis I leading a public penitential procession (1528), in protest against Lutheran outrages within Paris. (Bibliothèque Nationale, Paris. Photograph: Photographie Giraudon.)

PLATE 4 German anti-Catholic cartoon (1520), contrasting Lutheran preaching ('The Lord God says *this*') with that of their catholic opponents ('The Pope says *that*'). (Archiv für Kunst und Geschichte, Berlin.)

PLATE 5 Engraving of Guillaume Farel (1489–1565). (Archiv für Kunst und Geschichte, Berlin.)

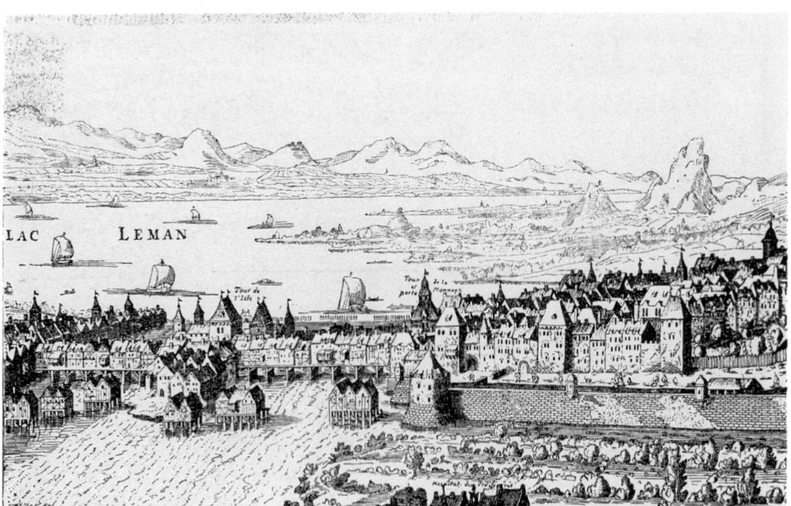

PLATE 6 View of the city of Geneva (1641), looking eastwards from the Rhone. The old city, centering on the cathedral of Saint-Pierre, is to the right of the illustration.

PLATE 7 (opposite) Portrait of John Calvin (1509–64). (Archiv für Kunst und Geschichte, Berlin.)

IOANNES, CALVINVS

PLATE 8 Engraving of John Calvin, *c.* 1562. (Archiv für Kunst und Geschichte, Berlin.)

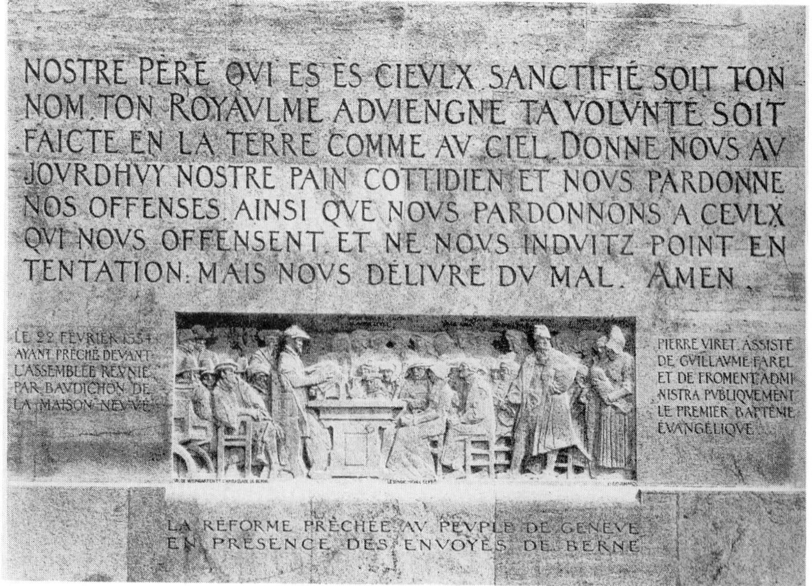

PLATE 9 Section of the International memorial to the Reformation, Promenade des Bastions, Geneva (1916), depicting the preaching of the Reformation to the Genevans in the presence of Bernese envoys (February 1534). (Archiv für Kunst und Geschichte, Berlin.)

PLATE 10 Section of the International Memorial to the Reformation, Promenade des Bastions, Geneva (1916), depicting the reformers Guillaume Farel, John Calvin, Théodore de Bèze, and John Knox. (Archiv für Kunst und Geschichte, Berlin.)

PLATE 11 Portrait of Théodore de Bèze (1519–1605). (Musée du Protestantisme, Paris. Photograph: Photographie Giraudon.)

PLATE 12 Portrait of the French Calvinist leader Gaspard de Coligny (1519–72). (Bibliothèque du Protestantisme, Paris. Photograph: Photographie Giraudon.)

PLATE 13 A satirical view of the religious struggles within Germany (1598), depicting Luther, the Pope and Calvin squabbling furiously (left panel), to the dismay of a pious believer (right panel).

8

Christianity according to Calvin: The Message

To understand Calvin it is necessary to *read* Calvin. Just as a guide-book to his native France cannot hope to be a substitute for first-hand experience of that country, so there is no adequate alternative to a personal engagement with Calvin's own writings. Many presentations of his thought have a certain 'second-hand' feel to them – as, indeed, may this work. To gain an understanding of Calvin's mindset, his mode of analysis, his use of analogy, his exploitation of rhetoric, and the manner in which potential difficulties and misunderstandings are forestalled, it is necessary to take time to read his *Institutes*. The present chapter is conceived as an introduction to that reading.

The analogy of a guidebook may serve to explain the intended purpose of this chapter. It is like a map, locating the various components of the *Institutes*, and allowing the reader to gain a preliminary understanding of their relation to one another. It is intended to draw attention to certain features worthy of attention, and provide such background information as may be necessary or appropriate to understand the importance of items singled out in this way. But above all, it is an aid to discovery, a stimulus to encounter, an incentive to first-hand experience.

The Priority of the *Institutes*

The most convenient way – and, as we shall suggest, the most reliable – of presenting an outline of Calvin's understanding of Christianity is to pick out the main themes of the 1559 edition of the *Institutes of the Christian Religion*. Calvin himself explicitly identified the *Institutes* as the sole authoritative exposition of his religious ideas. This is not to say that there are other potential sources for these ideas – for example, his biblical commentaries or his sermons – which are totally eclipsed by the *Institutes*. Nor is it to downplay Calvin's remarkable abilities as a biblical commentator or preacher. It is certainly true that, at least in some cases, it is possible to construct the main outlines of his doctrines from a survey of his biblical commentaries.[1] Further, the commentaries generally lack the petulant and irritable tone, occasionally verging on the cantankerous, characteristic of certain sections of the 1559 *Institutes*. Calvin's unattractive authorial persona, probably reflecting the increasingly distressing debilitations of both his ageing and his illness, is generally regarded as one of the work's chief shortcomings. His treatment of his opponents, particularly Andreas Osiander, is aggressive and dismissive, with a regrettable tendency to combine criticism of ideas with criticism of the personality of those who entertain them. The contrast with Thomas Aquinas is particularly pointed: the *Summa Theologiae* is characterized by considerable restraint, even at those points at which Aquinas is clearly presenting ideas he regards as erroneous. Calvin's commentaries, on the other hand, are a markedly more pleasant reading experience. Nevertheless, two potential dangers of prioritizing the commentaries must be noted.

In the first place, Calvin's rigorous conception of the role of the commentator upon a text, evident as early as the Seneca commentary, places severe restrictions upon his freedom to make the crucial hermeneutical transition between scriptural exposition and theological affirmation. Calvin does not understand 'theology' simply to mean 'biblical exposition', although he has no intention whatsoever of detaching theology from scriptural exposition.[2] While he regards theology as 'an echo of the biblical text',[3] it is not, strictly speaking, so much a *commentary* upon that text as an *interpretative framework* by which the text may be understood. It is clear that, in commenting upon texts, Calvin often feels it improper to provide a full-blown exposition of the total doctrinal implications of a given passage. In part, this reflects his awareness of the need to deal with the historical, linguistic and literary points raised by that passage. It also, however, rests upon his evident assumption that his readers will refer to the *Institutes* as the primary source of his theology – and hence his method of interpreting scripture – in its entirety. Commentaries may clarify points of detail within scriptural texts; the *Institutes* provides a general framework within which the broad thrust of the scriptural proclamation may be grasped and understood. Calvin clearly regarded his biblical commentaries as subordinate to the *Institutes* at points; they were not intended to be, and cannot be treated as if they are, an independent substitute. If there is one single aid to the reading of scripture which stands out above all others among his writings, and which was intended as such by Calvin himself, it is the *Institutes* itself, rather than any commentary upon a specific biblical work.

In the second place, Calvin's theological expositions often rest upon a detailed analysis of the interrelation of various constituent parts of his system, including the exploration of possible difficulties and the evaluation of rival alternatives. This enterprise is realistic within the context of the *Institutes*, especially the edition of 1559. The full nuances, emphases and subtleties of Calvin's thought may thus be identified and evaluated. In dealing with any given topic in the 1559 edition, the reader can rest assured that he or she will encounter everything Calvin regarded as essential to grasping his position on that topic. This comprehensiveness will not be encountered by the reader of the biblical commentaries, attempting to determine Calvin's position by considering his exposition of potentially relevant biblical passages. One is in effect obliged to consult the *Institutes* to determine whether some essential component of Calvin's thought on a given theme has been omitted, thereby conceding the priority of that work.

The Structure of Calvin's Thought

Calvin is widely regarded as a cool and dispassionate systematizer, a mind rather than a personality, a withdrawn and socially isolated figure who felt more at home in the world of ideas than in the real world of flesh, blood and human relationships.[4] The popular conception of Calvin's religious thought is that of a rigorously logical system, centring upon the doctrine of predestination. Influential though this popular icon may be, it bears little relation to reality; important though the doctrine of predestination may be for later Calvinism (see pp. 208–18), this is not reflected in Calvin's exposition of the idea. Yet this popular belief raises an important question. Can one speak of Calvin's thought as being a *system* in the first place? The word 'system' implies underlying assumptions of unity.[5] It makes claims to coherence. Yet Calvin shared the intense distaste of the humanist republic of letters for the scholastic theologicians, whose watchwords might have been 'systematization' and 'coherence'. To speak of Calvin as a theological systematizer is to imply a degree of affinity with medieval scholasticism which contradicts his known attitudes. It is also to suggest a significant dislocation between Calvin and his culture, which neither possessed the intellectual resources nor perceived any particular reason for producing works of 'systematic theology'[6] – a literary genre which was anyway firmly identified as the preserve of the much despised scholasticism. It is only by considering the *Institutes* as consistent with, rather than a radical exception to, the biblical humanism of Calvin's age that the work's full significance can be appreciated.[7]

It is certainly true that the 1559 *Institutes* has frequently been compared to Thomas Aquinas' *Summa Theologiae* – with its 512 questions, 2,669 articles, and more than 10,000 objections and replies – in its comprehensiveness and influence. Yet this is to confuse sheer literary bulk and historical influence with theological affinity. As a study of the evolution of the *Institutes* indicates (pp. 136–40), Calvin originally conceived the work in modest terms, with no claims to methodological comprehensiveness. The rearrangement of the material between editions in the period 1536 to 1559 reflects pedagogical, rather than methodological, considerations; Calvin's concern is humanist, rather than scholastic – to aid his readers, rather than impose method upon his own thought. The 1559 *Institutes* combine the cardinal virtues of the humanist educationalist – clarity and comprehensiveness – allowing its readers access to a clear and thorough presentation of the main points of the Christian faith, as Calvin wished it to be understood. At no point is there any evidence to suggest that a leading principle, axiom or doctrine – save that of clarity of presentation – has governed the form or the substance of the work. It is an expression of *eloquentia*, so highly prized by the Renaissance, both in its structure and its prose.

The analyst who, for whatever reason, presupposes a unifying principle within Calvin's thought is naturally predisposed to find one. Calvin scholarship possesses an abundance of studies which, presuming that there existed a unifying principle within Calvin's thought, have proceeded to identify it in his doctrine of predestination,[8] his doctrine of the knowledge of God,[9] or his doctrine of the church.[10] A more modest (and, it must be added, more realistic) approach involves conceding the obvious, and allowing that there is *no* central doctrine within Calvin's thought.[11] The very idea of a 'central dogma' has its origins in the deductive monism of the Enlightenment, rather than in the theology of the sixteenth century.[12] One may identify certain centrally important themes, certain fundamental root metaphors, which allow insights into Calvin's religious thought – but the notion of a central doctrine or axiom which controls it cannot be maintained. There is no 'hard core', no 'basic principle' or 'central premise', no 'essence' of Calvin's religious thought.

It is, however, evident that throughout his discussion of the relation of God and humanity Calvin regards a single paradigm as normative. The paradigm in question is that made available by the incarnation, specifically the union without fusion of divinity and humanity in the person of Jesus Christ. Time and time again, Calvin appeals to the Christologically grounded formula, *distinctio sed non separatio*;[13] at this point, two ideas may be *distinguished* but not *separated*. Thus the 'knowledge of God' and 'knowledge of ourselves' may be distinguished; they may not, however, be had in isolation from one another. Just as the incarnation represents a paradigmatic instance of this *complexio oppositorum*, so the same pattern is repeated and may be discerned throughout the various manifestations of the relationship between God and humanity. In that he stresses that theology is centred upon 'knowledge of God and knowledge of ourselves' (*Institutes* I.i.1), this paradigm is clearly of some importance. Throughout his works, Calvin displays a pervasive tendency to distinguish radically the human and divine realms – yet insist upon their unity. There is no possibility whatsoever of dividing God and the world, or God and human beings.

This principle can be seen in operation throughout the *Institutes*:[14] the relation between the word of God and the words of human beings in preaching; between the sign and thing signified in the eucharist; between the believer and Christ in justification, where a real communion of persons exists, yet not a fusion of being; between the secular and the spiritual power. Calvin's thought is thoroughly Christocentric, not merely in that it centres upon God's revelation in Jesus Christ, but also in that this revelation discloses a paradigm which governs other key areas of Christian thought. Wherever God and humanity come into conjunction, the incarnational paradigm illuminates their relation. If there is a centre of Calvin's religious thought, that centre may reasonably be identified as Jesus Christ himself.[15]

To suggest that it is not entirely appropriate to designate Calvin's religious thought as a 'system' is not for one moment to imply that it lacks coherence or internal consistency. Rather, it is to underscore the skill with which Calvin, apparently acting as a biblical rather than a philosophical theologian, was able to integrate a number of elements within the overall structure of his thought. He may not have developed a 'theological system', in the rigorous sense of the term; nevertheless, he was unquestionably a systematic thinker, who fully recognized the need to ensure internal consistency between the various components of his thought.

With the passing of Calvin's age, a new concern for method dawned. A significant shift in the intellectual climate took place, as a new humanist interest in methodological questions developed, with the pivotal result that systematization was no longer regarded as the exclusive preserve of the much despised scholastic theologians. In part, this is due to the increasing influence of the humanist school at Padua, whose stress upon the importance of method (and the contributions of Aristotle to this science) gained an increasingly sympathetic hearing in the later Renaissance. If it was to maintain intellectual respectability and credibility, Calvinism had to recast itself in the new systematic mould. Calvin's successors in the later sixteenth century, confronted with the need to impose method upon his thought, found that his theology was eminently suited to recasting within the more rigorously logical structures suggested by the Aristotelian methodology favoured by the later Italian Renaissance (pp. 212–14). This has perhaps led to the too easy conclusion that Calvin's thought itself possesses the systematic cast and logical rigour of later Reformed Orthodoxy, and has allowed Orthodoxy's preoccupation with the doctrine of predestination to be read back into the 1559 *Institutes*. As we shall suggest (pp. 208–18), there is a subtle difference between Calvin and Calvinism at this point, marking and reflecting a significant turning point in intellectual history in general. If Calvin's followers developed his ideas, it was in response to a new spirit of the age, which regarded systematization and a concern for method as intellectually respectable and desirable. Lutheranism failed to recognize the significance of this decisive shift in the intellectual climate; by the time Lutheran writers adopted the new methods, virtually an entire generation had passed, and the intellectual superiority of Calvinism seemed assured.

Before considering the main features of Calvin's thought, it may be helpful to identify at least some of the more significant influences upon his views. In the first place, it must be stressed that Calvin is a biblical theologian. The first and foremost source of his religious ideas was the Bible. Calvin's work as a biblical commentator serves to reinforce the overall impression one gains from a close reading of the *Institutes*: that he regarded himself as an obedient expositor of the Bible. Texts, however, require interpretation. Calvin had access to, and had little hesitation in using, the major new techniques of literary theory, textual criticism and philological analysis which the Renaissance had placed at his disposal. He was a humanist, and harnessed the techniques of the republic of letters to his service as a biblical expositor.

While Calvin's major concern was the interpretation of scripture, his reading of this text was enriched and informed by the Christian tradition.[16] He had no hesitation in developing the thesis he originally defended at the Lausanne Disputation – that the Reformation represented a recovery of the authentic teaching of the early church, with the distortions and spurious additions of the medieval period eliminated. Above all, Calvin regarded his thought as a faithful exposition of the leading ideas of Augustine of Hippo.[17] 'Augustine is totally ours!'[18] He had high regard for some of the earlier medieval writers, such as Bernard of Clairvaux.[19] Although he tended to regard later medieval theology as something of an irrelevance, it is evident that Calvin has incorporated at least some of its methods and presuppositions into his thought.[20] His voluntarism and subtle appeal to the logico-critical method are illustrations of an affinity, not necessarily with any *specific* writer or school of thought, but with the standard intellectual furniture of contemporary theology. Finally, his debt to the first generation of reformers is everywhere evident – to Luther, to his Strasbourg friend Bucer, and to the erudite Philip Melanchthon, to name but three.[21]

It is clearly impossible to give a detailed analysis of Calvin's thought in the space available. It is therefore proposed to present an overview of Christianity according to Calvin, as presented in the *Institutes*.

The 1559 *Institutes:* An Overview

The material which Calvin presents in the *Institutes* is broken down into four books, as follows. Book I deals with the doctrine of God, especially the ideas of creation and providence. Book II deals with the foundations of the doctrine of redemption, including a discussion of human sin, and an extended analysis of the person and work of the redeemer, Jesus Christ. Book III deals with the application of this redemption to the individual, including analysis of the doctrines of faith, regeneration, justification and predestination. Book IV deals with the life of the redeemed community, considering various matters of direct relevance to the church – its ministry, its sacraments, and its relation to the state.

The size of the *Institutes* makes any attempt to simplify its structure welcome. It is thus helpful to regard the work as possessing a Trinitarian structure: Book I dealing with God the Father, Book II with God the Son, Book III with God the Holy Spirit, and Book IV with the church. While such an overview facilitates location of material within the work, it must not be regarded as having been in Calvin's mind as he organized the material. For example, he fails to refer to the Holy Spirit in his own summary of the contents of Book III.

Book I

The first book of the *Institutes* opens with discussion of one of the fundamental problems of Christian theology: how do we know anything about God? Even before turning to discuss this question, however, Calvin stresses that 'knowledge of God and knowledge of ourselves are connected' (I.i.1). Without a knowledge of God, we cannot truly know ourselves; without knowing ourselves, we cannot know God. The two forms of knowledge are 'joined together by many bonds'; although they are distinct, they cannot be separated. It is impossible to have either in isolation. This principle is of fundamental importance to an understanding of Calvin's strongly world-affirming theology: knowledge of God cannot be detached from, nor allowed to merge with, knowledge of human nature or of the world. A dialectic is constructed, resting upon a delicately balanced interplay between God and the world, the creator and his creation.

In dealing with our knowledge of God as the 'creator and sovereign ruler of the world', Calvin affirms that a general knowledge of God may be discerned throughout his creation – in humanity, in the natural order, and in the historical process itself. Two main grounds of such knowledge are identified, one subjective, the other objective. The first ground is a 'sense of divinity' (*sensus divinitatis*) or a 'seed of religion' (*semen religionis*), implanted within every human being by God (I.iii.1; I.v.1). God himself has endowed human beings with some inbuilt sense or presentiment of his existence. It is as if something about God has been engraved in the hearts of every human being (I.x.3). Calvin identifies three consequences of this inbuilt awareness of divinity: the universality of religion (which, if uninformed by the Christian revelation, degenerates into idolatry: I.iii.1), a troubled conscience (I.iii.2), and a servile fear of God (I.iv.4). All of these, Calvin suggests, may serve as points of contact for the Christian proclamation.

The second such ground lies in experience of and reflection upon the ordering of the world. The fact that God is creator, together with an appreciation of his wisdom and justice, may be gained from an inspection of the created order, culminating in humanity itself (I.v.1–15). 'God has revealed himself in such a beautiful and elegant construction of heaven and earth, showing and presenting himself there every day, that human beings cannot open their eyes without having to notice him' (I.v.1). It is difficult to read this section of the *Institutes* without being reminded of the deism of later writers such as Herbert of Cherbury, or Isaac Newton – a significant fact to which we shall return later, as we consider Calvin's impact upon the natural sciences.

It is important to stress that Calvin makes no suggestion whatsoever that this knowledge of God from the created order is peculiar to, or restricted to, Christian believers. Calvin is arguing that *anyone*, by intelligent and rational reflection upon the created order, should be able to arrive at the idea of God. The created order is a 'theatre' (I.v.5) or a 'mirror' (I.v.11) for displaying the divine presence, nature and attributes. Although God is himself invisible and incomprehensible, he makes himself known under the form of created and visible things. The invisible God makes himself known by donning the garment of creation (I.v.1).

Calvin thus commends the natural sciences (such as astronomy), on account of their ability to illustrate further the wonderful ordering of creation, and the divine wisdom which this indicates (I.v.2). Significantly, though, he makes no appeal to specifically *Christian* sources of revelation. His argument is based upon empirical observation and ratiocination. If Calvin introduces scriptural quotations, it is to consolidate a general natural knowledge of God, rather than to establish that knowledge in the first place. There is, he stresses, a way of discerning God which is common to those inside and outside the Christian community (*exteris et domesticis communem:* I.v.6).

Having thus laid the foundations for a general knowledge of

God, Calvin stresses its shortcomings; his dialogue partner here is Cicero, whose *de natura deorum* is perhaps one of the most influential classical expositions of a natural knowledge of God.[22] The epistemic distance between God and humanity, already of enormous magnitude, is increased still further on account of human sin. Our natural knowledge of God is imperfect and confused, even to the point of contradiction, on occasion. A natural knowledge of God serves to deprive humanity of any excuse for ignoring him; nevertheless, it is inadequate as the basis of a fully fledged portrayal of the nature, character and purposes of God. Calvin thus introduces the notion of biblical revelation; scripture reiterates what may be known of God through nature, while simultaneously clarifying this general revelation and enhancing it (I.x.1). 'The knowledge of God, which is clearly shown in the ordering of the world and in all creatures, is still more clearly and familiarly explained in the Word' (I.x.1). It is only through scripture that the believer has access to knowledge of the redeeming actions of God in history, culminating in the life, death and resurrection of Jesus Christ (I.vi.1–4). For Calvin, revelation is focused upon the person of Jesus Christ; our knowledge of God is mediated through him (I.vi.1).

In that Jesus Christ is known only through the scriptural record, the centrality and indispensability of scripture to theologian and believer alike are assured. Calvin adds, however, that scripture can only be properly read and understood through the inspiration of the Holy Spirit (I.vii.1). Nevertheless, he does not develop a mechanical or literal understanding of the inspiration of scripture. It is certainly true that he occasionally uses images which might suggest a mechanical view of inspiration – for example, referring to the biblical authors as 'clerks' or 'scribes', or speaking of the Holy Spirit 'dictating'. However, these images are almost certainly to be understood metaphorically, as accommodations or visual figures. The content of scripture is indeed divine – yet the form in which that content is embodied is human. Scripture is the *verbum Dei*, not the *verba Dei*. It is the *record* of the Word, not the Word itself. There is unquestionably an implicit parallel with the incarnation at this point, as at so many other points in Calvin's thought: divine and human coexist, without compromising or destroying each other. Scripture represents the word of God mediated through the form of human words, weighted with divine authority on account of their origin.

God may thus only be fully known through Jesus Christ, who

may in turn only be known through scripture; the created order, however, provides important points of contact for and partial resonances of this revelation. Having thus identified the manner in which God may be known, Calvin proceeds to consider what may be known concerning him. At this point, nature is left behind. The doctrine of the Trinity, the first major aspect of his understanding of the nature of God to be expounded, is treated as a biblical doctrine resting upon special revelation, rather than an insight which may be gained from general revelation or nature. Many reformers found this doctrine to pose difficulties, not least on account of its arcane terminology (particularly the terms 'person' and 'substance'). Martin Bucer initially found himself hesitant over using non-biblical terms in expounding any aspect of the doctrine of God. Calvin himself proposed the principle 'never to attempt to search after God anywhere than in his holy word, or to speak or think of him further than we have it as our guide' (I.xiii.21); how then could the doctrine of the Trinity, which is not actually articulated in anything even approaching a fully developed form in scripture, be justified? Calvin's basic response is that 'while God declares his unity, he clearly sets this before us as existing in three persons' (I.xiii.2). The three persons are to be understood as arising from a distinction, not a division, within the Godhead (I.xiii.17).

Orthodox precisely on account of its unoriginality, Calvin's account of the Trinity assumes the function of a defensive doctrine, safeguarding primarily the divinity of Christ (I.xiii.22–8). His stress upon the epistemic and soteriological mediatorship of Jesus Christ requires him to establish the divinity of Christ at as early a stage as possible in his exposition. Both salvation and knowledge of God and ourselves are channelled through this mediator; such is the edifice that Calvin constructs upon this foundation that it must be demonstrated to rest upon secure grounds.

Calvin opened the *Institutes* with a declaration that 'our wisdom . . . consists almost entirely of two parts: the knowledge of God and of ourselves' (I.i.1). Having dealt with the basic features of the doctrine of God, he now turns to consider a cluster of questions relating to human nature. After a remarkable and lengthy digression into the nature and habits of angels (I.xiv.3–19), Calvin moves to a discussion of human nature as 'the most noble and excellent specimen of the righteousness, wisdom and goodness of God' (I.xv.1). Humans are created in the image and likeness of God, and endowed with a free will which was compromised by the Fall. Humans are clothed with a certain dignity which distinguishes them from other animals. By virtue of being created in the image and likeness of God, humans may be said to be 'mirrors of divine glory' (I.xv.4). Nevertheless, human nature as we now know it reflects that glory in an imperfect manner; it is only in Christ that we see that glory fully revealed. Even at this early stage, the strongly Christocentric character of Calvin's theology becomes apparent: true human nature is disclosed in the person of Jesus Christ. There is simultaneously a continuity and a discontinuity between our human nature and that of Jesus Christ, revealing both the possibility and the necessity of our renovation if we are to be restored to full communion with God.

Calvin's discussion of God the creator ends with an exposition of the notion of divine providence. This doctrine was not allocated a chapter of its own in the 1536 edition of the work; the edition of 1539, however, discussed the doctrine alongside that of predestination. It now appears, emancipated from predestination, as an aspect of the doctrine of creation. Why? It seems that Calvin wishes to affirm that God's providence is an extension of his creation. Having created the world, God continues to care for it, directing and sustaining it (I.xvii.1). Everything within creation is subject to the wise and benevolent influence of its creator.

Book II

The second book deals with the knowledge of God 'in as much as he has shown himself to be our redeemer in Jesus Christ'. Although knowledge of God the creator may be gleaned, albeit in a partial and piecemeal manner, from the created order itself, knowledge of God the redeemer can only be had through Jesus Christ, as he is attested to by scripture. Calvin opens his discussion of redemption through Christ with an analysis of its presuppositions – the Fall and its consequences, the relation of law and gospel, and the relation of Old and New Testaments within scripture itself.

There is perhaps a slight degree of repetition from Book I as Calvin expounds his understanding of the nature of sin and its consequences for human nature. Humanity, as originally created by God, was good in every respect. On account of the Fall (which Calvin regards as having had catastrophic consequences), natural human gifts and faculties have been radically impaired. The notion of the solidarity of the human race underlies his insistence that all of humanity now shares in Adam's fall from grace (II.i.7). The human free will, though not destroyed, is rendered powerless to resist sin. We have 'not been deprived of will, but of a healthy will' (II.iii.5). As a consequence, both human reason and will are contaminated by sin. Unbelief is thus seen as an act of will as much as of reason; it is not simply a failure to discern the hand of God within the created order, but a deliberate decision *not* to discern it and *not* to obey God.

Calvin develops the consequences of this at two distinct, although related, levels. At the epistemic level, humans lack the necessary rational and volitional resources to discern God fully within the created order. At the soteriological level, humans lack what is required in order to be saved; they do not *want* to be saved (on account of the debilitation of the mind and will through sin), and they are *incapable* of saving themselves (in that salvation presupposes obedience to God, now impossible on account of sin). True knowledge of God and salvation must both therefore come from outside the human situation. In such a manner, Calvin lays the foundations for his doctrine of the mediatorship of Jesus Christ.

He then turns to the historical preparation for the coming of the mediator. The giving of the law to Abraham and his successors is seen by Calvin as the first step in the providential strategy to redeem the human situation. He makes it clear that he understands the word 'law' to designate 'the form of religion delivered at the hand of Moses', and not merely the Ten Commandments (II.vii.1). The law was a gift of grace to the Jewish people, pointing ahead to the future coming of Jesus Christ as the fulfilment of the law's hints and promises. Calvin treats much of that law with scant respect, regarding it as little more than antiquated Jewish tradition or superstition whose origins lay in a peasant rural economy of the ancient near east:

> What could be more pointless or stupid than the idea that you can reconcile yourself to God by offering him the fat and stinking entrails of animals? Or getting rid of stains on your soul with a few splashes of blood or water? In short, if this was all the good that the law did (assuming that it did not point ahead to something else, or symbolize some corresponding truth), it would seem to be some kind of joke.

The whole purpose of the Jewish religion, according to Calvin, is to point ahead to Jesus Christ.

Developing this point, he formulates a set of principles which allows readers of the Old Testament to make sense of some of the more peculiar (and frankly primitive) practices and ideas described within its pages. A distinction may be drawn between the moral, ceremonial and judicial aspects of the law: the two latter – which included detailed instructions on the correct methods of ritual slaughter of animals, purification rites and various food prohibitions – were now to be regarded as obsolete. To use the language of a later period, they were to be recognized as radically conditioned, both historically and culturally. (Calvin, incidentally, will later make a similar point relating to the Old Testament prohibition of lending money at interest: p. 231.) At points, he sounds like an Enlightenment rationalist, scorning the primitive character of Old Testament religion; nevertheless, he insists that beneath the cultural rituals and stipulations, there may be discerned patterns of behaviour and conduct which are of relevance for Christians today. These moral regulations, as set out, for example, in the Ten Commandments, remain binding on Christians.

What functions might this moral law now have? In common with other reformers, such as Bucer and Melanchthon, Calvin identifies three functions. In the first place, it possesses an educational or pedagogical aspect (the *usus theologicus legis*), an ability to bring home the reality of sin, and thus prepare the ground for redemption (II.vii.6–7). In the second, it has a political function (the *usus civilis legis*): to constrain the unregenerate and unconverted from degenerating into moral chaos (an important consideration for European cities anxious at the threat of the development of internal instability). Finally, it possesses a third use, the so-called *tertius usus legis*, by which it encourages believers to submit themselves more completely to the will of God, in much the same way as a whip might encourage a lazy ass (II.vii.12). For many of Calvin's critics, particularly those with Lutheran backgrounds, this appears to confuse law and gospel, and has frequently opened Calvin to the charge of encouraging some form of Christian legalism.

This might seem to place the Old Testament on the same level as the New. Calvin is thus obliged to define more precisely the relationship of the two, identifying both their similarities and their differences. He argues that there exists a fundamental similarity and continuity between Old and New Testaments on the basis of three considerations. First, he stresses the immutability of the divine will. God cannot do one thing in the Old Testament, and follow it by doing something totally different in the New. There must be a fundamental continuity of action and intention between the two. Second, both celebrate and proclaim the grace of God manifested in Jesus Christ. The Old Testament may only be able to witness to Jesus Christ 'from a distance and darkly'; nevertheless, its witness to the coming of Christ is real. In the third place, both Testaments possess the 'same signs and sacraments' (II.x.5), bearing witness to the grace of God.

In terms of their substance and content, Calvin thus effectively argues that the Testaments are identical. There is no radical discontinuity between them. The Old Testament happens to occupy a different chronological position in the divine plan of salvation than the New; its content (rightly understood), however, is the same. Calvin proceeds to identify five points of difference between Old and New Testaments, relating to form, rather than substance.

1 The New Testament possesses greater clarity than the Old (II.xi.1), particularly in relation to invisible things. The Old Testament tends to be pervaded by a certain preoccupation with things visible and tangible, which might obscure the invisible goals, hopes and values which lie behind them. Calvin illustrates this point with reference to the land of Canaan; the Old Testament tends to treat this earthly possession as an end in itself, whereas the New Testament regards it as a reflection of the future inheritance reserved for believers in heaven. The Jews were thus given the hope of immortality using the analogy of worldly successes and achievements; this inferior method has now been set to one side.

2 The Old and New Testaments adopt significantly different approaches to imagery (II.xi.4). The Old Testament employs a mode of representation of reality which Calvin suggests leads to an indirect encounter with the truth, through various figures of speech and visual images; but the New Testament allows an immediate experience of truth. The Old Testament presents 'only the image of truth, . . . the shadow instead of the substance', giving a 'foretaste of that wisdom which would one day be clearly revealed' (II.xi.5); the New Testament presents the truth directly in all its fullness.

3 A third difference between the two Testaments centres on the distinction between law and gospel, or the letter and the spirit (II.xi.7). The Old Testament points to (but cannot effect) the empowering activity of the Holy Spirit, whereas the New is able to deliver this power. The law can thus command, forbid and

promise, but lacks the necessary resources to effect any fundamental change within human nature which renders such commands necessary in the first place. The gospel is able to 'change or correct the perversity which naturally exists in all humans'. It is interesting to note that the radical antithesis between law and gospel, so characteristic of Luther (and Marcion before him), is quite lacking. Law and gospel are continuous with each other, and do not stand in diametrical opposition.

4 Developing this previous distinction, Calvin argues that a fourth can be discerned in the differing emotions evoked by the law and the gospel. The Old Testament evokes fear and trembling, and holds the conscience in bondage, whereas the New produces a response of freedom and joy (II.xi.9).

5 The Old Testament revelation was confined to the Jewish nation; the New Testament revelation is universal in its scope (II.xi.11). Calvin restricts the sphere of the old covenant to Israel; with the coming of Jesus Christ, this partition was broken down, as the distinction between Jew and Greek, between those who were circumcised and those who were not, was abolished. The calling of the Gentiles thus distinguishes the New from the Old Testaments (II.xi.12).

Throughout this discussion of the distinctions between the Old and New Testaments, and the superiority of the latter over the former, Calvin is careful to allow that certain individuals within the old covenant – for example, the patriarchs – were able to discern hints of the new covenant. At no point did God change his mind, or radically alter his purposes; he merely made them clearer, in accordance with the limitations imposed upon human understanding. Thus, to give but one example, it was not as if God had originally determined to restrict his grace to the Jewish nation alone, and then changed his mind, making it available to everyone else as well; rather, the evolutionary thrust of the divine plan was only made clear with the coming of Jesus Christ (II.xi.12). Calvin summarizes this general principle with the assertion that 'where the entire law is concerned, the gospel differs from it only in clarity of presentation' (II.ix.4). Christ is shown forth and the grace of the Holy Spirit is offered in both Old and New Testaments – but more clearly and more fully in the latter (IV.xiv.26).

Having stressed the common, if unequal, witness of both Old and New Testaments to the coming of Jesus Christ, Calvin judges the moment to be right to turn to a discussion of the identity and significance of this figure. Nevertheless, it will be clear that his stress upon the unity of the Old and New Testaments raises a very serious difficulty: there appears to be no fundamental difference between the old and new covenants, save that of clarity of expression. This would appear to suggest that no fundamental alteration has resulted from the life, death and resurrection of Jesus Christ, save that of clarification of some obscurities within the Old Testament. This point is given added weight through a consideration of the soteriology of the *via moderna*, which also declined to recognize a fundamental difference between old and new covenants, and thus found itself obliged to explain the significance of Jesus Christ in terms of explanatory enhancement.[23]

In fact, however, Calvin insists that quite the reverse is the case. The person and work of Jesus Christ are of central importance to the divine plan of salvation. Without the achievement of Jesus Christ, there could be no redemption, and hence no covenant of grace. The achievement which is presented to us, in differing ways, in Old and New Testaments alike, is dependent upon what God achieved through Christ. In other words, it is not the New Testament, but both the Old and New Testaments taken together, which reflect his presence and work. The New Testament is not to be contrasted with the Old in this respect; rather, the Old and New, taken together, are to be contrasted with the order of unredeemed nature.

Calvin's analysis of the knowledge of God and of human sin lays the foundation for his Christology. Jesus Christ is the mediator between God and humanity. In order to act as such a mediator, Jesus Christ must be both divine and human (II.xii.1). In that it was impossible for us to ascend to God, on account of our sin, God chose to descend to us instead. Unless Jesus Christ was himself a human being (we avoid using the term 'man', as Calvin attaches no importance to Christ's *maleness*, but rests his entire case upon his *humanity*), other human beings could not benefit from his presence or activity. 'The Son of God became the Son of Man, and received what is ours in such a way that he transferred to us what is his, making that which is his by nature to become ours through grace' (II.xii.2).

In order for Christ to redeem us from sin, it was necessary, Calvin argues, for the primordial human disobedience towards God to be outweighed by an act of human obedience. Through his obedience to God *as a human being*, Christ presented an offering to his father which compensated for sin, discharging any debt and paying any penalty which might be due on its account (II.xii.3). Through his suffering, he satisfied the debt of sin; through his defeat of death, he broke the power of death over the human race. Interestingly, Calvin is reluctant to allow that Christ's humanity participates in every feature of his divinity – a doctrine especially associated with Luther. Later writers dubbed this aspect of Calvin's thought the *extra Calvinisticum*: although the Son of God took upon himself human nature at the incarnation, he did not become a prisoner of our human natures. God became incarnate, and yet may still be said to have remained in heaven (II.xiii.4). God, in all his totality, cannot be said to be concentrated into the single historical existence of Jesus Christ. The words of a famous Christmas hymn, due to St Germanus, express perfectly the point which Calvin stressed:

> The Word becomes incarnate,
> And yet remains on high!

Having dealt with questions relating to the person of Christ, Calvin turns to a cluster of issues centring on the work of Christ. Drawing on a tradition going back to Eusebius of Caesarea, Calvin argues that Christ's work may be summarized under three offices or ministries (the *munus triplex Christi*) – prophet, priest and king (II.xv.2). The basic argument is that Jesus Christ brings together in his person the three great offices of the Old Testament. In his prophetic office, Christ is the herald and witness of God's grace. He is a teacher endowed with divine wisdom and authority. In his kingly office, Christ has inaugurated a kingship which is heavenly, not earthly; spiritual, not carnal (II.xv.3–4). This kingship is exercised over believers through the action of the Holy Spirit. It also extends over the wicked, whose rebellion is frustrated by the exercise of his authority (II.xv.5). Finally as priest, Christ is able to reinstate us within the divine favour, through offering his death as a satisfaction for our sin (II.xv.6). In all these respects, Christ picks up and brings to fulfilment various Old Testament ministries, allowing them to be seen in a new and clearer light.

Calvin then details the manner in which Christ's obedience, especially his death, is connected with the obtaining of redemption (II.xvi.1–19). Salvation, he insists, only derives through Jesus Christ. This raises the question of the basis of the meritorious work of Christ (II.xvii.1–5). Why is it that the death of Jesus

Christ was regarded as possessing sufficient value to allow it to merit the redemption of sinful humanity? Is it that there is something *intrinsically* valuable about the death of Christ? This was certainly the position taken by Luther, who argued that the divinity of Jesus Christ gave rise to the unique value of his sufferings and death. Calvin, however, declines to adopt this solution. Instead, he aligns himself with the medieval voluntarist tradition, already evident in the writings of Duns Scotus, but receiving mature expression in the writings of the *via moderna* and the *schola Augustiniana moderna*, both associated with the University of Paris. The merit of Christ's death depended on the value God chose to assign it, rather than its intrinsic value. This is perhaps one of the most important affinities between Calvin's thought and that of the later medieval period.[24]

Book III

Having shown how redemption is related to the person and work of Jesus Christ, Calvin proceeds to discuss 'the manner of obtaining the grace of Christ, the benefits which it confers, and the effects which result from it'. The logical sequence is that of a shift of discussion from the *grounds* of redemption to its *actualization*. The order of the topics which follows has been a continual source of puzzlement to Calvin scholarship. Calvin discusses a series of matters in the following order: faith; regeneration; the Christian life; justification; predestination. On the basis of his discussion of the relation of these entities in the order of salvation, it might be expected that the order should be somewhat different; in particular, it would have been supposed that predestination would precede a discussion of justification, and regeneration follow such a discussion. Calvin's ordering appears to reflect educational considerations, rather than theological precision.

He opens his discussion of the appropriation of the benefits of Christ by noting that they remain external to us unless something happens by which they can be internalized. So long as we are separated from Christ, all that he achieved upon the cross is of no importance (III.i.1). It is by faith that these benefits are appropriated by the believer. The first major matter to be discussed is thus the nature of faith itself. Calvin defines it thus: 'a steady and certain knowledge of the divine good will towards us, which, being grounded upon the truth of the gracious promise in Christ, is both revealed to our minds and sealed in our hearts by the Holy Spirit'

(III.ii.7). This carefully constructed definition of faith requires explanation at several points.

Faith is not directed towards *God* as its object, but towards his will and work towards us, as revealed in scripture (III.ii.6). 'It is not so much our concern to know who God is in himself, as what he wills to be towards us . . . we hold faith to be a knowledge of God's will towards us, perceived from his Word' (III.ii.6). Nor is scripture itself the object of faith; although faith believes every word of God (III.ii.7), it has as its specific object the divine promises of mercy.

> Since the human heart is not roused to faith by every divine word, we must inquire further as to what it is in the Word that faith relates to. The declaration of God to Adam was, 'You shall surely die', and to Cain, 'The voice of your brother's blood cries to me from the ground.' Yet these are more likely to disturb faith rather than to establish it! This is not to deny that it is proper for faith to subscribe to divine truth whenever, whatever and however God may speak; rather, it is to inquire what faith finds in the Word to lean upon and rest upon. (III.ii.7)

The foundation of faith is the gracious promise of mercy towards us, even to the point where faith and gospel may be regarded as correlative terms (III.ii.29).

The value of faith, however, lies in what it mediates. Faith is a means, rather than an end, which gives rise to the presence of the real and living Christ within the believer. Through faith, Christ 'ingrafts us into his body, and makes us not only partakers of all his benefits, but also of himself' (III.ii.24). It is not merely some abstract qualities or some impersonal characteristics of Jesus Christ which become ours through faith: it is a personal relationship with the living Christ himself. (Calvin spends some time distinguishing his understanding of the nature of this relationship from that of Andreas Osiander, which he regards as little more than a crass confusion of Christ with human nature.)[25] The promises upon which faith depends, and which it gratefully appropriates, offer us more than sight or knowledge of Christ; they offer us a communication in his person (III.xvii.1). Faith thus channels the presence of Jesus Christ into the life of the believer, transforming it. 'We receive and possess Jesus Christ, as he is given to us by the benevolence of God, and by participation in him we have a double grace. First, we are reconciled to God by his innocence . . . Second, we are sanctified by his Spirit' (III.xi.1). With this, Calvin goes on to identify the consequences of our union with Christ through faith, and moves the discussion on to consider the doctrines of justification and sanctification.

The doctrine of justification by faith is widely regarded as the central doctrine of the Reformation, the 'article by which the church stands or falls'. It is central to the origins of Luther's reforming theology, and remained of central importance throughout his life.[26] However important the doctrine may have been to the first generation of reformers, it had become of lesser importance to the second. Although Calvin refers to justification by faith as 'the principal article of the Christian religion' (III.xi.1), it seems that he is acknowledging its importance to an earlier generation. It is not central to *his* conception of the Christian faith. The first wave of the Reformation may indeed have made a sustained appeal to the doctrine of justification, and its relevance to troubled individual consciences within a works-orientated catholic piety; nevertheless, the second wave of the Reformation saw the battleground shift to questions, such as church structures and disciplines, appropriate to the needs of urban societies.[27] Luther's individualist conception of Christian existence, conditioned by his territorial context and illustrated by his doctrine of justification, stands in contrast to a more corporate conception of that existence associated with the urban reformers of the south-west, such as Zwingli, Bucer and Calvin.

Nevertheless, the issues raised by the doctrine of justification remained live, even in Calvin's day. Two of those issues stand out as of particular importance. The first concerns the manner in which Jesus Christ is involved in justification. Philip Melanchthon had developed a concept of forensic justification, in which justification was understood as 'declaring right through the imputation of the righteousness of Christ'. Although this development achieved a significant degree of terminological clarification, it was at the price of involving Christ in a purely extrinsic and impersonal manner. Justification involves the imputation of an attribute of Christ, or quality or benefit deriving from him, to the believer – but *not* the personal encounter of Christ and the believer, a central element of Luther's conception of justification. Was there any way in which Melanchthon's doctrine of forensic justification could be maintained, while restoring Luther's emphasis upon the real presence of Christ himself – rather than the mere imputation of some impersonal attribute?

The second issue concerns the relation of God's initiative and the human response. How can the utterly gratuitous justification of the sinner before God be reconciled with the demands of obedience subsequently laid upon him or her? Luther seemed to suggest that works had no place in the Christian life, on account of the utter unconditionality of God's gift of grace – an incorrect perception, as it happened, but an understandable interpretation of his stress upon the gratuity of justification. Zwingli resolved this problem by making justification dependent upon moral regeneration; in justification, God confirms or seals the believer's self-achieved moral status. Luther seemed to deny any place to obedience in the Christian life; Zwingli to make the Christian life dependent upon such obedience. It was clear that clarification was necessary.[28]

It is to Calvin's credit that he resolved both these difficulties. The first is resolved through his conception of the 'insertion of the believer in Christ' (*insitio in Christum*). Through faith, the believer is united with Jesus Christ in a spiritual union, in such a way that we are 'not only partakers of all his benefits, but also of himself' (III.ii.24). All that Christ is becomes ours through faith. Through participating in him, we share in his benefits. The real presence of Christ within believers (Luther's particular stress) is thus shown to be consistent with, and is maintained simultaneously with, the sharing of Christ's benefits, such as his righteousness (Melanchthon's emphasis).

The second follows on from this immediately. Acceptance in the sight of God (justification) is not dependent upon moral improvement or regeneration (sanctification); nor does justification render sanctification superfluous. For Calvin, justification and sanctification are both direct consequences of the believer's incorporation into Christ. If the believer has been united with Christ through faith, he or she is at one and the same time made acceptable in the sight of God (justification), and launched on the path to moral improvement (sanctification). By treating these two elements, which had hitherto been regarded as independent entities requiring correlation, as subordinate to the believer's union with Christ, Calvin is able to uphold both the total gratuitousness of our acceptance before God and the subsequent demands of obedience placed upon us.

If justification is not central to Calvin's thought, then neither is predestination. Just as some writers, familiar with Luther's considerable stress upon the doctrine of justification, have projected this emphasis on to Calvin, so others have read back into his writings the particular concern within later Reformed Orthodoxy for predestination. Calvin himself, however, adopts a distinctly low-key approach to the doctrine, devoting a mere four chapters to its exposition (III.xxi–xxiv). Predestination is defined as 'the eternal decree of God, by which he determined what he wished to make of every man. For he does not create everyone in the same condition, but ordains eternal life for some and eternal damnation for others' (III.xxi.5). Predestination is something which should induce a sense of awe within us. The *decretum horribile* (III.xxiii.7) is not a 'horrible decree', as a crude translation, insensitive to the nuances of the Latin, might suggest; rather, it is an 'awe-inspiring' or 'terrifying' decree.

The very location of Calvin's discussion of predestination in the 1559 edition of the *Institutes* is significant. It follows his exposition of the doctrine of grace. It is only after the great themes of this doctrine – such as justification by faith – have been expounded that he turns to consider the mysterious and perplexing subject of predestination. Logically, predestination ought to precede such an analysis; predestination, after all, establishes the grounds of an individual's election, and hence his or her subsequent justification and sanctification. Yet Calvin declines to be subservient to the canons of such logic. Why?

For Calvin, predestination must be considered in its proper context. It is not the product of human speculation, but a mystery of divine revelation (I.ii.2; III.xxi.1–2). It has, however, been revealed in a specific *context* and in a specific *manner*. That manner relates to Jesus Christ himself, who is the 'mirror in which we may behold the fact of our election' (III.xxiv.5).[29] The context relates to the efficacy of the gospel proclamation. Why is it that some individuals respond to the Christian gospel, and others do not? Is the failure of some to respond to be put down to some lack of efficacy, some inherent inadequacy, in that gospel? Or is there some other reason for this divergence in responses?[30]

Far from being arid and abstract theological speculation, Calvin's analysis of predestination begins from observable facts. Some do, and some do not, believe the gospel. The primary function of the doctrine of predestination is to explain why some individuals respond to the gospel, and others do not. It is an *ex post facto* explanation of the particularity of human responses to grace. Calvin's predestinarianism is to be regarded as *a posteriori* reflection upon the data of human experience, interpreted in the light of scripture, rather than something which is deduced *a priori* on the basis of preconceived ideas concerning divine omnipotence. Belief in predestination is not an article of faith in its own right, but is the final outcome of scripturally informed reflection on the effects of grace upon individuals in the light of the enigmas of experience. Experience teaches that God does not touch every human heart (III.xxiv.15). Why not? Is this due to some failure or omission on God's part? In the light of scripture, Calvin feels able to deny the possibility of any weakness or inadequacy on the part of God or the gospel: the observable pattern of responses to the gospel reflects a mystery by which some are predestined to respond to, and others to reject, the promises of God. 'Some have been allocated to eternal life, others to eternal damnation' (III.xxi.5).

This is, it must be stressed, no theological innovation. Calvin is not introducing a hitherto unknown notion into the sphere of Christian theology. The 'modern Augustinian school' (*schola Augustiniana moderna*), exemplified by such leading medieval theologians as Gregory of Rimini and Hugolino of Orvieto, had also taught a doctrine of absolute double predestination – that God allocates some to eternal life, others to eternal condemnation, without any reference to their merits or demerits. Their fate rests totally upon the will of God, rather than their individualities.[31] Indeed, it is possible that Calvin has actively appropriated this aspect of late medieval Augustinianism, which certainly bears an uncanny resemblance to his own teaching.

Salvation thus lies outside the control of the individual, who is powerless to alter the situation. Calvin stresses that this selectivity is not in any way peculiar to the matter of salvation. In every area of life, he argues, we are forced to reckon with the mystery of the inexplicable. Why is it that some are more fortunate than others in life? Why does one person possess intellectual gifts denied to another? Even from the moment of birth, two infants may find themselves in totally different circumstances through no fault of their own: one may find a full breast of milk to suck and thus gain nourishment, while another may suffer malnutrition through having to suck a breast that is nearly dry.[32] For Calvin, predestination is merely a further instance of a general mystery of human existence, in which some are inexplicably favoured with material or intellectual gifts which are denied to others. It raises no difficulties which are not already presented by other areas of human existence.

Does not this idea of predestination suggest that God is dispensed from common notions of goodness, justice or rationality?

Although Calvin specifically repudiates the conception of God as an absolute and *arbitrary* power, his discussion of predestination has raised the spectre of a God whose relationship to his creation is whimsical and capricious, and whose conception and exercise of power are not bound to any law or order. At this point, Calvin clearly aligns himself with the late medieval discussion of this contentious issue, particularly within the *via moderna* and *schola Augustiniana moderna*, concerning the relation of God to the established moral order. God is not subject in any sense to law, in that this would place law above God, an aspect of creation – or even something outside of God *prior* to creation – above the creator. The will of God is not arbitrary, so that one could speak of God being outside law; rather, his will is the foundation of existing conceptions of morality (III.xxiii.2). These terse statements represent one of Calvin's clearest affinities with the late medieval voluntarist tradition.

In the end, Calvin argues that predestination must be recognized to rest in the inscrutable judgements of God (III.xxi.1). We cannot know why he elects some, and condemns others. Some scholars have suggested that this attitude may reveal the influence of late medieval discussions of the 'absolute power of God' (*potentia Dei absoluta*), by which a whimsical or arbitrary God is perfectly at liberty to do whatever he pleases, without being obliged to justify his actions.[33] This suggestion, however, rests upon a serious misunderstanding of the role of the dialectic between the two powers – absolute and ordained – of God in late medieval thought.[34] God must be free to choose whom he wills, otherwise his freedom is compromised by external considerations; the creator becomes subject to his creation. Nevertheless, God's decisions reflect his wisdom and justice, which are upheld, rather than contradicted, by the fact of predestination (III.xxii.4, xxiii.2).

Far from being a central premise of Calvin's theological 'system' (a quite inappropriate term, in any case), predestination is thus an ancillary doctrine, concerned with explaining a puzzling aspect of the consequences of the proclamation of the gospel of grace. Yet as Calvin's followers sought to extend and recast his thinking in the light of new intellectual developments, it was perhaps inevitable (if this lapse into a potentially predestinarian mode of speaking may be excused) that alterations to his structuring of Christian theology might occur.

Book IV

The final book of the *Institutes* centres on a cluster of issues relating to the church. In turning to deal with 'the outward means or aids by which God calls us into fellowship of Christ his Son, and keeps us in it', Calvin is able to draw upon both his considerable practical experience as an organizer, and his substantial theoretical analysis of the nature of the church, its ministry and its sacraments. Throughout this analysis, the spectre of abstraction is avoided. Calvin is prepared to enter into concrete particulars, and avoids the temptation of degenerating into general abstractions. In effect, the *Institutes* is a manual for church planting, growth, organization and discipline. The *Institutes* opens with a vigorous theological analysis; it ends by grounding its analysis in the realities of everyday human life.

Why is there any need for a church – understood, that is, as an institution, rather than a building – in the first place? Just as God redeemed human beings within the historical process through the incarnation, so he sanctifies them within that same process by founding an institution dedicated to that goal. God uses certain definite earthly means to work out the salvation of his elect; although he is not absolutely bound by these means, he normally works within them. The church is thus identified as a divinely founded body, within which God effects the sanctification of his people. Calvin confirms this high doctrine of the church by citing the two great ecclesiological maxims of Cyprian of Carthage: 'You cannot have God as your father unless you have the church for your mother'; 'Outside the church there is no hope of remission of sins nor any salvation' (IV.i.4).

Calvin then proceeds to draw an important distinction. At one level, the church is the community of Christian believers, a visible group. It is also, however, the fellowship of saints and the company of the elect – an *invisible* entity. In its invisible aspect, the church is the assembly of the elect, known only to God; in its visible aspect, it is the community of believers on earth (IV.i.7). The former consists only of the elect; the latter includes both good and evil, elect and reprobate. The former is an object of faith and hope, the latter of present experience. Calvin stresses that all believers are obliged to honour and to remain committed to the visible church, despite its weaknesses, on account of the invisible church, the true body of Christ. Despite this, there is only one church, a single entity with Jesus Christ as its head.

The distinction between the visible and invisible churches has two important consequences. In the first place, it is to be expected that the visible church will include both the elect and the reprobate. Augustine of Hippo had made this point against the Donatists, using the parable of the tares (Matthew 13:24–31) as his basis. It lies beyond human competence to discern the difference between the elect and the reprobate, correlating human qualities with divine favour (in any case, Calvin's doctrine of predestination precludes such grounds of election). In the second place, however, it is necessary to ask which of the various visible churches corresponds to the invisible church. Calvin thus recognizes the need to articulate objective criteria by which the authenticity of a given church may be judged. Two such criteria are stipulated: 'Wherever we see the Word of God preached purely and listened to, and the sacraments administered according to the institution of Christ, we cannot doubt that a church exists' (IV.i.9). It is thus not the quality of its members, but the presence of the authorized means of grace, which constitutes a true church. Interestingly, Calvin does not follow Bucer, and make discipline a mark of the true church; although passionately concerned with the need for the charitable discipline of church members (IV.xii.1), Calvin does not regard this as essential to the definition or evaluation of the credentials of a church.

Whereas Luther regarded the organization of the church as a matter of historical contingency, not requiring theological prescription, Calvin held that a definite pattern of church government was prescribed by scripture. Curiously, the lists of ecclesiastical offices (IV.iii.3; IV.iii.4; IV.iv.1) which Calvin presents within the *Institutes* do not harmonize, and leave both the status of elders (or presbyters) and the number of ministries in some doubt.

The church is endowed with 'spiritual power' (IV.viii.1), although Calvin is careful not to explain this in any manner that might suggest a comparison with the canon law of the medieval church. Further, its spiritual authority does not encroach on that of the civil authority. Note that the magistrate is never subject to the church, an important point in refuting the bizarre suggestion that Calvin laid the theoretical foundation for a theocratic dictatorship. The two powers, religious and secular, are to be regarded as theoretically complementary. In practice, however, their relationship was somewhat more turbulent.

Having earlier defined one of the 'marks of the church' (*notae ecclesiae*) as the administration of the sacraments, Calvin now turns to a detailed consideration of these (IV.xiv–xix). The medieval church had defined seven sacraments: baptism, eucharist, orders, penance, confirmation, marriage and unction. The reformers reduced these to two – baptism and eucharist – insisting that the true sacraments of the gospel were those ordained by Christ himself. (Although the reformers themselves tended to refer to the sacrament of the eucharist as 'the thanksgiving', 'the Lord's Supper', or simply 'the supper', we shall follow the general modern trend in this respect, and use the term 'eucharist' – (literally, 'thanksgiving'). No theological point is being made by this decision, which is intended to achieve greater clarity of word and felicity of expression than would otherwise be the case.)

Calvin offers two definitions of a sacrament, as 'an external symbol by which the Lord seals on our consciences his promises of good will towards us, in order to sustain the weakness of our faith', and as a 'visible sign of a sacred thing, or a visible form of an invisible grace' (IV.xiv.1). The former is Calvin's own definition; the latter is due to Augustine (although Calvin suggests that its brevity leads to obscurity). Insisting that a sacrament must be based upon 'a promise and a command of the Lord' (IV.xix.5), he rejected five of the seven sacraments traditionally accepted by the catholic church (IV.xix.1). Only baptism and the eucharist remained.

The 1520s saw a serious dispute develop between Luther and Zwingli over the nature of the sacraments.[35] Luther maintained that the eucharistic bread and wine really were the body and blood of Jesus Christ; Zwingli, at the other extreme, held that they were merely symbols of the body and blood of Christ. Luther thus held that the sacramental sign was equivalent to the thing which it signified, while Zwingli insisted that sign and thing signified were radically different. These two irreconcilable positions may be taken as marking the boundaries of the Reformation debates over the nature of the sacraments.

Calvin may be regarded as occupying a position roughly midway between these two extremes. In the sacraments, he argues, there is such a close connection between the sacramental symbol and the spiritual gift which it symbolizes that we can 'easily pass from one to the other'. The sign is visible and physical, whereas the thing signified is invisible and spiritual – yet the connection between the sign and the thing signified is so intimate that it is permissible to apply the one to the other (IV.xvii.21). The thing that is signified is effected by its sign (IV.xvii.3). Calvin's insistence upon the parellelism or coincidence – but not *identity*, which he regards as an untenable catholic idea – of sign and effect rests partly on an analysis of the power of symbols, and partly on his understanding of the divine wisdom: would God ever offer us an empty symbol (IV.xvii.10)? Sign and thing signified are distinct (IV.xvii.34). Yet here again we may see Calvin's Christologically grounded formula *distincto sed non separatio* in operation (see p. 149); sign and thing signified may be *distinguished*, yet not *separated*.

It might be possible to regard Calvin's position as an attempt to reconcile the views of Zwingli and Luther, an exercise in ecclesiastical diplomacy at an opportune moment in the history of the Reformation. In fact, there is little evidence to support this suggestion; Calvin's theology of the sacraments is consistent with his general outlook, and cannot be regarded as a compromise reached on political grounds.

His understanding of baptism may be seen as combining both Zwinglian and Lutheran elements. Nodding in Zwingli's direction, Calvin argues that baptism is a public demonstration of our allegiance to God (IV.xv.1). Just as Zwingli had asserted that sacraments are primarily ecclesial events, serving to demonstrate the loyalty of believers to the church or civic community, so Calvin stresses the declaratory role of the sacrament. However, he incorporates the characteristically Lutheran stress upon baptism as a sign of the remission of sins and the new life of believers in Jesus Christ (IV.xv.5).

In common with all the magisterial reformers, Calvin upholds the propriety of infant baptism. The practice, he argues, is an authentic tradition of the early church, and not a later medieval development (IV.xvi.8). Zwingli had justified the practice by an appeal to the Jewish rite of circumcision. By this rite and through this outward sign, he had argued, infant males were shown to be members of the covenant community. In a similar manner, baptism is the mark that an infant belongs to the church, the community of the new covenant.[36] The rising influence of Anabaptists, which Calvin had experienced at first hand during his Strasbourg period, demonstrated the importance of justifying the practice of infant baptism, which Anabaptists vigorously rejected. Calvin thus reiterates and extends Zwingli's covenantal justification of infant baptism: if Christian infants cannot be baptized, they are at a disadvantage in relation to Jewish infants, who were publicly and outwardly sealed into the covenant community through circumcision (IV.xvi.6). Calvin thus argues that infants should be baptized, and not denied the benefits which this conveys.

In his discussion of the eucharist, Calvin distinguishes three aspects of the spiritual truth which is presented (*monstretur*) and offered through the visible elements of bread and wine. The *signification or meaning* is the divine promises, which are included or enclosed within the sign itself; believers are reassured, particularly through the words of institution, that the body and blood of Jesus Christ have been broken and shed for them. The sacrament 'confirms the promise in which Jesus Christ declares that his flesh is food indeed, and his blood drink indeed, and that they feed us with eternal life' (IV.xvii.4). The *substance*[37] or matter of the eucharist concerns our reception of the body of Christ: God communicates to us what he has promised us. In receiving the sign of the body of Christ (in other words, the bread), we are simultaneously receiving the body of Christ itself (IV.xvii.10). Once more, we find the principle *distinctio sed non separatio* in operation; sign and thing signified may be different – but they are inseparable. Finally, the *virtue or effect* of the eucharist is located in the *beneficia Christi* – the benefits won for the believer by Christ through his obedience. The believer participates by faith in all the benefits of Christ, such as redemption, righteousness and eternal life (IV.xvii.11).

This, in the briefest of outlines, is the contents of the most significant work of Christian theology to emerge from the sixteenth-century Reformation. Its characteristic lucidity, linked with its comprehensiveness, gave it an enormous advantage over its rivals, both Lutheran and Roman Catholic. It remains a significant resource and dialogue partner for modern Christian theology. In that Calvin's historical significance is in part due to his ideas and the manner in which he presented and disseminated them, it may also be suggested that they are of relevance to the historian. This may be illustrated by considering one of the great invasions of ideas, as Calvin's religious thought began to have a major effect upon his native land – France.

9

The Invasion of Ideas: Calvin and France

After his return in near-triumph to Geneva in 1541, Calvin seems never to have returned to his native France from his place of exile. Although, as we saw earlier, one Jean Cauvin was prosecuted at Noyon in 1551–2 for immoral behaviour (he had maintained *une femme de mauvaise gouvernement* in his house),[1] it is clear that the Calvin on whom our narrative centres was otherwise occupied with the political crises of Geneva and his deteriorating position within the city at the time. However, the total defeat of the Perrinist faction – noted, incidentally, for its anti-French attitudes – in the revolution of April 1555 allowed Calvin and his colleagues a new freedom of activity. Geneva having been secured for the cause of the Reformation, their eyes turned towards France. In April 1555, under conditions of great secrecy, the Venerable Company of Pastors began a deliberate and systematic process of infiltration of personnel into France. The seeds of the French Wars of Religion had been sown.[2]

The present chapter is concerned with the origins and development of Calvin's influence upon the French church. It is, in many ways, a remarkable tale, lending added weight to those who would compare Geneva with Moscow as the symbol of a revolutionary ideology. Our story must, however, begin with the events which laid the foundations for Calvin's influence in his native country.

The Growth of Calvin's Influence in France

In the introduction to this work (pp. 4–13), we sketched the state of French religious life on the eve of the Reformation. The need for reform was obvious. This reform, however, must not be thought of in purely spiritual or religious terms. Social and economic factors conspired to point to the need for change, creating propitious circumstances for any revolutionary movement which appeared capable of offering social and economic, as much as religious, reform. The events within the diocese of Meaux in the 1520s and 1530s point to the perception of a link between evangelical spirituality and socio-economic reform,[3] as catholic clergy became increasingly distanced from the needs and concerns of the rural population. The catholic church was viewed as too enmeshed in the concerns of the gentry to allow it to contribute to the programmes of education, relief of poverty and elimination of disease which were widely regarded as essential by informed lay opinion – which increasingly tended towards heterodox religious views. Those who founded municipal colleges in the city of Paris (which competed directly with cathedral schools) and hospitals for the relief of the poor usually came from this new nucleus of lay activism.[4]

As survey after survey of French urban existence in the 1520s and 1530s indicates, a fundamental sense of restlessness may be detected within the newly-emerging literate *bourgeoisie*.[5] The Parisian interest in both humanism and 'Lutheranism' – a term which, as used by the Paris authorities, is too broad to designate simply the views of Luther – points to the emergence of a literate lay urban culture, which was largely based upon printed works. An amalgam of forces, informed by the new learning of humanism and the religious questioning of Luther, emerged. In Paris, and other intellectual centres of France, there was a growing tendency to adopt an attitude towards both the doctrinal assertions and the institutional manifestations of the catholic church which was simultaneously sceptical and critical.

It would have been difficult for Calvin to be unaware of such fundamental shifts in French society. Not merely had he lived in Paris and a number of other French cities; he had built up a network of personal contacts in such cities as Angoulême, Bourges, Orléans, Paris and Poitiers. His period as pastor to the congregation of French refugees at Strasbourg (1538–41) would have kept him abreast of developments in French life and political matters. Geneva itself served as an observatory from which he could survey the momentous developments in France, aided by correspondents, by an increasing host of French émigrés who sought refuge within Geneva's walls in the 1550s,[6] and by personal contacts with French merchants, who were taking advantage of the growing trade links between Geneva and major French cities, such as Lyons, from the early 1540s onwards.[7]

It is important to appreciate that the evangelicalism which initially achieved a considerable following within France predates Calvin, and was more influenced by Luther than Zwingli. *L'oraison de Jésuchrist* (1525), a devotional manual associated with the Meaux reforming group, includes Luther's preface to Romans, and represents one of the clearest expositions of his reforming programme and its implications. *Le livre de vraye et parfaicte oraison* (1528), a devotional manual which is clearly inoffensively catholic in its spirituality, included a number of Luther's writings. Claude d'Epence's devotional tract *Consolation en adversité* (1547), dedicated to Marguerite of France, turned out on closer inspection to be a translation of one of Luther's works. While generalizations are dangerous, it is reasonable to suggest that French evangelicalism up to about 1541 saw no irreconcilable contradiction between Lutheranism and catholicism. While rejecting papal authority, it saw no need whatsoever to break with the catholic church of its day. Calvin had yet to make his mark on French evangelicalism.[8]

The extent of Calvin's involvement in French affairs may be judged from his diplomatic initiatives in the 1530s and early 1540s. Making the best possible use of Geneva's alliance with Berne, Calvin pressed the Swiss city to apply what influence it could on the French authorities to exercise tolerance in relation to *évangéliques*.[9] Francis I, although virtually permanently alienated from Protestantism by this stage, nevertheless required the political goodwill of certain Swiss cantons, especially Berne. The seemingly permanent tension between France and Savoy on the one hand, and Francis I and the Holy Roman Emperor Charles V on the other, made it imperative that France had the political support of the north-western Swiss cantons.[10] Calvin's strategy was thus perfectly realistic, even if its results were unimpressive. However, his diplomatic activities are completely overshadowed by his influence upon France through the written word.

The most important contribution which Calvin was able to make to the French Reformation was at the level of ideas and their application. Without Calvin, French Protestantism would have been little more than an inchoate fissiparous sect, prone to introspection and internal dissent, lacking any real political power. Initially Calvin was able to give the movement advice, a sense of direction, and above all inspiration. We find him writing to advise the *évangéliques* at Rouen in 1540; inspiring enthusiasm at Poitiers in the same year; establishing contact with the *Vaudois* of Dauphiné and Provence in 1541;[11] warning the *évangéliques* of Lyons of a possible threat in 1542.[12]

A crucial turning point is marked by the publication of the French-language edition of the *Institutes* in 1541. Suddenly, coherently expressed and carefully justified radical reforming doctrines were available within France in the vernacular. Someone seems to have pressed a panic button. On 1 July 1542, the Parisian *parlement* directed that all works containing heterodox doctrines, especially Calvin's *Institutes*, should be surrendered to the authorities within three days.[13] That same year, a martyr died at Rouen with a quotation from the preface to the 1541 edition of the *Institutes* on his lips.[14] The visitation of bookshops became an important element of the official attempt to suppress the growing heterodox movement. The following year the faculty of theology, after due inquiries, drew up a list of sixty-five titles, twenty-two in Latin and forty-three in French (although two items are unwittingly duplicated, making forty-one in total), which were to be censured with immediate effect. Of the thirty-six texts which it is possible to identify and date with anything approaching probability, twenty-three were printed in Geneva.[15] Calvin's *Institutes* were thus seen as the spearhead of a Genevan assault upon the French church, mediated through the printed word. On 23 June 1545, an extended list of prohibited works was published with the full authority of *parlement*. Of its 121 titles in French, almost half were printed in Geneva. The reaction from the booksellers of Paris was immediate: they protested that they would be ruined if they were prohibited from selling such books. It seems there was a not insubstantial market for works which were considered heretical by the faculty of theology – further evidence of the importance of a literate and affluent laity in promoting the ideas of the Calvinist Reformation.

Yet the flood of Genevan literature into Paris continued. An extended list of prohibited works appeared in 1551, adding eighteen new titles (thirteen of which originated in Geneva). However, the total output of the Genevan presses far exceeded the number of works which were condemned. Without access to the catalogues of Genevan printers such as Girard or Crespin, the French authorities were unable to stem the flood of French-language material propagating the ideals of Calvin's Reformation. For example, during the period 1546–51, at least twelve French-language works by Calvin appeared which are not noted by the 1551 list of

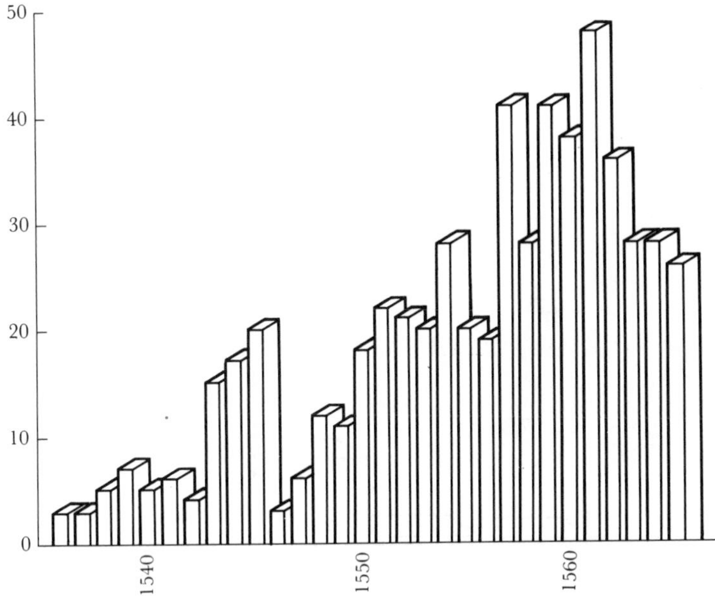

FIGURE 9.1 Books published at Geneva, 1536–65, demonstrated by the number of new titles issued per year

prohibited works. Furthermore, the attempt to regulate the public sale of books to exclude those originating from Geneva merely forced the trade to go underground. Until the Wars of Religion finally put a brake on the expansion of the Genevan publishing industry's sector of the French religious market in the years 1565–80, it was not difficult to obtain such works in Paris.[16] Laurent de Normandie, Calvin's friend and bookseller, found the contraband book trade so profitable that he emigrated to Geneva, in order that he might publish such books, rather than just sell them. (His edition of de Bèze's *Psalter* was one of his more notable productions.) In 1559, a member of the Parisian *parlement* was tried for heresy; he admitted that his unorthodox religious ideas came from reading 'the works of Calvin and others bought from those packmen who come and go between countries'. The Wars of Religion made such traffic problematical from about 1565 onwards; but by that stage, Calvin was dead, and the damage was done.

To illustrate the accelerating infiltration of Calvinist ideas, the records of the *parlement* of Toulouse, responsible for the Languedoc

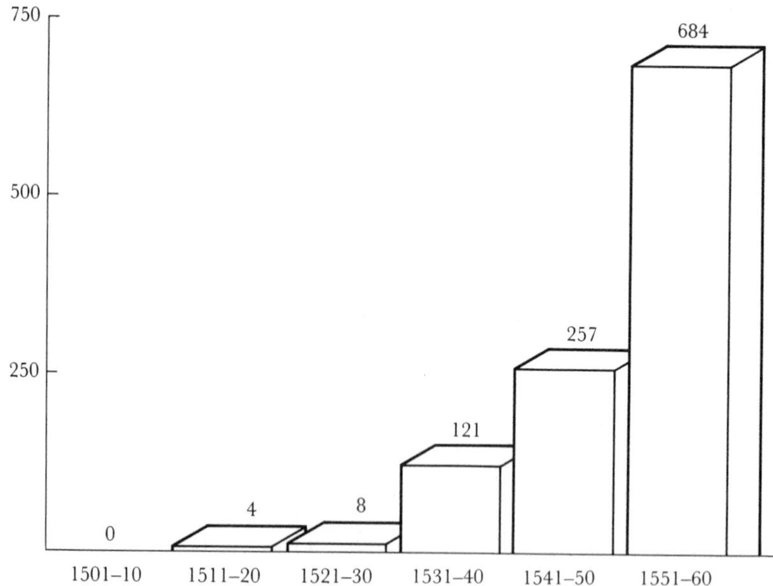

FIGURE 9.2 Numbers of accused heretics brought before the *parlement* of Toulouse, 1500–60

region, may be considered. Of the 1,074 cases of heresy brought before this body over the period 1500–60, a decade-by-decade analysis reveals the pattern shown in Figure 9.2.[17] A peak was reached in 1554, with 208 individuals arraigned for heresy. The rapid growth evident in the final decade points to Calvinist influence reaching new heights, a pattern which is repeated throughout France.

Which sections of French society were affected by Calvin's ideas and values in the period 1540–55? It is clear that his support was consistently greatest amongst artisans. Eight hundred and seventeen individuals were charged with heresy at Montpellier in 1560, of which 561 gave details of their professions. Three hundred and eighty-seven (69 per cent) were artisans. A similar pattern emerges at Bézier in 1568.[18] Of the French refugees seeking asylum in Geneva in the period 1549–60, 68.5 per cent were artisans.[19] Calvinism was initially the *religion des petits gens* (Henri Hauser). Why did Calvinism possess such an attraction for sections of the French middle classes? In part, the answer lies in its lending religious dignity to social values and productive activities which were deeply embedded within the more dynamic middle sections of French society (see pp. 234–7).

In contrast, Calvin's influence within the aristocracy was initially restricted. The potential anti-aristocratic bias of his work ethic, linked with the Genevan distaste for aristocracy in general,[20] was possibly a contributing factor to this social polarization. In addition, such factors as tradition, family loyalty and connections (most of the French bishops were members of the aristocracy), and a general distaste for *les petits gens*, combined to reinforce initial aristocratic prejudice against Calvinism. Just as the French Revolution would have its champions within the aristocracy, and the Bolshevik Revolution its supporters within the bourgeoisie, so Calvin was not totally without aristocratic backing; until 1555, however, this was not significant in its extent.

Finally, it may be noted that Calvinism appears to have been virtually without influence upon the peasantry. Despite the potentially anti-aristocratic bias of the movement, it failed to make significant headway among *les paysans*. A number of reasons may be advanced in explanation of this observation. Calvinism made intellectual demands, however modest, which were beyond the reach of the uneducated peasantry. It lent support to ideas and values which were alien to this social grouping. It was, at least to a certain extent, a 'religion of the book', which reduced its appeal to an illiterate rural peasantry, unable to afford books, let alone to read them. In any case, the rural population knew little French, the language used by Calvinists in their evangelization efforts; local patois still dominated the linguistic map of France.

There is, however, another consideration which merits attention. The popular religion of the French peasantry was firmly grounded in the rhythms, patterns and concerns of rural life.[21] A certain degree of flexibility within catholic spirituality allowed the teachings of the church to be accommodated to these, with cults orientated towards the cares and preoccupations of a rural peasant population. Calvinism had no time for such generous accommodations, which it regarded as something of an amalgam of superstition and idolatry. Its religious rigour in these matters rendered it devoid of spiritual appeal to the peasantry. This section of the population would retain its traditional allegiance to the catholic church and its beliefs.

Calvin's influence over France in the years 1536–55 is too easily overstated; unquestionably, he had many admirers, but he was able to exercise little influence in the corridors of power. For example, until the 1550s, his circle of correspondents within France included no members of the power-broking aristocracy. The potential influence of the evangelical movement was diminished by the phenomenon of Nicodemitism, which Calvin denounced in 1543–4. Although evangelicalism was widely diffused, especially within the southern cities, there was a marked tendency for those with evangelical sympathies to conform outwardly to catholic practices. Fearing the reaction of the catholic authorities, evangelical conventicles met clandestinely in private houses, often at night (hence occasioning the comparison with Nicodemus, who visited Jesus at night for fear of what the representatives of the old religion might say: John 3:1–2).[22] Nevertheless, as the official response to the 1541 edition of the *Institutes* makes clear, more and more reform-minded individuals were looking to Calvin for guidance and leadership. The French evangelical groupings could not expect to continue indefinitely without pastors, sacraments or church structures. The massacre of the *Vaudois* (Waldensians) (1545) and the martyrdom of five evangelical students at Lyons (1551), reinforced by the appearance of Jean Crespin's *Livre des Martyrs* (Geneva, 1554), made clear the cost and difficulties of being an evangelical in an increasingly hostile France. With the consolidation of Calvin's power-base at Geneva in 1555, the way was open to a more ambitious means of gaining further influence over the French church: the infiltration of agents to support existing churches, and plant new ones. The invasion of ideas was to be supplemented by an invasion of men from Geneva.

The Men from Geneva

In April 1555, the registers of the Venerable Company of Pastors listed, for the first time, agents sent out from Geneva to evangelize foreign parts. The entry for 22 April notes that Jehan Vernou and Jehan Lauvergeat had been sent to Piedmont, an area once associated with the Waldensian heretics and likely to be fertile ground for Calvinism.[23] Others followed rapidly, in response to requests for help from French Calvinist congregations. The first agent despatched to France, Jacques l'Anglois, was sent to Poitiers in response to a plea from the congregation in that city.

Secrecy was essential to the entire operation, at both the Genevan and the French ends. Safe houses, complete with hiding places, were established in the deep valleys of the Alpes Dauphinoises, set a day's journey apart. An underground network, similar to that employed by the French Resistance during the Second World War, allowed men from Geneva to slip across the ill defined frontier into France. The Company of Pastors made every effort to maintain total secrecy, even to the point of concealing its operations from the theoretically all-knowing city council. By 1557, however, the Company of Pastors realized it could not hope to keep its activities abroad clandestine indefinitely; late that year Calvin appeared before the city council to explain the situation, and request permission to send further agents. The council was evidently aware of the serious danger posed to the city by these activities: if it were thought that the Genevan government itself was organizing the infiltration of religious activists, it could be held guilty of seditious action against its larger neighbour, with unpredictable (but probably unpleasant) consequences. The council, however, agreed to the secret continuation of the policy, providing that they could not be held to be associated with it.

The wisdom of this decision became evident in January 1561. A courier arrived in Geneva from the court of Charles IX, the new king of France. The substance of his message to the city council was that the king had discovered that the recent disturbances within France were linked with preachers sent from Geneva. It seemed that the Genevans had embarked on a policy of systematic subversion of authority within France. He demanded that Geneva's agents should be recalled, and that no more should be sent under any conditions.[24] The council replied that *they* had not sent any such individuals into France; it was indeed the case that the Company of Pastors had done such a thing, but the city council could not accept responsibility for the actions of a private ecclesiastical organization. A serious rupture between Geneva and France was thus averted through what was little more than a fiction.

Geneva may have supplied pastors for France; local churches, however, were expected to provide the remainder of the ecclesiastical apparatus laid down by Geneva, such as the consistory. In 1555 a Calvinist church was established in Paris, complete with a consistory of elders and deacons. The *églises plantées* – little more than religious study groups, meeting for prayer, worship and Bible-reading – were gradually replaced by the more structured *églises dressées* in the years 1555–62. The little groups that had sprung up throughout France, meeting regularly for prayer and mutual edification, were gradually transformed into disciplined bodies with regular church structures. The consistorial structure was made obligatory by the Venerable Company of Pastors in 1557. Poitiers established a consistory in 1555, Orléans in 1557, La Rochelle in 1558, and Nîmes in 1561. At the opening of the momentous year 1562, the number of consistories in France had risen to 1,785.[25] Geneva was prepared to provide pastors for such congregations; elders and deacons, however, were to be provided locally.

In the end, Geneva proved herself unable to provide the vast numbers of pastors requested by the burgeoning Calvinist churches within France. Calvin's guidelines for the selection of pastors made heavy educational demands, which seriously restricted the number of those eligible for such positions. In practice, pastors tended to be French-speaking bourgeois from outside Geneva – a consideration which tended to lead to their being viewed as outsiders by native-born Genevans. In 1564, the year of Calvin's death, Geneva itself possessed a mere twenty-two such pastors. The Genevan Academy, founded to train pastors to the high standards required by Calvin,[26] was inaugurated on 5 June 1559, too late to meet the surge of demands for pastors trained and recognized by Geneva. Calvin had, in effect, created a demand he was incapable of meeting.

A study of eighty-eight agents sent out on 105 missions during the period 1555–63 allows important insights into the early successes of Calvinism, confirming the impression that the movement held a special appeal to the urban middle class. Six were sent to Poitiers, five to Paris and Lyons, and three to Bergerac, Dieppe (an important jumping-off point for England and Scotland), Issoudun and Orléans.[27] Interestingly, all these cities were on principal trade routes, confirming that Calvinism – like Islam – was often spread through commercial contacts, once more demonstrating its appeal to those involved in such spheres of activity, such as artisans and merchants. Henri Hauser once paid tribute to the vital role of the humble packman, with Calvinist tracts concealed among his pins and combs, in propagating the new religion.

The Political Dimensions of French Calvinism

In part, the appeal of Calvinism rests in its perceived economic significance; as we shall indicate later (pp. 234–7), *une adaptation française du calvinisme* emerged, which amalgamated certain religious views of Calvin with the proto-capitalist economic policies of the city of Geneva itself. The appeal of these liberating economic views upon the third estate, newly emerging as a social grouping of substantial importance within France, appears to have been considerable. Although the economic appeal of Calvinism – where Calvinism is understood to designate what Calvin and his agents were perceived to represent, rather than what they actually represented – to the French third estate must not be underestimated, there was also a significant political appeal. To illustrate the point in mind, we may turn to consider an analogous development in south-east Asia more than two millennia earlier.

Why did Buddhism emerge as a new religion? Its origins in the sixth century BC are perhaps best explained as a protest movement directed against the rigorous and intensely constricting class or caste system of Vedic Hinduism. The emergence of Buddhism corresponds to a period in Indian civilization in which urbanization became of major social significance. The emergence of a relatively wealthy urban class led to the development of considerable tensions within the rigidities of the Hindu caste system, which allocated individuals to a caste on the basis of the circumstances of their birth. The caste system was given some religious justification in the Vedic 'Hymn of the Cosmic Man', which suggested that this ordering of society rested upon cosmic foundations. With the emergence of social groupings who possessed the means to shape their own destiny, a certain impatience with the tradition-bound ordering of Vedic Hinduism emerged. The Buddha's stress upon personal responsibility and the individual's ability to influence his or her destiny appears to have had considerable appeal for such alienated city dwellers (there is some evidence to suggest that his first followers were drawn from urban households). Social order, and specifically the position of an individual within that order, came to be seen as something which could be changed, rather than something laid down as inviolable, somehow built into the very fabric of the universe. Frustration with the rigidity of existing social structures, particularly an oppressive tradition-bound class system, appears to have been a factor of some religious significance at this moment in human civilization, commending the virtues of Buddhism to individuals hitherto content to remain Hindu.

Since the early nineteenth century there has been a tendency on the part of some historians to suggest that the Protestant, and specifically the Calvinist, Reformation may be regarded as laying the foundations of modern progressive political thought.[28] In part, this tendency was based on a romantic liberal view of the Reformation as a movement crusading for personal liberty in an age of ecclesiastical oppression. Whatever Calvin's Geneva may have been, it certainly failed to gain an international reputation at the time for libertarianism, religious or otherwise, being seen rather as an icon of ecclesiastical and civil discipline. Calvin's political thought itself is generally regarded as largely unoriginal and uninteresting.[29] As Calvinism went forth from Geneva to seek fresh woods and pastures new, however, it proved able to develop and adapt its foundational inheritance, adopting and modifying ideas not included within, or necessarily suggested by, its founder.

One such idea concerns the 'givenness' of existing social structures.[30] It has been argued that Calvinism was instrumental in effecting the change between a medieval notion of worldly order, founded upon 'an order imagined to be natural and eternal', and a modern order 'founded upon change'. In other words, the medieval world-view was static: one was allocated a position within society on the basis of birth and tradition, and it was not possible to alter this situation. Calvinism, on the other hand, offered an 'ideology of transition', in that the individual's position within the world was declared to rest, at least in part, upon his or her efforts.[31] The attractiveness of such a suggestion to the French third estate – or, indeed, to the bourgeoisie throughout Europe – will be evident. To a social class frustrated by their inability to make significant headway in a society dominated by tradition and familial ties, the doctrine of the fundamental *changeability* of existing social orders would clearly have had considerable appeal. The use made of this principle by the English Calvinists John Ponet and Christopher Goodman, who developed theories of justifiable regicide (in direct contradiction of Calvin's refusal to permit regicide) on its basis, demonstrates a fundamental break with the medieval notion that existing power structures are somehow ordained by God, and are thus inviolable and unalterable.[32] The implications of this doctrine for the Reformation in Scotland will be evident.

Similar ideas developed within France in the aftermath of the St Bartholomew's Day Massacres. Initially, French Calvinism had limited its political reflections to the general area of liberty of conscience.[33] Throughout the 1550s, as Calvinist influence in France grew steadily more significant, the main burden of French Calvinist political agitation concerned religious toleration. There was, it was suggested, no fundamental contradiction between being a Calvinist and being French; to be a Frenchman and a Calvinist (or a Huguenot, for the terms designate much the same) implied no disloyalty to the French crown. The neat logic and persuasiveness of this position, which commended it to Calvin among others, was shattered in May 1560 through the *conjuration d'Amboise*, in which the aristocrat Godefroi de La Renaudie, apparently aided and abetted by a number of Calvinist pastors (to Calvin's irritation), attempted to kidnap Francis II.[34] It was, however, the massacres of St Bartholomew (1572) which precipitated the radical shift in French Calvinist political thinking.

The emergence of the monarchomachs – those who wished to place severe restrictions upon the rights of kings, and to uphold the *duty* (not merely the *right*) of the people to resist tyrannical monarchs – was a direct response to the atmosphere of shock which persisted in the aftermath of St Bartholomew.[35] In 1559, Calvin – perhaps beginning to recognize the practical and political importance of the question – had conceded that a ruler might exceed the bounds of his authority by setting himself against God; by doing this, he suggested, such a ruler had abrogated his own power. The magistrates (but not private individuals) might thus be in a position to take some (unspecified) action against him.[36] These ideas were developed and extended by Calvin's French followers in the aftermath of the events of 1572. François Hotman produced the celebrated *Franco-Gallia*, Théodore de Bèze his *Droits des Magistrats*, Philippe Duplessis-Mornay his *Vindiciae contra tyrannos*, and other minor writers produced pamphlet after pamphlet, all making the same point: tyrants are to be resisted. The duty to obey God is to be placed above any obligation to obey a human ruler.

These radical new theories, forged within the crucible of French Calvinism (even though in opposition to Calvin's own teaching), may be seen as marking an important point of transition between feudalism and modern democracy, with the notion of natural human rights being articulated and defended on theological grounds. Although most French Calvinists abandoned outright opposition to monarchy during the reign of Henri IV, particularly after the promulgation of the Edict of Nantes, important new theories had been let loose in the French political arena. It is arguable that they would resurface, in purely secular forms, in the French Enlightenment. The notion of natural human rights, shorn of its theological trimmings, was amalgamated with the republicanism of Calvin's Geneva in Jean-Jacques Rousseau's *thèse républicaine* which – in opposition to Voltaire's modernized *thèse royale* and

Montesquieu's *thèse nobilaire* – declared that sixteenth-century Geneva was a model republic, charged with assimilative possibilities of direct relevance to and potential for the situation of eighteenth-century France. Thus it was that Calvin's Geneva became a vibrant and potent ideal, which seized the imagination of pre-Revolutionary France. Was the French Revolution of 1789 a child of the Genevan revolution of 1535? But this is to pose questions which properly belong elsewhere in this study. We must return to the realities of France in the 1550s, and consider once more the appeal of Calvinism to its inhabitants.

The Social Profile of French Calvinism

Calvinism thus presented a complex cluster of ideas and values – political, religious and economic – of potential appeal to the French middle classes, and it is perhaps not surprising that the movement initially gained its adherents from this social stratum. In part, this also reflects upon the social background of the Genevan agents sent to France, who were virtually entirely middle-class and French-speaking, perhaps ideally suited to the needs of the urban middle classes. This was especially the case in the south, which was always conscious – indeed, proud – of its historic French linguistic affiliations. Yet French was but little understood in the countryside, where patois still ruled. In Languedoc – the region around Toulouse, in which the *langue d'oc* was spoken – French was seen almost as a foreign language. The Genevan agents belonged to a different world – socially and linguistically – from the rural population of France. Yet there was virtually nothing the Venerable Company of Pastors could do. They could only send men whom they had at their disposal, drawn from the middle and upper social strata, and conversant with French as their first language. A study of the background of forty-two such agents demonstrated that not a single one had any affiliation whatsoever with the peasantry.[37] From its beginnings, the great Genevan evangelization process was thus locked into a social spiral from which the peasantry were excluded.

This point was not, however, deemed of great importance by the Venerable Company of Pastors, who regarded themselves as riding the crest of a wave. In 1561, the company found itself overwhelmed by requests for pastors from France. Nicolas Colladon recorded 151 individuals as having been despatched to French missions during this year.[38] Genevan pastors were prone simply to disappear without public warning, subsequently to turn up in remote corners of France. Local Genevan parishes were stripped of their pastors in order to supply the burgeoning demand from French churches. Even the city of Lausanne found itself without pastors for a period, as its clergy heeded the call for volunteers to assist in the great work of evangelization in France. The decision of regent Catherine de Médicis to adopt a tolerant attitude towards Protestants facilitated this infiltration to no small extent: the policy of absolute secrecy was relaxed, and Genevan refugees began to return to their native France, apparently to the relief of the indigenous population of the city.

At least superficially, it seemed that the Genevan policy of evangelizing France was producing remarkable results. Evangelical congregations were springing up throughout the country, and calling upon Geneva for support, guidance and advice. Yet an important change had taken place within France itself. Calvinism had gained important converts among her aristocracy. A religion whose primary appeal was initially to *les petits gens* had become acceptable, even attractive, to the *Seigneurie*.[39]

According to Lucien Romier, the character of French Calvinism was irreversibly altered during the years 1558–62 through massive conversions within the aristocracy.[40] The French economy, long in need of radical overhaul, finally began to fail. Studies of the French fiscal and patronage system reveal an economy in crisis by 1557, and virtually in ruins by 1559.[41] A decline in ecclesiastical income attended this economic downturn, as revenue from such traditional catholic rites as prayers and masses for the dead began to dry up.[42] The aristocracy were no longer shielded against the brute facts of economics. The economic disincentives to conversion to Calvinism no longer had anything like the force they once had. The failure of traditional patterns of patronage and finance effectively led to the emergence of a section within the aristocracy caught up in a tension between assumed, traditional patterns, and new forces for which patterns had yet to emerge. Traditional aristocratic alliances and allegiances began to falter.

It is in the light of this degenerating economic situation that the growing alliance of the second and third estates against the first (that is, the nobility and the bourgeoisie against the clergy) in the period 1559–61 must be seen.[43] Elements of the urban elite, hitherto publicly hostile or indifferent to Calvinism, began to openly associate with it.[44] Criticism of the church and its wealth became increasingly strident within the second estate: the meeting of the *Etats-généraux* at Orléans in 1560 saw an open alliance of nobles and bourgeois in what appears to have been a Calvinist-inspired attack on the privileges and wealth of the church. The forging of this alliance between the second and third estates is of considerable importance: its advent meant that the Wars of Religion would not be primarily a class conflict, but rather the clash of two rival aristocratic-led factions.

The death of Henri II precipitated a period of uncertainty. The kingdom was initially in the hands of Francis II, then aged fifteen; he was succeeded by his younger brother Charles IX in December 1560. As he had yet to attain the age of majority (fourteen, under French law), Catherine de Médicis was able to seize power, and proclaim herself regent. The weakness of the central government during this period made it impossible to continue Henri II's policy of persecuting Calvinism within France. The Edict of Amboise (March 1560) may be seen as tacit recognition of this point,[45] as may the *lettres de cachet* issued by Catherine on 28 January 1561,[46] releasing those imprisoned on account of their religious beliefs and suspending heresy proceedings. Finally, the edict of St-Germain-en-Laye, issued on 17 January 1562, allowed Calvinists to meet for public worship, although under restricted conditions.[47]

Throughout this time, Calvin and his associates were attempting to control developments as best they could. Yet there is ample evidence that they failed to exploit the French situation to full advantage. In part, this may reflect inadequate planning; it may also, however, be due to Calvin and his circle having been caught unawares by the very success of their enterprise. They had not thought big enough, and had exercised caution where audacity was required. The period 1555–62 offered the Genevan church the opportunity to take this tide in the affairs of men at its flood; it proved unable to do so. Calvin himself remained locked into a politically unrealistic approach to the French situation, waiting upon the French court, the Elector Palatine, the Duke of Württemburg and divine providence in about equal measure.[48] There is ample evidence that Calvin, believing that the French king might be persuaded to reform the French church along acceptable lines, deliberately restricted the growth and development of evangelical churches.[49] The decision to impose a consistorial structure on congregations may be viewed as an attempt to restrain the growth of *églises plantées* for political reasons. If this is the case, it must be regarded as a serious misjudgement, resting upon uninformed optimism concerning the intentions of the French monarch.

This same approach is evident in Calvin's attitude towards the publication of a confession of faith for the French Reformed church. It seems that the need to consolidate the position of the Reformed church within France by convening an assembly of all its representatives was first mooted towards the end of 1558 at Poitiers, with Antoine de la Roche-Chandieu being invited to make the appropriate arrangements. The Parisian minister François de Morel thus wrote to Calvin, asking for his advice on how to proceed. It is evident that Calvin never received this letter.[50] His hostility towards the idea of such an assembly publishing a declaration of faith is well known, and undoubtedly reflects his cautious approach towards the French situation. To issue a public declaration of faith was to court persecution. We possess a letter from an English embassy to France, Nicholas Throckmorton, dated 15 May 1559, which explicitly identifies this possibility:

> I have learned that about 15,000 people of the provinces of Gascognne, Guyenne, Anjou, Poitou, Normandy and Maine had subscribed a confession similar to that of Geneva. This confession they intend soon to present to the king. Among those people were many of importance. In the same circles, it is said that as soon as they have presented this confession to the king the church will be forced to receive his assurance that they will be completely wiped out.[51]

Calvin's wishes, however, were ignored. The first national synod of the Reformed church in France was held in secret at Paris in the period 25–29 May 1559,[52] and drew up a confession of faith in thirty-five articles. This was published as *Confession de foy faicte d'un commun accord par les églises qui sont dispersées en France*, and was presented to Francis II the following year. The feared persecution, however, failed to materialize.

Despite his excessive prudence, Calvin's influence over France had reached major proportions by 1562. There had been an explosion in the growth of Calvinist congregations and influence; the complete reformation of France seemed a real possibility. Perhaps one third of the nobility had signalled their acceptance of his religious ideas. According to a list prepared for Admiral de Coligny in March 1562, there were 2,150 Huguenot churches in France at that point. It is difficult to verify these figures; it would,

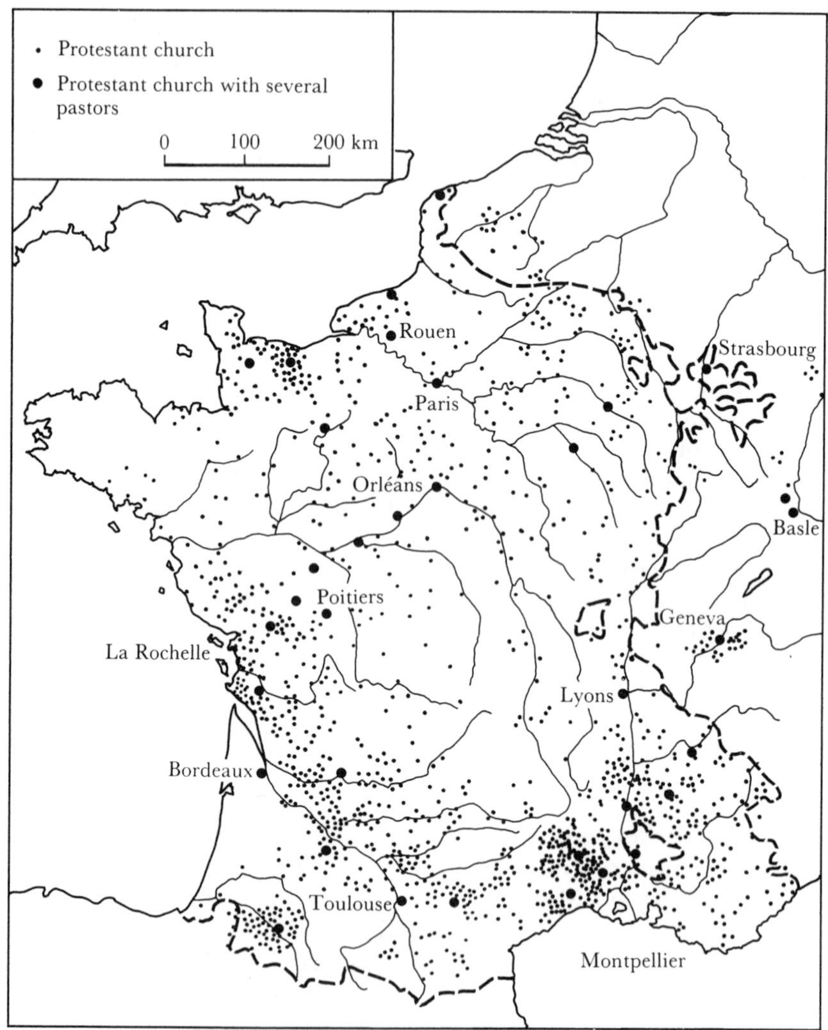

FIGURE 9.3 Calvinist churches in France, 1562

however, seem reasonable to suggest that there were at least 1,250 such churches, with a total membership in excess of two million out of a national population of twenty million.[53] The distribution of known Protestant churches throughout France is uneven, reflecting only partly understood considerations of political geography, local patronage and cultural and linguistic factors. Of particular interest is the so-called 'Huguenot crescent', stretching from La Rochelle on the Atlantic coast to the Dauphiné in the east, with a particularly strong concentration in the Midi.

This, then, was the extent of Calvin's influence on the eve of the Wars of Religion. If he ever entertained the idea that France would be united under his version of Christianity, such a vision would have perished when confronted with the reality, as war broke out over the 'matter of religion' at Orléans in April 1562. The Wars of Religion (1562–98) made clear that France was divided – regionally, socially and politically – by Calvinism. So deep were the rifts within French society that they proved incapable of being healed by the time-honoured means of pragmatic diplomacy. It is brutal and chilling memories of the Wars of Religion and especially the massacres of St Bartholomew[54] – ominously hinting at the excesses later to be unleashed in the revolutionary Reign of Terror – which render Calvin's reputation so ambiguous within his native France. Although other factors undoubtedly contributed to the origins of the Wars of Religion, they were first and foremost wars which centred on religious issues – above all, the agenda laid down in Geneva by John Calvin. Within a generation, the Calvinist struggle for supremacy within France would become a lost cause; its status was at best that of a tolerated *imperium in imperio*, a state within a state, under the conciliatory terms of the Edict of Nantes (1598). But by then its losses in France had been matched by gains elsewhere. Calvinism had become an international movement.

10

The Genesis of a Movement

By the early spring of 1564, it was obvious that Calvin was seriously ill. His attendance at the weekly Consistory meeting had become increasingly infrequent in the winter of 1563–4,[1] reflecting his decline in health. From of a list of symptoms which he described to a group of consulting physicians at Montpellier that year, it is possible to infer that Calvin suffered from symptoms consistent with migraine, gout, pulmonary tuberculosis, intestinal parasites, thrombosed haemorrhoids and irritated bowel syndrome. He preached for the last time from the pulpit of Saint-Pierre on the morning of Sunday 6 February. By April, it was clear that he had not much longer to live. He found breathing difficult, and was chronically short of breath.[2] Despite this, he managed to bid farewell to the ministers of Geneva on Friday 28 April.[3]

The *Discours d'adieu aux ministres* is a moving document, at times verging on the pathetic. Calvin confessed that he was, and had always been, little more than a poor and timid scholar,[4] who had been pressed into the service of the Christian gospel. One section of the document is of especial interest; in what might at first seem little more than rambling digressions, he catalogued some of the various disasters which had befallen him during his period in Geneva. People had fired their arquebuses in front of his door, and set their dogs on him. The significance of this portion of the *Discours d'adieu* has not been fully appreciated; Calvin is clearly influenced by the 'catalogues of hardships' found in writings of the classical period.[5] He would have known this literary genre through two sources: the Corinthian correspondence in the New Testament – Rudolf Bultmann characterized 1 Corinthians 4:9–13 and

2 Corinthians 4:8–9, 6:4–10, as *Peristasenkatalogen* (catalogues of difficult circumstances) – and the writings of the classical moralists, such as Seneca. Hardship seems to have been a constitutive element in Calvin's conception of his calling.

Calvin died at eight o'clock on the evening of 27 May. At his own request, he was buried in a common grave, with no stone to mark his own. There was to be no personality cult based upon him at Geneva. In death, as in life, Calvin proved self-effacing. Yet with his death, his influence upon the world proved to have only begun.

Urbi et Orbi: The Expansion of Calvin's Influence

By the end of the third quarter of the sixteenth century Calvinism was established as an international religion, convinced of its ability and right to cast society in a new mould.[6] Its proponents saw no need to compromise by adapting their principles to social realities; in theory – and, it must be said, in the light of the American experience (see p. 258), often in practice – society could be changed to meet the demands of the new religion. There is some truth in Emile G. Léonard's suggestion that Calvin's greatest achievement was the creation of a new type of human being[7] – the Calvinist, with a 'can-do' attitude to life, grounded in a sense of God's calling and empowerment.

The European situation in the 1530s and early 1540s gave virtually no indication that Calvin's thought was to receive such attention and achieve such influence in the remainder of the century. It was Luther's version of the Reformation which made inroads throughout Europe in the first half: his ideas attracted much comment in the aftermath of the Leipzig Disputation with Johann Eck (June–July 1519), as a consequence of which Luther was widely perceived to be a champion of liberal humanist values. The origins of his influence at Paris may be dated from late 1519, when the faculty of theology was invited to consider his Leipzig proposals; by the mid-1520s, his influence had spread far and wide within the city, embracing academics, clerics and ordinary citizens. The first Lutheran was publicly burned in 1524. In the following year, during Francis I's imprisonment at Madrid after his defeat at the battle of Pavia, the queen mother ordered the total elimination of 'the evil and damnable sect and heresy of Luther' from her son's kingdom. Even as far east as Vienna, Luther received attention; in the immediate aftermath of the Leipzig Disputation, the Viennese faculty of theology devised a six-point plan to minimize his scandalous influence in their university.[8] Yet despite such measures, Luther's influence over western European religion grew stronger during the 1520s and early 1530s. Some devotional literature in circulation in France in the 1530s even managed to mingle a catholic spirituality with elements of Luther's theology (pp. 176–7).

In England, Luther's writings were circulated widely from 1520 onwards, with English reformers such as William Tyndale and Robert Barnes publicly aligning themselves with the Saxon (even to the point of attending his University of Wittenberg).[9] Luther's ideas were influential within evangelical movements in the Netherlands in the 1520s to an extent which is only now becoming apparent.[10] Despite inauspicious beginnings, Lutheranism gradually gained influence in Scotland during the 1520s and 1530s, eventually reaching its (abortive) climax in 1543.[11] Similar patterns can be discerned within Spain and France. The Council of Trent, meeting in the 1540s to counter the Reformation, brought their heavy theological artillery to bear on Luther and his circle; no one else seemed worth bothering about. The Religious Peace of Augsburg (1555), which aimed to settle the religious question in Germany by adopting the principle *cuius regio eius religio* – 'your region decides your religion' – did not even find it necessary to acknowledge the existence of Calvin or his movement; Lutheranism and Roman Catholicism were the recognized alternatives in the stakes for Christian loyalty. In short, Luther was widely identified with the cause of Reformation. To be a reformer was to be a Lutheran.

With the death of Luther (1546) and the defeat of the Schmalkaldic League (1547), Lutheranism became intellectually moribund, increasingly weakened by severe internal dissent and landlocked within the German territories. Luther's little system had had its day, and the initial dynamism of the Lutheran Reformation seemed to be spent. The first wave of the Reformation had crashed against its shore, and spent itself; a second now followed. Calvin's star rose, and was soon in the ascendancy. A number of factors appear to have been instrumental in engineering this development.

Calvin's *Institutes* were widely read and appreciated, often to the point of being cited extensively in other works. The anonymous Italian treatise *Il Beneficio di Cristo* of 1541 – which rapidly attained the status of a religious best-seller before being suppressed by the Inquisition – draws heavily upon the 1539 edition of the *Institutes*,[12] without bothering to draw attention to the fact. Calvin's work was evidently familiar to front-rank Protestant theologians in the Netherlands by the late 1550s.[13] The work rapidly established itself as a neat and elegant one-stop and free-standing introduction to the ideas of the second wave of the Reformation. As we have seen (pp. 141–2), the 1541 French translation went into edition after edition, to meet the demands of its public. It was but a small step from the digestion of its ideas to calls for appropriate action.

As we have noted, Geneva actively propagated the programme of reform advocated by the *Institutes* by dispatching French-speaking pastors, whose influence soon proved to extend beyond France itself: the origins of Calvin's influence within the French-speaking provinces of the Netherlands is to be dated from around 1550. Other Calvinist-minded intellectuals travelled abroad to propagate his ideas, perhaps most successfully in England. Under the reign of Edward VI, leading divines, either Calvinist or sympathetic to Calvinism, were encouraged to settle in England and give a sense of theological direction to the nascent Reformed church. Individuals such as Martin Bucer, Pietro Martire Vermigli (perhaps better known as Peter Martyr) and John à Lasco gave the Church of England a new impetus which moved it away from its earlier flirtations with Lutheranism, and towards at least some of the ideas associated with Calvin's Geneva. In May 1559, John Knox returned to his native Scotland after a period of exile in Geneva; within days of his arrival, riots broke out at Perth, precipitating the Reformation crisis.[14]

The phenomenon of the refugee and the place of refuge played no small part in the propagation of Calvinism. Geneva was but one of a number of European centres (such as Frankfurt, Emden and Strasbourg) which played host to exiled Protestants. Much to the irritation of the indigenous Genevans, who disliked the presence of foreigners (and showed it by their support for the Perrinist faction in the early 1550s), Calvin secured Geneva as a place of refuge for those with Reformed views. During their period of exile, such refugees often absorbed Calvin's outlook, and, upon their return to their native lands, proceeded to propagate Calvinism. The French exiles were by far the most numerous, but they were supplemented by others, such as English Protestants seeking safety from the Marian persecutions. (Twelve of the eighteen bishops appointed by Elizabeth I in the aftermath of the mass resignations of 1559 had sought refuge in Europe during Mary's reign.) Other countries, by receiving Calvinist refugees, nourished centres of Calvinist activities which had the potential to extend their influence beyond their congregations.[15]

To these must be added a number of other factors, social, political and economic, which reflect the nature of Calvin's thought itself, rather than the historical means through which it was disseminated. We shall consider these in due course; it is, however, worth noting at this stage that Calvinism was often regarded as progressive, associated in many minds with a decisive break with obsolete institutions, customs and practices fettering individuals to the legacy of the feudal past. Where Luther seemed cautious and conservative, Calvin appeared bold and forward-looking (an impression apparently fostered, at least in part, by the progressive political policies and structures of the city of Geneva). The future seemed to belong to him. The adoption of Calvinism by the Palatinate, along with the formulation of the enormously influential Heidelberg Catechism (1563),[16] seemed to symbolize the new ascendancy of the French reformer over the German, even on the latter's home territory.

By 1591, Calvinism seemed to have made irreversible gains throughout Europe. The German Calvinist Abraham Scultetus (1566–1624) wrote thus of the sense of achievement, even of destiny (which Calvinist writers were careful to speak of only in terms of divine providence), that pervaded the movement:

> I cannot fail to recall the optimistic mood which I and many others felt when we considered the condition of the Reformed churches in 1591. In France there ruled the valiant King Henri IV, in England the mighty Queen Elizabeth, in Scotland the learned King James, in the Palatinate the bold hero John Casimir, in Saxony the courageous and powerful Elector Christian I, in Hesse the clever and prudent Landgrave William, who were all inclined to the Reformed religion. In the Netherlands everything went as Prince Maurice of Orange wished, when he took Breda, Zutphen, Hulst and Nijmegen. . . . We imagined that *aureum seculum*, a golden age, had dawned.[17]

This rapid international expansion of Calvinism in the second half of the century, to be supplemented by its remarkable gains in the New World in the half-century which followed, should be seen in the context of the erosion of its original power-base, the city of Geneva.[18] As early as 1575, informed rumours of its decline were

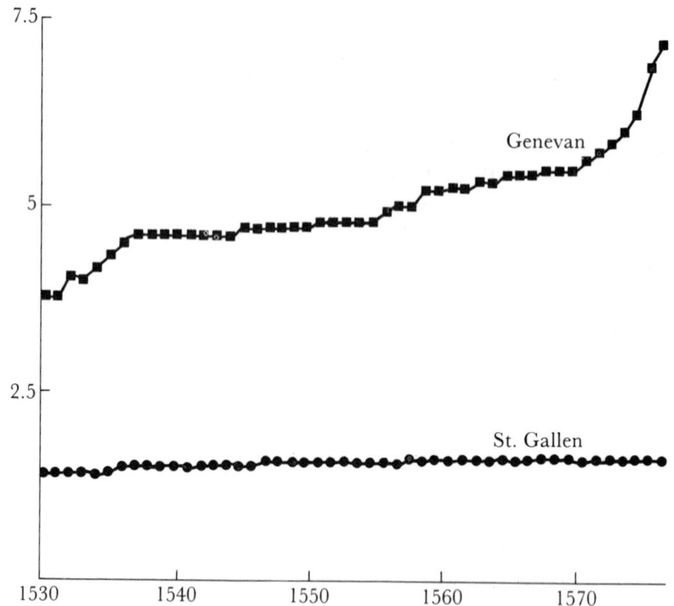

FIGURE 10.1 The depreciation of the Genevan and St Gallen florins against the French *écu d'or*, 1530–77

in circulation.[19] In part, this reflects the serious economic situation faced by the city: the Genevan florin was depreciating rapidly against the French *écu d'or*. In a study of 1934, the Swiss historian Charles Gilliard suggested that there appeared to have been a serious collapse of currency in the area of western Switzerland in the second half of the sixteenth century. This has now been confirmed by detailed studies of currency fluctuations in the region, which have revealed patterns of depreciation directly corresponding to political geography.[20] The currencies of the cities of eastern Switzerland and the Rhine valley (such as St Gallen and Basle) remained relatively stable during the period, while those of the cities of central Switzerland (such as Zurich, Schaffhausen, Lucerne and Berne) depreciated slightly. The cities of western Switzerland, however, saw their currencies depreciate seriously. Fribourg and Lausanne were badly affected; as the most westward city, Geneva was by far the worst hit. Whereas the value of the St Gallen florin remained virtually constant against the French *écu d'or* over the critical period 1550–90, the Genevan florin decreased in value by some 30 per cent over the period 1570–7 alone.

This deteriorating economic situation was accompanied by a decline in the fortunes of the Genevan church. Without the considerable personal authority of Calvin to contend with, the city council was gradually able to gain control over areas of city life hitherto regarded as the province of the pastors. The process of secularization, begun in 1535 and redirected (rather than ended) through the influence of Calvin, was now extended, as the secular powers increased their sphere of authority, eroding the position of the pastors within the city. Although the Company of Pastors, under Théodore de Bèze, was able to exercise at least some degree of influence, however limited, over the public affairs of the city, this virtually ceased when de Bèze resigned its moderatorship in 1580. It became increasingly obvious that the pastors possessed a purely moral authority, and lacked any statutory or constitutional authority within the city. From 1580 they lacked a representative with anything even approaching the personal authority of de Bèze, let alone of Calvin himself.

In part, Geneva's international reputation rested upon its academy, founded by Calvin in 1559. Yet even this illustrious academy soon lost its appeal; as Calvinism became an international movement, an increasing number of universities became favourably disposed towards the new religion. The Universities of Leiden and Heidelberg rapidly gained an international reputation both as centres of learning and as strongholds of Calvinism, eclipsing the more modest reputation of Calvin's personal foundation. These new seats of learning were supplemented by the new Calvinist academies located strategically at cities such as Herborn in Hanau (the location of the celebrated Wechsel presses),[21] and especially those founded in France after the Edict of Nantes – at Die, Montauban, Saumur and Sedan. The foundation of Harvard College (1636) established the intellectual hegemony of Calvinism in New England, ensuring the survival of the by then not-so-new faith in the New World.

With the passing of its monopoly on clerical education, Geneva's star slipped from the ascendancy. Calvinist pastors found cosmopolitan institutions at places such as Heidelberg, Saumur and Sedan more attractive than that of Geneva, despite the powerful and evocative links with Calvin which still lingered at that city.[22] Although Geneva continued to figure prominently in the iconography of Calvinism, this came increasingly to rest upon mythical foundations.[23] The seductive (and, it must be added, not entirely accurate) memory of a 'golden period' under Calvin increasingly overshadowed the harsher realities of the city's religious situation. By 1585 Geneva had become little more than a symbol for the new religion, where once it had been its source.

It is dangerously easy to settle upon a single event as marking a turning point in the development of a movement. The risk, however, seems worth taking. The death of Calvin in 1564 may be identified as a watershed in the history of Calvinism. It may be suggested that, with the death of its founder, Calvinism was able to break its original – and highly restrictive – links with a small city, and assume its place in the international forum. Its institutional links with Geneva would remain, however notional these might be in practice; but the personal links with Calvin were decisively broken. Calvin's death allowed the increasingly tenuous and unhelpful link between an international movement and its city of origin to be set aside. But, perhaps more importantly, it also allowed that movement to develop independently of its founder. With the death of Calvin, Calvinism began to establish its own character. The transition is of such importance that it merits closer attention.

From Calvin to Calvinism

In the sixth decade of the sixteenth century, a new expression entered the polemical literature of the churches of the Reformation. The term 'Calvinism' appears to have been introduced by the German Lutheran polemicist Joachim Westphal to refer to the theological, and particularly the sacramental, views of the Swiss reformers in general, and John Calvin in particular.[24] Once introduced, the term rapidly passed into general use within the German Lutheran church. In part, this rapid acceptance of the new term reflected intense disquiet within the Lutheran camp concerning the growing influence of Reformed theology in regions of Germany hitherto regarded as historically Lutheran.[25] Under the terms of the Religious Peace of Augsburg (September 1555), the particular form of Protestantism recognized in the German territories was defined as Lutheranism. The expansion of Calvin's influence in the Palatinate, especially evident in Elector Frederick III's introduction of the celebrated Heidelberg Catechism in 1563, was the cause of particular concern. The defection of the Elector from Lutheranism to the form of Protestantism associated with Calvin was widely regarded as an open infringement of the Peace of

Augsburg, and a destabilizing influence in the region. The introduction of the term 'Calvinist' appears to have been an attempt on the part of alarmed German Lutherans to stigmatize and discredit Calvin's ideas as a foreign influence in Germany. Calvin himself was alarmed at the use of the term, which he rightly regarded as a thinly veiled attempt to discredit the Elector's espousal of the Reformed faith.[26] By then, however, Calvin had only months to live, and his protest was ineffective. The term 'Calvinism' was thus introduced to refer to the religious outlook of Calvin's followers *by their opponents*. Modern students of the Reformation period find themselves unwilling heirs to this most dubious bequest of early Protestant internecine politics. The precise relationship between Calvin and Reformed thought and polity, particularly in the period after his death, is considerably more complex than might be expected, and the use of the term 'Calvinism' to refer to that theology is fraught with potential danger. History, however, cannot be conducted in a psychological vacuum, in which words and their associated memories are set to one side. 'Calvinism' remains firmly embedded within the historian's vocabulary.

It is, all the same, an amorphous and ill-defined term. It is possible to lend rigour and precision to the notion by defining it in terms of the religious orthodoxy laid down by the Synod of Dort (1618–19) or the *Consensus Helveticus* (1675). Such refinements, however desirable from the standpoint of theological meticulousness, would oblige us to limit alarmingly the number of Calvinists, forcing a wedge between an ideal 'Calvinist' and many of those who, as a matter of history, chose to regard themselves as Calvinists. For example, those Huguenot pastors who chose to seek refuge in Switzerland after the revocation of the Edict of Nantes (October 1685) had little sympathy with the allegedly Calvinist stipulations of the *Consensus Helveticus*. The Calvinists of history were not – despite all the efforts of preachers, confessions of faith and catechisms – necessarily loyal and rigid adherents to strict systems of doctrine, but were, rather, individuals who conformed to a general social type. Their character, although shaped and informed by the great beliefs and values of Calvin and his heirs, was ultimately detachable from its theological roots. In understanding Calvinism as an historical force, which did so much to mould western European and North American culture, it is necessary to consider the moral and social deposit of faith which, although originally *shaped* by the faith, would remain behind after it departed. The cultural landscape of modern America is littered with such deposits, as a secular Calvinism – devoid of its original religious vitality, but retaining much of its moral and social worldview – began to emerge, eventually to gain the ascendancy.

Our attention initially focuses on the relation of Calvin and Calvinism. The study of the relation of men and their movements has proved one of the most stimulating aspects of intellectual history. Whilst certain objections might be raised against the suggestion that 'the history of the world is but the biography of great men' (Thomas Carlyle), it is beyond dispute that certain individuals injected an impulse into the historical process which proved to be of major importance, providing a focus and foundation for a more or less coherent movement. Jesus of Nazareth and Karl Marx might serve as examples of this phenomenon. These two historic individuals also highlight a major question which the historian of Calvinism is obliged to address. In what way does the movement which originates with a specific human existence relate to that individual?

A preliminary response to this question might run like this. Calvinism is the body of ideas historically associated with John Calvin. In fact, however, this assumption is potentially vulnerable. The point at issue may be illustrated and developed from some remarks of J. L. Austin concerning the term 'Fascism' in his essay 'The Meaning of a Word.'[27] The term 'Fascism' is usually understood to mean forms of polity historically derived from the inspiration of the political ideas and enterprises of Mussolini. However, certain political ideas in circulation prior to Mussolini (for instance, those of Charles Maurras and the *action française*)[28] may legitimately be termed 'Fascist', despite the absence of this pattern of historical causation, in that they conform to the paradigm of Mussolini's movement. Just as the term 'Fascist' cannot thus simply mean '*historically derived* from Mussolini', so the term 'Calvinist' could conceivably refer to persons or ideas historically prior to Calvin. For example, the most radical survivors of the Hussite movement in Bohemia, the *Jednota bratrská*, came to be known as *Calviniani ante Calvinum* for precisely such reasons.[29] In practice, however, it is reasonably clear that Calvinism designates a coherent body of beliefs whose inspiration ultimately derives, at least in part, from Calvin himself. Despite clear parallels between certain aspects of his thought and those of earlier writers, Calvin's system (we use this term loosely) as a totality represents an original and creative synthesis. There is a clear paradigm of historical causation linking Calvin with those writers usually designated 'Calvinist' and the movement known as 'Calvinism'.

'To be great is to be misunderstood' (Ralph Waldo Emerson). In considering the relationship between the generative individual and the generated movement, particular importance is to be attached to accounting for the transition between the individual and the movement. An initial consideration is suggested by some remarks of the Oxford literary critic C. S. Lewis:

> All theology of the liberal type involves at some point – and often involves throughout – the claim that the real behaviour and purpose and teaching of Christ came very rapidly to be misunderstood and misrepresented by his followers, and he has been recovered or exhumed only by modern scholars. Now long before I became interested in theology I had met this kind of theory elsewhere. The tradition of Jowett still dominated the study of ancient philosophy when I was reading Greats. One was brought up to believe that the real meaning of Plato had been misunderstood by Aristotle and wildly travestied by the neo-Platonists, only to be recovered by the moderns. When recovered, it turned out (most fortunately) that Plato had really all along been an English Hegelian, rather like T. H. Green.[30]

('Greats' is an Oxford colloquialism which designates the study of *literae humaniores*, generally referred to as 'classical studies' elsewhere.) The question Lewis obliges us to consider is whether Calvin was misunderstood or misrepresented by his followers.

It is perhaps inevitable that a delicately balanced and complex agglomerate of ideas, such as that developed by Calvin, will be vulnerable to tension and distortion, at least to *some* extent, as it is extended by later adherents. The rapid development of right- and left-wing Hegelian movements in the 1830s illustrates this phenomenon particularly well; what Hegel had held together, his followers rent asunder. Perhaps Calvin perceived this danger as he lay dying: 'Ne changer rien, ne innover!'[31] Yet, unless Calvin's heirs were merely to passively reiterate the dicta of their master, some shifts were inevitable, as they responded to specific needs, situations and opportunities. Many Calvin scholars appear reluctant to allow such shifts, apparently on the basis of the suspicion that any deviation from Calvin's original ideas marks a form of degeneration. Yet development, it must be stressed, is an historical concept, devoid of value judgement. No movement of the calibre and dynamism of international Calvinism could survive, let alone prosper, without modifying itself at least to some extent, in the face of the specific situations it faced. It is the task of the historian to identify such shifts, and for the theologian to assess their significance. The crude denial of any such shifts is, however, historically untenable.

The significance of the question of the manner in and extent to which a movement appropriates the ideas of its founder may be illustrated by considering the relation of Marxism to Marx.[32] 'Marxism' designates a broad movement which, although based upon the writings of Marx, nevertheless represents a considerable elaboration and refinement of his ideas. Marxism cannot adequately be defined as 'the ideas of Karl Marx', as if Marx were appropriated in a crudely unreconstructed manner by his followers; rather, the term designates the broad spectrum of manners in which Marx has been appropriated, remastered and applied in the light of the needs and opportunities of given socio-economic situations.[33] To account for the genesis and development, the successes and failures, of Marxism, it is necessary to consider the Marxian ideational origins of the movement and the manner in which this heritage was found to be applicable to situations which were not necessarily identical with those envisaged by Marx himself. The debate between Karl Kautsky and Edward Bernstein reflects a perception that Marxism could become irrelevant to the needs of western societies as a result of economic development,[34] on account of an overemphasis within Marxism on the specific socio-economic situation addressed by Marx. With the erosion of this original situation through historical development, Marxism could, in Bernstein's view, become an irrelevance, unless it adapted itself to the new situation.

Similarly, to account for the origins and development of Calvinism, including its successes and failures, it is necessary to ask in what manner and to what extent Calvin's ideas were appropriated by his followers. How were these ideas found to be applicable to social, political and economic situations which bore little relation to those of sixteenth-century Geneva, within which they were originally formulated? Subtle shifts of balance and emphasis may reflect perceptions on the part of Calvin's agents and followers of the need to be selective in relation to his ideas in order to address new situations and their opportunities. For example, Calvin himself was unyielding in his opposition to armed insurrection against legally constituted governments (for instance, *Institutes* IV.xx.25); many French Calvinists, however, chose to ignore or overlook this point, and lent overt support to the *conjuration d'Amboise* (1560), an unsuccessful attempt to further the cause of the French Reformation by removing certain of its opponents by force.[35] Particularly in the political sphere,[36] Calvinism developed ideas and outlooks which went far beyond the modest recommendations emanating from Geneva, even if they were ultimately inspired by Calvin's proposals. The extraordinary success of Calvinism suggests that Calvin's heritage was remarkably fruitful in this respect.

A further complication arises through the influence of individuals who, although clearly associated with theological systems bearing some relation to Calvin's thought, cannot be regarded as 'Calvinists' in the strict sense of the term. Examples of such individuals would include Pietro Martire Vermigli and Giralmo Zanchi, whose Italian origins led them to adopt an approach to theological method quite distinct from that of Calvin.[37] Although their ideas were, in many ways, similar to those of Calvin, they resulted from the application of a quite distinct theological method. Later Calvinism appears to have drawn appreciatively upon the writings of these two individuals, apparently without realizing the extent or nature of the subtle differences between them and Calvin. 'Calvinism' thus came to include a number of elements, chiefly relating to theological method, which were perceived to be authentically Calvinist – yet paradoxically did not owe their origins to Calvin himself. The full implications of this process of assimilation are perhaps best seen in the later Calvinist discussion of predestination, where the influence of Vermigli and Zanchi appears to outweigh that of Calvin himself (see pp. 208–18).

The term 'Calvinism' is thus potentially misleading, in that it suggests a movement primarily concerned with the appropriation of the intellectual heritage of Calvin. Yet it may be shown that theologians historically regarded as 'Calvinist' in their outlook regarded themselves at liberty to draw upon theological and methodological resources other than the writings of Calvin himself. Calvin may have been the most significant luminary in the Calvinist firmament; there were, nevertheless, others, whose ideas and methods modified him at points. It is for this reason that the term 'Reformed' is perhaps to be preferred to 'Calvinist', in that it implies no *exclusive* dependence upon Calvin himself.

International Calvinism was not an intellectual abstraction, but – like any other international movement – took quite definite local forms which were subject to a number of historical contingencies. It was localized within, and thus shaped by, regional forces, within a number of very different societies. Each of these societies had its own history, its own particular concerns and accepted conventions, its own internal tensions and needs.[38] We have already seen how, in response to local circumstances, French Calvinism came to develop political ideas in the 1570s which bore little resemblance to those known to be associated with Calvin (see pp. 186–8). 'Calvinism' thus came to mean something different in each of its local manifestations, reflecting local factors which combined to give it a different shape, a different persona, in its various locations. The American colonies, city-states such as Geneva or La Rochelle, European powers such as the Netherlands, principalities such as the Palatinate: all may be described in a too easy generalization as 'Calvinist' – yet the 'Calvinism' in question was specific to each situation. The historian is obliged to account for this diversity within the movement, and assess its significance.

A Religious System

Calvinism possessed a relentless inner momentum for systematization, nourished by an acute awareness of the need to defend itself initially in the face of Roman Catholic opposition,[39] and stimulated still further by important shifts in the intellectual climate in western Europe. As the influence of the Renaissance began to wane, hostility towards systematization declined. The new insights of the humanist Aristotelians of Padua began to gain a more sympathetic and appreciative hearing, as a new awareness of the importance of the possibility of developing a universal method, applicable to all the sciences – theology included – dawned. Calvinist writers, always more sensitive to their intellectual environment than many of their opponents, responded by developing sophisticated theological systems capable of exploiting the resources and attitudes of the new academic climate; in this, they were possibly as much as a generation ahead of Lutheranism, contributing further to the relative eclipse of the latter outside its German strongholds. By the middle of the seventeenth century, Calvinism was firmly established as a leading academic movement in many European universities, as well as Harvard College, Massachusetts.[40] The question of how this academic form of Calvinism, often referred to as 'Calvinist scholasticism', developed is of considerable interest.

Even by the time of Calvin's death (1564), Calvinism had become established as the most formidable alternative to Roman

Catholicism in western Europe, assisted to no small extent by Calvin's brilliance in recognizing the importance of ecclesiastical organization and structuring to the survival of a movement. His successors recognized the importance of extending this process to his religious thought, in order to supplement Calvinist ecclesiastical institutions with equally resilient intellectual structures. In the course of this, a new emphasis came to be placed upon the doctrine of predestination. The extent and intensity of the disputes over this doctrine within later Calvinism (illustrated particularly by the Arminian controversy) indicated its considerable importance to Calvin's followers. Calvinism places an emphasis upon this doctrine which is largely lacking in Calvin's thought. Two major reasons may be given for this development, one sociological and the other theological.

The Social Function of the Doctrine of Predestination

Recent analyses of the origins, nature and function of Christian doctrine have drawn attention to the manner in which doctrines function as social demarcators.[41] There is an obvious need for a religious group to define itself in relation to other religious groups, and to the world in general. The general phenomenon of 'doctrine' – although not specific *doctrines* – is linked with the need for social definition, especially when other factors do not adequately define a group. An ideology which legitimates the existence of that group is required. Thus Niklas Luhmann, perhaps the most significant recent writer to address the question of the social function of Christian doctrine, stresses that doctrine arises partly in response to perceived threats to the distinctive religious identity of a group, which may come about through encounters or conflict with other religious systems. Doctrine is, according to Luhmann, the self-reflection of a religious community, by which it maintains its identity and regulates its relations with other such communities and the whole social system in general. The social function of doctrine is particularly evident and significant in cases in which a religious group originates through rupture with an older grouping (for example, in the case of Christianity's appearance from within the matrix of Judaism, or the emergence of the churches of the Reformation from the medieval catholic church).

In the early stages of the Reformation, the recognition of the social importance of doctrine is especially associated with Martin Luther. The Lutheran faction at Wittenberg chose to define itself in relation to an explicitly doctrinal criterion: the doctrine of justification by faith alone. It was on the basis of this doctrine that the Lutheran faction, soon to become the Lutheran church, would take its stand against the world and the papacy. Once the Lutheran church became established as a serious and potentially credible alternative to the medieval church, self-definition through doctrinal formulations once more became of crucial importance to the catholic church. The significance of the Council of Trent lies in its perception of the need for the catholic church to define *itself* – rather than define *heretics* – at the doctrinal level. Earlier medieval councils had tended simply to condemn heretical opinions, thus defining views which placed those who entertained (or were prepared to admit to entertaining) them as heretical and therefore as lying outside the bounds of the church. In other words, they defined who was *outside* the bounds of the church, on the assumption that all others, whose views did not require definition, were *within* its bounds. The Council of Trent, in discussing the doctrine of justification, felt obliged to do more than simply censure Lutheran ideas: it provided an explicit definition of the intellectual (and hence the social) bounds of the church.

This development reflected the growing need to demarcate catholics from evangelicals in sixteenth-century Europe, especially in disputed regions such as Germany. The catholic church was obliged to offer a criterion of self-identity, in order that its bounds might be defined in the face of the threat from Protestantism. The Reformation may therefore be regarded as precipitating the reclamation of doctrine as a criterion of social demarcation, a function which had not been of decisive importance during the medieval period.

The importance of doctrine as a criterion of social demarcation in certain geopolitical regions of Europe during the sixteenth century is evident from events in Germany during the period of the so-called 'Second Reformation',[42] as Lutheran and Reformed communities found themselves entering a period of increased tension in the 1560s and 1570s due to the expansion of the Reformed church in what had hitherto been regarded as exclusively Lutheran territory. The principle *cuius regio eius religio* – 'your region decides your religion' – established by the Religious Peace of Augsburg (1555), appeared to allow political geography to function as a criterion of religious demarcation: this possibility was eliminated through the rise of Calvinism (not envisaged by the Peace), again forcing social demarcation to be grounded on doctrinal criteria.

The late sixteenth-century phenomenon of 'Confessionalization', by which both Lutheran and Reformed communities defined themselves by explicit and extensive doctrinal formulations, represents the inevitable outcome of a quest for self-definition on the part of two ecclesial bodies within the same geographical region, both claiming to be legitimate outcomes of the Reformation. At the social and political level, the communities were difficult to distinguish; doctrine therefore provided the most reliable means by which they might define themselves over and against one another.

Yet Lutheranism and Calvinism were, in many respects, remarkably similar at the doctrinal level. Both placed considerable emphasis upon the priority of scripture, worship in the vernacular and the positive function of preaching; both rejected papal authority, communion in one kind (that is, allowing the laity to receive only bread, and not wine, at the communion) and the ministerial structures of the Roman Catholic church. In terms of their religious practices, the two groups were remarkably similar. It is certainly true that there were doctrinal differences between them; yet most of the differences between Lutheranism and Calvinism were so subtle that it was difficult for a non-theologian to grasp them fully. The doctrine of predestination thus provided a dramatic (and easily understood) theological difference between the two groups.[43] And the need to differentiate them as social entities naturally led to this doctrine being given a certain degree of priority, not necessarily on account of any particular emphasis placed upon it by Calvinists, but on account of its utility as a means of allowing two otherwise similar groups to be distinguished.

The Theological Function of the Doctrine of Predestination

As noted earlier (p. 147), it is incorrect to speak of Calvin developing a 'system' in the strict sense of the term. His religious ideas, as presented in the 1559 *Institutes*, are *systematically arranged*, on the basis of pedagogical considerations; they are not, however, *systematically derived* on the basis of a leading speculative principle.[44] Calvin knows nothing of any fundamental methodological distinction between biblical exposition and systematic theology which would become characteristic of later Reformed thought.

In the period after his death, however, a new concern for method gained momentum. Reformed theologians, the heirs to Calvin's religious ideas, found themselves under increasing pressure to defend their ideas against both their Lutheran and their Roman

Catholic opponents. So significant was this struggle that theologians such as Théodore de Bèze, Lambert Daneau, Pietro Martire Vermigli and Giralmo Zanchi were prepared to use every weapon at their disposal in order to ensure at least their survival, if not an outright victory, in the face of such opposition. Reason, regarded with a certain degree of suspicion by Calvin, was now seized upon as an ally.[45] It became increasingly important to demonstrate the internal consistency and coherence of Calvinism. As a result, many Calvinist writers turned to later Renaissance writings on method, in the hope that this might offer hints as to how their theology might be placed upon a firmer rational foundation.

Four characteristics of this new approach to theology may be discerned.[46] First, Christian theology is presented as a logically coherent and rationally defensible system, derived from syllogistic deductions based upon known axioms. Second, human reason is assigned a major role in the exploration and defence of Christian theology. Third, theology is understood to be grounded upon Aristotelian philosophy, and particularly Aristotelian insights into the nature of method; later Reformed writers are better described as philosophical, rather than biblical, theologians. Fourth, theology is concerned with metaphysical and speculative questions, especially relating to the nature of God, his will for humanity and creation, and above all the doctrine of predestination.

But how did this happen? How did a movement initially opposed to scholasticism in general, and Aristotelianism in particular, come to develop an Aristotelian scholasticism so soon after the death of its founder? And why did such emphasis come to be placed upon the doctrine of predestination? To explore these questions, it is necessary to consider the theories of method drawn upon by Calvinist writers such as de Bèze and Zanchi.

Throughout the later Renaissance, the university of Padua stood out from the remainder of humanism as a stronghold of Aristotelianism; this was not, however, the Aristotle of the medieval scholastics, concerned primarily with metaphysical matters, but an Aristotle concerned with questions of method.[47] For writers of the Paduan school, culminating in Giacomo Zabarella (1532–89), it was possible to develop a universal method, applicable in principle to every science; this method was, in principle, to be identified with logic.[48] It was inevitable that Aristotelian logic, with its pronounced emphasis upon the role of syllogisms, would thus become of major importance. If theology was a science, as the majority of its later sixteenth-century practitioners believed to be the case, it should, in theory, be capable of conforming to the general rules of method laid down for all disciplines by the Paduan school. Thus in his inaugural lecture at Heidelberg, Zanchi stressed that theology must be able to lay its foundations and establish its principles with as much care as, if not more than, logic or mathematics.[49]

By the 1560s, Aristotelianism was established widely throughout the universities of Europe, including many major centres hitherto associated with the Reformation. Philip Melanchthon had introduced Aristotle to the curriculum at Wittenberg, as de Bèze had at Geneva.[50] Possible rivals – such as the system of Pierre Ramus – had been eliminated. Lutheran universities, however, were generally reluctant to readmit Aristotle; it was only by the second decade of the seventeenth century that Aristotelianism became acceptable at these centres.

The impact of Aristotle upon later sixteenth-century Reformed theology is evident: formal deductive syllogisms are to be found everywhere, especially in the writings of Zanchi. The starting point of theology is general principles, not a specific historical event.[51] It may, however, be stressed that these general principles are not to be understood as purely rational; rather, they are the deliverances of divine revelation. It is this development which allows us to understand the new importance which came to be attached to the doctrine of predestination.

Where Calvin adopts an inductive and analytic approach to theology, focusing upon the specific historical event of Jesus Christ and moving out to explore its implications,[52] de Bèze adopts a deductive and synthetic approach, beginning from general principles and proceeding to deduce their consequences for Christian theology.[53] (It is possible that de Bèze derived these ideas directly from the writings of the Paduan Aristotelian Pietro Pomponazzi;[54] nevertheless, the possibility that this Paduan methodology may have been mediated through Vermigli or Zanchi remains open.) These general principles – the divine decrees – are determined with reference to the doctrine of predestination, which thus assumes the status of a controlling principle, affecting the location and discussion of doctrines as diverse as that of the Trinity, of the two natures of Christ, of justification by faith, and of the nature of the sacraments.[55] The actuality of predestination is taken to imply a divine decision or decree to predestine; and it is this divine decree of predestination which adopts a leading position within the context of de Bèze's doctrine of God. (It is interesting to note that Calvin treats predestination as an incidental aspect of the doctrine of salvation, where de Bèze follows Thomas Aquinas in making it an aspect of the doctrine of God.) De Bèze stresses that the divine decrees are not speculative construction of the human imagination, but are to be derived from scripture; the manner in which they are to be derived, however, involves treating scripture as a set of propositions from which the divine decrees may be deduced, rather than a witness to the central event of Jesus Christ, from which the nature of predestination may be inferred.

The centrality of the doctrine of predestination may be appreciated by considering de Bèze's celebrated *ordo rerum decretarum*, which arranges in the form of a chart his understanding of the nature and execution of the divine decrees of election (Figure 10.2). Everything in the history of salvation is shown to be the logical execution in time of the 'eternal and immutable purpose of God' (*propositum eius aeternum et immutabile*).

One major consequence of this development may be noted. For whom did Christ die? The question had been raised in the great predestinarian controversy of the ninth century, in which the Benedictine monk Godescalc of Orbais developed a doctrine of double predestination similar to that later to be associated with Calvin and his followers.[56] Pursuing with relentless logic the implications of his assertion that God has predestined some to eternal damnation, Godescalc pointed out that it was thus quite improper to speak of Christ dying for such individuals; if he had, he would have died in vain, for their fate would be unaffected. Hesitant over the implications of this assertion, Godescalc proposed that Christ died *only for the elect*. The scope of his redeeming work was limited to those who were predestined to benefit from his death. Most ninth-century writers reacted with disbelief to this assertion. It was, however, to resurface in later Calvinism.

An examination of de Bèze's 'description and distribution of the causes of the salvation of the elect and of the destruction of the reprobate' brings out the point at issue. It is only the elect who benefit from Christ's death. Indeed, Christ is only to be found on the left-hand side of the chart, dealing with the fate of the elect; there is no mention of him on the right-hand side, outlining the progress of the reprobate towards eternal death. Although Vermigli and Zanchi fail to provide their readers with graphic diagrams by which they may trace their route to salvation, their published works bear abundant witness to the same point: only the elect

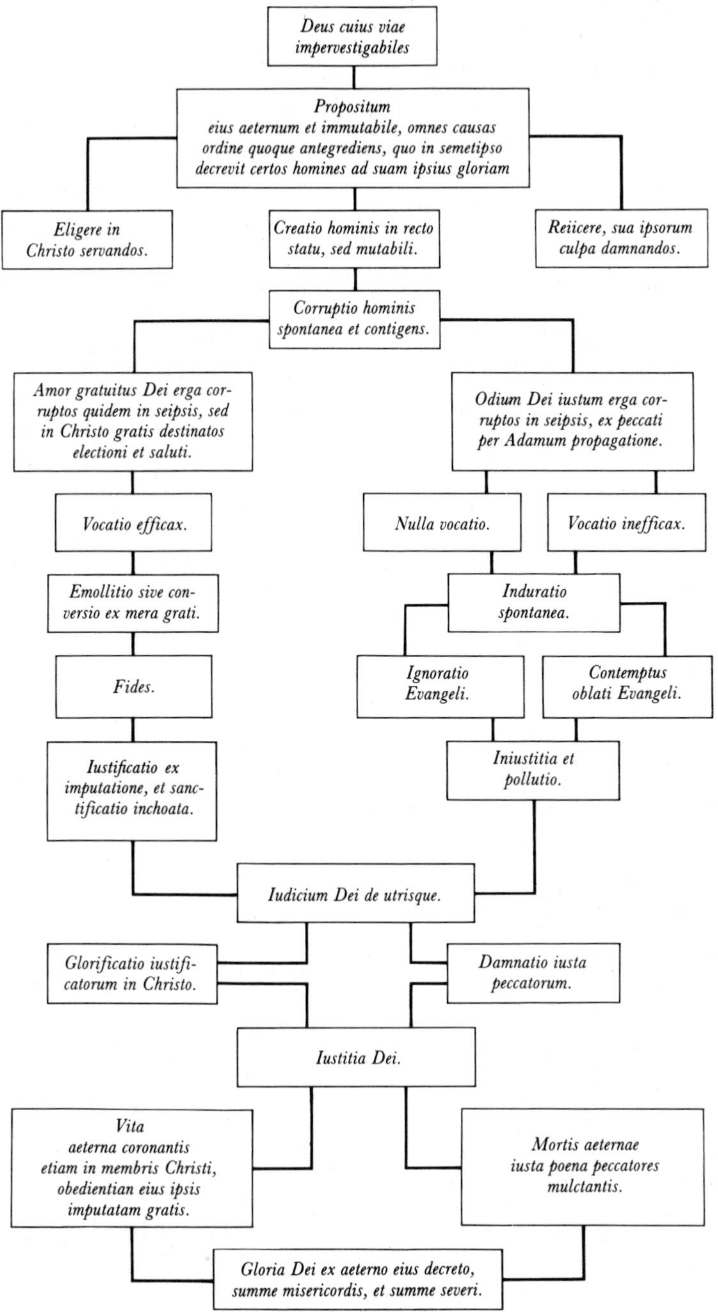

FIGURE 10.2 Théodore de Bèze's diagram representing the logical sequence of human redemption, showing the divine decrees of election

may expect to benefit from the incarnation, death and resurrection of Jesus Christ.[57] It may be stressed that at no point does Calvin himself suggest that Christ died only for the elect; the Calvinist doctrine of limited atonement appears to result, at least in part, from the influence of these two Italian writers and the growing awareness of the need to tie up theological loose ends. This serves to remind us of the variety of sources upon which Calvinism felt able to draw, and the subtlety of its relationship with Calvin himself.

The doctrine of absolute double predestination, and its logical corollary of limited atonement, divided Calvinism into two warring factions, particularly in the Low Countries. Arminius argued vehemently, on both pastoral and methodological grounds, for the modification of the Bezan understanding of the nature and function of predestination. His comments are of particular importance, in that they point to his recognition of the role of methodological considerations in shaping attitudes to predestination. For Arminius, the Bezan approach to theology via predestination is the result of the application of a deductive and synthetic method; the correct theological method, he argues, is inductive and analytic:

> It has long been a maxim with those philosophers who are the masters of method and order, that the theoretical sciences ought to be delivered in a synthetical manner [*ordine compositivo*], but the practical in an analytical order [*vero resolutivo*], on which account, and because theology is a practical science, it follows that it must be treated according to the analytical method [*methodo resolutiva*]. [58]

For Arminius, to treat theology as a theoretical science – which is the procedure of de Bèze, following Zabarella – is quite improper.

A similar reaction against the Bezan doctrine of predestination may be discerned within the French Protestant Academy of Saumur in the seventeenth century, again for methodological reasons. Under the influence of de Bèze, Aristotelian syllogistic logic became an essential component of the curriculum of the Genevan Academy.[59] De Bèze's refusal to allow Pierre Ramus a teaching position at the academy was based upon his hostility towards Ramus' anti-Aristotelian programme, evident in his logic. Although the Genevan Aristotelian pattern was adopted by many Reformed academies throughout Europe, Ramus' logic was taught at the Protestant Academy of Saumur – and on the basis of this logic, which declined to deduce the particular from the general, the later Salmurian academicians, such as Moses Amyraut, challenged the foundations of the orthodox doctrine of predestination.[60] Underlying both these challenges to this doctrine, as developed by de Bèze, was a critique of the methodological presuppositions, inherited from the Paduan school, on which it was perceived to be based.

The Remonstrants, a party sympathetic to the views of Arminius, argued that Christ had died for all, and fully merited their salvation; yet only those who believe in him receive the benefit of salvation.[61] In other words, Christ died for all, in such a manner that his death was sufficient and efficacious for any who chose to respond to him in faith. The doctrine of predestination was reinterpreted to refer to a general principle of fidelity; God has predestined any who turn to Christ in faith to receive salvation. For the majority, however, predestination had a specifically individual reference; it was the divine decision to elect a given person to life or death.[62]

The Synod of Dort (1618–19) met to settle the divisions within the Reformed church in the Low Countries arising from disagreement over the doctrine of predestination and limited atonement.[63] The outcome is generally regarded as a victory for the Bezan school. Although the Netherlands had yet to establish its reputation as a centre for the cultivation of tulips, the English-speaking world may have anticipated this development. The 'Five Points' of the Synod can be summarized thus in the TULIP mnemonic:

T – total depravity of human nature.
U – unconditional election of the individual.
L – limited atonement: Christ died only for the elect.
I – irresistable grace: God is able to effect what he wills.
P – perseverance of the saints: those whom God elects will not defect from their calling.

In noting that these views are not identical with those of Calvin, we are not suggesting that later Calvinism distorted the views of its founder. Rather, we are drawing attention to the variety of sources upon which later Calvinism felt able to draw. It is historically inept to suggest that Calvinism was simply the appropriation of Calvin's heritage; other writers, such as Vermigli and Zanchi, were appropriated in addition. Later Calvinism is a complex amalgam of elements deriving from a number of sources, of which Calvin is but one. The received view of Calvinism may be that of a movement which drew solely upon Calvin, contenting itself with the reiteration of his doctrines; the intellectual historian, however, knows of a very different phenomenon – a dynamic and creative movement, sensitive to the latest developments in intellectual circles, which drew upon the doctrines of Reformed writers other than Calvin and appropriated (it is not clear whether directly from writers such as Pomponazzi or indirectly through writers such as Zanchi) notions of system, method and reasoning apparently unknown to Calvin, in the interests of developing a coherent system of Christian doctrine.[64]

The general theme of predestination, which received such emphasis within later Calvinism, may appear to be utterly irrelevant to the business and concerns of this world. How, it might reasonably be asked, could such an abstract and intangible notion have any bearing upon mundane affairs? Such an obsession with predestination might seem to lead to a lack of interest in and engagement with the present world, in favour of an obsession with the mysterious mechanics of eternity. In fact, however, the Calvinist notion of predestination served to shape attitudes to everyday life which appear to have been of considerable social and economic importance. It is possible that Calvin's doctrine of predestination, as modified by his successors, may be responsible, at least in part, for the generation of outlooks upon work which are of decisive importance for an understanding of the nature and purpose of human labour, and may well have been implicated in the genesis of modern capitalism. It is this subtle interaction of religious, social and economic attitudes which is the substance of the following chapter.

11

Commitment to the World: Calvinism, Work and Capitalism

THE SIXTEENTH century scholar Roland H. Bainton remarked that, when Christianity takes itself seriously, it must either renounce or master the world.[1] Both these stances can be illustrated from the great upheaval which was the European Reformation. Many of the radical reformers rejected the coercive structures of contemporary society, refusing to swear oaths, hold any magisterial office, serve in any military capacity, or even bear arms.[2] Such a radically apolitical and world-renouncing attitude inevitably entailed separation from the world. Perhaps with the pre-Constantinian church – which existed within, but not as part of, the Roman Empire – as a model, the radicals often conceived of their communities as an 'alternative society' within, but not part of, the greater society which surrounded them.

The contrast with Calvinism could not be more marked. If any religious movement of the sixteenth century was world-affirming, it was Calvinism. Yet Calvinism affirmed the world in order to master it, addressing its specific situations rather than luxuriating in abstract speculation. Time and time again, in both his theology and his spirituality, Calvin refuses to indulge in easy generalizations or abstractions. In a highly perceptive comparison of Karl Barth's *Church Dogmatics* and Anthony Trollope's *Doctor Wortle's School*, Stanley Hauerwas points to the peculiarly abstract character of Barth's ethics, which lends his account of the moral life an aura of unreality; this abstractness is made all the more evident through the comparison with Trollope's concreteness, in that his account of morality is grounded in individual persons and societies, rather than impersonal principles.[3] In short, Barth's ethical thought is not adequately grounded in the realities of human existence.

This weakness is conspicuously absent from Calvin. Throughout his writings, we find a determination to engage with the objective social existence of human beings, along with the problems and possibilities this brings with it. It seems that Calvin learned in Strasbourg the lessons which Reinhold Niebuhr learned in downtown Detroit during the 1920s. In his *Leaves from the Notebook of a Tamed Cynic* (1929), Niebuhr wrote:

> If a minister wants to be a man among men he need only stop creating a devotion to abstract ideals which everyone accepts in theory and denies in practice, and to agonize about their validity and practicability in the social issues which he and others face in our present civilization. That immediately gives his ministry a touch of reality and potency.

Precisely this pattern stands out in Calvin's spiritual and homiletic writings. Calvin addresses real and specific human situations – social, political and economic – with all the risks that this precision entails. Even his analysis of anxiety – a major element of sixteenth-century thought[4] – led his followers to regard the overcoming of anxiety as a specifically worldly, rather than other-worldly, activity.[5] It is perfectly fair to describe Calvin's thought as 'theology anti-theological',[6] providing this is understood not to entail the *absence* of a theology, but to highlight the distinctly world-affirming and anti-speculative trajectory of his ideas. Calvin's 'secularization of holiness' (Henri Hauser) involved bringing the entire sphere of human existence within the scope of divine sanctification and human dedication. It is this sanctification of life, of which the sanctification of work is the chief pillar, which stamped its impression upon Calvin's followers.

As we shall see, his heirs shared and benefited from this relentless drive to relate theory and practice. It has often been noted that an extreme preoccupation with worldly means dominates the writings of Théodore de Bèze, lending them a curiously non-religious tone; however, it is easily demonstrated that this preoccupation itself stems directly from de Bèze's world-affirming theology.[7] The political philosopher Leo Strauss has suggested that the later Calvinist involvement in worldly affairs represented a subsequent development of Calvin's thought, a 'carnal interpretation of a spiritual teaching'.[8] This is untenable; Calvin's theology is itself radically orientated towards worldly action,[9] a tendency which was developed and placed on a more rigorous ideological foundation by his successors. The Calvinist propensity for resolute activity in the secular realm is nourished and informed by deep theological springs, too easily overlooked by the historian.

Yet a note of caution must be entered. Those who seem to master the world are often those who have been mastered by it. Those Christians who are judged to be successes in the world are all too often those Christians who have capitulated to the standards of the world. The strongly affirmative attitude which undergirds the Calvinist outlook on life is perennially vulnerable; the delicate balance between church and world can too easily be disturbed, leading to their radical separation on the one hand, or – and herein the greater danger was perceived to lie – their coalescing on the other. For latent within Calvinism is a purely profane approach to life, in that the failure to maintain a proper dialectic between God and the world leads to the collapse of the divine into the secular. Calvinist moral, economic, social and political structures and values, although firmly *grounded* in theology, could easily become detached from those theological foundations, and maintain an independent existence. The emancipation of such structures and values from faith itself through a process of cultural erosion is one of the most significant aspects of the western reception and assimilation of Calvinism, especially in North America.

Calvin himself constructed a sophisticated dialectic between faith and the world which allowed scope for positive action within the world while identifying and averting the risks which this entailed.[10] The form of life which is most praiseworthy in the sight of God is that which is useful to society: 'however much we may admire celibacy or a philosophical life cut off from everyday life', the persons best fitted to govern church and society alike are those who have immersed themselves in the experience and practice of everyday life.[11] Christians are encouraged, even required, to invest in and commit themselves to the world. There is no place in Calvin's thought for the medieval monastic attitude towards society, which led to the situation in which individuals renounced the world, while the institutions which they served affirmed it (*Institutes* III.xi.3–4). Yet the Christian, while immersing himself or herself in the affairs and anxieties of the world, must learn to keep it at a critical distance. Outward investment in and commitment to the world must be accompanied by inward detachment and the fostering of a critical attitude towards the secular. Believers must actively immerse themselves in the secular sphere, without passively allowing themselves to be submerged by it. 'We are to learn to pass through this world as though it were a foreign country, treating lightly all earthly things and declining to set our hearts upon them.'[12]

With such an attitude, it is only to be expected that Calvinism would develop theories of society, capital and political authority of potentially the same calibre and comprehensiveness as its religious system. Our attention is thus claimed by the broad theme 'Calvinism and capitalism', which neatly summarizes the perceived economic importance of this movement. Calvinism, it is widely believed, is capitalism-friendly. Before beginning a sustained analysis of the origins and specific character of the attitudes of Calvin and his heirs to capitalism, it is appropriate to introduce the theory which has dominated scholarly discussion of this theme – the Weber thesis.

The Weber Thesis

In *Das Kapital*, Karl Marx declared that the origins of capitalism were to be located in the sixteenth century. Amintoni Fanfani, giving vent to his intense dislike of both Protestantism and capitalism, argued that medieval catholicism was radically and inalienably anti-capitalist.[13] A more historically informed approach negates these assertions. The operations of medieval financial institutions, such as the Medicis or the Fuggers, are clear evidence of capitalist assumptions and methods in the period prior to the Reformation. On the eve of the Reformation, cities such as Antwerp, Augsburg, Liège, Lisbon, Lucca and Milan were all heirs to capitalism in its medieval forms. Nor can the religious importance of capitalism prior to the Reformation be ignored: the ability of the Medici family to purchase outright the papacy, and that of the Fuggers to control virtually every episcopal appointment of importance in Germany, Poland and Hungary (while financing the election of Charles V as emperor) points to the importance of capitalism as a religious force on the eve of the Reformation. The pope (Leo X) who excommunicated Luther in 1520 was a Medici who had liquidated his bank in order to gain the papacy. The pioneering studies of Raymond de Roover – an accountant turned medieval historian – demonstrated that capitalist assumptions and methods were deeply ingrained within medieval society as a whole,[14] and not merely in the purchase of ecclesiastical appointments. More recent studies have confirmed that capitalism was an integral part of medieval life, both social and intellectual.[15] To suggest, though, that capitalism was the invention of, or is somehow due to, Protestantism is clearly absurd.

Weber made no such suggestion. The popular version of the Weber thesis – that capitalism is a direct consequence of the Protestant Reformation – is as historically untenable as it is alien to Weber's stated aims. Weber stressed that he had 'no intention whatsoever of maintaining such a foolish and doctrinaire thesis as that the spirit of capitalism . . . could only have arisen as a result of certain effects of the Reformation. In itself, the fact that certain important forms of capitalistic business organizations are known to be considerably older than the Reformation is a sufficient refutation of such a claim.'[16] The Weber thesis is considerably more subtle and merits closer attention.

Weber argued that capitalism existed long before the Reformation.[17] A lust after wealth or possessions is as characteristic of the medieval merchant princes as it is of traditional peasant societies. What requires to be explained is a new 'spirit of capitalism', which Weber detected emerging in the early modern period. It is not so much *capitalism* as *modern* capitalism which Weber regarded as requiring explanation. He identified the characteristics of 'modern capitalism' by comparing it with what he called the 'adventurer capitalism' of the medieval period. Adventurer capitalism, he argued, was opportunistic and unscrupulous; it tended to consume its capital gains in flamboyant and decadent lifestyles. Modern capitalism, however, was rational, possessing a strong ethical basis; it practised personal asceticism in respect to the use of material goods. Modern capitalism, he argued (although the evidence adduced to support his statements is dangerously flimsy),[18] was devoid of hedonism, almost to the point of deliberately avoiding the direct enjoyment of life. How, Weber asked, could such a dramatic turnabout be explained?

A religious explanation seemed to be implicated. Weber noted that, although medieval society tolerated money-making activities, they were nevertheless generally regarded as unethical. Basing his analysis on fourteenth- and fifteenth-century Florence, with occasional appeals to the history of the Fuggers' banking house at Augsburg, Weber noted the perceived tension between the accumulation of capital on the one hand, and the salvation of the souls of those who accumulated it on the other. Jakob Fugger, for example, was aware of a serious divergence between his banking activities and those actions which were traditionally regarded by the catholic church as conducive to attaining salvation.

With the rise of ascetic Protestantism, however, a new attitude towards the accumulation of capital developed. Weber saw this attitude particularly well illustrated by a number of seventeenth- and eighteenth-century Calvinist writers such as Benjamin Franklin, whose writings combined commendation of the accumulation of capital through engagement with the world, while criticizing its consumption. Capital was to be increased, not consumed. Christopher Hill summarizes thus the difference between Protestant and catholic attitudes: 'Successful medieval businessmen died with feelings of guilt, and left money to the church to be put to unproductive uses. Successful Protestant businessmen were no longer ashamed of their productive activities whilst alive, and at death left money to help others to imitate them.'[19] Protestantism, then, generated the psychological preconditions essential to the development of modern capitalism. Indeed, it is fair to suggest that Weber located the fundamental contribution of Calvinism as lying in its generation of psychological impulses on account of its belief-systems. He laid especial stress upon the notion of 'calling', which he linked with the Calvinist idea of predestination.[20] The Calvinist could find assurance of his salvation in a manner impossible for his catholic contemporary, though engaging in worldly activity. Providing capital was not obtained by unacceptable means nor consumed in a profligate manner, its generation and accumulation were devoid of moral difficulties.

The importance of the emergence of modern capitalism is of such magnitude to the shaping of western civilization that, if a link with John Calvin can be established, the reformer may be credited – for better or worse – with the instigation of a fundamental impulse of the modern world.

But can he? Is there such a link? Weber's analysis relates primarily to the seventeenth century. The chief witnesses to Weber's case – John Bunyan and Richard Baxter – were English Calvinists, writing a century after Calvin's death within a totally different social context.[21] Can one trace continuity between Calvin and the attitudes of later Calvinists, which – if Weber is right – accounts for the origins of modern capitalism? This question leads us to investigate Calvin's attitude to capitalism, and trace its transformation in the writings of his later followers.

Early Genevan Capitalism

Many early sixteenth-century cities witnessed serious internal division arising from tensions between the established patriciate, whose social position rested upon a mingling of such factors as tradition, inertia, inherited wealth and political structures which favoured the status quo, and the rising mercantile and artisan classes, who felt that their moment had come. To give but one example, the Reformation struggle at Zurich may be viewed in the light of this tension between the tradition-bound forces of the patriciate and the new power of the economically and politically progressive artisans.[22] This observation raises an important question: might there not be a case for suggesting that the Reformation and capitalism had a common appeal to the emerging urban elites?

If this is the case, it becomes pointless to speak of Protestantism 'causing' a new spirit of capitalism. A specific social stratum with a predisposition towards the form of economic dynamism which Weber designates 'modern capitalism' may have regarded adopting the Reformation as a means of furthering their political and economic ends. In other words, there may be an historically contingent association between capitalism and Protestantism of such a nature that one cannot speak of the latter causing the former; rather, both may have been associated with shifts within the power structures of urban society in the early modern period. Capitalism and Protestantism appear to have been regarded as possessing economic and religious affinities with the rising artisan and mercantile urban classes, allowing them a degree of self-expression and fulfilment hitherto unattainable within the matrix of the restricted economic and religious beliefs and practices of the late medieval period.

In turning to consider the case of Geneva, it may be noted that the struggle between the pro-Savoyard Mammelukes and pro-Swiss Eiguenots may be broadly interpreted as a conflict between tradition and progress. The Mammelukes, with long-standing traditional familial links with Savoy, favoured the retention of Geneva's dependency upon the duchy; the Eiguenots generally represented the more progressive faction, who saw their personal political and economic futures as linked with the liberties by then associated with alliance with Swiss cities.[23] The economically dynamic constituents of the city thus saw the development of links with Berne and Fribourg during the 1520s as eminently desirable. At this stage, however, there was no hint of any association with Protestantism; Berne and Fribourg were still both catholic cities. Their appeal lay in their being Swiss, with the economic and political benefits which an alliance seemed to offer. When Berne adopted the Zwinglian Reformation, Protestantism became a religious factor – but not necessarily a *constitutive* factor – in an already complicated economic and political equation.

As we noted earlier, in the year 1535, Geneva finally achieved political liberation from the neighbouring duchy of Savoy, to become an independent Protestant city-state. Religious and political independence were achieved virtually simultaneously, and, through a series of crucial historical contingencies, were seen to be interrelated. Political independence, however, was not without its economic foundations. For Geneva to retain her hard-won independence, it was necessary for her to achieve some degree of economic self-sufficiency. Since the thirteenth century, her economy had been dependent upon her trade fairs, which had gained her international fame.[24] Standing at the junction of several major trade routes, Geneva was able to establish herself as the leading entrepôt of western Europe by the dawn of the fifteenth century. Leading Italian banking families – including the Medici – deemed it worth their while to open branches in the city.[25] By the middle of the century, Geneva was a major centre of what Weber would term 'old-style capitalism'.

As the century progressed, Geneva's situation became less favourable. During the years 1464–6 Italian merchants began to cease attending her fairs in favour of those of neighbouring Lyons.[26] Indeed, an 'economic cold war' (Bruno Caizzi) set in between the two cities. The Italian bankers, sensing the way the wind was blowing, closed their Genevan branches. Although Italian merchants would still frequent Geneva, the loss of the banks and the growing political instability within the city during the period 1520–35 caused it to lose its favoured status as a trading centre.[27] Paradoxically, it was the influx of traders which contributed to that instability: German merchants trading within the city brought with them Lutheran publications, which seem to have found as ready a market as their more customary wares.[28] Although a period of considerable economic expansion may be detected in the years 1518–23, this was soon reversed through political uncertainty. From 1524 to 1534, depression set in.[29] Although compounded by local difficulties, the Genevan situation paralleled similar economic difficulties in the Swiss cities in general.[30]

Deprived of much of its traditional economic role as an entrepôt, the city was faced with a significant challenge to its survival in the year of its independence (1535). An impoverished city locked into a cycle of stagnation and depression could not support itself, let alone strengthen its defences (at considerable cost) against the threat of invasion from predatory states in the vicinity. Although the period 1535–40 saw an economic recession begin in several Swiss cities,[31] Geneva witnessed a remarkable recovery. This was further consolidated during 1540–59, when growing economic activity throughout the region further assisted her recovery.[32] How is this to be accounted for?

In part, the determination of the city to ensure its independence contributed to its economic success.[33] There was a corporate will to retain the freedoms gained in the struggle for independence. Recently, however, attention has been focused on a major contribution to the economic viability of the republic of Geneva in its make-or-break period – the Swiss Protestant financial solidarities.[34] The origins of the modern Swiss banking system, particularly its heavy involvement in international corporate financial ventures, may be traced to the opening of the fourth decade of the sixteenth century. As we saw earlier, a significant contribution to this development was the establishment of *combourgeoisies* between cities of the Helvetic Confederation and other cities: the *combourgeoisie* of 1519 between Lausanne and Berne, and that of 1526 between Geneva and Berne, are particularly important examples of this trend.

Initially, it seems that the primary object of the *combourgeoisies* was to provide political and military support for allied cities in times of need. In the years 1530–1, however, this was extended to include financial support. Zurich faced a political and economic crisis in the aftermath of the First Peace of Cappel. In order to safeguard the integrity of its Protestant ally against its catholic opponents, the city of Basle offered a loan of 14,300 écus to see Zurich through its difficulties. After further reverses in Protestant fortunes within the Helvetic Confederation towards the end of 1531 and the beginning of 1532, the city of Berne was able to raise a loan of 12,750 écus through Basle.[35] The Swiss Wars of Religion in the early 1530s may thus be regarded as marking both the emergence of a financial system capable of sustaining Protestant cities in times of difficulty, and the establishment of

Basle as the centre of that system.

Until Geneva accepted the Reformation, she was not in any position to draw upon such financial resources. From 1536 onwards, however, she was able to draw upon funds at Basle for the purposes of fortification, defence, and so forth. The *trésor de l'Arche* was established in the aftermath of the revolution of 1536 to coordinate confederate loans.[36] Geneva would begin to draw extensively upon other sources of foreign capital from 1567 onwards; by 1590, the city had received some 211,000 écus from various Protestant financial sources in England, France, Germany, Hungary, the Low Countries and the Swiss cities.[37] With access to such funds, Geneva was able to retain economic independence in the face of her catholic neighbours. The creation of new financial institutions within Geneva itself – such as the establishment of the *change public* in 1567[38] – further consolidated the city's potential to survive as an independent entity.

Nevertheless, there was a growing awareness within Geneva of the need to develop independent sources of capital. A note in the city's financial archives for 1551 speaks of the need for Geneva to 'reduce her dependence upon Basle' (*se débasler*). One of the major contributions to this process was the development of manufacturing industries within the city itself, as a source of foreign capital. Although traces of this trend may be discerned in the early 1540s, the most significant period in its evolution appears to overlap with the massive influx of foreign refugees. During the years 1549–60, some 4,776 refugees arrived in Geneva from France; of those, 1,536 are known to have been artisans,[39] doubtless encouraged by the generally anti-aristocratic attitude of the Genevan authorities.[40] Most of the refugees had been engaged in small-scale manufacturing, craftsmanship or trading in their native France, and many had little difficulty in resuming their activities once settled in Geneva.[41]

Some examples may serve to illustrate the growth of manufacturing industries in the city. Within a short period of time, Geneva became a centre for the manufacture of clocks and watches, on account of the arrival of French refugees whose specialities lay in this area.[42] A significant publishing industry developed, along with ancillary industries, such as paper-making and the production of type.[43] The immigration of French families associated with the cloth and drapery trades – such as the Bordiers and the Mallets[44] – led to the growth of these industries at Geneva. The silk industry developed as a substantial export industry, drawing on the expertise of skilled French and Italian refugees and the capital provided by shrewd Italian merchant bankers.[45] The abolition of the old seigneurial ecclesiastical and guild system – in effect, the final secular obstacle to 'modern capitalism' – meant that such newcomers could set up in business and begin manufacturing and trading without serious restrictions.

As a result, an exceptionally high density of skills became concentrated in the city which, linked with the availability of capital, led to it becoming a major centre of the form of economic dynamism which Weber terms 'modern capitalism'. Geneva's fairs, once the distribution point for Italian goods in western Europe, now became the centre of a distribution network for Genevan-manufactured items. As the Swiss economic historian Jean-François Bergier points out, three factors essential to the development of a modern capitalist society – capital, manufacturing skills and capacity, and a distribution network – arose virtually simultaneously within Geneva at this period.[46]

It must, however, be stressed that it is not strictly correct to portray Geneva as a capitalist society in the *modern* sense of the term. If capitalism is to be identified with the system of economic relationships which developed in the wake of the industrial revolution,[47] it is difficult to speak of Geneva as capitalist. For example, the central capitalist maxim of *laissez-faire* was vigorously opposed by the Genevan city council. No commercial activity within the city was immune from central scrutiny and intervention. This can be illustrated from the considerable restrictions imposed at every level upon the printers Henri and François Estienne.[48] Economic transactions were probed by the city council, and subject to a series of severe restrictions. The rigorous control which the council exercised over every aspect of the life of Geneva – moral, economic and political – severely inhibited the development of a fully capitalist society. Sixteenth-century capitalism happens to be rather different from its nineteenth-century descendant; it is capitalism, none the less.

What, then, might the influence of Calvin be upon these developments? In one sense, they appear to be accidental, a mere concatenation of historical circumstances favourable to the development of dynamic capitalism. Genevan capitalism arose and developed in response to factors which were primarily *indirectly* due to the religious ideas of Calvin. For example, the presence of large numbers of economically active immigrants at Geneva in the 1540s and 1550s is clearly due to Calvin's religious ideas, in that these ideas were the cause of their perceived need to emigrate from their native France in the first place, and to settle in Geneva in the second. The importance of such immigrants, irrespective of their religious loyalty, in promoting European capitalism at the time of the Reformation has been stressed by Hugh Trevor-Roper;[49] the importance of Calvin may thus be located, at least in part, in his being a precipitating cause of migration within an economically dynamic stratum of French society.

Equally, the development of the Swiss confessional financial solidarities antedates Calvin; the financial organizations and mechanisms which would contribute significantly to the concentration of capital within the city during the period of Calvin owed nothing to him. Neither can Geneva's decision to accept the Reformation, thus allowing it access to such capital, be put down to Calvin's influence. There are thus excellent reasons for suggesting that the initial association of capitalism and Calvinism is centred upon the city of Geneva itself, which became a focus for both economic and religious activism at more or less the same time. This association is, it must be stressed, largely accidental; there is no necessary historical or ideological connection between them.

Further, it is reasonable to suggest that Geneva's development of a capitalist economy was primarily a consequence of her need to maintain her political independence, initially from Savoy and subsequently from Berne, rather than of her decision to accept the Reformation. In that the historical evolution of the republic of Geneva proceeded in such a manner as to intertwine religious and political developments, the two cannot be totally disentangled. Nevertheless, it is reasonable to suggest that it was the perceived need to maintain Geneva's economic, and hence political, autonomy which fuelled the city's adoption of overtly capitalist strategies, particularly during the 1550s. Religion, although inevitably implicated within this process, was largely of marginal importance.

Nevertheless, it must be conceded that one of the circumstances under which Genevan capitalism flourished was Calvin's benign attitude towards its evolution. A comparison with Luther will bring out one point at issue. Luther's economic outlook – like his social thought in general – is heavily conditioned by the social realities of the unsophisticated rural German territory he set out to reform. It was a world preoccupied with the perennial problems of late feudal rural life, such as the tensions between peasantry and nobility. Although Luther is clearly aware of some of the economic issues of his day – such as whether money should be loaned at interest[50] – he appears to lack awareness of the issues dominating urban finance. He had no conception of the economic forces which were beginning to transform Germany from a feudal nation of peasant agriculturalists into a society with an emergent capitalist economy. In his treatise *Von Kaufshandlung und Wucher*, 'On Trade and Usury', written in the summer of 1524, he tends to adopt a heavily critical attitude towards those engaged in any form of commercial activity. For Luther, the German term *Fynanzte*, far from having a neutral meaning, carried totally negative overtones of fraud, deception and excessive profiteering. The fact that Luther's economic thought – if one can dignify it with such a title – was hostile to any form of capitalism largely reflects his unfamiliarity with the sophisticated world of finance then emerging in the great free cities.

Calvin, however, was perfectly aware of the financial realities at Geneva, and their implications.[51] Although he does not develop an 'economic theory' in any sense of the term, he appears to have been fully cognizant of the basic principles of capital. The productive nature of both capital and human work is fully recognized.[52] The division of labour is praised, both for its economic benefits and for its merits as a means of emphasizing human interdependence and the importance of social existence. The right of individuals to possess property, denied by the radical wing of the Reformation, is upheld. Passages in the book of Deuteronomy, relating to business ethics, are recognized to be located in the social realities of a bygone age: Calvin refuses to let certain injunctions relating to a primitive Jewish agrarian society have binding force upon a progressive modern urban society, such as sixteenth-century Geneva.[53] For example, the absolute prohibition upon lending money at interest (known as usury) is dismissed as an accommodation to the specific needs of primitive Jewish society; there is no similarity between such a society and Geneva. Interest is merely rent paid on capital.[54] Calvin's willingness to allow a variable rate of interest shows an awareness of the pressures upon capital in a more or less free market. The ethical interests served by such a prohibition could in any case be safeguarded by other means. Furthermore, he was aware of the importance of generating new industries through injection of capital, as is evident from his lobbying for a state-sponsored cloth industry in the 1540s.[55]

Calvin's elimination of such religious barriers to capitalism is supplemented by the articulation of a work ethic which strongly encouraged its development. The believer is called to serve God in the world. Calvin's insistence that the individual believer could be called by God to serve him in every sphere of worldly existence lent a new dignity and meaning to work. The world is to be treated with contempt to the extent that it is not God, and is too easily mistaken for God; yet, in that it is the creation of God, it is to be affirmed. 'Let believers get used to a contempt of the present life that gives rise to no hatred of it, or ingratitude towards God' (*Institutes* III.xi.3). 'Something that is neither blessed nor desirable in itself can become something good for the devout' (III.xi.4). Christians are thus to inhabit the world with joy and gratitude, without becoming trapped within it. To use modern existential categories, the world must be seen as our *Spielraum*. A degree of critical detachment must accompany Christian affirmation of the world as God's creation and gift. Christians are to live in the world, while avoiding falling into that world, becoming immersed within and swallowed by it.

Calvin thus treats the notion of the 'contemplative life' with a certain degree of cynicism, insisting that Christian meditation and prayer must take place in the midst of, rather than detached from, the cares and concerns of everyday mundane life (IV.xii.10, 16). The believer is not called to leave the world and enter a monastery, but to enter fully into the life of the world, and thus to transform it. In one sense, this doctrine must be regarded as anti-aristocratic, in that it implicitly censured those who regarded themselves as above manual labour.[56] Calvin cites with approval Paul's dictum, 'If a man will not work, he shall not eat' (1 Thessalonians 3:10). Commentators on his work ethic, perhaps with the unemployment situation of the 1920s in mind, have seen in this a lack of regard for the circumstances of the unemployed. In fact, Calvin's remarks were directed specifically against the aristocracy, including French aristocrats exiled in Geneva, who traditionally regarded themselves as above manual labour.[57] The targets of Calvin's stress upon the dignity of human labour and his critique of indolence are the magnificent courts and possessions of princes of the church and the formidable dead weight of the aristocracy. Despite the fact that Calvin's colleague Théodore de Bèze came from a noble French family, Genevan society had little patience with the archaic social outlook of his class. We possess an intriguing contemporary record of the reactions of the French aristocracy to the fact that former aristocrats who had sought refuge in Geneva were being obliged to work. The French aristocrat Pierre de Bourdeille Brantôme registered his shock on visiting Geneva and seeing the former noble François d'Aubeterre earning his living as *faiseur de boutons*. Why, he asked, should someone from such a noble family have to degrade himself by making buttons? The account illustrates graphically the radically different attitudes towards work in general and manual labour in particular, associated with the old French aristocracy and the new Genevan entrepreneurs.[58] Work, it seems, was the great Genevan social leveller.

While acknowledging that it is impossible to condense Calvin's complex work ethic into a sentence, it is worth noting that Paul's injunction to the Corinthian Christians captures much of its essence: 'Each one should retain the place in life that the Lord assigned to him and to which God has called him' (1 Corinthians 7:17). Each believer is summoned to *une vocation juste et approuvée* (*Institutes* IV.xii.10, 16).[59] Mundane labour became an integral part of Calvin's spirituality,[60] lending a new meaning to the medieval monastic slogan *laborare est orare*, 'to labour is to pray'.[61] Manual labour was not simply the norm at Geneva; it was the religiously sanctioned ideal. For the first time, the ordinary everyday activity of even the most petty producer was given a religious significance. Action in the world was dignified and sanctified. Perhaps the English poet George Herbert might be allowed to express Calvin's insights with more eloquence than the Genevan reformer himself achieved:

> Teach me, my God and King,
> In all things thee to see;
> And what I do in anything
> To do it as for thee.
> A servant with this clause
> Makes drudgery divine;
> Who sweeps a room, as for thy laws,
> Makes that and the action fine.

These attitudes, although not themselves explicitly capitalist, taken collectively can be said to favour the growth of capitalism, particularly in the form historically associated with Geneva. Calvin's contribution may be regarded as functioning at two levels: at one, disincentives (such as the social and religious opprobrium with which the generation of capital was invested in the medieval period) were removed; at the other, positive incentives encouraged the fostering of attitudes and practices favourable to the emergence of capitalism. Bourgeois values – thrift, diligence, perseverance, hard work and dedication – were all religiously sanctioned by Calvin's theories. Capitalism is, however, a spin-off, rather than the intended product, of his religious outlook. (It may be stressed, incidentally, that Weber himself at no point suggested that Calvinism explicitly encouraged the accumulation and reinvestment of capital; rather, he argued that these were unintentionally fostered as a consequence of the Calvinist stress upon diligence in one's calling and this-worldly asceticism).

Yet this religious sanction of a cluster of attitudes conducive to capitalism is of somewhat limited importance in explaining the rise of that phenomenon in the republic of Geneva. Genevan capitalism was born of economic necessity, rather than religious instigation. The very survival of the city was seen to be dependent upon its economy. Political autonomy rested upon economic self-sufficiency. The development of the Genevan economy was primarily due to a more fundamental impulse than even Calvin's powerful religious dynamism – the primitive and perennial human instinct to survive. Calvin may have been implicated in fostering religious and social attitudes generally conducive to the development of some form of capitalism; it was the city of Geneva itself, however, which gave shape and specification to the form that capitalism would take, fleshing out the bare bones of Calvin's somewhat indeterminate attitudes with quite definite proposals, policies and institutions. In effect, Calvin appears to have sanctified existing or emerging Genevan attitudes and institutions, demonstrating yet again the importance of that city in the shaping of the contours of international Calvinism.

The economic attitudes commended by Calvin were not, however, merely capitalism-friendly; they were also radically anti-feudal. It is this aspect of Calvin's thought which goes some considerable way towards explaining its influence in France – to which we now turn.

Calvinism and Capitalism: The Case of France

The strongholds of Calvinism within France in the 1550s lay in the cities, and supremely among the skilled craftsmen and merchants of the urban populations. It is certainly true that there was support for Calvin's programme of reform among members of the French aristocracy; however, on closer inspection these aristocrats often turn out to be merchants who acquired the titles and lifestyles of the nobility late in their careers. The barons of Anduze and Barroux, for example, both major supporters of Calvin's Reformation, had been merchants until 1535 and 1545 respectively.[62] Thus the aristocracy who favoured the cause of reform tended to be 'new' rather than 'old' nobility (although this subtle differentiation is distinctly vulnerable). They were often men who had risen from the ranks of the bourgeoisie. Yet the bulk of Calvin's support came from artisans – a varied and heterogeneous social class including journeymen, shopkeepers, apprentices, merchant manufacturers and rural craftsmen. Florimond de Raemond, a catholic convert to Calvinism who subsequently reverted to his former religion, wrote scathingly of the 'goldsmiths, masons, carpenters and other miserable wage-earners, who became excellent theologians overnight'. Detailed analysis of those arraigned for heresy in France during the period 1540–60 has demonstrated that the vast bulk – perhaps as many as 70 per cent – were often drawn from this social stratum.[63] In part, this reflects the widespread perception that the French catholic church was aristocratic in its leadership and concerns (see pp. 9–10), without any real connection with or concern for the restless lower classes. Many members of the third estate were anti-clerical in their outlook at this time, yet declined to express this by adopting Calvinism. Their hopes appear to have rested in a reform of the French church. The Calvinist parties in the cities of France may be regarded as the tip of a very large anti-clerical iceberg.

More significantly, however, the artisans represented an embryonic middle class, whose values and aspirations were lent dignity and religious value through Calvin's religious ideas, and whose economic future seemed to lie with the adoption of economically dynamic policies, such as those then associated with the city of Geneva. Within a society still influenced by feudalism, dominated by a church whose social vision lay firmly in the past, the new ideas emanating from Geneva were viewed as progressive and liberating. Capitalism seemed to hold the key to the liberation of the French economy, and with it the emancipation of *les petits gens* for whom Calvinism had such an attraction.

The contemporary appeal of such policies within France can be seen in Bernard Palissy's *Recepte véritable*, which laid down policies which would transform French agriculture and avert food crises similar to those which had plagued France earlier in the sixteenth century.[64] A study of wheat prices at Paris between 1560 and 1580 indicates the frequency with which crises occurred during the period. Apart from advocating the merits of scientific manuring, Palissy identified a central problem underlying France's economic malaise in general, and its agriculture in particular: agriculture was so underdeveloped and under-resourced that it could not sustain an expansion of the secondary sector. It was only through the capitalization of agriculture that the situation could be changed.[65] Agricultural investment and increases in productivity were the solution to a problem which arose from a failure to make proper use of the land and its resources. Land was regarded as a convenient source of rent, rather than a commodity which was susceptible to intensive exploitation. Capital existed within France; it was, however, put to non-productive uses. Furthermore, a new attitude to work on the land was needed. Work was not something to be left to peasants; to work was the allotted role of the bourgeoisie, the land-possessing class, as well.

The importance of Palissy's work lies in its evident endorsement of financial measures and a work ethic already associated with Geneva. It also points to a quite definite economic, as much as religious or social, element within the appeal of Calvinism to French artisans. Not merely was Calvinism perceived to be anti-aristocratic and hostile to the French ecclesiastical establishment; it was seen to possess policies which, if implemented in France, might transform the French economy.

The French artisans – a large and amorphous group who might be described as the 'makers and doers' of sixteenth-century France – thus seem to have discerned in Calvinism a belief-system which endorsed and legitimized the values and aspirations of the productive classes in French society. Their present situation and future prospects were radically restricted by the French seigneurial– ecclesiastical establishment, which placed barriers to their economic and social progress. Geneva had dismantled such an establishment in the revolution of 1535 and opened the way to the emancipation of this social class. Calvin's role in this development was peripheral; nevertheless, Geneva's religious, political and economic systems in the 1550s and 1560s were generally regarded as a unity by those who looked from France with envy and, unwilling to leave and seek refuge within Geneva, sought to establish her values within their own sphere of influence. The appeal of Calvinism to France is undoubtedly due in part to Calvin's religious ideas; but it was also due to the new political and economic order ushered in by the Genevan revolution of 1535 – an order which, it must be noted, owed virtually nothing to the ideas and actions of Calvin, yet was generally regarded as an integral part of Calvinism by those viewing it from afar. It is reasonable to suggest that the theme 'Calvinism and capitalism' is actually an historically contingent amalgam of Calvin's religious attitudes and existing Genevan economic policies and institutions. Calvin and Geneva tended to coalesce in the public imagination, with 'Calvinism' thus including significant economic (not to mention political) elements which were Genevan, rather than Calvinian, in origin.

The Calvinist Work Ethic and Capitalism

Capitalism and Calvinism were virtually coextensive by the middle of the seventeenth century. It is this phenomenon which has attracted such attention on the part of social theorists. To give but one example: Flanders – hitherto culturally homogeneous – was torn apart by Protestant revolt and Spanish catholic reconquest. For two hundred years, the Protestant zone was bustling and prosperous, and the catholic area depressed and unproductive. Even in catholic countries – such as France or Austria – it was Calvinists who developed their industrial and capital potential. It was not Protestants in general, but Calvinists in particular, who developed capitalism. When the two great early seventeenth-century champions of Lutheranism, Christian IV of Denmark and Gustavus Adolphus of Sweden, wished to mobilize the financial and industrial resources of their respective countries, they turned to Dutch Calvinists for help; so successful was the outcome that a Dutch Calvinist capitalist aristocracy was soon established in Scandinavia.[66] Countless other examples might be given: between northern and southern Europe, between the north and south of Ireland, or the two Americas. Where Calvinism flourished, there too did capitalism.

In part, the appeal of Weber's thesis lies in its obvious consonance with the observable. The demonstrable affinity of Calvinism and capitalism functions as a premise, rather than a conclusion, in Weber's analysis. It is something which requires to be explained, rather than to be demonstrated. There is little doubt that the economic elite of early seventeenth-century Europe – in both catholic and Protestant countries – was Calvinist. It seemed that Calvinism alone was able to mobilize industry and finance, and inject a vital impulse into the commercial life of cities and nations.

The suggestion that Calvinism somehow caused – however remotely – the development of conditions under which capitalism might flourish is clearly highly plausible. It is, however, the *religious* explanation of this tendency which raises difficulties for the theologian. To put it pointedly, it is difficult for a Christian theologian, familiar with the religious thought of the period, to discern the close connection between Calvinist spirituality and the 'spirit of modern capitalism' which Weber detects.

If there is any serious criticism which may be directed against the vast body of literature dealing with the relation of Calvinism and capitalism, it is that it is generally the work of writers who lack the necessary *theological* equipment to appreciate the implications of certain religious doctrines and attitudes. Weber himself exemplifies this difficulty: throughout his writings, he tends to slip haphazardly, in discussion, from the 'capitalist mentality' to the Calvinist doctrine of 'calling'. The link between the two is frequently asserted, rarely clarified, and never justified at a *theoretical* level. The new *emphasis* placed upon divine predestination by Calvin's followers has often been misunderstood as a new *doctrine* in itself, as if the idea of divine election were a theological novelty unknown before the Reformation – and even then, only within a section of Protestantism. As we have seen (pp. 208–18), the centrality accorded to questions relating to 'calling' – such as predestination, election and providence – within later Calvinist thought reflects both a new concern for theological systematization and method (to allow the development of a system at least as watertight as those of Roman Catholic theologians such as Thomas Aquinas) and a recognition of the need to distinguish Calvinism as a social entity from Lutheranism (which adopted a somewhat different stance on this specific matter), on account of the rivalry between the two movements in Germany (see pp. 209–11). Herbert Lüthy has rightly complained of the tendency of historians to 'plunge headlong into crude attempts to psychoanalyse the Calvinist concept of predestination as a path to success',[67] isolating the specifically Calvinist notion from its theological matrix in the late medieval and early Reformation periods. Calvin's doctrine of double predestination has its roots in an Augustinian renaissance of the fourteenth century,[68] and cannot be regarded as a theological novelty which is somehow linked with the development of the 'spirit of modern capitalism'. Gregory of Rimini and Hugolino of Orvieto – to note but two fourteenth-century theologians who vigorously defended a doctrine of double predestination as rigorous as that of Calvin – show no obvious inclination to economic activism or protocapitalist attitudes as a result of their predestinarianism.

Furthermore, Weber fails to distinguish the different levels of Calvinist commitment to the doctrine of absolute double predestination. The Arminians virtually abandoned the idea (pp. 216–17), while orthodox Calvinism retained it, even to the point of strengthening it. Yet it was Arminian Amsterdam which created the remarkable wealth of the United Provinces, while Calvinist Gelderland remained economically backward. Weber's theory clearly suggests the reverse should have occurred.

It is important to examine in more detail the notion of a 'work ethic', upon which Weber places such interpretative weight. The origins of the Calvinist work ethic are simultaneously pastoral and theological. One of the central questions debated within the early Reformation concerned the relation between divine grace and human moral action. Was God's grace conditional upon prior human action or merit? And if grace was prior to human actions, how could the threat of 'antinomianism' – spiritual anarchism, for want of a better term – be avoided? How could the gift character of grace be upheld without snapping the vital link between grace and the human moral response?

The early Reformation period witnessed the generation of a consensus upon this point, to which Calvin was heir.[69] God's grace was an unconditional gift, prior to and independent of any human work or merit. Nevertheless, grace possessed a transformational dimension, an ability to work within its recipient. To receive grace is to be renewed by grace. An essential part of that process of renewal and regeneration (which, by Calvin's time, had become known as 'sanctification') was the motivation and empowering of the believer to perform good works. Good works were seen as the outward and visible sign of the presence and activity of grace within the believer.

Calvin, like Luther before him, stresses the utter gratuity of grace. Grace is a gift, not a reward. It is not something which God is under any obligation to give. Its gift reflects his generosity, rather than any obligation upon his part. Grace is only given to some, not to all. The doctrine of predestination, according to Calvin, serves to emphasize the gift character of grace (*Institutes* III.xxi.1):

> We shall never be clearly persuaded (as we should be) that our salvation flows from the spring of the mercy of God until we come

> to know his eternal election. This casts light on the grace of God, by contrasting the fact that he does not indiscriminately adopt everyone into the hope of salvation, but gives to some what he denies to others.

Grace, in other words, is only given to the elect. This being the case, an obvious question arises. How can anyone know whether he or she is among the elect? Given that grace is invisible and beyond human detection, may its presence be discerned by its effects?

Although Weber argued that Calvin did not regard such questions as problematical, the evidence suggests quite the reverse. A struggle with unbelief, Calvin suggested, was a permanent feature of the Christian life (*Institutes* III.ii.17–18). Although he indicated certain theological or spiritual means by which such doubts may be countered – for example, by looking to the promises of God as they are revealed and grounded in Jesus Christ (III.xxiv.24) – he also appealed to more practical considerations: good works. Although Calvin stressed that works are not the grounds of *salvation*, he nevertheless allowed it to be understood that they are the grounds of *assurance*. Works may be regarded as 'the testimonies of God dwelling and ruling within us' (III.xiv.18). Believers are not saved by works (III.xiv.6–11); rather, their salvation is demonstrated by works (III.xiv.18). 'The grace of good works . . . demonstrates that the spirit of adoption has been given to us' (III.xiv.18). This tendency to regard works as evidence of election may be seen as the first stage in the articulation of a work ethic with significant pastoral overtones: it is by worldly activism that the believer can assure his or her troubled conscience that he or she is among the elect.

Anxiety over this question of election is subsequently a pervasive feature of Calvinist spirituality, and is generally treated at some length by Calvinist preachers and spiritual writers. The basic answer given, however, remains substantially the same: the believer who performs good works has indeed been chosen. Théodore de Bèze makes the point as follows:

> For this cause St Peter admonishes us to make our vocation and election sure by good works. Not that they be the cause of our vocation and election . . . But forasmuch as good works bring

> testimony to our conscience that Jesus Christ dwells within us, and consequently we cannot perish, being elected to salvation. [70]

Again, we find the same point being made: works testify to, but do not cause, salvation; they are the consequence, not the precondition, of salvation. By a process of *a posteriori* reasoning, the believer may infer his or her election from its consequences (good works). In addition to glorifying God and demonstrating the believer's thankfulness to him, such human moral action serves a vital psychological role for the anxious Christian conscience, by assuring the believer that he or she is indeed among the elect.

This idea was often stated in terms of the 'practical syllogism', which rested upon an argument constructed along the following lines:

> All who are elected exhibit certain signs as a consequence of that election.
> But I exhibit those signs.
> Therefore I am among the elect.

This *syllogismus practicus* thus locates the grounds of certainty of election in the presence of certain signs (*signa posteriora*) in the life of the believer.[71] There was thus a significant psychological pressure to demonstrate one's election to oneself and the world in general by exhibiting its signs – among which was the wholehearted commitment to serve and glorify God by labouring in his world.

This idea was placed on a firmer foundation through the introduction of a 'covenant theology'.[72] This concept, laden with considerable political import, placed Calvinist spirituality and pastoral theology upon a more secure theoretical foundation. The Cambridge writer William Perkins (1558–1602) argued, especially in his significantly entitled work *A treatise tending unto a declaration whether a man may be in the estate of damnation or in the estate of grace* (1589), that the elect stood within a covenant with God:

> God's covenant is his contract with man, concerning the obtaining of life eternal, upon a certain condition. This covenant consists of two parts: God's promise to man, man's promise to God. God's promise to man is that whereby he bindeth himself to man to be his God, if he perform the condition. Man's promise to God is that

> whereby he voweth his allegiance unto his Lord, and to perform the condition between them. [73]

God has entered into a contract with believers by which they are assured of salvation upon condition that they perform certain moral actions. Upon performing these actions, the believer may rest assured that he or she is to be numbered among the elect.

The early Calvinist propensity towards moral, economic and political activism may thus be seen to rest upon important theological foundations. By active involvement in the affairs of the world, subject to the guidance of scripture, the believer could clinch his or her calling, and gain peace of mind (always a prized and elusive commodity within Puritan circles) concerning his or her election. The notion of 'calling' (*vocatio*) must be interpreted in this light: the imperative to perform good works is not necessarily linked with a specific worldly vocation (for example, to be a butcher, a baker, or a candlestick-maker), but with the need to demonstrate one's *divine* calling to oneself and the world at large. The grounds of this work ethic may be illustrated from the writings of the Scottish divine John Davidson (1549–1603), whose *Catechisme* made the following statement:

> TEACHER: Whilk are their effects, whereby we are to witnesse that we are truely saved?
>
> DISCIPLE: The glorifying of God, and the edifying of our selves and our neighbours, by shewing fourth the frutes of our new birth in sanctification.[74]

By the middle of the seventeenth century, it had become clear that there was a general consensus among the European churches, Protestant or Roman Catholic, in the sphere of everyday ethics. Whatever their differences might be in relation to matters of doctrine or church polity, the main churches – Roman Catholic, Lutheran and Calvinist – all stressed the same basic qualities necessary for everyday life: moral earnestness, dedication, and conscientiousness.[75] What seems to distinguish Calvinism at this juncture is not so much its moral earnestness as the theological and spiritual function which this was understood to serve. The notion of a 'calling' remained characteristic of Calvinism, and its peculiar existential importance was linked with anxieties occasioned by the Calvinist doctrine of predestination. It is undoubtedly true that this doctrine contained the seeds of worldly activism. At the theoretical level, predestination might seem to encourage quietism: if one is elected, why bother doing anything active? In fact, however, its effect was quite the reverse: to ensure that one *is* elected, one must throw oneself wholeheartedly into appropriate action within the world.

In the sixteenth century, this affirmative and dynamic attitude to work propelled Calvinists into the forefront of progress. Yet by the middle of the seventeenth century, this distinctiveness on the part of Calvinism appears to have been subjected to considerable historical erosion. Other Protestant groupings of the period – such as Arminians, Mennonites, Independents, Pietists and Quakers – who did not share the orthodox Calvinist understanding of predestination and the anxieties which this is held to engender, may also be shown to have thrown themselves wholeheartedly into worldly activity. Lacking any theoretical framework which indicated a need to confirm one's election through work, they nevertheless appear to have adopted patterns of social activity which paralleled those of Calvinism. It is as if Calvinism's distinctive commitment to mundane activity and investment had been detached from its theological basis, and become absorbed within western European society *independent* of its original religious roots. What may have been distinctive of Calvinism in the sixteenth or early seventeenth centuries seems to have become the common coinage of the northern European bourgeoisie by about 1650.

This erosion of the theological basis of the Calvinist work ethic is lent credibility through Trevor-Roper's observation that many of the great Calvinist entrepreneurs of the mid-seventeenth century were actually far from orthodox in their religious views.[76] Their 'Calvinism' would but rarely conform to the rigid doctrinal criteria which led to stress upon the doctrine of predestination and to the existential anxieties that it engendered, which Weber discerned as underlying their commitment to worldly activism. It is that commitment which remained for these individuals, while the religious considerations which originally occasioned it appear to have largely evaporated. The secular attitudes persisted, while their religious foundations were rejected, forgotten or set to one side. It may be argued with some cogency that the general later seventeenth-century attitude towards work and secular activism – upon which Calvinism by then had lost its monopoly – is the residue of the *Angst* of an earlier period over the issue of divine election. The manner in which this anxiety could be resolved may initially have catapulted Calvinism into the forefront of western European economic activity; others, however, would draw level as the seventeenth century progressed, feeling able to adopt Calvinism's attitudes and methods without subscribing to the religious pressures which originally generated them.

A fundamental difficulty with the Weber thesis is that it fails to forge a specific link between the work ethic on the one hand, and the accumulation and reinvestment of capital on the other; indeed, there is no specific connection with *economic* activity in general. To the strictly limited extent that there is *any* peculiarly economic application of the Calvinist work ethic, this may indeed be grounded, as Weber suggests, in the asceticism which is initially so pervasive and distinctive a feature of orthodox Calvinist spirituality. If the believer is prohibited from enjoying the financial rewards of his labours (and the social controls placed upon such enjoyment in early Calvinist societies were often considerable), he or she has little option but to accumulate or reinvest the capital thus gained.[77]

Yet although Calvinism may have carried with it the imperative to clinch one's election and demonstrate it to oneself and the world through appropriate worldly activity, the specific form which this activity might take was left open. Historical analysis suggests that these forms were a matter of historical contingency, varying from one age and historical location to another. For example, English Calvinism (or Puritanism, as it is generally known) during the period 1603–40 was characterized by a flurry of political activism, culminating in the Civil War, the routing of Charles I, and the inauguration of the Puritan commonwealth. As Michael Walzer observes, politics was 'made into a kind of work'.[78] After the failure of the commonwealth and the restoration of Charles II in 1660, Puritans found themselves on the fringes of English political life, and so concentrated upon hard work and dedication in whatever fields were open to them. This deliberate decision to withdraw from the political arena led to a period of economic dynamism within Puritanism. It is significant that Weber's case for the link between Calvinism and economic activism rests largely upon the English Puritans Richard Baxter and John Bunyan, both writing in the period after 1660.[79] This might seem to suggest that Weber had erected a substantial theoretical construction upon a mere historical contingency.

However, a connection between Calvin's world-affirming theology and capitalism seems inevitable. Such a connection is presupposed by the English preacher and theologian of the eighteenth century, John Wesley, who wrote: 'I do not see how it is possible in the nature of things for any revival of religion to continue for long. For religion must necessarily produce both industry and frugality, and these cannot but produce riches. But as riches increase, so will pride, anger, and love of the world in all its branches.' While Wesley regards prosperity as bringing religious difficulties in its wake, it is evident that he believes that evangelical Christianity 'must necessarily produce both industry and frugality', a cornerstone of capitalism.

Whatever the precise relation between Calvinism and capitalism may prove to be, it may be said that one of Calvinism's greatest legacies to western culture is a new attitude towards work, and, supremely, manual labour.[80] Work, far from being merely an inevitable and somewhat tedious means of obtaining the basic necessities for existence, is perhaps the most praiseworthy of all human activities, surpassing all others in this respect. To be 'called' by God does not entail withdrawing from the world, but demands critical engagement with every sphere of worldly life. To speak of a 'Protestant work ethic' is not to decry those who cannot work, but to censure those – such as French aristocrats seeking exile in Geneva – who *will* not work. 'Work', it may be added, is not understood as 'paid employment', but as diligent and productive use of whatever resources and talents one has been given.

Work is thus viewed as a profoundly spiritual activity, a productive and socially beneficial form of prayer. Physical and spiritual activity are combined in this one action, by which socially useful functions may be discharged and personal assurance of salvation may be gained. It may indeed be that this new attitude towards work is conducive to the development of capitalism. But it also brings a new depth of meaning to the everyday mundane activities of *les petits gens*. Social distinctions (to which Calvinism had an inbuilt aversion) are levelled through the common imperative to 'redeem time' (Richard Baxter).

The transformation of the status of work from a distasteful and degrading activity, to be avoided if possible, to a dignified and glorious means of affirming God and the world he created is one of the most important contributions of Calvinism to western culture, and we shall explore it further in the concluding chapter. But what other aspects of modern western culture may reasonably be put down to the legacy of Calvin and his city? To what extent has Calvinism shaped, or contributed to the shaping of, attitudes and outlooks within the modern world? To conclude this study, we shall consider some aspects of the impact of Calvin upon modern western culture.

12

Calvin and the Shaping of Modern Western Culture

In this work, we have aimed to sketch the outlines of Calvin's career and thought, as well as tracing the development of the movement which owed its origins and much of its form to his inspiration, and attempting to indicate the appeal which it possessed for the later sixteenth century and beyond. That appeal lay partly in its novelty, partly in its intellectual rigour, and partly in its obvious attractions for those who felt that their creativity and potential were being stifled by the restrictions of a semi-feudal society. With the advent of Calvinism as an international movement, it seemed to many that change was in the air. The movement seemed charged with the potential to liberate western Europe from the remaining shackles of the Middle Ages. C. S. Lewis stresses this aspect, and insists upon the need to grasp 'the freshness, the audacity, and (soon) the fashionableness of Calvinism' to the sixteenth century.[1] As we have stressed throughout, Calvinism was far more than a theology; it was perceived as a progressive world-view which seemed capable of taking that world by storm, and made a deep impact upon the culture of the period.

At first sight, it might seem quite inappropriate to suggest that Calvinism affected western culture, except in a purely negative sense. Is not Calvinism the opponent of culture? For example, Calvinism has often been portrayed as the enemy of the arts. At one level, there is considerable evidence to support this suggestion. If there is one point at which Calvin's theology approaches that of Islam, it is in his attitude to decoration in buildings designed for public worship. No portrayals of God in human form were to be permitted within churches. It was, he suggested, all too easy for something created to be confused with the creator.[2] It was to open the way to idolatry, 'to imagine or possess something in which to put one's trust in place of or in addition to the one true God who has revealed himself in his word.'[3]

Underlying this prohibition, however, was a more substantial point: it is not merely that God should not be pictured; he is inherently incapable of being pictured.[4] In the period immediately following the Council of Trent, Roman Catholic churches – soon to be followed by their Lutheran counterparts – adopted a baroque style of ornamentation, with extensive use of visual aids to piety in the form of religious images and portraits. These were, however, rigorously excluded from Calvinist places of worship. There is perhaps more than a hint of intellectual superiority in the Heidelberg Catechism (1563): Calvinists do not need visual images of God, being perfectly capable of understanding and making full use of the wide range of verbal images conveyed in scripture:

> Q: But may not pictures be allowed in churches instead of books for the laity?
>
> A: No. We must not try to be more clever than God, who does not want his people to be taught through dumb idols, but through the living preaching of his word.[5]

However, no significant restrictions were placed upon the activities of Calvinist artists outside the specific sphere of ecclesiastical ornamentation: indeed, the growing wealth of Calvinist communities, not totally unconnected with their association with capitalism, led to the emergence of patterns of patronage similar to those associated with the Italian Renaissance. The wealthy Calvinist burgers of Flanders appear to have been just as aware of the importance of the decoration of buildings and homes as their Renaissance predecessors. Further, the Calvinist hostility to pictorial representations of God was fundamentally theological in its foundation, and did not extend to other subject matters. Calvinist painters were prohibited from representing God in their paintings, but not from painting itself (and it should be recalled in this context that artists were among the earliest supporters of the Calvinist Reformation in the Low Countries);[6] happily, this prohibition far from exhausted the possibilities open to them, as the new interest in landscapes, townscapes, domestic scenes and portraits characteristic of seventeenth-century Flemish art makes clear. Similarly, the new Puritan emphasis upon 'the factual record of divine providences in biographies and histories, or of the natural environment about them',[7] led to such subjects becoming ideal material for Calvinist artists. They might not portray God; but as God could be known through his creation, a new religious motivation was given to the portrayal of nature and history. (This fundamental impulse to depict nature is also linked with the Calvinist interest in the natural sciences, to which we shall return presently.)

Even in catholic countries, Calvinist artists were active and well received. In France, the Bourbon monarchy embarked upon an ambitious programme of urban development in Renaissance style within Paris and elsewhere. A benign fiscal system under Richelieu created the fortunes of the financiers, who sought socially acceptable means of expending their accumulated wealth. The great *hôtels* of the Ile Saint-Louis and an extensive programme of patronage of the arts were tangible expressions of this new wealth.[8] Although the Edict of Nantes (1598) had designated Calvinism as a tolerated religion, it was nevertheless generally regarded as deviationist in its behavioural patterns, and something of a threat to national security – a perception which hardened during the English Civil War and which persuaded Mazarin and his advisors that Calvinists were potential revolutionaries.[9] However, even during this period, Calvinist architects and painters enjoyed status and success far exceeding their numbers, a fact which points to both a certain degree of religious toleration on the part of the French establishment and the genuine artistic commitment and ability of Calvinists. Their success may be illustrated by the fact that of the twenty-three founding members of the *Académie royale de peinture*, established in 1648, seven (30.5 per cent) were Calvinists.[10] Louis Testelin, the first secretary of the academy, was openly recognized as a Calvinist, although – as a later oration put it – 'he was not as obstinate as is usual for those who are infected with such errors, and he avoided seditious controversies.'

'Culture', however, designates a broader entity than the fine arts. In its widest sense, it embraces a series of attitudes, outlooks, practices and beliefs which shape patterns of human existence at specific junctures in history. In dealing with the impact of Calvin's legacy upon western culture, we are concerned with its contribution to the shaping and forging of a world-view. In their study of contemporary attitudes in modern America, Robert Bellah and his colleagues conducted interviews with more than two hundred individuals. Commenting on those interviews, they remarked, 'In talking to our contemporaries, we were also talking to our predecessors. In our conversations, we were listening not only to voices present, but to voices past. In the words of those we talked to, we heard John Calvin.'[11] Yet not one of these individuals appears to have mentioned Calvin specifically, or recognized his influence upon them. That influence is subtle, anonymous, even unrecognized. In bringing this work to a close, it seems fitting to highlight some areas of modern western culture to which Calvinism appears to have made a major contribution, whether this is explicitly recognized or not. We are not so much concerned with the evaluation of those contributions, as with their identification in the first place.

Three general themes stand out as central to an understanding of the impact of Calvin's heritage upon the west:

1 The *international* character of Calvinism, which rapidly managed to disinvest itself of any features which linked it specifically with its original Genevan situation (see pp. 201–2). Calvinism proved remarkably adept at adapting itself to local situations, a feature which has been identified by twentieth-century theoreticians of Christian missions as essential to the implantation of forms of Christianity in alien cultures.[12] Calvinism was able to entrench itself in a variety of contexts, European and American, bearing little relation to that of sixteenth-century Geneva, and addressing directly specific issues – political, economic and religious – within those societies.

2 The strongly *world-affirming* character of Calvin's thought, especially as developed by his later followers (pp. 219–22). Calvinism must not be thought of as a set of abstract and irrelevant religious principles, but as a religion firmly entrenched within the concrete realities of human existence (particularly, it may be added, urban existence). Even the doctrine of predestination, perhaps the most abstract of all Calvinist ideas, proves to be orientated towards engagement with the everyday world. Calvinism proved capable of engaging with western culture to the point at which, perhaps more than any other modern version of Christianity, it was able to transform it from within. The Calvinist was encouraged to engage directly with the world, rather than to retreat from it.

3 Calvinism proved vulnerable to *secularization*: with the evaporation of its religious core, a quite definite residue of political,

social and economic values remained. Hugh Trevor-Roper has suggested that one of Calvinism's distinctive features is that it is more easily discarded than catholicism;[13] once discarded, however, it proves to have shaped the attitudes and outlooks of those who formerly adopted it. Where the original power of Calvinism waned, it none the less left a distinctive imprint upon the outlook of the west.

The story is told of an Englishman who was confronted by a group of youths on the streets of Northern Ireland, noted for its sectarian strife between Roman Catholics and Protestants. 'Are you a Protestant or a Catholic?,' they asked him, menacingly. He hesitated, before replying, 'I'm an atheist.' The youths were quick to riposte, 'Yes, but are you a *Protestant* atheist or a *Catholic* atheist?' There is much truth in their question. Atheism arises when the religious core of a movement such as Calvinism evaporates, leaving a distinctive residue. That residue takes the form of a cluster of social, political, moral and economic attitudes, originally linked with religious faith, but apparently proving to be capable of continuing in its absence. Although it might at first sight seem absurd to speak of 'Calvinist atheism', the phrase captures a crucial insight concerning the impact of Calvinism upon western culture: the persistence of a crater in the cultural landscape, when the original force of its explosion has been spent.

With these points in mind, we turn to consider several areas in which Calvinism may be argued to have shaped some significant areas of modern western culture, especially in North America. The aspects chosen are illustrative, rather than exhaustive; to trace the full impact of Calvin's legacy upon the west would require a work in itself.

The Religious Legitimation of Economic Activism

The previous chapter documented the emergence of economically dynamic attitudes within Calvinism, heterodox and orthodox, supremely during the seventeenth century. The Calvinist work ethic has now been largely secularized; the attitude remains, while its underlying religious causes are forgotten. The origins of this trend towards a secular work ethic may perhaps be perceived within Calvinism over the period 1550–1680. For earlier Calvinist writers, including Calvin himself, 'calling' expresses primarily the fact that an individual has been elected by God, and only secondarily the worldly vocation (*une vocation juste et approuvée*) in which this calling finds expression. In Restoration England, the emphasis falls primarily upon one's calling within the world, rather than one's eternal calling by God; although this latter element remains essential, there is nonetheless a distinct tendency to prioritize action in the world over and against its theological foundations. In this may be seen the origins of the modern trend to secularize the notion of 'calling' or 'vocation': for most individuals within modern western culture, it is not *God* who has called them into a particular sphere of activity; one is called by society, or by an inner sense of purpose, to enter a given field of action. The predisposition of many in the west to throw themselves into activism[14] of one sort or another may be traced, in part, to the attitudes of their Puritan forebears. Thus Stephen Foster points out how many of the Puritan economic attitudes which account for the expansion of New England during its first century of settlement are to be put down to the Calvinist work ethic.[15] And Robert Bellah, in his survey of individualism and commitment in modern American life, suggests that a 'reappropriation of the idea of vocation or calling'[16] may hold the key to the reshaping of American culture. The Calvinist idea of calling gives every indication of living on, even if in a new secular clothing. It also lives on, in a form probably unrecognizable to Calvin himself, in the North American 'theologies of prosperity', which we may briefly consider.

The impact of the Calvinist work ethic upon North American culture appears to have been enormous. In 1831, Alexis de Tocqueville remarked that it was often difficult to tell whether American preachers were concerned to 'procure eternal felicity in the other world or prosperity in this'. In his masterly study of the religious history of the United States, Sidney Ahlstrom noted the emergence of a distinct trend in the nineteenth century, which became more marked in the twentieth – wealth is regarded as a sign of divine election.[17] Thus, to note but two of the individuals who dominated the American financial scene in the late nineteenth century, John D. Rockefeller Sr regarded his wealth as some kind of divine reward for his faith, while Andrew Carnegie spoke of 'The Gospel of Wealth'. Personal and national wealth came to be seen as signs of special divine favour. The rise of 'the theology of prosperity' in the 1970s in the United States may be regarded as the inevitable outcome of this distorted version of the Calvinist work ethic. Frederick Price speaks for this movement when he asserts that 'we need to realize that prosperity is the will of God. It is God's perfect will that everyone prosper in every area of life. Primarily, we are dealing with material and financial prosperity.'[18] The same theme is echoed in Gloria Copeland's significantly titled work, *God's Will is Prosperity* (1978), and Norval Hayes' *Prosperity now!* (1986). The close link presupposed between individual and national prosperity is generally regarded as underlying an alliance between 'the theology of prosperity' and a resurgent American nationalism. While the extent of the influence of Calvinism upon this significant and expanding development within modern American religious culture is debatable, there are sufficient points of contact to allow a *prima facie* case for Calvin's indirect influence. Calvin may be argued to have eliminated the religious and social stigma attached to wealth.

But for some, the most significant memorial to the Calvinist work ethic is perhaps still to be found in Calvin's Geneva itself. The casual visitor can hardly fail to notice how the city centre is dominated by banks and other financial institutions. As we have suggested, the link between Calvin and capitalism is perhaps more nuanced and historically conditioned than might be thought, and is due more to the needs, institutions and policies of the republic of Geneva than to Calvin himself. He may not have set out to promote capitalism, and may have done little more than sanctify existing or developing Genevan economic attitudes, policies and institutions; it may, however, reasonably be suggested that the new impetus given to capitalism and an enterprise culture was a significant – if unintended – result of his thought, and the popular perception of what Calvinism was and what it entailed. If this is the case, modern western culture has been indelibly marked and decisively shaped – whether directly or indirectly, whether for better or for worse – by this religious thinker.

Calvin and the Natural Sciences

The origins of modern natural science are complex and controversial. For instance, Lewis S. Feuer has argued vigorously that modern science was the direct result of a 'hedonist–libertarian spirit'.[19] Theories which attempt to explain the remarkable development of the natural sciences in terms of one single controlling factor are, however, ambitious and generally unconvincing. It is clear that a number of contributing factors are implicated; one of those is unquestionably religious, and related to John Calvin.

There is a large body of sociological research, stretching back more than a century, which demonstrates that there are consistent differences between the abilities of the Protestant and Roman Catholic traditions within Christianity to produce first-class natural scientists. These differences, which span a wide range of countries, can be summarized thus: Protestants seem to be much better at fostering the natural sciences than Roman Catholics. In his major study of the foreign membership of the Parisian *Académie des Sciences* over the period 1666–1883, Alphonse de Candolle found that Protestants by far outnumbered Roman Catholics. On the basis of population, de Candolle estimated that 60 per cent of that membership should have been Roman Catholic, and 40 per cent Protestant; the actual figures turned out to be 18.2 per cent and 81.8 per cent.[20] Although Calvinists were considerably in a minority in the southern Netherlands during the sixteenth century, the vast majority of the region's natural scientists were drawn from this constituency. The early membership of the Royal Society of London was dominated by Puritans.[21] As survey after survey indicates, both the physical and the biological sciences were dominated by Calvinists during the sixteenth and seventeenth centuries. This remarkable observation clearly requires some sort of explanation.

Calvin may be regarded as making two major contributions to this debate. At one level, he positively encouraged the scientific study of nature; at the other, he removed a major obstacle to the development of that study. His first contribution is specifically linked with his stress upon the orderliness of creation; both the physical world and the human body testify to the wisdom and character of God.

> In order that no one might be excluded from the means of obtaining happiness, God has been pleased, not only to place in our minds the seeds of religion of which we have already spoken, but to make known his perfection in the whole structure of the universe, and daily place himself in our view, in such a manner that we cannot open our eyes without being compelled to observe him . . . Hence the author of the Letter to the Hebrews elegantly describes the visible world as images of the invisible, the elegant structure of the world serving as a kind of mirror in which we may see God, who is otherwise invisible . . . To prove his remarkable wisdom, both the heavens and the earth present us with countless proofs – not

> just those more advanced proofs which astronomy, medicine and all the other natural sciences are designed to illustrate, but proofs which force themselves on the attention of the most illiterate peasant, who cannot open his eyes without seeing them. (*Institutes* I.v.1–2).

Calvin thus commends both astronomy and medicine – indeed, he even confesses to being slightly jealous of them – in that they are able to probe more deeply into the natural world, and thus uncover further evidence of the orderliness of the creation and the wisdom of its creator. (The idea that Calvin rubbished Copernicus is a complete myth, as we noted earlier: p. xiv.)

It may thus be argued that Calvin gave a fundamental religious impulse and legitimation to the scientific investigation of nature, in that it was seen as a means of discerning the wise hand of God in creation, thus enhancing both belief in his existence and the respect in which he was held. The *Confessio Belgica* (1561), a Calvinist statement of faith which exercised particular influence in the Low Countries (to become particularly noted for its botanists and physicists), declared that nature is 'before our eyes as a most beautiful book in which all created things, whether great or small, are as letters showing the invisible things of God to us'.[22] God can thus be discerned through the detailed study of his creation. Perry Miller has drawn attention to the manner in which nature could become the 'altar of God', a factual revelation of the divine in the 'vast sea and the terrible forest'.[23] An ethos which clearly reflects similar views was pervasive within the Royal Society in the seventeenth century.[24] Thus Richard Bentley (1662–1742) delivered a series of lectures in 1692, based on Newton's *Principia Mathematica* (1687), in which the regularity of the universe, as established by Newton, is interpreted as evidence of design. In a letter written to Bentley as he was preparing his lectures, Newton declared that 'when I wrote my treatise about our system, I had an eye on such principles as might work with considering men for the belief of a Deity; and nothing can rejoice me more than to find it useful for that purpose.' There are unambiguous hints here of Calvin's reference to the universe as a 'theatre of the glory of God', in which humans are an appreciative audience (*Institutes* I.vi.2).

In the second place, Calvin may also be regarded as eliminating a major obstacle to the development of the natural sciences – biblical literalism. This emancipation of scientific observation and theory from crudely literalist interpretations of scripture took place at two distinct levels: first, in the declaration that the natural subject matter of scripture is not the structure of the world, but God's self-revelation and redemption, as concentrated in Jesus Christ; second, in the insistence upon the accommodated character of biblical language. We shall consider both these points individually.

Calvin indicates (although he is not totally consistent in this respect) that the Bible is to be regarded as primarily concerned with the knowledge of Jesus Christ. It is not to be treated as an astronomical, geographical or biological textbook. Perhaps the clearest statement of this principle is to be found in a paragraph added in 1543 to Calvin's preface to Pierre Olivétan's translation of the New Testament (1534): the whole point of scripture is to bring us to a knowledge of Jesus Christ – and having come to know him (and all that this implies), we should come to a halt, and not expect to learn more.[25] Scripture provides us with spectacles (I.v.8, vi.1), through which we may view the world *as God's creation and self-expression*; it does not, and was never intended to, provide us with an infallible repository of astronomical and medical information. The natural sciences are thus effectively emancipated from theological restrictions.

On 4 June 1539, Luther commented caustically upon Copernicus' theory – to be published in 1543 – that the earth revolved around the sun: did not scripture insist that the contrary was the case? And so the heliocentric theory of the solar system received a somewhat curt dismissal. Such crude biblical literalism appears to have been typical of the German reformer. In his controversy with Zwingli over the meaning of the famous words spoken by Jesus over the bread at the last supper – 'this is my body' (Matthew 26:26) – Luther insisted that the word 'is' could only be interpreted as 'is literally identical with'. This struck Zwingli as a religious and linguistic absurdity, totally insensitive to the various levels at which language operated. In this case, 'is' meant 'signifies'.[26]

Calvin, as we have seen (pp. 130–2), develops a sophisticated theory of 'accommodation'. God, in revealing himself to us, has accommodated himself to our levels of understanding and our innate preference for pictorial means of conceiving him. God reveals himself, not as he is in himself, but in forms adapted to our human capacity. Thus scripture speaks of God having arms, a mouth, and so on – but these are just vivid and memorable metaphors, ideally suited to our intellectual abilities. God reveals himself in ways suitable to the abilities and situations of those to whom the revelation was originally made. Thus the biblical stories of the creation and Fall (Genesis 1–3) are accommodated to the abilities and horizons of a relatively simple and unsophisticated people;[27] they are not intended to be taken as *literal* representations of reality.

The impact of these ideas upon English scientific theorizing, especially during the seventeenth century, was considerable. For example, Edward Wright defended Copernicus' heliocentric theory of the solar system against biblical literalists by arguing, in the first place, that scripture was not concerned with physics, and in the second, that its manner of speaking was 'accommodated to the understanding and way of speech of the common people, like nurses to little children'.[28] Both these arguments derive directly from Calvin.

Since the nineteenth century, religion and science have often seemed to be locked in mortal combat within western culture. Some writers have suggested that this reflects an excessive influence of Calvin upon western Christianity. Yet, paradoxically, it is precisely on account of Calvin having had *too little* influence upon his later followers. The infamous Scopes Trial (1925), centring upon the allegedly non-biblical character of the theory of evolution, bears witness to the inadequacies of a crudely literal interpretation of the Genesis creation accounts. Yet for Calvin, even the idea of the 'six days of creation' was a divine accommodation to human cognitive abilities;[29] it was not to be taken as literally true. Had Calvin had a greater influence over his contemporary followers, perhaps one of the central aspects of modern western culture – the notion of a tension between religion and science – would have been averted. The entire evolutionary debate would have taken a radically different course had he had a greater influence over his later followers.

This, however, is to speculate on what might have happened; our concern is to analyse what did happen. It is evident that there is a fundamental religious impulse to the rapid expansion of the natural sciences in the sixteenth century and beyond, and that this can be put down, at least in part, to the ideas and influence of John Calvin.

The Phenomenon of American Civil Religion

The Calvinist stress upon predestination is specifically linked with the idea of 'election' – being chosen by God. Whereas its chief Protestant rival, Lutheranism, de-emphasized the notion of predestination, in effect reducing it to little more than an affirmation of God's constancy and fidelity, Calvinism regarded the doctrine as giving religious inspiration and moral and social legitimation to the international expansion of the movement. Election was not understood merely to refer to individuals, but to the communities to which they belonged. The Calvinist communities had been chosen by God, set apart in order to achieve God's purposes. It was therefore natural that Calvinists should notice and exploit the obvious parallels between their own situation and that of ancient Israel. Where Israel was the chosen people of God in the ancient near east, the Calvinists were their successors in the early modern period. And, like their Israelite predecessors, they looked forward to the triumphant entry into the new promised land. Menna Prestwich notes this development, and its potential significance:

> The doctrine of predestination, which came into the forefront when Beza [de Bèze] succeeded Calvin, led Calvinists to identify themselves with the Elect and the children of Israel. The Old Testament was for them a mirror and a guide, in which they found inspiration for their victories over the forces of Babylon and consolation for their tribulations in the desert or wilderness on their way to the Promised Land. Providence and the dispensations of God had immediacy and reality for them. When Coligny crossed a ford on the Loire in 1568 this was at once compared to the crossing of the Red Sea. [30]

With the accession of Elizabeth I, many Calvinist writers regarded England as having been given 'most favoured nation' status in the sight of God. This perception, however, was relatively short-lived. It was not long before Puritan writers turned their eyes and imaginations towards America.

The early history of the colonization of North America, whether by English or Dutch Calvinists, was widely regarded as the entry of God's exiled people into a new promised land. As Perry Miller has shown, the first and unquestioned premise of the original New Englanders was that they had entered into a covenant with God to establish godly commonwealths.[31] The true America was a prototype of the new Jerusalem, the 'city on a hill' predestined from all eternity yet in the process of actualization in New England. This perception was enhanced through the religious revivals of the Great Awakening, and through the Treaty of Paris (1763), which returned to Protestant hands the vast catholic empires of France and Spain in North America. Perhaps most significantly, the American Revolution saw the link between American independence and its divine calling being further strengthened; Robert Smith's Pennsylvania declaration – 'the cause of America is the cause of Jesus Christ' – appears to reflect a widespread perception within American society at this time. The congregationalist minister John Devotion declared that God had singled out America as his chosen nation: 'All nations hear the great Jehovah's will; America, henceforth separate, shall sit as queen among the nations.'

As Sidney Ahlstrom has noted, a recurring theme of much American historiography from this point onwards concerns the providential guidance and strengthening of America.

> Only an occasional very eccentric American ever doubted that the Star-Spangled Banner waved over the Lord's Chosen Nation. In many minds the American was conceived as a new Adam in a new Eden, and the American nation as mankind's great second chance. Nothing better illustrates the continuity of this tradition than the patriotic hymns that were entered in the national book of Psalms – from *America*, struck off in an inspired moment by an Andover seminarian for a Fourth of July observance in 1832, to *The Battle Hymn of the Republic*, written by Julia Ward Howe as if by the hand of God in 1861, to *America the Beautiful*, published in the *Congregationalist* in 1893. This mythic theme of America as a beacon on a hill and an exemplar for the world became a constituent element in historical interpretations of the nation's religious life. [32]

The notion of predestination is easily secularized into that of 'fate' or 'destiny'. The proximity of the notions of providence and predestination was indicated by Calvin himself, who treated the two subjects together within a single chapter of an early edition of the *Institutes*. As the religious core of Calvinism began to evaporate within sections of American society in the late nineteenth and twentieth centuries, a secular notion of providence or destiny began to replace the more specifically religious idea of predestination. A secularized America was still able to think of itself as singled out among nations, with its institutions (for example, the presidency) and symbols (for example, the flag) endowed with quasi-divine or sacramental significance. The origins of this notion of national destiny are to be traced to America's Puritan past, which – for some at least – is still present.

Calvinism and Natural Human Rights

The implication of Calvinism in the development of concepts of natural human rights in Europe and North America has been stressed in several recent studies.[33] The hostile attitude of sixteenth-century French monarchs towards their Calvinist subjects raised with acute force the questions of whether there existed limits to regal authority, and the obligation of subjects to obey it. The massacres of St Bartholomew (1572) may be regarded as precipitating intense debate within Calvinist circles over the proper use of violence, the place of obedience, and the limits of civil authority (see pp. 186–8). The success of the Calvinist Reformation in Scotland raised much the same questions, particularly in the aftermath of the deposition of Mary Queen of Scots (1567).[34] An amalgam of biblical notions of justice and fidelity (which the Old Testament linked with the concept of a covenant between God and his people) with the ideas of later medieval contractarian writers resulted, centring upon the notion of government by justice, rather than oppression. If these ideas originated in late sixteenth-century Europe, they were appropriated with vigour by American revolutionaries, determined to break what they regarded as the tyranny of the British monarchy over their existence. Jonathan Mayhew (1720–66) linked his politics with his religion when he declared that 'the hereditary, indefensible, divine right of kings, and the doctrine of non-resistance, which is built upon the supposition of such a right, are altogether as fabulous and chimerical as transubstantiation.' The outcome of this North American debate was the emergence of a covenantal understanding of human rights which, when linked with Calvin's appeal to natural law, gave rise to the notion of all humanity being created equal, with certain inalienable human rights to life, liberty and the pursuit of happiness.[35]

If this notion of human rights characterized the American Revolution and its aftermath, it was not shared by all Calvinist writers. Two significant exceptions may be noted, sharing a common alternative approach to human rights. Whereas the Calvinist writers of the northern American states insisted that all humanity was created with equal rights, a number of southern Calvinist writers – such as Robert Lewis Dabney, Benjamin Morgan Palmer and James Henley Thornwell – argued that God created individuals with ethnic and social diversity of status. Where the northern theologians appealed to one notion of natural law, their southern colleagues appealed to one quite different in its origins and emphases.[36] As a result, these southern Calvinist writers felt able to justify both the doctrine of separate racial development for whites and negroes and the continuation of the existing practice of slavery. On the eve of the American Civil War, two radically different Calvinist conceptions of human rights thus found themselves locked in mortal combat. The southerners would lose this particular battle, but their ideas live on in other places; until recently the Dutch Reformed churches in South Africa appealed to a similar notion in defending the doctrine of apartheid, just as some Ulster Protestants defend, on the same grounds, the existence of the border between the predominantly Protestant north of Ireland from the predominantly Roman Catholic south. Diversity within Calvinism here finds its outworking in significant political controversies which are an integral part of the controversies of modern history.

The full history of the impact of Calvinism upon western culture has yet to be written; the points noted above are merely a tentative indicator to its extent and potential importance. Nevertheless, the modest findings of this last chapter allow a significant conclusion to be drawn: to study Calvin is not merely to study the past – it is also to gain a deeper understanding of the present. Modern western culture continues to be shaped by memories of the past. Although Calvin lies buried in an unmarked grave somewhere in Geneva, his ideas and influence live on in the outlooks of the culture he helped to create.

Appendix 1

A Glossary of Theological and Historical Terms

THE USE OF at least some potentially obscure theological and historical terms in a work of this nature is inevitable. As much of this terminology may be unfamiliar to the general reader, the present Appendix is intended to achieve some degree of clarity without sacrificing accuracy within the body of the work itself.

ACCOMMODATION

The principle, especially associated with Calvin, that God reveals himself in words and images which are appropriate to the human capacity to visualize and comprehend. Scripture is thus not to be taken literally at every point; it often uses non-literal ideas and images (pp. 130–2). The principle is of major importance in understanding how Calvinism came to be so favourably disposed towards the new natural sciences, especially astronomy (pp. 253–7); biblical literalism was removed as an obstacle from this new field of human inquiry.

ADIAPHORA

Literally, 'matters of indifference'. Beliefs or practices which the reformers regarded as tolerable, in that they were neither explicitly rejected nor stipulated by scripture. For example, what ministers wore at church services was often regarded as a 'matter of indifference', upon which variations could be tolerated without compromising essential beliefs. The concept is of importance in that it allowed the reformers to adopt a pragmatic approach to many beliefs and practices, thus avoiding unnecessary confrontation. For example, Calvin tended to adopt this attitude to bishops.

Amyraldianism

A Calvinist heresy, based on the teachings of Moïse Amyraut, professor at the Protestant Academy of Saumur, a designated *place de sûreté* under the terms of the Edict of Nantes. Like Arminianism, Amyraldianism involved the criticism of the Calvinist notion of predestination, arguing for a return to a concept more akin to that associated with Calvin rather than his later interpreters.

Anabaptism

Literally, 're-baptism'. A term used to refer to the radical wing of the Reformation, based on thinkers such as Menno Simons and Balthasar Hubmaier. The radicals generally defended the right of every individual to interpret scripture for him- or herself, rejected the intrusion of civil authority into the realm of religion, and adopted a critical attitude towards most existing social, religious and political institutions.

Anti-Pelagian writings

The writings of Augustine relating to the Pelagian controversy, in which he defended his views on grace and justification. See 'Pelagianism'.

Apostolic era

For humanists and reformers alike, the definitive period of the Christian church, bounded by the resurrection of Jesus Christ (c.AD 35) and the death of the last apostle (c.AD 90?). The ideas and practices of this period were widely regarded as normative in humanist and reforming circles.

Arminianism

A Calvinist heresy associated with Jakob Arminius. In contrast to Théodore de Bèze, who asserted that all are individually predestined to eternal life or death, Arminius taught that predestination refers to the general divine decree to the effect that all who believe shall be saved. Arminianism was explicitly condemned by the Synod of Dort (1618–19).

Articulants

The faction within Geneva, especially during the period 1535–8, opposed to Guillaume Farel. Also known as the Artichauds.

Augustinianism

A term used in two major senses. First, it refers to the views of Augustine of Hippo concerning the doctrine of salvation, in which the need for divine grace is stressed (see pp. 43–4). In this sense, the term is the antithesis of Pelagianism. Second, it is used to refer to the body of opinion within the Augustinian Order during the Middle Ages, irrespective of whether these views derive from Augustine or not. The first sense of the term dominates the present study.

Calvinism

An ambiguous term, used with two quite distinct meanings. First, it refers to the religious ideas of religious bodies (such as the Reformed church) and individuals (such as Théodore de Bèze) who were profoundly influenced by John Calvin, or by documents written by him. In that 'Calvinism' drew upon theological resources other than Calvin (see pp. 202–8), the use of the word is slightly confusing; the term 'Reformed theology' is preferred by many writers. Second, it refers to the religious ideas of John Calvin himself. The more clumsy term 'Calvinian' is often used in preference to designate this latter meaning.

Catechism

A popular manual of Christian doctrine, usually in the form of question and answer, intended for religious instruction. With its considerable emphasis upon religious education, the Reformation saw the appearance of a number of major catechisms, most notably Luther's Lesser Catechism (1529), Calvin's Geneva Catechism (1545), and the celebrated Heidelberg Catechism (1563).

Christology

The section of Christian theology dealing with the identity of Jesus Christ, particularly the question of the relation of his human and divine natures. Apart from being the subject of a disagreement between Luther and Zwingli at Marburg in 1529, Christology, like the doctrine of the Trinity, was of little relevance to the Reformation, in that it was not regarded as central to the Reformation struggle.

Confession, Confessionalism

Although the term refers primarily to the admission of sin, it acquired a rather different technical sense in the sixteenth century – that of a document which embodies the principles of faith of a Protestant church. Thus the Augsburg Confession (1530) embodies the ideas of early Lutheranism, and the First Helvetic Confession (1536) those of the early Reformed church. The term 'Confessionalism' is often used to refer to the hardening of religious attitudes in the later sixteenth century during the so-called 'Second Reformation', as the Lutheran and Reformed churches became involved in a struggle for power in Germany.

Consistory

The Genevan institution created by Calvin in his *Ordonnances* of 1541, apparently based upon medieval marital courts, which was responsible for ecclesiastical discipline at Geneva. The scope of the authority of this body was the subject of intense debate within Geneva in the early 1540s and 1550s. See pp. 111–14.

Council of Two Hundred (*Conseil des Deux Cents*)

The Genevan council, modelled on comparable institutions at Berne and Zurich, which constituted the electoral college for the *Petit Conseil*. See pp. 107–8.

Donatism

A North African sectarian movement of the late classical period, opposed by Augustine of Hippo, which made especially rigorous demands of church members, including that they be rebaptized.

Ecclesiology

The section of Christian theology dealing with the theory of the church (Greek: *ekklesia*, 'church'). At the time of the Reformation, controversy centred upon the question of whether the Protestant churches could be regarded as continuous with mainstream Christianity – in other words, were they a reformed version of Christianity, or something completely new, having little or no connection with the previous 1,500 years of Christian history?

Église dressée, église plantée

The two main forms of Calvinist congregations in the France of the 1550s. An *église plantée* was little more than an amorphous group meeting clandestinely for bible study and prayer. An *église dressée* possessed a consistorial structure with elders and deacons (obligatory from 1555 onwards).

Eiguenots

The pro-Bernese party within Geneva prior to the revolution of 1536. The term is a corrupted form of the Swiss–German word *Eidgnoss*, 'confederate'.

Estates

A way of referring to the upper strata of French society: the first estate (the clergy), the second (the nobility) and the third (the bourgeoisie). Representatives of the three met at the *Etats-généraux* (Estates General).

Evangelical

A term used to refer to the nascent reforming movements, especially in Germany and Switzerland, in the 1510s and 1520s. The term was later replaced by 'Protestant' in the aftermath of the Diet of Speyer (1529), although this latter term had connotations specifically associated with the German situation at the time.

Évangéliques

A term often used to refer to the French reforming movement, especially in the 1520s and 1530s, centring upon figures such as Margaret of Navarre and Guillaume Briçonnet, committed to a moderate Fabrisian programme of reform.

Exegesis

The science of textual interpretation, usually referring specifically to the Bible. The term 'biblical exegesis' basically means 'the process of interpreting the Bible'. The specific techniques employed in the exegesis of scripture are usually referred to as 'hermeneutics'.

Fabrisian

The reforming views associated with Jacques Lefèvre d'Etaples, which assumed particular importance at Paris and elsewhere in France in the 1520s. Although developing views, particularly on the authority and interpretation of scripture, which foreshadowed those of the reformers, Lefèvre did not regard these as necessitating or implying a break with the catholic church. It was a movement for reform *within* the church.

Fathers

An alternative term for 'patristic writers'.

General Council (*Conseil Général*)

The largest Genevan council, which was originally the electoral college of the medieval city. By Calvin's time, this function had been taken over by the *Conseil des Deux Cents*; the *Conseil Général* was now ordinarily summoned only twice a year, for two strictly limited purposes: the election of syndics in February, and the fixing of corn and wine prices in November. See pp. 107–8.

Guillermins

The faction within Geneva, especially during the period 1535–8, which centred upon Guillaume Farel.

Habits of grace, created

A concept introduced by writers of the thirteenth century, such as Thomas Aquinas, as an intermediate between God and human nature in the process of salvation. It was argued that, as God could not deal *directly* with fallen human nature, it was necessary for an intermediate state between divinity and humanity to be established as a sort of 'bridgehead' from which the process of salvation could proceed. This intermediate state was known as a 'created habit of grace'.

Heresy

A formal denial of any central defined doctrine of the Christian faith. In historical terms, however, heresies were not merely intellectual in origin; they were often a response to certain social and political pressures. Thus Donatism was partly a reaction on the part of native North African Berbers to Roman settlers, while Hussitism was closely linked with the emergence of Bohemian nationalism.

Hermeneutics

The principles underlying the interpretation, or exegesis, of a text, particularly of scripture. The first phase of the Reformation witnessed the development of a number of ways of interpreting scripture, deriving from both humanism and scholasticism. Zwingli initially used a hermeneutical scheme deriving from Erasmian humanism, and Luther a scheme deriving from scholastic theology.

Huguenot

A term used to refer to French Calvinists, particularly during the Wars of Religion.

Humanism

The general trend, especially associated with the Renaissance, to regard classical style as normative, and the study of classical literature as a means of promoting such style in the present day. See pp. 52–8. Renaissance humanism was not a secular or atheistic movement, as the modern use of the term might suggest.

Intellectualism

In medieval thought, the belief that the divine intellect takes precedence over the divine will. An intellectualist approach to human merit rests on the belief that the divine intellect recognizes the inherent moral value of a human act, and thus allocates it a proportional meritorious value. This approach is to be contrasted with *voluntarism*, which assigned priority to the divine will.

Justification by faith, doctrine of

The section of Christian theology dealing with how the individual sinner is able to enter into fellowship with God. Although of major importance to Martin Luther and his colleagues at Wittenberg, the doctrine was actually of relatively little interest to the Swiss reformers, such as Zwingli, and subsequently to Calvin. Whereas the first wave of the Reformation (deriving largely from Luther) would centre on this doctrine, the second (especially associated with Calvin) centred primarily on issues relating to church order and discipline.

Liturgy

The written text of public services, especially of the eucharist. As liturgy was predetermined by theology in the Reformation, the reform of the liturgy was regarded as being of particular importance.

Lutheranism

The religious ideas associated with Martin Luther, particularly as expressed in the Lesser Catechism (1529) and the Augsburg Confession (1530). A series of internal disagreements within Lutheranism after Luther's death (1546) between hardliners (the so-called 'Gnesio-Lutherans' or 'Flacianists') and moderates ('Philippists') led to their resolution by the Formula of Concord (1577), which is usually regarded as the authoritative statement of Lutheran theology.

Magisterial Reformation

A term used to distinguish the Lutheran and Reformed wings of the Reformation from the radical wing (Anabaptism). The term denotes the positive attitude to the authority of the magistrates (or city councils) characteristic of Luther, Zwingli, Bucer and Calvin.

Mammelukes

The pro-Savoyard party within Geneva prior to the revolution of 1536.

Messieurs de Genève

A term used to designate the *Petit Conseil* and syndics of the city of Geneva – in other words, the city's ruling body.

Nicodemism

A derogatory term referring to those evangelicals within catholic contexts, especially in France, who were reluctant to draw attention publicly to their faith for fear of the consequences.

Nominalism

Strictly speaking, the theory of knowledge opposed to realism. The term is, however, still used occasionally to refer to the *via moderna*. See pp. 41–5.

Patristic

An adjective used to refer to the first centuries in the history of the church, following the writing of the New Testament (the 'patristic period'), or thinkers writing during this period (the 'patristic writers'). For the reformers, the period thus designated seems to be c.100–451 (in other words, the period between the closing of the New Testament and the Council of Chalcedon). The reformers tended to regard the New Testament and, to a lesser extent, the patristic periods as normative for Christian belief and practice.

Pelagianism

An understanding of how humans are able to merit their salvation which is diametrically opposed to that of Augustine of Hippo, placing considerable emphasis upon the role and value of human works and playing down the idea of divine grace. See pp. 43–5.

Petit Conseil

The Little Council of the city of Geneva, often referred to simply as 'the council', which was responsible for virtually every aspect of Genevan life. See pp. 107–8.

Predestination

The doctrine that God has in some way predetermined the destiny of individuals. The most common form of the doctrine – *praedestinatio ad vitam* or 'predestination to life' – treated predestination as a mystery by which God was actively involved in the salvation of believers, even before they came to faith. The more radical form of the doctrine, associated with the *schola Augustiniana moderna*, Calvin and later Calvinism, was known as *praedestinatio gemina*, 'double predestination'. According to this doctrine, God has predetermined the fate of all, whether believers or non-believers, in a sovereign act of will (see pp. 208–18). It was seen by many Calvinist writers as a forceful statement of divine sovereignty over his creation.

Protestantism

A term used in the aftermath of the Diet of Speyer (1529) to designate those who 'protested' against the practices and beliefs of the Roman Catholic church. Prior to 1529, such individuals and groups had referred to themselves as 'evangelicals'.

Puritanism

A somewhat loose term generally used to refer to the form of Calvinism especially associated with England, and subsequently America, in the late sixteenth and early seventeenth centuries.

Radical Reformation

A term used with increasing frequency to refer to the Anabaptist movement – in other words, the wing of the Reformation which adopted a generally negative approach to secular authority, and a radical approach to common property. It was widely perceived as a destabilizing influence by city councils, especially at Zurich and Strasbourg.

Sacrament

In purely historical terms, a church service or rite which was held to have been instituted by Jesus Christ himself. Although medieval theology and church practice recognized seven such sacraments, the reformers argued that only two (baptism and eucharist) were to be found in the New Testament itself. The theory of the sacraments came to be intensely divisive, with Luther and Zwingli proving unable to reach agreement between themselves concerning what the sacraments actually achieved. Calvin's theology of the sacraments is generally regarded as eirenic, mediating between these two positions.

Schism

A deliberate break with the unity of the church, condemned vigorously by influential writers of the early church, such as Cyprian and Augustine. The Donatist controversy centred on the question of whether it was legitimate for a group dissatisfied with the behaviour of the church or its leaders to break away from it and found their own sect. The reformers were branded as 'schismatics' or 'sectarians' by their opponents, and thus found themselves placed in the difficult situation of upholding Augustine's views on grace, but disregarding his views on the unity of the church.

Schola Augustiniana moderna

A form of late medieval scholasticism which laid emphasis upon Augustine's doctrine of grace, while adopting a nominalist position on the question of universals. See pp. 41–5.

Scotism

The scholastic philosophy associated with Duns Scotus.

Scripture principle

The theory, especially associated with Reformed theologians such as Calvin, that the practices and beliefs of the church should be grounded in scripture. Nothing that could not be demonstrated to be grounded in scripture could be regarded as binding upon the believer. The phrase *sola scriptura*, 'by scripture alone', summarizes this principle.

Septuagint

The Greek translation of the Old Testament, dating from the third century BC.

Sorbonne

In its precise sense, this refers to the *Collège de la Sorbonne*, one of the most important and oldest constituent colleges of the University of Paris. In the sixteenth century, the term was usually employed in a derogatory sense, to mean the faculty of theology of the University of Paris.

Soteriology

The section of Christian theology dealing with the doctrine of salvation (Greek: *soteria*).

Syndics

The four leading members of the *Petit Conseil* of Geneva. See pp. 107–8.

Terminism

A more precise way of designating 'nominalism'.

Thomism, *via Thomae*

The scholastic philosophy associated with Thomas Aquinas.

Transubstantiation

The medieval doctrine according to which the bread and the wine are transformed into the body and blood of Christ in the eucharist, while retaining their outward appearance.

Universals

An abstract or general concept (e.g., 'whiteness') regarded as having a real or mental existence (cf. Realism). One of the central tenets of Terminism or Nominalism is the denial of such universals.

via antiqua

A term used to designate forms of scholastic philosophy, such as Thomism and Scotism, which adopted a realist position on the question of universals.

via moderna

A term used broadly in two senses. First, forms of scholastic philosophy which adopted a nominalist position on the question of universals, in opposition to the realism of the *via antiqua*. See pp. 00–00. Second, and more importantly, the form of scholasticism (formerly known as 'nominalism') based upon the writings of William of Ockham and his followers, such as Pierre d'Ailly and Gabriel Biel. See pp. 41–5.

Voluntarism

The medieval doctrine that the divine will takes precedence over the divine intellect. A voluntarist approach to human merit argues that God determines, by an act of will, what the meritorious value of a given human action will be. The intrinsic moral value of this action is argued to be irrelevant; it is what God wills the action to be worth that is of central importance. This approach is to be contrasted with intellectualism, which gave priority to the divine intellect. Calvin, in common with most of his generation, tended towards voluntarism.

Vulgate

The Latin translation of the Bible, largely deriving from Jerome, upon which medieval theology was mainly based. Strictly speaking, 'Vulgate' designates Jerome's translation of the Old Testament (except the Psalms, which were taken from the Gallican Psalter); the apocryphal works (except Wisdom, Ecclesiasticus, 1 and 2 Maccabees, and Baruch, which were taken from the Old Latin Version); and all the New Testament. The recognition of its many inaccuracies was of fundamental importance to the Reformation. See pp. 56–8.

Zwinglianism

The term is used generally to refer to the thought of Huldrych Zwingli, but is often used to refer specifically to his views on the sacraments, especially on the 'real presence' (which for Zwingli was more of a 'real absence').

Appendix 2

Referring to Works by Calvin

TWO MAIN primary sources have been referred to extensively throughout the present work: the 1559 edition of the *Institutes*, and the *Corpus Reformatorum* edition of Calvin's works. The latter is especially valuable as a source for his biblical commentaries, sermons and correspondence, as well as documents concerning the relation of Calvin to the Genevan authorities. The present Appendix aims to explain the most commonly encountered means of referring to these works.

THE *INSTITUTES OF THE CHRISTIAN RELIGION*

Calvin's *Institutes of the Christian Religion* is almost invariably referred to in the edition of 1559. This edition is divided into four main books, each dealing with a broad general theme. Each book is then divided into chapters, each of which is further subdivided into sections. A reference to the 1559 edition of this work will therefore include *three* numbers, identifying the *book*, the *chapter* and the *section*. The book number is usually given in capital Roman numerals, the chapter in small Roman numerals, and the section in Arabic numerals. Thus book two, chapter twelve, section one, is generally referred to as II.xii.1, although a reference might read II, 12, 1 or 2.12.1. The first system is used in the present work.

In addition, reference may be given to an edition (for example, the *Corpus Reformatorum* or *Opera Selecta*) or an English translation. For example, the reference *Institutes* III.xi.1; *OS* 4.193.2–5 is a reference to book three, chapter eleven, section one of the 1559 edition of the *Institutes*, specifically the section to be found on lines 2–5 of page 193 of the fourth volume of the *Opera Selecta*.

The *Corpus Reformatorum* Edition of Calvin's Works

Reference to Calvin's commentaries and sermons usually involves the *Corpus Reformatorum* edition, which is referred to simply by volume and page number. Thus OC 50.437 is a reference to page 437 of volume 50. The volume number will be in the range 1–59. Where a volume exists in several parts, these are designated by lower-case letters – thus OC10a.160–5 is a reference to pages 160–5 of the first part of volume 10.

Occasionally, unfortunately, confusion can result from an irritating practice, generally confined to older studies of Calvin. The *Corpus Reformatorum* edition consists of the works of Melanchthon (vols 1–28), Calvin (vols 29–87) and Zwingli (vols 88–). Volume one of Calvin's works is thus volume 29 within the series – and older works sometimes refer to Calvin's works using this higher volume number. If you find reference to this edition of Calvin with a volume number in the region 60–87, you should subtract 28 to obtain the correct volume number. If you find an isolated reference to Calvin, especially in an older work, which doesn't seem to make sense, you should subtract 28, and try again.

Abbreviations

Annales ESC	*Annales économies, societés et civilisations*
ARG	*Archiv für Reformationsgeschichte*
BSHPF	*Bulletin de la société d'histoire du protestantisme française*
BHR	*Bibliothèque d'histoire de la Renaissance*
HThR	*Harvard Theological Review*
JHI	*Journal of the History of Ideas*
NAK	*Nederlands Archief voor Kerk Geschiedenis*
OC	Ioannis Calvini opera quae supersunt omnia (Corpus Reformatorum)
RHR	*Revue d'Humanisme et Renaissance.*
RHPhR	*Revue d'histoire et de philosophie religieuse*
RThAM	*Recherches de théologie ancienne et médiévale*
SCJ	*Sixteenth-Century Journal*
SJTh	*Scottish Journal of Theology*
WA	D. Martin Luthers Werke: kritische Gesamtausgabe
Z	Huldreich Zwinglis sämtliche Werke (Corpus Reformatorum)

Notes

Preface

1 Dufour, 'Le mythe de Genève au temps de Calvin'.
2 Morgan, *The Puritan Family*, 16. The conventional Puritan stereotype is 'largely a post-Restoration creation': C. Hill, *The Intellectual Origins of the English Revolution*, 293.
3 Rosen, 'Calvin's Attitude towards Copernicus'.

Chapter 1 Introduction

1 On the early history of Geneva, see Martin, 'Les origines de la civitas et de l'évêché de Genève'; idem, *Histoire de Genève des origines à 1798*; Broise, *Genève et son territoire dans l'antiquité*. For the history of the diocese of Geneva, see Baud, *Le diocèse de Genève-Annecy*.
2 D. Hay, *Europe: The Emergence of an Idea* (Edinburgh, 2nd edn, 1968).
3 E.g., see J. Toussaert, *Le sentiment religieux en Flandre à la fin du Moyen Age* (Paris, 1963).
4 See P. Saenger, 'Silent Reading: Its Impact on Late Medieval Script', *Viator* 13 (1982), 367–414, especially 408–13.
5 P. Imbart de la Tour, *Origines de la Réforme* (4 vols: Melun, 2nd edn, 1946), vol. 3, 127, 324, 335–6.
6 A. Labarre, *Le livre dans la vie amiénoise au XVIe siècle* (Paris, 1971).
7 See R. Stupperich, 'Das Enchiridion Militis Christiani des Erasmus von Rotterdam', *ARG* 69 (1978), 5–23.
8 For example, see G. Strauss, *Manifestations of Discontent in Germany on the Eve of the Reformation* (Bloomington, Ind., 1971).
9 See B. Moeller, 'Piety in Germany around 1500', in S. Ozment (ed.), *The Reformation in Medieval Perspective* (Chicago, 1971), 50–75.
10 On which see K. Stendahl, 'The Apostle Paul and the Introspective Con-

science of the West', in *Paul among Jews and Gentiles* (Philadelphia, 1976), 78–96.

11 B. Collett, *Italian Benedictine Scholars and the Reformation* (Oxford, 1985), 1–76.

12 R. Lecotte, *Recherches sur les cultes populaires dans l'actuel diocèse de Meaux* (Paris, 1953), 260.

13 For the practices in France, see S. Lebecq, 'Sur la mort en France et dans les contrées voisines à la fin du Moyen Age', *Information Historique* 40 (1978), 21–32.

14 A. E. McGrath, *Reformation Thought* (Oxford/New York, 1988), 78–82.

15 Clerval, *Registre des procès-verbaux*, 237.

16 D. Hay, *The Italian Renaissance* (Cambridge, 2nd edn, 1977), 49–57.

17 M. Venard, 'Pour une sociologie du clergé du XVIe siècle: recherches sur le recrutement sacerdotal dans la province d'Avignon', *Annales ESC* 23 (1968), 987–1016.

18 H. Heller, *The Conquest of Poverty: The Calvinist Revolt in Sixteenth-Century France* (Leiden, 1986), 11–12, 53–4.

19 E. Le Roy Ladurie, *Les paysans de Languedoc* (2 vols: Paris, 1966), vol. 1, 320–6.

20 T. Boutiot, *Etudes historiques: recherches sur les anciennes pestes de Troyes* (Troyes, 1857), 15–23; A. Croix, *Nantes et pays nantais au XVIe siècle* (Paris, 1974), 109–10; H. Heller, 'Famine, Revolt and Heresy at Meaux, 1521–25', *ARG* 68 (1977), 133–57.

21 M. M. Edelstein, 'Les origines sociales de l'épiscopat sous Louis XII et François Ier', *Revue d'histoire moderne et contemporaine* 24 (1977), 239–47.

22 E. Marcel, *Le Cardinal de Givry, évêque de Langres, 1529–1561* (2 vols: Dijon, 1926), vol. 1, 69–109.

23 P. Benedict, *Rouen during the Wars of Religion* (Cambridge, 1981), 10.

24 Lefranc, *Jeunesse de Calvin*, 34.

25 The origins of the Reformation at Strasbourg are thought to reflect this tension: F. Rapp, *Réformes et réformation à Strasbourg* (Paris, 1979).

26 A. E. McGrath, *The Intellectual Origins of the European Reformation* (Oxford/New York, 1987), 12–28.

27 A. E. McGrath, *Luther's Theology of the Cross* (Oxford/New York, 1985), 8–12.

28 E. Droz, 'Fausses adresses typographiques', *BHR* 23 (1961), 380–6, 572–4.

29 Desmay, 'Remarques sur la vie de Jean Calvin', 388 (1621). Other local traditions, all dating from the early seventeenth century, are preserved in Le Vasseur, *Annales* (1633), and Masson, *Elogia varia* (1638).

30 Walzer, *Revolution of the Saints*, 310, 313–14.

31 G. Berthoud, *Antoine Marcourt, réformateur et pamphlétaire du 'Livre des Marchands' aux placards de 1534* (Geneva, 1973), 157–222. For the text of the placards, see 287–9.

32 See *Ordonnance du Roy François contre les imitateurs de la secte Luthérienne* (1 February 1535), Bibliothèque Nationale *F.* 35149, cited *Recueil général des anciennes lois françaises*, ed. F. Isambert, A. Jourdain and A. Recosy (20 vols: Paris, 1821–33), vol. 12, 50–75.

33 See Colladon's account, OC 21.56. Cf. Doumergue, *Jean Calvin*, vol. 1, 354.

34 Ibid., vol. 1, 127.

35 See McGrath, *Luther's Theology of the Cross*, 95–181.

36 OC 5.411–13.

37 OC 31.21–4.
38 Stauffer, 'Le discours à la première personne dans les sermons de Calvin'.
39 As Pfeilschifter has shown in the case of modern French Roman Catholic writings relating to Calvin: Pfeilschifter, *Das Calvinbild bei Bolsec.*
40 OC 31.26.
41 Calvin remarked that one of his chief objectives as a young man had been to live a secluded life, escaping public attention: OC 31.19–34.
42 See Hall, 'The Calvin Legend'; idem, 'Calvin against the Calvinists'; Stauffer, *L'humanité de Calvin*, 9–17.

Chapter 2 Paris: the formation of a mind

1 Wendel, *Calvin*, 17–18; Stauffer, 'Calvin', 16.
2 Desmay, 'Remarques sur la vie de Jean Calvin', 388.
3 Thurot, *Organisation de l'enseignement dans l'université de Paris*, 94; Dupon-Ferrier, 'Faculté des arts dans l'université de Paris', 70–1. Other sources, however, suggest that fifteen would have been the normal age for beginning an arts course: Farge, *Orthodoxy and Reform*, 11.
4 Lefranc, *Jeunesse de Calvin*, 195. Calvin is then described as being 12 years old, when he would in fact have been 11. Lefranc provides a useful series of relevant extracts from the Noyon registers relating to Calvin: 193–201.
5 OC 21.36. In his study of Sainte-Barbe, Quicherat claims Calvin as an alumnus on the basis of de Bèze's statement: Quicherat, *Histoire de Sainte-Barbe*, vol. 1, 203–18.
6 Ménager, 'Théodore de Bèze, biographe de Calvin'.
7 OC 21.54.
8 OC 21.56.
9 OC 21.121: '. . . In Gymnasio Marchiano Mathurinum Corderium.'
10 See C. E. Delormeau, *Un maître de Calvin: Mathurin Cordier, l'un des créateurs de l'enseignement secondaire moderne* (Neuchâtel, 1976), 24–9. A list of Parisian colleges with which Cordier was associated may be found in the *Colloquia* of 6 February 1564, reprinted Delormeau, 122–6, especially 122.
11 E.g., Quicherat, *Histoire de Sainte-Barbe*, vol. 1, 206.
12 Farge, *Orthodoxy and Reform*, 88.
13 Bibliothèque Nationale MS Lat 5657A. Rashdall, *Universities of Europe*, vol. 1, 528–9.
14 Archives de l'Université MSS Reg 89 fol. 41v; Reg 90 fols 33v, 43r. There is also some relevant material in Bibliothèque Nationale MS Lat 12846 (e.g., fol. 161r–v) certifying that a number of named individuals lectured in theology at a variety of colleges other than the Sorbonne and Navarre in the 1520s. This document dates from the seventeenth century, summarizing now-lost sixteenth century originals. It is evident that the information given is purely illustrative of the original archive material, suggesting that theology was taught more widely within the university than even this important source indicates.
15 For the Paris theological curriculum, see Farge, *Orthodoxy and Reform*, 16–28.
16 A third ground which gave rise to the suggestion that Calvin might have been associated with more than one college at Paris may be noted, but is not of relevance to Calvin. It was not uncommon for university faculty members,

such as regent masters, to have multiple college affiliations, reflecting their involvement in teaching at a number of colleges.

17 Godet, *Congrégation de Montaigu*; Féret, *Faculté de théologie*, vol. 1, 3–5.

18 See A. Renaudet, 'Jean Standonck un réformateur catholique avant la Réforme', *Humanisme et Renaissance, Travaux* 30 (1958), 114–61 for further details. The statutes then introduced are noted by Godet, *Congrégation de Montaigu*, 143–70.

19 E.g., A. Renaudet, *Préréforme et l'humanisme à Paris pendant les premières guerres de l'Italie (1496–1517)*, (Paris, rev. edn, 1953) 26; Wendel, *Calvin et l'humanisme*, 13.

20 See R. R. Post, *The Modern Devotion* (Leiden, 1968), 13–15.

21 Renaudet, 'L'humanisme et l'enseignement de l'université', 153; Garcia Villoslada, *Universidad de París durante los estudios de Francisco de Vitorio*, 87, 106–26.

22 OC 21.54.

23 Based on Thurot, *Organisation de l'enseignement dans l'université de Paris*, appendixes 3–5. For a selection of student estimates in the period 1500–50, see Matos, *Les Portugais à l'université de Paris*, 111 n. 1.

24 Note the reference by Goulet to the 'cingulum super vestem': Quicherat, *Histoire de Sainte-Barbe*, 331. Suggestions for reform are noted in 1539: Du Boulay, *Historia Universitatis Parisiensis*, vol. 6, 334–5.

25 Berty, *Topographie historique du vieux Paris: région centrale de l'université*, passim, supplemented by Archives Nationales collections S 6211, S 6482–3.

26 See Godet, *Congrégation de Montaigu*, 34.

27 Godet, *Congrégation de Montaigu*, 33 n. 5. Full details of the foundation and titles possessed by the college are located in Archives Nationales manuscripts S 6211 and S 6482–3.

28 J. Verger, 'Le rôle social de l'université d'Avignon au XVe siècle', *BHR* 33 (1971), 489–504.

29 Le Goff, 'La conception française de l'université à l'époque de la Renaissance', 94–100.

30 Note Calvin's later recollection: OC 31.22. Cf. the comment of de Bèze, 'son coeur tendit entièrement à la Théologie' (OC 21.29).

31 Ganoczy, *The Young Calvin*, 174.

32 Thurot, *Organisation de l'enseignement dans l'université de Paris*; Cobban, *Medieval Universities*.

33 An annotated list may be found in J. M. Prat, *Maldonet et l'université de Paris* (Paris, 1856), 527–37.

34 OC 21.121.

35 On which see Kibre, *Nations in the Medieval Universities*.

36 Farge, *Orthodoxy and Reform*, 60, 72–5, 81. These figures relate to students graduating in arts, and subsequently studying theology, whose institutional affiliations are known. The affiliations of as many as one-half of such students are unknown.

37 Goulet, *Compendium*. We have used the section to be found in Quicherat, *Histoire de Sainte-Barbe*, vol. 1, 325–31.

38 Thurot, *Organisation de l'enseignement dans l'université de Paris*, 101.

39 Quicherat, *Histoire de Sainte-Barbe*, vol. 1, 330.

40 For the reverence attached to Aristotle, see Goulet's comment, 'in logica summe colatur Aristoteles': Quicherat, *Histoire de Sainte-Barbe*, vol. 1, 330.

For full details of the works laid down by statute for study, see Garcia Villoslada, *Universidad de París*, 74–5.

41 Garcia Villoslada, *Universidad de París*, 133. This should not, however, be taken to mean that Mair was thoroughly Aristotelian in his outlook: for example, he was a leading exponent at Paris of anti-Aristotelian ideas, such as an extra-cosmic void and an infinity of worlds: Kaiser, 'Calvin's Understanding of Aristotelian Natural Philosophy', 87.

42 E.g., see C. B. Schmidt, *Aristotle and the Renaissance* (Cambridge, Mass., 1983); E. F. Rice, 'Humanist Aristotelianism in France: Jacques Lefèvre d'Etaples and His Circle', in A. H. T. Levi (ed.), *Humanism in France at the End of the Middle Ages and in the Early Renaissance* (Manchester 1970), 132–49.

43 Paris, Bibliothèque Nationale MS Lat 6535 fol. 228v.

44 Kaiser, 'Calvin's Understanding of Aristotelian Natural Philosophy'.

45 Quicherat, *Histoire de Sainte-Barbe*, vol. 1, 330.

46 Colladon refers us to two Spaniards (OC 21.54), and de Bèze to one who taught him dialectic (OC 21.121): 'translatus deinde in Gymnasium ab Acuto Monte cognominatum Hispanum habuit doctorem non indoctum: a quo exculto ipsius ingenio, quod ei iam tum erat acerrimum, ita profecit ut . . . ad dialectices et aliarum quas vocant artium studium, promoveretur.'

47 Reuter, *Grundverständnis der Theologie Calvins*, 20–1, 28. For a summary, see A. E. McGrath, *Reformation Thought*, (Oxford/New York, 1988) 63–4. This thesis is modified slightly in Reuter's more recent study, *Vom Scholaren bis zum jungen Reformator*. His earlier position is uncritically accepted by McDonnell, *John Calvin*, 7–13.

48 Torrance, 'Intuitive and Abstractive Knowledge'. Cf. his earlier study 'La philosophie et la théologie de Jean Mair ou Major'. Epistemological similarities are also detected by Richard, *Spirituality of John Calvin*, 181.

49 Wendel, *Calvin*, 19.

50 Dankbaar, *Calvin*, 5.

51 Ganoczy, *Young Calvin*, 168–78. For a detailed breakdown of Calvin's use of Peter Lombard and Gratian in the 1536, 1539, 1543 and 1559 editions of the *Institutes*, see Smits, *Saint Augustin dans l'oeuvre de Jean Calvin*, 210.

52 Reuter, *Vom Scholaren bis zum jungen Reformator*, 6–12.

53 Goumaz, *Doctrine du salut*, 92.

54 C. G. Nauert, 'The Clash of Humanists and Scholastics: An Approach to Pre-Reformation Controversies', *SCJ* 4 (1973), 1–18; J. Overfield, 'Scholastic Opposition to Humanism in Pre-Reformation Germany', *Viator* 7 (1976), 391–420; A. H. T. Levi, 'The Breakdown of Scholasticism and the Significance of Evangelical Humanism', in G. R. Hughes (ed.), *The Philosophical Assessment of Theology* (Georgetown, 1987), 101–28.

55 Erasmus, *Opera Omnia*, vol. 6, 962D–967C.

56 There was! Whether God could become a cucumber (or an ass, or a stone for that matter) concerned personification in the incarnation: A. E. McGrath, '*Homo Assumptus*? A Study in the Christology of the *Via Moderna*, with Special Reference to William of Ockham', *Ephemerides Theologicae Lovanienses* 60 (1985), 283–97. Whether he could undo the past concerned the problem of future contingents: W. J. Courtenay, 'John of Mirecourt and Gregory of Rimini on whether God can undo the past', *Recherches de Théologie ancienne et médiévale* 39 (1972), 244–56; 40 (1973), 147–74.

57 For an elementary introduction, see McGrath, *Reformation Thought*, 50–66,

especially 53–61. For a more detailed analysis, see A. E. McGrath, *Intellectual Origins of the European Reformation* (Oxford/New York, 1987), 69–121, especially 70–93.

58 See E. Gilson, *History of Christian Philosophy in the Middle Ages* (London, 1978), 489–98.

59 A. L. Gabriel, '"Via Moderna" and "Via Antiqua" and the Migration of Paris Students and Masters to the German Universities in the Fifteenth Century', in A. Zimmermann, (ed.), *Antiqui und Moderni: Traditionsbewusstsein und Fortschrittsbewusstsein im späten Mittelalter* (Berlin/New York, 1974), 439–83.

60 Reuter discerns six major points of contact between Calvin and the terminism of John Mair: Reuter, *Vom Scholaren bis zum jungen Reformator*, 6–12.

61 This possibility was first outlined in McGrath, 'John Calvin and Late Medieval Thought'.

62 For the historical development of the Pelagian controversy, and the issues involved, see P. Brown, *Augustine of Hippo* (London, 1975), 340–407.

63 A. E. McGrath, *Iustitia Dei: A History of the Christian Doctrine of Justification* (2 vols: Cambridge, 1986), vol. 1, 163–79.

64 Scotus, *Opus Oxoniense* III dist. xix q.1 n.7: 'dico, quod omne aliud a Deo, ideo est bonum, quia a Deo volitum, et non est converso: sic meritum illud tantum bonum erat, pro quanto acceptabatur.'

65 *Responsio ad aliquot Laelii Socini Senensis quaestiones*: OC 10a.160–5. The 1554 edition of the *Institutes* gives a purely cursory analysis of the question (vii, 18: OC 1.523–4).

66 *Institutes* II.xvii.1.

67 See, e.g., A. Gordon, 'The Sozzini and their School', *Theological Review* 16 (1879), 293–322.

68 Reuter, *Grundverständnis der Theologie Calvins*, 21.

69 Mair, *In I Sent.*, preface (Paris, 1530).

70 A copy of this work (though not necessarily Calvin's personal copy) was included in the library of the Genevan Academy in 1572: see Ganoczy, *La bibliothèque de l'Académie de Calvin*, 102–5.

71 For the university statute identifying William of Ockham and Gregory of Rimini as the doctors of the *via nominalium*, see Garcia Villoslada, *Universidad de París*, 118.

72 Dankbaar, *Calvin*, 26.

73 Clerval, *Registre des procès-verbaux*, 370.

74 Paris, Archives Nationales X 1530, fols 33v–34r; letter of the king to the *Parlement* of Paris.

75 See Cristiani, 'Luther et la faculté de théologie de Paris' for details.

76 E.g., that of 14 August: the registers record that 'in materia de Leuter [sic] de qua fuerat articulus, non fuit conclusio pacifica.' Clerval, *Registre des procès-verbaux*, 273.

77 Text in Du Boulay, *Historia Universitatis Parisiensis*, vol. 6, 116–27. This document does not really represent a response to the Leipzig theses, as noted by Hempsall, 'Luther and the Sorbonne'.

78 Cf. A. E. McGrath, 'Forerunners of the Reformation? A Critical Examination of the Evidence for Precursors of the Reformation Doctrines of Justification', HThR 75 (1982), 221.

79 For full documentation, see F. M. Higman, *Censorship and the Sorbonne: A Bibliographical Study of Books in French Censured by the Faculty of Theology of the*

University of Paris, 1520–1551 (Geneva, 1979); Farge, *Orthodoxy and Reform*, 169–208.

Chapter 3 The years of wandering: Orléans and the encounter with humanism

1 The phrase is de Bèze's: OC 21.121–2. For discussion of the controverted date of the move to Orléans, see Parker, *John Calvin*, 189–91.
2 OC 21.29, 54, 121.
3 A. E. McGrath, *Intellectual Origins of the European Reformation* (Oxford/New York, 1987), 125–7.
4 For a review of recent studies of the nature of Renaissance humanism, see McGrath, *Intellectual Origins of the European Reformation*, 32–68.
5 P. O. Kristeller, *La tradizione aristotelica nel Rinascimento* (Padua, 1972).
6 Idem. 'The European Diffusion of Italian Humanism', in *Renaissance Thought II: Humanism and the Arts* (New York, 1965), 69–88.
7 P. Bietenholz, *Der italienische Humanismus und die Blütezeit des Buchdrucks in Basel* (Basle, 1959).
8 R. Stupperich, 'Das Enchiridion Militis Christiani des Erasmus von Rotterdam', *ARG* 69 (1978), 5–23.
9 For what follows, see McGrath, *Intellectual Origins of the European Reformation*, 122–39.
10 Hall, 'Calvin, the Jurisconsults and the *Ius Civile*'.
11 G. Kisch, *Humanismus und Jurisprudenz: Der Kampf zwischen mos italicus und mos gallicus an der Universität Basel* (Basle, 1955), 9–76.
12 For possible lines of influence, see R. Abbondanza, 'Premières considérations sur la méthodologie d'Alciat', in *Pédagogues et Juristes* (Paris, 1963), 107–18.
13 For the drafts, see OC 10a.125–46.
14 Grislis, 'Calvin's Use of Cicero in the Institutes I:1–5'.
15 Cf. OC 10b.16–17, 19–20.
16 OC 10b.19–20, 20–1. Cf. Battles and Hugo, *Commentary on Seneca*, 387–91.
17 Note the bold suggestion (OC 5.32): 'errat tamen Erasmus.'
18 J. Boisset, *Sagesse et sainteté dans la pensée de Calvin* (Paris, 1959), 248.
19 Calvin may have used collections of patristic quotations in much the same manner later in his career. For example, Hermann Bodius' *Unio Dissidentium* was printed frequently between 1527 and 1602, and it is possible that Calvin may have derived some of his patristic references from it, or a similar work.
20 Doinel, 'Jean Calvin à Orléans'.
21 Lefranc, *La jeunesse de Calvin*, 200.
22 For what follows, see Bourrilly and Weiss, 'Jean du Bellay, les protestants et la Sorbonne, 1529–1535'.
23 Duplessis d'Argentré, *Collectio judiciorum* 2/1, 78.
24 Duplessis d'Argentré, *Collectio judiciorum*, 2/1, 96–7. 'Broder' can also bear the equally apposite meaning 'embroider'.
25 Paris, BN MS N Acq Lat 1782 fols 259v–260r.
26 Paris, BN MS N Acq Lat 1782 fols 265v–269r, indicating the faculty's insistence that it had not actively condemned the poem; the censure took place *ipso facto*, they argued, through a failure of her publisher to meet existing regulations. For a different interpretation of these events, see F. M. Higman,

Censorship and the Sorbonne: A Bibliographical Study of Books in French Censured by the Faculty of Theology of the University of Paris, 1520–1551 (Geneva, 1979).

27 OC 10b.25–6. The reference to 'pridie Simonis' is to be interpreted as 'the eve of the feast of St Simon' – i.e., 27 October. A later reference in Colladon's biography (OC 21.123) suggests Calvin resided at the Collège de Fortet (*Gymnasium quod Fortretum vocant*) during this period.

28 Ganoczy, *The Young Calvin*, 77–8.

29 A. Renaudet, *Préréforme et l'humanisme à Paris pendant les premières guerres de l'Italie 1496–1517* (Paris, rev. edn, 1953), 210.

30 According to Du Boulay, *Historia Universitatis Parisiensis* vol. 6, 238, he took up his duties on 10 October.

31 E.g., Wendel, *Calvin*, 40.

32 H. de Vocht, *Monumenta humanistica Lovaniensia* (Louvain, 1934), 434–41, esp. 438.

33 For the text, see Rott, 'Documents strasbourgeois', 43–9.

34 De Vocht, *Monumenta*, 430–58 for the full text of the letter and copious notes.

35 This emerges from a letter, dated 11 December, from Jacques Colin to Jean du Bellay; cf. Bourrilly and Weiss, 'Jean du Bellay, les protestants et la Sorbonne', 218–19 n. 3.

36 Our source here is Manrique: De Vocht, *Monumenta*, 440.

37 Paris, Archives Nationales MS X 1537 fol. 29r. (It is possible that the king may have confused Cop with Pierre Cornu, and that 'Recteur' ought to read 'docteur': cf. Rott, 'Documents strasbourgeois', 35 n. 39.) Note also the earlier instructions to *parlement* to prosecute with vigour the 'damnable Lutheran sect' (fols 28v–29r); Cop is clearly associated with this group in the king's mind.

38 For details, see Rott, 'Documents strasbourgeois'.

39 This seems to be implied by his letter to François Daniel, to be dated 18 January 1534: OC 10b.15–16 (the published date, 1532, is clearly incorrect).

40 Witness the letter to Daniel, dated 27 December 1533: OC 10b.11–12.

Chapter 4 From humanist to reformer: the conversion

1 See P. Fredricksen, 'Paul and Augustine: Conversion Narratives, Orthodox Traditions and the Retrospective Self', *Journal of Theological Studies* 37 (1986), 3–34.

2 This widespread attitude, it must be stressed, rests upon misunderstandings of the views of both late Judaism and late medieval catholicism on justification: cf. A. E. McGrath, *Iustitia Dei: A History of the Christian Doctrine of Justification* (2 vols. Cambridge, 1986), vol. 1, 70–91; E. P. Sanders, *Paul, the Law and the Jewish People* (Philadelphia, 1983).

3 It is occasionally suggested that the *Reply to Sadoleto* may include clues concerning Calvin's conversion. In this work, two evangelicals – one a pastor, the other a layman – describe their 'conversions'. For some writers, these are not stereotypes or models, but reflect Calvin's personal experience: Doumergue, *Jean Calvin*, vol. 1, 347; Wendel, *Calvin*, 38–9. In response, it must be pointed out that the literary genre of this work is that of dramatic fiction. Calvin's literary model is forced upon him by Sadoleto's original, in which a priest and a 'common man' complain of the eccentricities and deviations

of evangelicalism. No autobiographical reference is implied, and none is immediately obvious, on the basis of what we know of Calvin's career: Ganoczy, *Young Calvin*, 254–9.

4 We here summarize OC 31.21–4.

5 Parker, *John Calvin*, 193, suggests that *subita* should be translated as 'unexpected', on the basis of Calvin's Seneca commentary. In this commentary, Calvin comments as follows: '*subita* – not only sudden (*repentina*) but also unexpected (*inconsiderata*)'. Cf. Battles and Hugo, *Commentary on Seneca*, 55–6; Parker, *John Calvin*, 193–4. However, at this point Calvin merely seems to be clarifying an unusual meaning of the term *subita*, in which Seneca allows the sense of 'unpremeditated' to assume priority over the normal meaning of 'sudden'. One may reasonably assume that most conversions are unpremeditated and unexpected, which appears to render Calvin's *subita conversio* tautologous; nevertheless, conversions are not necessarily *sudden*, in that they may take place over a prolonged period of time.

6 A. Rich, *Die Anfänge der Theologie Huldrych Zwinglis* (Zurich, 1949), 104–19.

7 See Ganoczy's excellent analysis of Calvin's consciousness of a divine call: *Young Calvin*, 287–307.

8 Identified and analysed by Sprenger, *Das Rätsel um die Bekehrung Calvins*, 36–41. For the texts, see OC 31.21 and 48.199–202.

9 McGrath, *Luther's Theology of the Cross* (Oxford/New York, 1985). Luther's recollections date from 1545, the year before his death; the events described date from 1513 to 1519, probably centring upon 1515.

10 Ganoczy, *Young Calvin*, 252–66.

11 De Raemond, *Histoire*, 883–5.

12 OC 13.681. De Raemond lists a number of individuals with whom Calvin fraternized during this period (although he mistakenly states that Calvin resided at Angoulême for a period of several years): *Histoire*, 883–5.

13 De Raemond, *Histoire*, 889.

14 The document is cited in Lefranc, *Jeunesse de Calvin*, 201.

15 Ibid., 201.

16 Cf. Doumergue, *Jean Calvin*, vol. 7, 575.

17 OC 12.68. The suggestion that Calvin was imprisoned by the Inquisition in April 1536 as he crossed the Val d'Aoste on his return from Italy (e.g., Dankbaar, *Calvin*, 42–3) is not confirmed by any contemporary source.

18 OC 21.57.

19 Calvin refers to this abortive meeting in 1554: OC 8.481.

20 G. Berthoud, *Antoine Marcourt, réformateur et pamphlétaire du 'Lire des Marchands' aux placards de 1534* (Geneva, 1973), 157–222. For facsimiles of the placards, see 287–9.

21 D. R. Kelley, *The Beginning of Ideology: Consciousness and Formation in the French Reformation* (Cambridge, 1981), 13–19.

22 For the distinction, see R. O. Allen and B. Spilka, 'Committed and Consensual Religion', *Journal for the Scientific Study of Religion* 6 (1967), 191–206.

23 Cf. H. R. Guggisberg, *Basel in the Sixteenth Century* (St Louis, 1982), for details.

24 P. Wernle, *Calvin und Basel bis zum Tode des Myconius* (Tübingen, 1909), 4; some further material in Plath, *Calvin und Basel in den Jahren 1552–1556*.

25 The memory of this event was still fresh in his mind in 1557: OC 31.24.

26 See especially the letter of Francis I to the German Protestant princes, dated 1 February 1535: Herminjard, *Correspondance des réformateurs*, vol. 3, 250–4.

27 OC 31.24 (the French is more expressive than the parallel Latin text).
28 The 'prefatory letter' is dated '10. Cal. Septembris'. The Basle printers, Thomas Platter and Balthasar Lasius, acting with the editorial assistance of Jean Oporin, took their time in producing the work: it would not be published until March the following year.
29 OC 21.58.
30 N. M. Sutherland, *Huguenot Struggle for Recognition* (New Haven/London, 1980), 30–1, 336.
31 Lefranc, *La jeunesse de Calvin*, 205.

Chapter 5 Geneva: the first period

1 OC 8.416.
2 OC 48.117–18.
3 Kingdon, 'Deacons of the Reformed Church'.
4 See Kingdon, 'Social Welfare in Calvin's Geneva'.
5 B. Moeller, *Imperial Cities and the Reformation* (Philadelphia, 1972).
6 T. A. Brady, *Ruling Class, Regime and Reformation at Strasbourg, 1520–1555* (Leiden, 1977).
7 S. E. Ozment, *The Reformation in the Cities: The Appeal of Protestantism to Sixteenth-Century Germany and Switzerland* (New Haven, 1975).
8 P. Broadhead, 'Popular Pressure for Reform in Augsburg, 1524–1534', in W. J. Mommsen (ed.), *Stadtbürgertum und Adel in der Reformation* (Stuttgart, 1979), 80–7; H. von Greyerz, *The Late City Reformation in Germany: The Case of Colmar* (Wiesbaden, 1980); W. Ehbrecht, 'Verlaufsformen innerstädtischer Konflicte in nord- und westdeutschen Städten im Reformationszeitalter', in B. Moeller (ed.), *Stadt und Kirche im 16. Jahrhundert* (Gütersloh, 1978), 27–47; idem, 'Köln, Osnabrück, Stralsund: Rat und Bürgerschaft hansischer Städte zwischen religiöser Erneuerung und Bauernkrieg', in F. Petri (ed.), *Kirche und gesellschaftlicher Wandel* (Cologne, 1980), 23–64; Guggisberg, *Basel in the Sixteenth Century*; S. Jahns, *Frankfurt, Reformation und schmalkaldischer Bund* (Frankfurt, 1976); E. Naujoks, *Obrigkeitsgedanke, Zunftverfassung und Reformation: Studien zur Verfassungsgeschichte von Ulm, Esslingen und schwäbische Gmünd* (Stuttgart, 1958); H.-C. Rublack, *Die Einführung der Reformation in Konstanz* (Gütersloh, 1971); idem, 'Forschungsbericht Stadt und Reformation', in B. Moeller (ed.), *Stadt und Kirche im 16. Jahrhundert* (Gütersloh, 1978), 9–26; R. W. Scribner, 'Civic Unity and the Reformation in Erfurt', *Past and Present* 66 (1975), 29–60; idem, 'Why was there no Reformation at Cologne?', *Bulletin of the Institute of Historical Research* 49 (1976), 217–41; H. Stratenwerth, *Die Reformation in der Stadt Osnabrück* (Wiesbaden, 1971); G. Strauss, *Nuremberg in the Sixteenth Century* (New York, 1966); W. Wettges, *Reformation und Propaganda: Studien zur Kommunikation des Aufruhrs in süddeutschen Reichstädten* (Stuttgart, 1978).
9 A. E. McGrath, 'Justification and the Reformation: The Significance of the Doctrine of Justification by Faith to Sixteenth-Century Urban Communities', *ARG* 81 (1990), forthcoming.
10 A point stressed by W. Becker, *Reformation und Revolution* (Münster, 1974).
11 The Swiss cities were often seen, however unrealistically, as models of civic liberty by their oppressed German counterparts: T. A. Brady, *Turning Swiss: Cities and Empire, 1450–1550* (Cambridge, 1985).

12 H. C. Peyer, *Leinwandgewerbe und Fernhandel der Stadt St Gallen von den Anfängen bis 1520* (2 vols: St Gallen, 1959–60).
13 Scribner, 'Civic Unity and the Reformation in Erfurt'.
14 N. Birnbaum, 'The Zwinglian Reformation in Zurich', *Past and Presents* 15 (1959), 27–47.
15 Borel, *Les foires de Genève au XVe siècle.*
16 Bergier, *Die Wirtschaftgeschichte der Schweiz*, 293–9.
17 Much useful information may be found in Monter, *Calvin's Geneva*, 29–63, and references therein.
18 Cf. W. Richard, *Untersuchungen zur Genesis der reformierten Kirchenterminologie des Westschweiz und Frankreichs* (Berne, 1959), 41–53.
19 Ammann, 'Oberdeutsche Kaufleute und die Anfänge der Reformation in Genf'.
20 van Berchem, 'Une prédication dans un jardin'.
21 Herminjard, *Correspondance des réformateurs*, vol. 3, 125–6.
22 For details of the military campaigns, see *Histoire militaire de la Suisse* (4 vols: Berne, 1913–17), passim.
23 F. J. C. Gingins la Sarra, *Histoire de la ville d'Orbe et son château* (Lausanne, 1855).
24 M. H. Körner, *Solidarités financières suisses au XVIe siècle* (Lucerne, 1980).
25 Monter, *Genevan Government*, 11–14.
26 OC 21.200–2 for details.
27 OC 31.24 (following the longer French version of the text). The briefer Latin text suggests that the 'studies' in question were somewhat recherché.
28 OC 21.30.
29 *La Dispute de Lausanne 1536: La théologie réformée après Zwingli et avant Calvin* (Lausanne, 1988).
30 OC 9.701–2.
31 OC 9.877–84. He also intervened, briefly, on 7 October: OC 9.884–6.
32 OC 9.879, 890.
33 See Calvin's letter from Lausanne to François Daniel, dated 13 October 1536: OC 10b.64.
34 Dankbaar, *Calvin*, 49.
35 A point stressed by Kingdon, 'Calvin and the Government of Geneva', 58.
36 OC 1.369–70.
37 OC 1.372–3.
38 OC 21.222.
39 The Bernese rites involved retaining baptismal fonts, wedding services and unleavened bread, as well as several religious feasts (Christmas, Easter and Pentecost) abolished by Farel.
40 OC 10b.185–6.
41 The letters to du Tillet, dated 10 July and 20 October 1538, are very revealing in this respect: OC 10b.201, 221.
42 Letter dated 7 September 1538: OC 10b.242–4.
43 Note the letter to Farel of September 1538, referring to his own 'inexperience, carelessness, negligence and mistakes': OC 10b.246. Much the same note is struck in a letter to 'the faithful of Geneva' of 1 October: OC 10b.253.
44 OC 10b.270–2.
45 For details, see Brady, *Ruling Class, Regime and Reformation at Strasbourg*; M. U. Chrisman, *Strasbourg and the Reform: A Study in the Process of Change* (New

Haven/London, 1967); idem, *Lay Culture, Learned Culture: Books and Social Change in Strasbourg, 1480–1599* (New Haven/London, 1982).
46 Note the letter to Farel, dating from the first phase of his new ministry: OC 10b.247.
47 Pannier, *Calvin à Strasbourg*, 39–40.
48 OC 6.336.
49 Höpfl, *Christian Polity of John Calvin*, 129–31.

Chapter 6 Geneva: the consolidation of power

1 Hall, 'The Calvin Legend', identifies and discredits the more influential of these myths. However, scholarship still has a long way to go before the influence of these inventions can be exorcised from the popular conception of the reformer.
2 A. Huxley, *Proper Studies* (London, 1949), 287.
3 Chenevière, *La pensée politique de Calvin*, 178. Cf. Mercier, 'L'esprit de Calvin', 32–7; Choisy, *La théocratie à Genève.*
4 A point stressed by Chenevière, *La pensée politique de Calvin*, 244.
5 At a later stage, Calvin was occasionally ridiculed by his opponents for having no children. He replied that, while this was true, he nevertheless had a myriad of children throughout the Christian world: OC 9.576.
6 Calvin's reflections on the death of his wife, which break in on a sermon on a passage from 1 Timothy, is one of the few occasions on which the reformer disclosed details of his private feelings in public: OC 53.254.
7 R. Doucet, *Les institutions de la France au XVIe siècle* (Paris, 1948), 37–56.
8 Monter, *Studies in Genevan Government*, 85–9.
9 *Le livre des bourgeois*, 266.
10 N. Z. Davis, 'The Sacred and the Body Social in Sixteenth-Century Lyon', *Past and Present* 90 (1981), 40–70, esp. 62.
11 OC 21.547.
12 Höpfl, *Christian Polity of John Calvin*, 90–102.
13 For the suggestion that Geneva's Reformation may be regarded as a revolution, see Kingdon, 'Was the Protestant Reformation a Revolution?'
14 W. Köhler, *Zürcher Ehegericht und Genfer Konsistorium* (2 vols: Leipzig, 1932–42).
15 Höpfl, *Christian Polity of John Calvin*, 94–5.
16 H. Morf, 'Obrigkeit und Kirche in Zürich bis zu Beginn der Reformation', *Zwingliana* 13 (1970), 164–71; R. C. Walton, 'The Institutionalization of the Reformation at Zurich', *Zwingliana* 13 (1972), 497–515.
17 For a full discussion, see J. W. Baker, *Heinrich Bullinger and the Covenant: The Other Reformed Tradition* (Athens, Ohio, 1980), 55–140. However, in 1553 the Zurich authorities suggested that Geneva's form of ecclesiastical discipline was perhaps not totally inappropriate, given the situation as it existed in that city: OC 14.699–700. An earlier letter from Bullinger to Calvin, however, suggests that the former brought pressure upon the city council to adopt a non-critical approach to the Genevan system: OC 14.697–8.
18 See the letter of Sulzer to the clergy at Geneva: OC 14.711–13.
19 See the letter of 1553 from Messieurs de Berne: OC 14.691.
20 For details, see J. W. Baker, 'Church Discipline or Civil Punishment: On the

Origins of the Reformed Schism, 1528–1531', *Andrews University Seminary Bulletin* 23 (1985), 3–18.

21 Z 11.199.

22 See K. Deppermann, *Melchior Hoffmann* (Edinburgh, 1987), 279-81.

23 Chrisman, *Strasbourg and the Reform*, 220–6, 229–32; Deppermann, *Melchior Hoffmann*, 296–311.

24 Courvoisier, *La notion d'église chez Bucer*, 137–9.

25 The idea of 'elders' is also absent: for this idea in Bucer, see H. Strohl, 'La théorie et la pratique des quatre ministères à Strasbourg avant l'arrivée de Calvin', *BSHPF* 84 (1935), 123–40.

26 Monter, 'Consistory of Geneva', 479.

27 An important contemporary witness to this controversy is the letter of Johann Haller to Bullinger (September 1553), which records the hostility towards ecclesiastical discipline among prominent Genevans: OC 14.625.

28 The sixteenth century witnessed the erosion of such judicial authority within French cities, as absolutism gained momentum. See Doucet, *Institutions de la France*, 45–55.

29 At this time the office of Procureur-Général, whose responsibilities were roughly equivalent to an American prosecuting attorney. The general framework of Genevan justice could be argued to have been set in place on 28 November 1529, which – despite minor modifications in 1563 – remained the cornerstone of the city's judicial system until the end of the eighteenth century. See Monter, *Studies in Genevan Government*, 61–7.

30 This is best studied from Guggisberg's splendid analysis of the manner in which Sebastian Castellio – who criticized Calvin's role in the Servetus affair – has been viewed, especially during the Enlightenment: H. Guggisberg, *Sebastian Castellio im Urteil seiner Nachwelt vom Späthumanismus bis zur Aufklärung* (Basle, 1956).

31 R. Mentzer, *Heresy Proceedings in Languedoc, 1500–1560* (New York, 1984), 100–1.

32 *Summa Theologiae* IIaIIae q. 11 a. 3.

33 See P. E. Sigmund, *St Thomas Aquinas on Politics and Ethics* (New York, 1988), xxvi.

34 See W. H. F. Frend, 'Heresy and Schism as Social and National Movements', *Studies in Church History* 9 (1972), 37–56.

35 J. M. Stayer, 'Christianity in One City: Anabaptist Münster, 1534–35', in H. J. Hillerbrand (ed.), *Radical Tendencies in the Reformation* (Kirksville, Mo., 1988), 117–34.

36 Deppermann, *Melchior Hoffmann*, 296–311.

37 Bullinger suggested it was due to divine providence, to allow Geneva to regain its reputation for orthodoxy: OC 14.624.

38 See Stayer, 'Anabaptist Münster', 130–1.

39 The manner in which the city council prosecuted individuals whom they regarded as unsalubrious may be illustrated from the forgery trial of George Battonat (1552). This has been fully documented from the archives by Naef, 'Un alchimiste au XVIe siècle'.

40 OC 14.628.

41 OC 8.761, 783, 789–90.

42 OC 8.789.

43 OC 8.808–23.

44 OC 36.830.

45 OC 14.656–7. Note the conclusion of Höpfl, *Christian Polity of John Calvin*, 136: 'there is nothing whatever to suggest that Calvin at any time favoured anything except quick and efficient executions.'

46 Monter, *Genevan Government*, 57.

47 The growing alienation of Basle from Geneva has been traced by Plath, *Calvin und Basel in den Jahren 1552–1556*.

48 Kingdon, 'The First Expression of Theodore Beza's Political Ideas'.

49 OC 21.560.

50 Perrenaud, *La population de Genève*, 37.

51 The number of refugees is unclear. For the suggestion that population figures require revision, with a considerable increase in the number of refugees resulting, see Monter, 'Historical Demography and Religious History in Sixteenth-Century Geneva'.

52 Mandrou, 'Les français hors de France', 665.

53 OC 7.362.

54 For the tensions these refugees caused between Calvin and Genevan nationalists (who resisted their residence within the city), see Biéler, *La pensée économique et sociale de Calvin*, 107–9.

55 *Livre des bourgeois*, 240.

56 Ibid., 241–4.

57 On St Gallen, see W. Ehrenzeller, *St. Gallischer Geschichte im spätmittelalter und in der Reformationszeit* (3 vols: St Gallen, 1931–47).

58 K. Spillmann, *Zwingli und die zürcherische Politik gegenüber der Abtei St. Gallen* (St Gallen, 1965).

59 See C. Bonorand, 'Joachim Vadian und Johannes Dantiscus: Ein Beitrag zu den schweizerisch–polnischen Beziehungen im 16. Jahrhundert', *Zeitschrift für die Geschichte und Altertumskunde Ermlands* 35 (1971), 150–70; idem, Joachim Vadians Beziehungen zu Ungarn', *Zwingliana* 13 (1969), 97–131.

60 C. Bonorand, *Vadians Weg vom Humanismus zur Reformation* (St Gallen, 1962).

61 See W. Naef, *Die Familie von Watt. Geschichte eines St. Gallischen Bürgergeschlechtes* (St Gallen, 1936).

62 E. Rüsch, '"Glücklich der Stadt, die einen solchen Bürgermeister hat." Die Gratulationen zur Wahl Vadians als Bürgermeister von St. Gallen', in *Vadian, 1484–1984: Drei Vorträge* (St Gallen, 1985), 63–76.

63 Witness the protests of December 1537: E. Rüsch, 'Politische Opposition in St. Gallen zur Zeit Vadians', *Schriften des Vereins für Geschichte des Bodensees und seiner Umgebung* 104 (1986), 67–113.

64 In common with most eastern Swiss reformers: E. Ziegler, 'Zur Reformation als Reformation des Lebens und der Sitten', *Rorschacher Neujahrblatt* (1984), 53–71.

65 The exception is MS 138, held in the Burgerbibliothek, Berne. It is not entirely clear how this MS – written in 1548, dealing with the Reformation of religious orders – came to migrate from St Gallen to Berne.

66 C. Bonorand, 'Dolfin Landolfi von Poschiano: Der erste Bündner Buchdrucker der Reformationszeit', in *Festgabe Leonhart von Muralt* (Zurich, 1970), 228–44.

Chapter 7 Christianity according to Calvin: the medium

1 Holl, 'Johannes Calvin', 267 (my emphasis).
2 For details, see G. P. Norton, 'Translation Theory in Renaissance France: Etienne Dolet and the Rhetorical Tradition', *Renaissance and Reformation* 10 (1974), 1–13; L. A. Sonnino, *A Handbook to Sixteenth-Century Rhetoric* (London, 1968).
3 For a brilliant analysis, see Girardin, *Rhétorique et théologique.*
4 For what follows, see Battles, 'God was accommodating Himself to Human Capacity'.
5 A. N. Wilder, *Early Christian Rhetoric: The Language of the Gospel* (London, 1964).
6 OC 26.387–8: 'Dieu s'est fait quasi semblable à une nourrice, qui ne parlera point à un petit enfant selon qu'elle feroit à un homme . . . nostre Seigneur s'est ainsi familièrement accommodé à nous.'
7 OC 29.70, 356; 36.134; 43.161.
8 OC 23.17, 20–3, 40.
9 OC 32.364–5.
10 Battles, 'God was accommodating Himself to Human Capacity', 20–1.
11 *Institutes* I.xiii.1.
12 Balke, 'The Word of God and Experientia according to Calvin'.
13 We here develop ideas to be found in F. M. Higman, 'The Reformation and the French Language', *L'Esprit créateur* 16 (1976), 20–36; idem, 'Theology in French: Religious Pamphlets from the Counter-Reformation', *Renaissance and Modern Studies* 23 (1979), 128–46; idem, 'De Calvin à Descartes: la création de la langue classique', *RHR* 15 (1986), 5–18.
14 Higman, 'Theology in French', 130.
15 Ibid., 138.
16 See further Higman, *Style of John Calvin.*
17 Marmelstein, *Etude comparative*, passim.
18 Note the contemporary comments of Pasquier, *Recherches*, 1067: 'Car aussi estoit il homme bien escrivant tant en Latin que François, & auquel nostre langue Françaises est grandement redevable pour l'avoir enrichie d'une infinité de beaux traicts.'
19 *Vadianische Briefsammlung*, Letter no. 884.
20 For a full analysis, see Ganoczy, *Young Calvin*, 137–68.
21 For full details of the various editions and the manner in which material is transposed within them, see Autin, *L'Institution chrétienne de Calvin.* For a comparison of the various Latin and French editions, see Marmelstein, *Etude comparative.*
22 OC 1.255.
23 E.g., Pannier, 'Une première *Institution* française dès 1537'.
24 W. Maurer, 'Melanchthons "Loci Communes" von 1521 als wissenschaftliche Programmschrift', *Luther Jahrbuch* 27 (1960), 1–50.
25 Fatio, 'Présence de Calvin à l'époque de l'orthodoxie réformée', for invaluable bibliographical material.
26 Parker, *Calvin's New Testament Commentaries*; idem, *Calvin's Old Testament Commentaries.*

27 McGrath, *The Intellectual Origins of the European Reformation* (Oxford/New York, 1987), 37–8.
28 Heller, *The Conquest of Poverty: The Calvinist Revolt in Sixteenth-Century France*, (Leiden, 1986), 121–5.

Chapter 8 Christianity according to Calvin: the message

1 For example, in the case of the doctrines of justification, anthropology and ecclesiology: Santmire, 'Justification in Calvin's 1540 Romans Commentary'; Torrance, *Calvin's Doctrine of Man*; Milner, *Calvin's Doctrine of the Church*. In his study of Calvin's sermons, Stauffer has indicated the manner in which Calvin's preaching relates to his theology, with reflections upon the consequences: Stauffer, *Dieu, la création et la providence dans la prédication de Calvin*.
2 Fatio, *Méthode et théologie*, 150–3. The origins of the tendency within later Calvinism to treat theology and scriptural exegesis as unrelated matters may be traced to Lambert Daneau's definition of theology, as given in his *Compendium*.
3 Rist, 'Méthode théologique de Calvin', 21.
4 For a useful discussion, see Selinger, *Calvin against Himself*, 72–84.
5 For the general problem within intellectual history (and not merely historical theology), see H. Kellner, 'Triangular Anxieties: The Present State of European Intellectual History', in D. LaCapra and S. L. Kaplan (eds), *Modern European Intellectual History* (Ithaca, N.Y., 1982), pp. 116–31.
6 A point rightly stressed by Bouwsma, *John Calvin*, 4–6.
7 See further Willis, 'Rhetoric and Responsibility in Calvin's Theology'.
8 Schweizer, *Die protestantischen Centraldogmen*, 1–18, 150–79. More generally, see L. Boettner, *The Reformed Doctrine of Predestination* (Grand Rapids, 1968).
9 Dowey, *Knowledge of God in Calvin's Theology*, 41–9.
10 Milner, *Calvin's Doctrine of the Church*, 1–5.
11 Partee, 'Calvin's Central Dogma Again'.
12 A point stressed by Bauke, *Die Probleme der Theologie Calvins*, 22, 30–1.
13 Milner, *Calvin's Doctrine of the Church*, 2–3.
14 See Niesel, *Theology of Calvin*, 247–50; Milner, *Calvin's Doctrine of the Church*, 191.
15 The suggestion of earlier writers, such as Ernst Troeltsch, that Calvin is less Christocentric than Luther rests upon then prevailing assumptions of Calvin scholarship – especially regarding the centrality of predestination – now long abandoned.
16 Lane, 'Calvin's Use of the Fathers and Medievals', provides a splendid analysis.
17 See the analysis of Smits, *Saint Augustin dans l'oeuvre de Jean Calvin*.
18 OC 8.266.
19 Lane, 'Calvin's Sources of St Bernard'.
20 Reuter, *Vom Scholaren bis zum jungen Reformator*, 6–12; McGrath, 'John Calvin and Late Medieval Thought'.
21 Ganoczy, *The Young Calvin*, 137–51, 158–68.
22 Grislis, 'Calvin's Use of Cicero in the Institutes I:1–5'.
23 A. E. McGrath, 'Some Observations concerning the Soteriology of the *Schola Moderna*', *RThAM* 52 (1985), 182–93.

24 McGrath, 'John Calvin and Late Medieval Thought'.

25 Niesel, 'Calvin wider Osianders Rechtfertigungslehre'; Zimmermann, 'Calvins Auseinandersetzung mit Osianders Rechtfertigungslehre'.

26 McGrath, *Luther's Theology of the Cross* (Oxford/New York, 1985); idem, *Iustitia Dei: A History of the Christian Doctrine of Justification* (2 vols: Cambridge, 1986), vol. 2, 3–20.

27 A. E. McGrath, 'Justification and the Reformation: The Significance of the Doctrine of Justification by Faith to Sixteenth-Century Urban Communities', *ARG* 81 (1990), forthcoming.

28 McGrath, *Iustitia Dei*, vol. 2, 3–39.

29 The Christological aspects of Calvin's doctrine of predestination have been stressed by Jacobs, *Prädestination und Verantwortlichkeit bei Calvin.*

30 OC 14.417 is of particular importance here, especially the explicit posing of the question of why the promises of God are not equally efficacious in the lives of all people.

31 Cf. McGrath, *Iustitia Dei*, vol. 1, 128–45 for an analysis of medieval views on predestination.

32 I.v.5; III.xxi.5; xxii.1, 5; xxiv.17.

33 See Wendel, *Calvin*, 127.

34 McGrath, *Iustitia Dei*, vol. 1, 119–28, for an analysis of the concepts and their theological implications. It may be pointed out that the last century has witnessed a near-total revision of our understanding of these ideas.

35 McGrath, *Reformation Thought* (Oxford/New York, 1988), 117–30.

36 W. P. Stephens, *The Theology of Huldrych Zwingli* (Oxford, 1986), 206–11.

37 It should be stressed that Calvin does not use the term *substantia* in an Aristotelian sense, such as that underlying the medieval theory of transubstantiation. For his refutation of this theory, see *Institutes* IV.xvii.12–18.

Chapter 9 The invasion of ideas: Calvin and France

1 Desmay, 'Remarques sur la vie de Jean Calvin', 390.

2 The two outstanding studies of the Genevan influence upon the French Protestant movement by Kingdon are essential reading: Kingdon, *Geneva and the Coming of the Wars of Religion in France 1555–1563*; idem, *Geneva and the Consolidation of the French Protestant Movement 1564–1572*.

3 See H. Heller, 'Famine, Revolt and Heresy at Meaux, 1521–25', *ARG* 68 (1977), 133–57.

4 E.g., see N. Z. Davis, *Society and Culture in Early Modern France* (London, 1975); G. Huppert, *Public Schools in Renaissance France* (Chicago, 1984).

5 A useful survey of recent literature may be found in M. Greengrass, *The French Reformation* (Oxford, 1987), 1–20.

6 On which see Geisendorf, 'Métiers et conditions sociales du premier refuge à Genève, 1549–87'.

7 Geisendorf, 'Lyon et Genève du XVIe siècle au XVIIIe siècle'.

8 Much the same situation existed in England, where Lutheranism seemed initially to have gained the upper hand: B. Hall, 'The Early Rise and Gradual Decline of Lutheranism in England', in D. Baker (ed.), *Reform and Reformation: England and the Continent* (Oxford, 1979), 103–31.

9 E.g., OC 4.70–3; E. Rott, *Histoire de la représentation diplomatique de la France auprès des cantons suisses I* (Berne, 1900), 456.
10 Rott, *Représentation diplomatique de la France*, 318–21.
11 See G. Audisio, *Les vaudois du Luberon: une minorité en Provence (1460–1560)* (Luberon, 1984), for details of such communities and their reception of Calvin's ideas and structures.
12 H. Heller, *The Conquest of Poverty: The Calvinist Revolt in Sixteenth-Century France* (Leiden, 1986), 123.
13 For the text, see N. Weiss, 'Un arrêt inédit du parlement contre l'Institution chréstienne', *BSHPF* 33 (1884), 16–21.
14 Heller, *Conquest of Poverty*, 116, 127.
15 F. Higman, 'Genevan Printing and French Censorship', in J.-D. Candaux and B. Lescaze (eds), *Cinq siècles d'imprimerie genevoise* (Geneva, 1980), 31–53, esp. 36–7. A further three titles may also have been printed at Geneva, although Neuchâtel is a possibility.
16 Bremme, *Buchdrucker und Buchhändler zur Zeit der Glaubenskämpfe*.
17 R. Mentzer, *Heresy Proceedings in Languedoc*, 1500–1560 (New York, 1984), 163. Sixty-two of these individuals were burned as a result of proceedings against them.
18 Ibid., 152–3.
19 Mandrou, 'Les français hors de France', 665. This figure is based on an analysis of those 2,247 individuals whose profession is known.
20 Cf. Dufour, 'De la bourgeoisie de Genève à la noblesse de Savoie'.
21 See R. Lecotte, *Recherches sur les cultes populaires dans l'actuel diocèse de Meaux* (Paris, 1953); R. Muchembled, *Culture populaire et culture des élites dans la France moderne, XVe–XVIIIe siècles* (Paris, 1978).
22 See Eire, 'Calvin and Nicodemitism'. More generally, see A. Autin, *La crise du nicodémisme 1535–1545* (Toulon, 1917); P. Fraenkel, 'Bucer's *Memorandum* of 1541 and a "littera nicodemitica" of Capito's', *BHR* 36 (1974), 575–87; C. Ginzburg, *Il Nicodemismo: simulazione e dissimulazione religiosa nell'Europa del'500* (Turin, 1970). The phenomenon was by no means restricted to France.
23 Kingdon, *Geneva and the Coming of the Wars of Religion*, 2.
24 Ibid., 34–5.
25 Prestwich, 'Calvinism in France, 1559–1629', 84–5.
26 For its development from the *haute école* of the Ecclesiastical Ordinances of 1541, see Courvoisier, 'La haute école de Genève au XVIe siècle'.
27 For details, see Kingdon, *Geneva and the Coming of the Wars of Religion*, 54–5, Appendix VI. Several individuals were sent out on more than one mission during this period.
28 Cf. Hancock, *Calvin and the Foundations of Modern Politics*, 1–20.
29 E.g., Q. Skinner, *Foundations of Modern Political Thought* (2 vols: Cambridge, 1978), vol. 2, 219–40.
30 A point stressed by Walzer, *Revolution of the Saints*.
31 Note the emphasis upon Calvinism's 'capacity to activate adherents and change the world': Walzer, *Revolution of the Saints*, 27.
32 Cf. Skinner, *Foundations of Modern Political Thought*, vol. 2, 227.
33 E.g, see R. M. Kingdon, 'Problems of Religious Choice for Sixteenth-Century Frenchmen', *Journal of Religious History* 4 (1966), 105–12.
34 Note the views expressed in *Histoire du tumulte d'Amboise* (1560).
35 Yardeni, 'French Calvinist Political Thought', 320–4; R. E. Giesey, 'The

Monarchomach Triumvirs: Hotman, Beza and Mornay', *BHR* 32 (1970), 41–56.

36 *Institutes* IV.xx.31. In his *Homily on the First Book of Samuel*, the intervention of the inferior magistrates is identified as a check upon monarchs: see Skinner, *Foundations of Modern Political Thought*, 214.

37 Kingdon, *Geneva and the Coming of the Wars of Religion*, 7–9.

38 Ibid., 79–92.

39 Cf. Prestwich, 'Calvinism in France, 1555–1629'.

40 L. Romier, *Royaume de Catherine de Médicis: la France à la veille des guerres de religion* (2 vols: Paris, 1925), vol. 2, 255–62.

41 E.g., M. Wolfe, *The Fiscal System of Renaissance France* (New Haven/London, 1972), esp. 112–13; R. R. Harding, *Anatomy of a Power Elite: The Provincial Governors of Early Modern France* (New Haven/London, 1978), 46–9.

42 D. J. Nicholls, 'Inertia and Reform in the pre-Tridentine French Church: The Response to Protestantism in the Diocese of Rouen, 1520–62', *Journal of Ecclesiastical History* 32 (1981), 185–97.

43 Heller, *Conquest of Poverty*, 234–46.

44 D. Richet, 'Aspects socio-culturels des conflicts religieux à Paris dans la seconde moitié du XVIe siècle', *Annales ESC* 32 (1977), 764–83.

45 N. M. Sutherland, *The Huguenot Struggle for Recognition* (New Haven/London, 1980), 347–8.

46 Ibid., 351–2.

47 Ibid., 354–6.

48 Prestwich, 'Calvinism in France', 85–8.

49 E. Trocmé, 'Une révolution mal conduite', *RHPhR* 39 (1959), 160–8.

50 This is evident from his letter of 17 May 1559: OC 17.525. Cf. J. Pannier, *Les origines de la confession de foi et la discipline des églises réformées de France* (Paris, 1936), 86–7.

51 Quoted in J. Poujol, 'L'ambassadeur d'Angleterre et la confession de foi du synode de 1559', *BSHPF* 105 (1959), 49–53.

52 Amyon, *Les synodes nationaux*, vol. 1, 98.

53 J. Garrison-Estèbe, *Les Protestants du Midi* (Toulouse, 1980), 64–7; cf. Kingdon, *Geneva and the Coming of the Wars of Religion*, 79–80.

54 We use the plural deliberately, in view of the chain of events precipitated by the killings in Paris: see J. Garrison–Estèbe, *Tocsin pour un massacre* (Paris, 1973).

Chapter 10 The genesis of a movement

1 Monter, 'Consistory of Geneva', 470.

2 OC 8.837.

3 OC 9.891–4.

4 OC 9.892: '. . . un pauvre escholier timide comme ie suis, et comme ie l'ay tousiors esté. . .'.

5 For which see J. T. Fitzgerald, *Cracks in an Earthen Vessel: An Examination of the Catalogues of Hardships in the Corinthian Correspondence* (Atlanta, Ga., 1989).

6 For a general account of this development, see McNeill, *History and Character of Calvinism*.

7 E. G. Léonard, *Histoire générale du protestantisme* (2 vols: Paris, 1961), vol. 1, 307.
8 Vienna, Universitätsarchiv, microfilm 75 Th3, fols 64v; 65v–66r (the transcript of the proceedings is virtually illegible).
9 B. Hall, 'The Early Rise and Gradual Decline of Lutheranism in England', in D. Baker (ed.), *Reform and Reformation: England and the Continent* (Oxford, 1979), 103–31. See further E. G. Rupp, *Studies in the Making of the English Protestant Tradition* (Cambridge, 2nd edn, 1966); W. A. Clebsch, *England's Earliest Protestants 1520–35* (New Haven/London, 1964).
10 Duke, 'Calvinism in the Netherlands, 1561–1618', 113.
11 Lynch, 'Calvinism in Scotland, 1559–1638', 225.
12 T. Bozza, *Il Beneficio di Cristo e la Istituzione della religione christiana* (Rome, 1961), 4–5.
13 Duke, 'Calvinism in the Netherlands 1561–1618', 120.
14 Lynch, 'Calvinism in Scotland', 227.
15 Collinson, 'Calvinism with an Anglican Face'.
16 On which see Neuser, 'Die Väter des Heidelberger Katechismus'.
17 Cited Cohn, 'Territorial Princes', 135.
18 See Lewis, 'Calvinism in Geneva'.
19 Fatio, *Méthode et théologie*, 6, especially n. 53.
20 Körner, *Solidarités financières suisses au XVIe siècle* (Lucerne, 1980), 58–63, with full data at 468–9.
21 Evans, *The Wechsel Presses*, provides invaluable information concerning the relation of humanism and Calvinism associated with this development.
22 E.g., see Meylan, 'Collèges et académies protestantes'; Stauffer, 'Calvinisme et les universités'.
23 Dufour, 'Le mythe de Genève'.
24 For example, his *Farrago confusanearum et inter se dissidentium opinionum de coena Domini ex sacramentariorum libris congesta* (Magdeburg, 1552). See E. Bizer, *Studien zur Geschichte des Abendmahlstreits im 16. Jahrhundert* (Gütersloh, 1940); J. Cadier, *La doctrine calviniste de la sainte cène* (Montpellier, 1951). For terms relating to Calvin in use in the French polemical literature of the 1560s and 1570s, see W. Richard, *Untersuchungen zur Genesis der reformierten Kirchenterminologie des Westschweiz und Frankreichs* (Berne, 1959), 37–40.
25 See further H. Leube, *Kalvinismus und Luthertum im Zeitalter der Orthodoxie I: Der Kampf um die Herrschaft im protestantischen Deutschland* (Leipzig, 1928); H. Schilling (ed.), *Die reformierte Konfessionalisierung in Deutschland: Das Problem der 'Zweiten Reformation'* (Gütersloh, 1986).
26 See the dedicatory epistle to the Jeremiah commentary, dated 23 July 1563, OC 20.73: 'Dum ergo *Calvinismum* obiciendo aliqua infamiae nota tua, Celsitudinem aspergere conantur, nihil aliud quam suam privitatem cum stultitia frustra et magno suo cum dedecore produnt.'
27 J. L. Austin, 'The Meaning of a Word', in *Philosophical Papers*, (Oxford, 2nd edn, 1970), 23–43.
28 P. C. Capitan, *Charles Maurras et l'idéologie d'Action Française* (Paris, 1972).
29 Evans, 'Calvinism in East Central Europe, 1540–1700', 169.
30 C. S. Lewis, 'Fern-seed and Elephants', in *Christian Reflections* (London, 1981), 191–208, esp. 197.
31 OC 9.893–4.
32 D. McLellan, *Marxism after Marx* (London, 1980).

33 Cf. L. Kolakowski, *Main Currents of Marxism* (3 vols: Oxford, 1978), for a thorough historical analysis.

34 See P. Gay, *The Dilemma of Democratic Socialism: Edward Bernstein's Challenge to Marx* (New York, 1962), for a fine analysis.

35 Kingdon, *Geneva and the Coming of the Wars of Religion*, 68–78.

36 Yardeni, 'French Calvinist Political Thought'.

37 Donnelly, 'Italian Influences on Calvinist Scholasticism'.

38 A point stressed by H. R. Trevor-Roper, 'Religious Origins of the Enlightenment', in *Religion, the Reformation and Social Change*, 193–236, 204–5.

39 Muller, 'Scholasticism Protestant and Catholic', 194. The rise of Calvinism within Germany in the 1560s and 1570s also necessitated engagement with Lutheranism.

40 Costello, *Scholastic Curriculum in Early Seventeenth-Century Cambridge.*

41 E.g., A. E. McGrath, *The Genesis of Doctrine* (Oxford/Cambridge, Mass., 1990), 37–52. What follows summarizes the more detailed analysis presented in this work.

42 See Schilling (ed.), *Die reformierte Konfessionalisierung in Deutschland.*

43 For a summary of their differences in relation to this doctrine, see A. E. McGrath, *Iustitia Dei: A History of the Christian Doctrine of Justification* (2 vols, Cambridge, 1986), vol. 2, 39–50.

44 Bauke, *Probleme der Theologie Calvins*, 22, 30–1.

45 A development rigorously documented by Platt, *Reformed Thought and Scholasticism*, with particular reference to arguments for the existence of God.

46 We follow Armstrong, *Calvinism and the Amyraut Heresy*, 32.

47 P. O. Kristeller, *La tradizione aristotelica nel Rinascimento* (Padua, 1972); idem, *Aristotelismo e sincretismo nel pensiero di Pietro Pomponazzi* (Padua, 1983). B. Nardi, *Saggi sull'Aristotelismo padovana dal secolo XIV al XVI* (Florence, 1958), is still helpful. For the importance of Aristotelian method in relation to ethical questions, see A. Poppi, 'Il problema della filosofia morale nella scuola padovana del Rinascimento: Platonismo e Aristotelismo nella definizione del metodo dell'ethica', in *Platon et Aristote à la Renaissance* (XVIe Colloque International de Tours: Paris, 1976), 105–46.

48 J. H. Randall, 'The Development of Scientific Method in the School of Padua', in *Renaissance Essays*, ed. P. O. Kristeller and P. P. Wiener (New York, 1968), 217–51.

49 Donnelly, 'Italian Influences on Calvinist Scholasticism', 90.

50 P. Petersen, *Geschichte der aristotelischen Philosophie im protestantischen Deutschland* (Leipzig, 1921), 19–108; G. Spini, 'Riforma italiana e mediazioni ginevine nella nuova Inghilterra', in D. Cantimori (ed.), *Ginevra e l'Italia* (Florence, 1959), 451–89.

51 Donnelly, 'Italian Influences on Calvinist Scholasticism', 90–9.

52 Jacobs, *Prädestination und Verantwortlichkeit bei Calvin.*

53 Kickel, *Vernunft und Offenbarung bei Beza*. This attitude is also characteristic of Vermigli and Zanchi: Donnelly, 'Italian Influences on Calvinist Scholasticism, 89–90; Gründler, *Die Gotteslehre Giralmo Zanchis.*

54 Note his request to Grataroli, dated 11 August 1563, for a copy of Pomponazzi's *De naturalium effectuum causis*, published by Grataroli at Basle in 1556: *Correspondance de Théodore de Bèze*, vol. 4, letter no. 282, pp. 182–3. This entry is interpreted by the editors as substantiation of de Bèze's scholastic

tendencies: *Correspondance*, vol. 4, p. 9, 183 n. 5. Cf. P. Bietenholz, *Der italienische Humanismus und die Blütezeit des Buchdrucks in Basel* (Basle, 1959), 131–2.
55 Kickel, *Vernunft und Offenbarung bei Beza*, 167–9.
56 See McGrath, *Iustitia Dei*, vol. 1, 130–1.
57 Donnelly, 'Italian Influences on Calvinist Scholasticism', 98.
58 Arminius, 'Private Disputation II', in *Works* vol. 2, 319.
59 See, e.g., Kingdon, *Geneva and the Consolidation of the French Protestant Movement*, 18, 120.
60 Moltmann, 'Prädestination und Heilsgeschichte bei Moyse Amyraut'; Laplanche, *Orthodoxie et prédication*; Armstrong, *Calvinism and the Amyraut Heresy*.
61 McComish, *The Epigones*, 86.
62 For the views of Puritan writers, see McGrath, *Iustitia Dei*, vol. 2, 111–21.
63 For a survey of the literature relating to this Synod, see McComish, *The Epigones*, 46–125.
64 Cf. Muller, '*Vera philosophia cum sacra theologia nunquam pugnat*'; idem, 'Scholasticism Protestant and Catholic'.

Chapter 11 Commitment to the world: Calvinism, work and capitalism

1 R. H. Bainton, *The Medieval Church* (Princeton, N.J., 1962), 42.
2 R. Friedmann, 'Das Täuferische Glaubensgut', *ARG* 55 (1964), 145–61.
3 S. Hauerwas, 'On Honour: By Way of a Comparison of Barth and Trollope', in N. Biggar (ed.), *Reckoning with Barth* (London, 1988), 145–69.
4 See Bouwsma, *John Calvin*, 32–65.
5 A point stressed by Walzer, *Revolution of the Saints*, 25.
6 Ibid., 24.
7 Ibid., 80.
8 L. Strauss, *Natural Right and History* (Chicago, 1950), 59.
9 A point stressed by Hancock, *Calvin and the Foundations of Modern Politics*.
10 This dialectic has been well summarized by Hancock: 'Calvin radically distinguishes politics and religion in order to unify them in worldly activity': Hancock, *Calvin and the Foundations of Modern Politics*, 163.
11 OC 46.570.
12 Geneva Catechism (1545), q. 107; E. F. K. Müller (ed.), *Die Bekenntnisschriften der reformierten Kirche* (Leipzig, 1903), 126, lines 38–40.
13 A. Fanfani, *Catholicism, Protestantism and Capitalism* (London, 1935).
14 E.g., see R. de Roover, *The Rise and Decline of the Medici Bank* (Cambridge, Mass., 1963); idem, *La pensée économique des scolastiques: doctrines et méthodes* (Montréal/Paris, 1971); idem, 'The Scholastic Attitude towards Trade and Entrepreneurship', *Explorations in Entrepreneurial History* 1 (1963), 76–87.
15 E.g., see M. Grice-Hutchinson, *The School of Salamanca: Readings in Spanish Monetary History, 1544–1605* (Oxford, 1952).
16 Weber, *Protestant Ethic and the Spirit of Capitalism*, 91.
17 We here follow Marshall, *In Search of the Spirit of Capitalism*.
18 Trevor-Roper points to the extravagant lifestyles of many Calvinist financiers in his critique of the historical foundations of Weber's hypothesis: H. R. Trevor-Roper, 'Religion, the Reformation and Social Change', in *Religion, the Reformation and Social Change* (London, 1967), 1–45.
19 C. Hill, 'Protestantism and the Rise of Capitalism', in F. J. Fisher (ed.),

Essays on the Economic and Social History of Tudor and Stuart England (Cambridge, 1961), 19.

20 Marshall, *In Search of the Spirit of Capitalism*, 97–100.

21 For the problems raised by 'Diaspora Calvinism' for Weber's thesis, see Trevor-Roper, 'Religion, the Reformation and Social Change', 20. There are excellent reasons for suggesting that the phenomenon of selective immigration by entrepreneurial individuals is as important as their religious affiliations.

22 Birnbaum, 'The Zwinglian Reformation in Zurich', *Past and Present* 15 (1959), 27–47. Note the reference to the 'united front of artisans and merchants behind Zwingli': p. 24.

23 A theme explored by T. A. Brady, *Turning Swiss: Cities and Empire, 1450–1550* (Cambridge, 1985).

24 Borel, *Les foires de Genève.*

25 On the Medici branch, see de Roover, *Rise and Decline of the Medici Bank*, 279–89.

26 The fairs subsequently migrated to Chambéry, then to Montluel in Savoy, and finally to Besançon from 1535 onwards: Gioffré, *Gênes et les foires de change.*

27 Bergier, 'Marchands italiens à Genève'.

28 Ammann, 'Oberdeutsche Kaufleute und die Anfänge der Reformation in Genf'.

29 See the careful analysis of M. H. Körner, *Solidarités financières suisses au XVIe siècle* (Lucerne, 1980), 79.

30 Ibid., 105.

31 Ibid., 105–6.

32 Ibid., 81–2.

33 Bergier, 'Zu den Anfängen des Kapitalismus – Das Beispiel Genf', 18.

34 See Körner, *Solidarités financières suisses au XVIe siècle.*

35 Ibid., 388.

36 Ibid., 135.

37 Ibid., 390.

38 Monter, 'Le change public à Genève, 1568–1581'.

39 Mandrou, 'Les français hors de France', 665. The occupations of 2,247 of these 4,776 are known; if this known fraction is typical, it may be estimated that 3,265 artisans entered Geneva in this period.

40 On which see Dufour, 'De la bourgeoisie de Genève à la noblesse de Savoie'.

41 For an excellent analysis, see Bürgli, *Kapitalismus und Calvinismus*, 108–22. The phenomenon was repeated, although perhaps not on quite the same scale, in Protestant cities throughout the Helvetic Confederation: W. Bodmer, *Der Einfluß der Refugiantenwanderung von 1550–1700 auf die schweizerisch Wirtschaft. Ein Beitrag zur Geschichte des Frühkapitalismus und der Textil-Industrie* (Zurich, 1946).

42 Babel, *Histoire corporative de l'horlogerie.*

43 Chaix, *Recherches sur l'imprimerie à Genève de 1550 à 1564.*

44 Bürgli, *Kapitalismus und Calvinismus*, 189–94.

45 Bodmer, *Der Einfluß der Refugiantenwanderung von 1550–1700 auf die schweizerisch Wirtschaft*, 22–3.

46 Bergier, 'Zu den Anfängen des Kapitalismus – Das Beispiel Genf', 21.

47 A point made by G. V. Taylor, 'Types of Capitalism in Eighteenth-Century

France', *English Historical Review* 79 (1964), 478–97, who stresses the difficulties in interpreting *ancien régime* capitalism in the light of such presuppositions.

48 Kingdon, 'The Business Activities of Printers Henri and François Estienne', 271–4.

49 Trevor-Roper, 'Religion, the Reformation and Social Change', 14–21.

50 T. Strohm, 'Luthers Wirtschafts- und Sozialethik', in H. Junghans (ed.), *Leben und Werk Martin Luthers von 1526 bis 1546* (2 vols: Berlin, 2nd edn, 1985), vol. 1, 205–23, 214–19.

51 See Bürgli, *Kapitalismus und Calvinismus*, 194–215.

52 Ibid., 201.

53 Ibid., 201–5 for an analysis of the relevant texts. A more detailed analysis may be found in Biéler, *La pensée économique et sociale de Calvin.*

54 For Calvin's views on rates of interest, see Martin, 'Calvin et le prêt à intérêt à Genève'.

55 Bodmer, *Der Einfluß der Refugiantenwanderung von 1550–1700 auf die schweizerisch Wirtschaft*, 19.

56 Dufour, 'De la bourgeoisie de Genève à la noblesse de Savoie'.

57 On social welfare in the city at the time, see Kingdon, 'Social Welfare in Calvin's Geneva'.

58 Heller, *The Conquest of Poverty: The Calvinist Revolt in Sixteenth-Century France* (Leiden, 1986), 240–2.

59 For this notion in later Calvinism, see Miegge, *Vocation et travail*, 11–30. There is a useful collection of relevant texts in Bouwsma, *John Calvin*, 198–201.

60 Biéler, *La pensée économique et sociale de Calvin*, 399– 402.

61 For the meaning of this slogan within a monastic context, see E. Delaruelle, 'Le travail dans les règles monastiques occidentales', *Journal de psychologie normale et pathologique* 41 (1948), 51–62.

62 Heller, *Conquest of Poverty*, 242.

63 R. Mentzer, *Heresy Proceedings in Languedoc, 1500–1560* (New York, 1988), 152–3.

64 Details of the work and an analysis of its significance may be found in Heller, *Conquest of Poverty*, 247–51.

65 The problems arising from the feudal legacy may be seen from G. Bois, *La crise du féodalisme: économie rurale et démographie en Normandie orientale du début du XIVe siècle au milieu du XVIe siècle* (Paris, 1976).

66 Trevor-Roper, 'Religion, the Reformation and Social Change', 7–8. This essay includes invaluable material relating to the Weber theory.

67 Lüthy, 'Variations on a Theme', 377.

68 McGrath, 'John Calvin and Late Medieval Thought'.

69 For references, see A. E. McGrath, *Iustitia Dei: A History of the Christian Doctrine of Justification* (2 vols, Cambridge, 1986), vol. 2, 1–39.

70 de Bèze, *Brief and Pithie Summe*, 37–8.

71 For this device in the works of William Perkins, see Kendall, *Calvin and English Calvinism*, 69–72.

72 For details, see McGrath, *Iustitia Dei*, vol. 2, 111–21 and references therein. A more detailed study may be found in D. A. Weir, *The Origins of the Federal Theology in Sixteenth-Century Reformed Thought* (Oxford, 1989).

73 Perkins, *Workes*, vol. 1, 32.

74 For an excellent discussion of Scottish Calvinist attitudes to work in the

sixteenth and seventeenth centuries, see Marshall, *Presbyteries and Profits: Calvinism and the Development of Capitalism in Scotland, 1560–1707*, 39–112. Quotation at p. 52.

75 See Lehmann, *Zeitalter des Absolutismus*, 114–23; Zeller, *Theologie und Frömmigkeit*, vol. 1, 85–116.

76 Trevor-Roper, 'Religion, the Reformation and Social Change', 14.

77 Although the origins of the phenomenon may lie in millenarian hopes rather than the doctrine of predestination: Lehmann, *Zeitalter des Absolutismus*, 123–35. For this phenomenon in English Puritanism, see Ball, *Great Expectation*.

78 Walzer, *Revolution of the Saints*, 318.

79 Miegge, *Vocation et travail*, 115–53, suggests that Baxter may have altered traditional Puritan attitudes towards calling and work.

80 There is much useful material on this subject in Tranquilli, *Il concetto di lavoro da Aristotele a Calvino*.

Chapter 12 Calvin and the shaping of modern western culture

1 C. S. Lewis, *English Literature in the Sixteenth Century* (Oxford, 1954), 43.

2 See C. M. N. Eire, *War against the Idols: The Reformation of Worship from Erasmus to Calvin* (Cambridge, 1986).

3 Heidelberg Catechism, q. 95. E. F. K. Müller (ed.), *Die Bekenntnisschriften der reformierten Kirche* (Leipzig, 1903), 709–10.

4 Heidelberg Catechism, q. 97. ibid., 710, lines 15–19.

5 Heidelberg Catechism, q. 98; ibid., 710, lines 23–7.

6 See Freeberg, *Iconoclasm and Painting in the Netherlands, 1566–1609*.

7 P. Miller, *Nature's Nation* (Cambridge, Mass., 1967), 22.

8 Prestwich, 'Le mécénat et les protestants'.

9 Labrousse, 'Calvinism in France, 1598–1685', 304–5.

10 Prestwich, 'Le mécénat et les protestants', 82.

11 R. Bellah et al., *Habits of the Heart: Individualism and Commitment in American Life* (Berkeley, 1985), 306. Two other thinkers were identified as exercising comparable covert influence over modern Americans: Thomas Hobbes and John Locke.

12 See H. M. Conn, *Eternal Word and Changing Worlds: Theology, Anthropology and Mission in Dialogue* (Grand Rapids, Mich., 1984).

13 Trevor-Roper, 'Religious Origins of the Enlightenment' in *Religion, the Reformation and Social Change* (London, 1967), 236.

14 Explored in H. Arendt, *The Human Condition* (Chicago, 1958).

15 Foster, *Their Solitary Way*, 99–126.

16 Bellah et al., *Habits of the Heart*, 287–300.

17 Ahlstrom, *Religious History of the American People*, 789–90.

18 F. K. C. Price, *High Finance: God's Financial Plan* (New York, 1984), 12.

19 L. S. Feuer, *The Scientific Intellectual* (New York, 1963).

20 A. de Candolle, *Histoire des sciences et des savants* (Geneva/Basle, 2nd edn, 1885), 329–31.

21 For further details, see R. Hooykaas, *Religion and the Rise of Modern Science* (Edinburgh, 1972), 98–9.

22 Müller, *Bekenntnisschriften*, 233, lines 14–16.

23 Miller, *Nature's Nation*, 213.

24 The religious aspects of this have been explored by H. R. McAdoo, *The Spirit of Anglicanism* (London, 1965), 240–315.
25 OC 9.815: 'Mais fault que nostre entendement soit du tout arresté à ce poinct, d'apprendre en l'Escriture à cognoistre Iesus Christ tant seulement'.
26 See A. E. McGrath, *Reformation Thought: An Introduction* (Oxford/Cambridge, Mass., 1988), 117–30.
27 OC 23.9–10, 17–18, 20–3.
28 Hooykaas, *Religion and the Rise of Modern Science*, 122–3.
29 OC 23.18.
30 M. Prestwich, 'Introduction', in *International Calvinism*, 7.
31 Miller, *Nature's Nation*, passim.
32 Ahlstrom, *Religious History of the American People*, 7.
33 For this theme, see Ritschl, 'Der Beitrag des Calvinismus für die Entwicklung des Menschenrechtsgedankens in Europa und Nordamerika'.
34 Cf. Torrance, 'Covenant Concept in Scottish Theology and Politics'.
35 For a full historical analysis, see J. Torrance, 'Interpreting the Word by the Light of Christ', in R. Schnucker (ed.), *Calviniana* (Kirksville, Mo., 1989), 255–67.
36 Ibid., 262–3.

Select Bibliography

Manuscript Sources

Berne, Burgerbibliothek
MS 138.
Geneva, Bibliothèque Publique et Universitaire
MSS Fr 145, 194.
Paris, Archives Nationales
MSS L 428; M 71; MM 247–8; S 6211; S 6482–3; X[1a] 1528–65.
Paris, Archives de l'Université
MSS Reg 13–14; Reg 63; Reg 89–90.
Paris, Bibliothèque Nationale (BN)
MSS Lat 5657A; 6535; 9943; 9959–60; 12846–51; 13884; 15445–6; 16576; N Acq Lat 1782.
St Gallen, Stadtsbibliothek (Vadiana)
MSS 59; 65.
Strasbourg, Archives Saint-Thomas
MSS 155; 174.
Vienna, Universitätsarchiv
Microfilms 65 Ph8; 66 Ph9; 75 Th3.

Works by Calvin

A full list of sixteenth-century editions of the *Institutio Christianae Religionis* may be found at table 7.1, pp. 141–2.

Barth, P., and Niesel, W. (eds)., *Ioannis Calvini Opera Selecta* (5 vols: Munich, 1926–62).
Battles, F. L. (trans.), *Institution of the Christian Religion* (Atlanta, 1975).
— and Hugo, A. M. (eds and trans.), *Calvin's Commentary on Seneca's 'De Clementia'* (Leiden, 1969).
Benoit, J. D. (ed.), *Institution de la religion chrestienne* (5 vols: Paris, 1957–63).
Ioannis Calvini opera quae supersunt omnia (59 vols: Braunschweig, 1863–1900).

McNeill, J. T. (ed.), and Battles, F. L. (trans.), *Institutes of the Christian Religion* (2 vols: Philadelphia/London, 1960).
Olin, J. C. (ed.), *John Calvin and Jacopo Sadoleto: A Reformation Debate. Sadoleto's Letter to the Genevans and Calvin's Reply* (New York, 1966).

Other Primary Sources

Agricola, R., *De inventione dialectica* (Cologne, 1527).
Amyon, J., *Tous les synodes nationaux des églises réformées de France* (2 vols: La Haye, 1710).
Arminius, J., *Works* (3 vols: London, 1825–75).
Beraldo, P., *Commentarii questionum Tusculanarum* (Paris, 1509).
de Bèze, T., *A Brief and Pithie Summe of the Christian Faith* (London, 1565(?)).
— *Correspondance de Théodore de Bèze* (11 vols: Geneva, 1960–83).
Bucer, M., *Metaphrases et enarrationes perpetuae epistolarum D. Pauli* (Strasbourg, 1536).
Bullinger, H., *In Pauli ad Romanos epistolam . . . commentarius* (Zurich, 1533).
Bunny, E., *Institutionis christianae religionis . . . compendium* (London, 1576).
Caesarius, J., *Rhetorica . . . in septem libros* (Lyons, 1539).
de Coulogne, D. (Colonius), *Analysis paraphastica Institutionum theologicarum Ioh. Calvini* (Leiden, 1628).
d'Epense, C., *Consolation en adversité* (Lyons, 1547).
Erasmus, *Opera Omnia*, ed. J. LeClerc (12 vols: Leiden, 1703; reprinted 1963).
— *Opus epistolarum D. Erasmi Roterodami*, ed. P. S. Allen, H. M. Allen, and H. W. Garrod (11 vols: Oxford, 1906–47).
— *Colloquies*, trans. C. Thompson (Chicago, 1965).
Histoire des églises réformées au Royaume de France (Geneva, 1580).
Histoire du tumulte d'Amboise (Strasbourg, 1560).
Launoy, J., *Opera Omnia* (5 vols: Cologne, 1731–2).
Lawne (Delaune), W., *Institutionis Christianae religionis . . . epitome* (London, 1584).
— *An Abridgement of the Institution of the Christian Religion* (Edinburgh, 1585).
Lefèvre d'Etaples, J., *Sancti Pauli epistolae XIV ex vulgata editione* (Paris, 1512).
Le livre de vraye et parfaicte oraison (Paris, 1528).
Mair, J., *Commentarius in III librum sententiarum* (Paris, 1528).
Masson, P., *Elogia varia* (Paris, 1638).
Olevianus, C., *Institutionis Christiae religionis epitome* (Herborn, 1586).
L'oraison de Jesuchrist (Paris, 1525(?)).
Pasquier, E., *Les recherches de la France* (Paris, 1607).
Perkins, W., *Workes* (3 vols: Cambridge, 1608–9).
Piscator, J., *Aphorismi doctrinae christianae ex Institutione Calvini excerpti* (Herborn, 1589).
de Raemond, F., *Histoire de la naissance, progrès et décadence de l'hérésie de ce siècle* (Paris, 1605).
Sadoleto, J., *Opera quae extant omnia* (Verona, 1737–8).
[Saunier, A.], *L'ordre et manière d'enseigner en la ville de Genève au collège* (Geneva, 1538).
Servetus, M., *De trinitatis erroribus libri septem* (place unknown, 1531).

Biographies and Biographical Sources of Calvin

Bouwsma, W. J., *John Calvin: A Sixteenth-Century Portrait* (Oxford, 1988).
Crottet, A., *Correspondance français de Calvin avec Louis de Tillet (1537–1538)* (Geneva, 1850).
Desmay, J., 'Remarques sur la vie de Jean Calvin, tirées des registres de Noyon, ville de sa naissance' (1621), in Cimber (alias Lafait), L. and Danjou, F., *Archives curieuses de l'histoire de France depuis Louis XI jusqu'à Louis XVIII* (15 vols: Paris, 1834–7), vol. 5, 387–98.
Doinel, J., 'Jean Calvin à Orléans. Date précise de son séjour d'après des documents inédits', *BSHPF* 26 (1877), 174–85.
Doumergue, E., *Jean Calvin: les hommes et les choses de son temps* (7 vols: Lausanne, 1899–1917).
Hall, B., *John Calvin* (London, 1956).
Herminjard, A. L., *Correspondance des réformateurs dans les pays de langue française* (9 vols: Geneva/Paris, 1866–97).
Lefranc, A., *La jeunesse de Calvin* (Paris, 1888).
Le Vasseur, J., *Annales de l'église cathédrale de Noyon* (Paris, 1633).
MacKinnon, J., *Calvin and the Reformation* (New York, 1962).
Ménager, D., 'Théodore de Bèze, biographe de Calvin', *BHR* 45 (1983), 231–55.
Pannier, J., *Calvin à Strasbourg* (Strasbourg, 1925).
Parker, T. H. L., *John Calvin* (London, 1975).
Rott, E., 'Documents strasbourgeois concernant Calvin. Un manuscrit autographe: la harangue du recteur Nicolas Cop', in *Regards contemporains sur Jean Calvin* (Paris, 1965), 28–43.
Stauffer, R., 'Calvin', in Prestwich, M. (ed.), *International Calvinism 1541–1715* (Oxford, 1985), 15–38.
Wallace, R. S., *Calvin, Geneva and the Reformation* (Edinburgh, 1988).
Wendel, F., *Calvin: The Origins and Development of His Religious Thought* (London, 1963).

University of Paris

Bernard-Maître, H., 'Les "théologastres" de l'université de Paris au temps d'Erasme et de Rabelais', *BHR* 27 (1965), 248–64.
Berty, A., *Topographie historique du vieux Paris: région centrale de l'université* (Paris, 1897).
Bourrilly, V.-L., and Weiss, N., 'Jean du Bellay, les protestants et la Sorbonne, 1529–1535', *BSHPF* 52 (1903), 97–127, 193–231; 53 (1904), 97–143.
Chartularium Universitatis Parisiensis, ed. H. Denifle and E. Chatelain (4 vols: Paris, 1889-97).
Clerval, J.-A., *Registre des procès-verbaux de la faculté de théologie 1503–23* (Paris, 1917).
Cobban, A. B., *The Medieval Universities: Their Development and Organization* (New York, 1975).
Crevier, M., *Histoire de l'Université de Paris* (Paris, 1761).

Cristiani, L., 'Luther et la faculté de théologie de Paris', *Revue de l'histoire de l'église de France* 32 (1946), 53–83.

Dubarle, E., *Histoire de l'Université de Paris* (Paris, 1844).

Du Boulay, C. E., *Historia Universitatis Parisiensis* (6 vols: Paris, 1665–73; reprinted Frankfurt, 1966).

Duplessis d'Argentré, C., *Collectio judiciorum de novis erroribus* (3 vols: Paris, 1725–36).

Dupon-Ferrier, G., 'La faculté des arts dans l'université de Paris et son influence civilisatrice', in Calvet, J. (ed.), *Aspects de l'Université de Paris* (Paris, 1949), 63–80.

Farge, J. K., *Biographical Register of Paris Doctors of Theology, 1500–1536* (Toronto, 1980).

— *Orthodoxy and Reform in Early Reformation France: The Faculty of Theology of Paris, 1500–1543* (Leiden, 1985).

Fechter, A., *Das Studienleben in Paris zu Anfang des XVI Jahrhunderts* (Basle, 1846).

Féret, P., *La faculté de théologie de Paris et ses docteurs les plus célèbres* (7 vols: Paris, 1900–10).

Fourier, M., *Les statuts et privilèges des universités de France* (Paris, 1890).

Garcia Villoslada, R., *La Universidad de París durante los estudios de Francisco de Vitorio O.P (1507–1522)* (Rome, 1938).

Godet, M., 'Le collège de Montaigu', *Revue des études rabelaisiennes* 7 (1909), 283–305.

— *La congrégation de Montaigu (1490–1580)* (Paris, 1912).

Goulet, R., *Compendium de multiplici Parisiensis Universitatis magnificentia, dignitate et excellentia* (Paris, 1517).

Hempsall, D., 'Martin Luther and the Sorbonne, 1519–21', *Bulletin of the Institute of Historical Research* 46 (1973), 28–40.

Kibre, P., *The Nations in the Medieval Universities* (Cambridge, Mass., 1948).

Le Goff, J., 'La conception française de l'université à l'époque de la Renaissance', in *Les universités européennes du XIVe au XVIIIe siècle: aspects et problèmes* (Geneva, 1967), 94–100.

Matos, L. de, *Les Portugais à l'université de Paris entre 1500 et 1550* (Coimbra, 1950).

Paqué, R., *Das Pariser Nominalistenstatut: Zur Entstehung des Realitätsbegriffs der neuzeitlichen Naturwissenschaft (Occam, Buridan und Petrus Hispanicus, Nikolaus von Autrecourt und Gregor von Rimini)* (Berlin, 1970).

Quicherat, J., *Histoire de Sainte-Barbe: collège, communauté, institution* (3 vols: Paris, 1860–4).

Rashdall, H., *The Universities of Europe in the Middle Ages* (2 vols: Oxford, 2nd edn, 1936).

Renaudet, A., 'L'humanisme et l'enseignement de l'université de Paris au temps de la Renaissance', in Calvet, J. (ed.), *Aspects de l'Université de Paris* (Paris, 1949), 135–55.

Thurot, C., *De l'organisation de l'enseignement dans l'université de Paris au Moyen Age* (Paris, 1850; reprinted 1967).

The City of Geneva

Ammann, H., 'Oberdeutsche Kaufleute und die Anfänge der Reformation in Genf', *Zeitschrift für württembergische Landesgeschichte* 13 (1954), 150–93.

Babel, A., *Histoire corporative de l'horlogerie, de l'orfèvrerie et des industries annexes* (Geneva, 1916).

— *Histoire économique de Genève des origines au début du XVIe siècle* (Geneva, 1963).

Baud, H., *Le diocèse de Genève-Annecy* (Histoire des diocèses de France 19: Paris, 1985).

van Berchem, V., 'Une prédication dans un jardin (15 avril 1533). Episode de la Réforme genevoise', in *Festschrift Hans Nabholz* (Zurich, 1934), 151–70.

Bergier, J.-F., 'Marchands italiens à Genève au début du XVIe siècle', in *Studi in onore di Armando Sapori* (Milan, 1957), 883–96.

— *Genève et l'économie européenne de la Renaissance* (Paris, 1963).

— 'Zu den Anfängen des Kapitalismus - Das Beispiel Genf', *Kölner Vorträge zur Sozial- und Wirtschaftgeschichte* 20 (1972), 3–29.

— *Die Wirtschaftgeschichte der Schweiz* (Zurich, 1983).

— and Kingdon, R. M. (eds), *Registres de la Compagnie des Pasteurs de Genève au temps de Calvin* (2 vols: Geneva, 1962–4).

Blondel, L., *Le développement urbain de Genève à travers les siècles* (Geneva/Nyon, 1946).

Borel, F., *Les foires de Genève au XVe siècle* (Geneva/Paris, 1892).

Borgeaud, C., *Histoire de l'Université de Genève I: L'Académie de Calvin, 1559–1798* (Geneva, 1900).

Bremme, H. J., *Buchdrucker und Buchhändler zur Zeit der Glaubenskämpfe: Studien zur genfer Druckgeschichte 1565–1580* (Geneva, 1969).

Broise, P., *Genève et son territoire dans l'antiquité* (Brussels, 1974).

Bürgli, A., *Kapitalismus und Calvinismus: Versuch einer wirtschaftsgeschichtlichen und religionsoziologischen Untersuchungen der Verhältnisse in Genf im 16. und beginnenden 17. Jahrhundert* (Winterthur, 1960).

Chaix, P., *Recherches sur l'imprimerie à Genève de 1550 à 1564* (Geneva, 1954).

— Dufour, A., and Moeckli, G., *Les livres imprimés à Genève de 1550 à 1600* (Geneva, 1966).

Choisy, E., *La théocratie à Genève au temps de Calvin* (Geneva, 1897).

Courvoisier, J., *La notion d'église chez Bucer dans son développement historique* (Paris, 1933).

— 'La haute école de Genève au XVIe siècle', *Theologische Zeitschrift* 35 (1979), 169–76.

Delarue, H., 'La première offensive évangélique à Genève, 1532–33', *Bulletin de la société d'histoire et d'archéologie de Genève* 9 (1948), 83–102.

Dufour, A., 'L'affaire de Maligny vue à travers la correspondance de Calvin et de Bèze', *Cahiers d'histoire* 8 (1963), 269–80.

— 'De la bourgeoisie de Genève à la noblesse de Savoie', in *Mélanges d'histoire économique et sociale en hommage Antony Babel* (Geneva, 1963), 227–38.

— 'Le mythe de Genève au temps de Calvin', in *Histoire politique et psychologie historique* (Geneva, 1966), 63–95.

Ganoczy, A., *La bibliothèque de l'Académie de Calvin* (Geneva, 1969). Gauthier, J.-A., *Histoire de Genève des origines à l'année 1691* (9 vols: Geneva, 1896–1914).

Gauthier, L., *L'hôpital général de Genève de 1535 à 1545* (Geneva, 1914).

Geisendorf, P.-F., *Les annalistes genevois du début du XVIIe siècle* (Geneva, 1942).

— *L'Université de Genève, 1559–1959* (Geneva, 1959).

— 'Lyon et Genève du XVIe siècle au XVIIIe siècle', *Cahiers d'histoire* 5 (1960), 65–76.

— 'Métiers et conditions sociales du premier refuge à Genève, 1549–87', in

Mélanges d'histoire économique et sociale en hommage Antony Babel (Geneva, 1963), 239–49.

Gioffré, D., *Gênes et les foires de change: de Lyon à Besançon* (Paris, 1960).

Guerdon, R., *La vie quotidienne à Genève au temps de Calvin* (Paris, 1973).

de Jussy, J., *Le levain du Calvinisme, ou commencement de l'hérésie de Genève* (Geneva, 1865).

Kaden, E.-H., *Le jurisconsulte Germain Colladon, ami de Jean Calvin et de Théodore de Bèze* (Geneva, 1974).

Kingdon, R. M., *Geneva and the Coming of the Wars of Religion in France, 1555–1563* (Geneva, 1956).

— 'The Business Activities of Printers Henri and François Estienne', in *Aspects de la propagande religieuse* (Geneva, 1957), 258–75.

— *Geneva and the Consolidation of the French Protestant Movement 1564–1572* (Geneva, 1967).

— 'The Deacons of the Reformed Church in Calvin's Geneva', in *Mélanges d'histoire du XVIe siècle* (Geneva, 1970), 81–9.

— 'Social Welfare in Calvin's Geneva', *American Historical Review* 76 (1971), 50–69.

— 'The Control of Morals in Calvin's Geneva', in Buck, L. P., and Zophy, J. W. (eds), *The Social History of the Reformation*, (Colombus, Ohio, 1972), 3–16.

— 'Was the Protestant Reformation a Revolution? The Case of Geneva', in Kingdon, R. M., (ed.), *Transition and Revolution: Problems and Issues of European Renaissance and Reformation* (Minneapolis, 1974), 53–76.

— 'Calvin and the Government of Geneva', in Neusner, W. H. (ed.), *Calvinus ecclesiae Genevensis custos* (Frankfurt/Berne, 1984), 49–67.

Labarthe, O., 'En marge de l'édition des Registres de la Compagnie des pasteurs de Genève: le changement du mode de présidence de la Compagnie, 1578–1580', *Revue d'histoire ecclésiastique suisse* 67 (1972), 160–86.

Mandrou, R., 'Les français hors de France aux XVIe et XVIIe siècles. I: A Genève, le premier refuge protestant (1549–1560)', *Annales ESC* 14 (1959), 663–75.

Martin, P.-E., 'Les origines de la civitas et de l'évêché de Genève', in *Mélanges d'histoire et de littérature offerts à Charles Gilliard* (Lausanne, 1944), 82–92.

— *Histoire de Genève des origines à 1798* (Geneva, 1951).

— 'Calvin et le prêt à intérêt à Genève', in *Mélanges d'histoire économique et sociale en hommage Antony Babel* (Geneva, 1963), 251–63.

Monter, E. W., 'Le change public à Genève, 1568–1581', in *Mélanges d'histoire économique et sociale en hommage Antony Babel* (Geneva, 1963), 265–90.

— *Studies in Genevan Government (1536–1605)* (Geneva, 1964).

— *Calvin's Geneva* (New York/London: Wiley, 1967).

— 'Crime and Punishment in Calvin's Geneva', *ARG* 69 (1973), 281–7.

— 'The Consistory of Geneva, 1559–1569', *BHR* 38 (1976), 467–84.

— 'Historical Demography and Religious History in Sixteenth-Century Geneva', *Journal of Inter-Disciplinary History* 9 (1979), 399–427.

Naef, H., 'Un alchimiste au XVIe siècle; ou Battonat, la Seigneurie de Genève, et le comte de Gruyère', *Mémoires et documents de la société d'histoire de la Suisse Romande* 2 (1946), 7–304.

— *Les origines de la Réforme à Genève* (2 vols: Geneva, 1968).

Olson, J. E., 'La Bourse française de Genève: les années d'origine', *Revue du vieux Genève* 17 (1987), 16–20.

Perrenaud, A., *La population de Genève, XVIe – XIXe siècles* (Geneva, 1979).
Roget, A., *Histoire du peuple de Genève depuis la Réforme jusqu'à l'escalade* (7 vols: Geneva, 1870–83).
Stadler, P., *Genf, die großen Mächte und die eidgenössischen Glaubensparteien 1571–1584* (Zurich, 1952).
Turchetti, M., *Concordia o tolleranza? François Badouin (1520–1573) e i 'Moyenneurs'* (Geneva, 1984).

Calvin's Thought

Alting von Geusau, L. G. M., *Die Lehre von der Kindertaufe bei Calvin* (Bilthoven/ Mainz, 1963).
Anderson, M., 'Theodore Beza: Savant or Scholastic?', *Theologische Zeitschrift* 43 (1987), 320–32.
— 'John Calvin: Biblical Preacher (1539–1564)', *SJTh* 42 (1989), 167– 81.
Autin, A., *L'Institution chrétienne de Calvin* (Paris, 1929).
Babelotsky, G., *Platonischer Bilder und Gedankengänge in Calvins Lehre vom Menschen* (Wiesbaden, 1977).
Balke, W., 'The Word of God and Experientia according to Calvin', in Neuser, W. H. (ed.), *Calvinus ecclesiae doctor* (Kampen, 1978), 19–31.
Barth, P., 'Die fünf Einleitungskapitel von Calvins Institutio', *Kirchenblatt für die reformierte Schweiz* 40 (1925), 41–2, 45–7, 49–50.
Battenhouse, R. W., 'The Doctrine of Man in Calvin and in Renaissance Platonism', *JHI* 9 (1948), 447–71.
Battles, F. L., 'God was accommodating Himself to Human Capacity', *Interpretation* 31 (1977), 19–38.
Bauke, H., *Die Probleme der Theologie Calvins* (Leipzig, 1922).
Biéler, A., *La pensée économique et sociale de Calvin* (Geneva, 1959).
— *Calvin, prophète de l'ère industrielle* (Geneva, 1964).
Blanke, F., 'Calvins Urteil über Zwingli', *Zwingliana* 11 (1959), 66–92.
Bohatec, J., *Calvin und das Recht* (Graz, 1934).
— 'Calvin et la procédure civile à Genève', *Revue historique de droit français et étranger* 17 (1938), 229–303.
— *Budé und Calvin: Studien zur Gedankenwelt des französischen Frühhumanismus* (Graz, 1950).
Breen, Q., 'John Calvin and the Rhetorical Tradition', *Church History* 26 (1957), 3–21.
— 'Some Aspects of Humanist Rhetoric and the Reformation', *NAK* 43 (1960), 1–14.
— *John Calvin: A Study in French Humanism* (Hamden, 2nd edn, 1968).
Büsser, F., *Calvins Urteil über sich selbst* (Zurich, 1950).
— 'Bullinger et Calvin', *Etudes théologiques et religieuses* 63 (1988), 31–52.
Cadier, J., 'Calvin et Saint Augustin', in *Augustinus Magister* (Paris, 1954), 1039–56.
Calvetti, C., *La filosofia di Giovanni Calvino* (Milan, 1955).
Chenevière, M. E., *La pensée politique de Calvin* (Paris, 1937).
Courvoisier, J., 'Réflexions à propos de la doctrine eucharistique de Zwingle et Calvin', in *Festgabe Leonhard von Muralt* (Zurich, 1970), 258–65.
— *De la Réforme au Protestantisme: essai d'ecclésiologie réformée* (Paris, 1977).

Dankbaar, W. F., *Calvin, sein Weg und sein Werk* (Neukirchen, 1959).
— 'L'office des docteurs chez Calvin', in *Regards contemporains sur Jean Calvin* (Strasbourg, 1964), 102–26.
Douglass, E. J. D., *Women, Freedom and Calvin* (Philadelphia, 1985).
Dowey, E. A., *The Knowledge of God in Calvin's Theology* (New York, 1952).
Eire, C. M. N., 'Calvin and Nicodemitism: A Reappraisal', *SCJ* 10 (1979), 45–69.
Engel, M. P., *Calvin's Perspectival Anthropology* (Atlanta, Ga., 1988).
Ganoczy, A., 'Calvin als paulinischer Theologe. Ein Forschungsansatz zur Hermeneutik Calvins', in Neuser, W. (ed.), *Calvinus Theologus* (Neukirchen, 1976), 36–69.
— *The Young Calvin* (Philadelphia, 1987).
— and Müller, K., *Calvins handschriftliche Annotationen zu Chrysostomus* (Wiesbaden, 1981).
— and Scheld, S., *Herrschaft, Tugend, Vorsehung: Hermeneutische Deutung und Veröffentlichung handschriftlicher Annotationen Calvins zu sieben Senecatragödien* (Wiesbaden, 1982).
Gerrish, B. A., 'The Word of God and the Word of Scripture: Luther and Calvin on Biblical Authority', in *The Old Protestantism and the New: Essays on the Reformation Heritage* (Chicago, 1982), 51–68.
Girardin, B., *Rhétorique et théologique: Calvin, le Commentaire de l'Epître aux Romains* (Paris, 1979).
Goumaz, L., *La doctrine du salut (doctrina salutis) d'après les commentaires de Jean Calvin sur le Nouveau Testament* (Lausanne/Paris, 1917).
Graham, W. F., *The Constructive Revolutionary: John Calvin and His Socio-Economic Impact* (Richmond, Va., 1971).
Grislis, E., 'Calvin's Use of Cicero in the Institutes I:1–5 – A Case Study in Theological Method', *ARG* 62 (1971), 5–37.
Hall, B., 'The Calvin Legend', in Duffield, G. E. (ed.), *John Calvin*, (Abingdon, 1966), 1–18.
— 'Calvin against the Calvinists', in Duffield, G. E. (ed.), *John Calvin*, (Abingdon, 1966), 19–37.
— 'John Calvin, the Jurisconsults and the *Ius Civile*', in Cuming, G. J. (ed.), *Studies in Church History*, (Leiden, 1966), 202–16.
Hancock, R. C., *Calvin and the Foundations of Modern Politics* (Ithaca, N.Y., 1989).
Higman, F. M., *The Style of John Calvin in His French Polemical Treatises* (Oxford, 1967).
Holl, K., 'Johannes Calvin', in *Gesammelte Aufsätze zur Kirchengeschichte* (3 vols: Tübingen, 1928), vol. 3, 254–84.
Höpfl, H., *The Christian Polity of John Calvin* (Cambridge, 1985).
Jacobs, P., *Prädestination und Verantwortlichkeit bei Calvin* (Kassel, 1937).
Kaiser, C. B., 'Calvin, Copernicus and Castellio', *Calvin Theological Journal* 21 (1986), 5–31.
— 'Calvin's Understanding of Aristotelian Natural Philosophy', in Schnucker, R. V. (ed.), *Calviniana: Ideas and Influence of Jean Calvin* (Kirksville, Mo., 1988), 77–92.
Koch, E., 'Erwägungen zum Bekehrungsbericht Calvins', *NAK* 61 (1981), 185–97.
Lane, A. N. S., 'Calvin's Sources of St Bernard', *ARG* 67 (1976), 253–83.

— 'Calvin's Use of the Fathers and Medievals', *Calvin Theological Journal* 16 (1981), 149–205.
McDonnell, K., *John Calvin, the Church and the Eucharist* (Princeton, 1967).
McGrath, A. E., 'John Calvin and Late Medieval Thought: A Study in Late Medieval Influences upon Calvin's Theological Thought', *ARG* 77 (1986), 58–78.
Marmelstein, J.-W., *Etude comparative des textes latins et français de l'Institution de la Religion chrestienne par Jean Calvin* (Paris/Groningen/The Hague, 1921).
Mercier, C., 'L'esprit de Calvin et la démocratie', *Revue d'histoire écclesiastique* 30 (1934), 5–53.
Milner, B. C., *Calvin's Doctrine of the Church* (Leiden, 1970).
Niesel, W., 'Calvin wider Osianders Rechtfertigungslehre', *Zeitschrift für Kirchengeschichte* 46 (1928), 410–30.
— 'Verstand Calvin deutsch?', *Zeitschrift für Kirchengeschichte* 49 (1930), 343–58.
— *The Theology of Calvin* (London, 1956).
Pannier, J., *Calvin et l'épiscopat* (Strasbourg, 1927).
— 'Une première *Institution* française dès 1537', *RHPhR* 8 (1928), 513–34.
Parker, T. H. L., *The Oracles of God: An Introduction to the Preaching of John Calvin* (London, 1962).
— *Calvin's Doctrine of the Knowledge of God* (Edinburgh, rev. edn, 1969).
— *Calvin's New Testament Commentaries* (London, 1971).
— *Calvin's Old Testament Commentaries* (Edinburgh, 1986).
Partee, C., *Calvin and Classical Philosophy* (Leiden, 1977).
— 'Calvin's Central Dogma Again', *SCJ* 18 (1987), 191–9.
Peter, R., 'Rhétorique et prédication selon Calvin', *Revue d'histoire et de philosophie religieuses* 55 (1975), 249–72.
Pfeilschifter, F., *Das Calvinbild bei Bolsec und sein Fortwirken im französischen Katholizismus bis ins 20. Jahrhundert* (Augsburg, 1983).
Plath, U., *Calvin und Basel in den Jahren 1552–1556* (Basle/Stuttgart, 1974).
Reid, W. S., *John Calvin: His Influence in the Western World* (Grand Rapids, 1982).
Reuter, K., *Das Grundverständnis der Theologie Calvins* (Neukirchen, 1963).
— *Vom Scholaren bis zum jungen Reformator: Studien zum Werdegang Johannes Calvins* (Neukirchen, 1981).
Richard, L. J., *The Spirituality of John Calvin* (Atlanta, 1974).
Rist, G., 'La modernité de la méthode théologique de Calvin', *Revue de théologie et philosophie* 1 (1968), 19–33.
Rosen, E., 'Calvin's Attitude towards Copernicus', *JHI* 21 (1960), 431–41.
Ruff, H., *Die französischen Briefe Calvins: Versuch einer stylistischen Analyse* (Glarus, 1937).
Santmire, P. H., 'Justification in Calvin's 1540 Romans Commentary', *Church History* 33 (1964), 294–313.
Schellong, D., *Das evangelische Gesetz in der Auslegung Calvins* (Munich, 1968).
—, *Calvins Auslegung der synoptsichen Evangelien* (Munich, 1969).
Scholl, H., *Calvinus Catholicus: Die katholische Calvinforschung im 20. Jahrhundert* (Freiburg, 1974).
Selinger, S., *Calvin against Himself: An Inquiry in Intellectual History* (Hamden, Conn., 1984).
Smits, L., *Saint Augustin dans l'oeuvre de Jean Calvin* (Louvain, 1957).
Sprenger, P., *Das Rätsel um die Bekehrung Calvins* (Neukirchen, 1960).
Stauffer, R., *L'humanité de Calvin* (Neuchatel, 1964).

— 'Le discours à la première personne dans les sermons de Calvin', in *Regards contemporains sur Jean Calvin* (Paris, 1965), 206–38.

— *Dieu, la création et la providence dans la prédication de Calvin* (Berne, 1978).

Steinmetz, D. C., 'Calvin and the Absolute Power of God', *Journal of Medieval and Renaissance Studies* 18 (1988), 65–79.

— 'Calvin and Abraham: The Interpretation of Romans 4 in the Sixteenth Century', *Church History* 57 (1988), 443–55.

Thompson, J. L., 'Creata ad imaginem Dei, licet secundo gradu: Woman as the Image of God according to John Calvin', *HThR* 81 (1988), 125–43.

Torrance, T. F., *Calvin's Doctrine of Man* (London, 1952).

— 'La philosophie et la théologie de Jean Mair ou Major (1469–1550)', *Archives de philosophie* 32 (1969), 531–47; 33 (1970), 261–94.

— 'Intuitive and Abstractive Knowledge from Duns Scotus to John Calvin', in *De doctrina Ioannis Duns Scoti: Acta tertii Congressus Scotistici Internationalis* (Rome, 1972), 291–305.

— *The Hermeneutics of John Calvin* (Edinburgh, 1988).

Tranquilli, V., *Il concetto di lavoro da Aristotele a Calvino* (Naples, 1979).

Trinkaus, C., 'Renaissance Problems in Calvin's Theology', in Peery, W. (ed.), *Studies in the Renaissance I* (Austin, 1954), 59–80.

Van't Spijker, W., 'Prädestination bei Bucer und Calvin', in Neuser, W. (ed.), *Calvinus Theologicus* (Neukirchen, 1976), 85–111.

Wallace, R. S., *Calvin's Doctrine of the Word and Sacrament* (Edinburgh, 1953).

— *Calvin's Doctrine of the Christian Life* (Edinburgh, 1959).

Warfield, B. B., *Calvin and Augustine* (Philadelphia, 1956).

— *Calvin et l'humanisme* (Paris, 1976).

Willis, E. D., *Calvin's Catholic Christology* (Leiden, 1966).

— 'Rhetoric and Responsibility in Calvin's Theology', in McKelway, A. J., and Willis, E. D. (eds), *The Context of Contemporary Theology* (Atlanta, Ga., 1974), 43–63.

Zeeden, E. W., 'Das Bild Luthers in der Briefen Calvins', *ARG* 11 (1959), 66–92.

Zimmermann, A., 'Calvins Auseinandersetzung mit Osianders Rechtfertigungslehre', *Kerygma und Dogma* 35 (1989), 236–56.

Calvinism

Ahlstrom, S., *A Religious History of the American People* (New Haven, 1972).

Armstrong, B. G., *Calvinism and the Amyraut Heresy: Protestant Scholasticism and Humanism in Seventeenth-Century France* (Madison, Wis., 1969).

Ball, B. W., *A Great Expectation: Eschatological Thought in English Protestantism to 1660* (Leiden, 1975).

Baron, H., 'Calvinist Republicanism and Its Historical Roots', *Church History* 7 (1939), 30–42.

Bercovitch, S., *The Puritan Origins of the American Self* (New Haven/London, 1975).

Besnard, P., *Protestantisme et capitalisme: la controverse post-wébérienne* (Paris, 1970).

Boettner, L., *The Reformed Doctrine of Predestination* (Grand Rapids, 1968).

Bohatec, J., '"Lutherisch" und "Reformiert"', *Reformiertes Kirchenblatt für Österreich* 28 (January, 1951), 1–3.

Bourchenin, D., *Etude sur les Académies Protestantes en France au XVIe et au XVIIe siècles* (Paris, 1882).

Cadix, M., 'Le calvinisme et l'expérience religieuse', in *Etudes sur Calvin et le calvinisme* (Paris, 1936), 173–87.

Caldwell, P., *The Puritan Conversion Narrative: The Beginnings of American Expression* (Cambridge, 1986).

Cohn, H. J., 'The Territorial Princes in Germany's Second Reformation', in Prestwich, M. (ed.), *International Calvinism 1541–1715* (Oxford, 1985), 135–66.

Collinson, P., 'Calvinism with an Anglican Face', in Baker, D. (ed.), *Reform and Reformation: England and the Continent* (Oxford, 1979), 71–102.

— 'England and International Calvinism, 1558–1640', in Prestwich, M. (ed.), *International Calvinism 1541–1715* (Oxford, 1985), 197–224.

Costello, W. T., *The Scholastic Curriculum in Early Seventeenth-Century Cambridge* (Cambridge, Mass., 1958).

Donnelly, J. P., 'Italian Influences on the Development of Calvinist Scholasticism', *SCJ* 7/1 (1976), 81–101.

— *Calvinism and Scholasticism in Vermigli's Doctrine of Man and Grace* (Leiden, 1976).

— 'Calvinist Thomism', *Viator* 7 (1976), 441–5.

Duke, A., 'The Ambivalent Face of Calvinism in the Netherlands, 1561–1618', in Prestwich, M. (ed.), *International Calvinism 1541–1715* (Oxford, 1985), 109–35.

Evans, R. J. W., *The Wechsel Presses: Humanism and Calvinism in Central Europe 1572–1627* (*Past and Present* Supplement 2: London, 1975).

— 'Calvinism in East Central Europe: Hungary and her Neighbours, 1540–1700', in Prestwich, M. (ed.), *International Calvinism 1541–1715* (Oxford, 1985), 167–96.

Fatio, O., *Méthode et théologie: Lambert Daneau et les débuts de la scholastique réformée* (Geneva, 1976).

— 'Présence de Calvin à l'époque de l'orthodoxie réformée: les abrégés de Calvin à la fin du 16e et au 17e siècle', in Neuser, W. H. (ed.), *Calvinus ecclesiae doctor* (Kampen, 1978), 171–207.

Foster, S., *Their Solitary Way: The Puritan Social Ethic in the First Century of Settlement in New England* (New Haven, 1971).

Freeberg, D. A., *Iconoclasm and Painting in the Netherlands, 1566–1609* (Oxford, unpublished thesis, 1972).

Goodzwaard, R., *Capitalism and Progress* (Grand Rapids, 1979).

Green, R. W. (ed.), *Protestantism and Capitalism: The Weber Thesis and Its Critics* (Boston, Mass., 1959).

— (ed.), *Protestantism, Capitalism and Social Science: The Weber Thesis Controversy* (Boston, Mass., 1973).

Greven, P., *The Protestant Temperament: Patterns of Child-Rearing, Religious Experience and the Self in Early America* (New York, 1977).

Gründler, O., *Die Gotteslehre Giralmo Zanchis* (Neukirchen, 1965).

Hill, C., *The Intellectual Origins of the English Revolution* (Oxford, 1965).

Jamieson, J. F., 'Jonathan Edwards's Change of Position on Stoddardeanism', *HThR* 74 (1981), 79–99.

Kendall, R. T., *The Influence of Calvin and Calvinism upon the American Heritage* (London, 1976).

— *Calvin and English Calvinism to 1649* (Oxford, 1980).

Kickel, W., *Vernunft und Offenbarung bei Theodor Beza* (Neukirchen, 1967).

Kingdon, R. M., 'The First Expression of Theodore Beza's Political Ideas', *ARG* 46 (1955), 88–99.

— 'Calvinism and Democracy: Some Political Implications of Debates on French Reformed Church Government, 1562–1572', *American Historical Review* 69 (1964), 393–401.

Labrousse, E., 'Calvinism in France, 1598–1685', in Prestwich, M. (ed.), *International Calvinism 1541–1715* (Oxford, 1985), 285–314.

Laplanche, F., *Orthodoxie et prédication: l'oeuvre d'Amyraut et la querelle de la grâce universelle* (Paris, 1965).

Lehmann, H., *Das Zeitalter des Absolutismus: Gottesgnadentum und Kriegsnot* (Stuttgart, 1980).

— 'The Cultural Importance of the Pious Middle Classes in 17th-Century Protestant Society', in von Greyerz, H. (ed.), *Religion and Society in Modern Europe* (London, 1984), 33–41.

Lewis, G., 'Calvinism in Geneva in the Time of Calvin and Beza', in Prestwich, M. (ed.), *International Calvinism 1541–1715* (Oxford, 1985), 39–70.

Liedtke, H., *Die Pädagogik der werdenden Orthodoxie: Ein Beitrag zur Bestimmung der Verhältnisses von Reformation und Humanismus* (Königsdorf, 1968).

Lüthy, H., 'Variations on a Theme by Max Weber', in Prestwich, M. (ed.), *International Calvinism 1541–1715* (Oxford, 1985), 369–90.

Lynch, M., 'Calvinism in Scotland, 1559–1638', in Prestwich, M. (ed.), *International Calvinism 1541–1715* (Oxford, 1985), 225–56.

McComish, W. A., *The Epigones: A Study of the Genevan Academy* (Allison Park, Pa., 1989).

McKim, D. K., *Ramism in William Perkin's Theology* (Berne, 1987).

McNeill, J. T., *The History and Character of Calvinism* (New York, 1954).

Marshall, G., *Presbyteries and Profits: Calvinism and the Development of Capitalism in Scotland, 1560–1707* (Oxford, 1980).

— *In Search of the Spirit of Capitalism: An Essay on Max Weber's Protestant Ethic Thesis* (London, 1982).

Meylan, H., 'Collèges et académies protestantes en France au XVIe siècle', in *Actes du 95e congrès national des sociétés savantes* 2 vols: Paris, 1971), vol. 1, 301–8.

Miegge, M., *Vocation et travail: essai sur l'éthique puritaine* (Geneva, 1989).

Moltmann, J., 'Prädestination und Heilsgeschichte bei Moyse Amyraut', *Zeitschrift für Kirchengeschichte* 65 (1954), 270–303.

Morgan, E., *The Puritan Family* (Boston, Mass., 1966).

Mosse, G. L., *Calvinism: Authoritarian or Democratic?* (New York, 1957).

Muller, R. A., '*Vera philosophia cum sacra theologia nunquam pugnat*: Keckermann on Philosophy, Theology and the Problem of Double Truth', *SCJ* 15 (1984), 341–65.

— 'Scholasticism Protestant and Catholic: Francis Turretin on the Object and Principles of Theology', *Church History* 55 (1986), 193–205.

Neuser, W., 'Die Väter des Heidelberger Katechismus', *Theologische Zeitschrift* 35 (1979), 177–94.

Nürenberger, R., *Die Politisierung des französischen Protestantismus: Calvin und die Anfänge des protestantischen Radikalismus* (Tübingen, 1948).

Platt, J., *Reformed Thought and Scholasticism: The Arguments for the Existence of God in Dutch Theology, 1575–1670* (Leiden, 1982).

Prestwich, M., 'Le mécénat et les protestants en France, 1598–1661: architectes et peintres', in Mesnard, J., and Mousnier, R. (eds), *L'Age d'Or du mécénat* (Paris, 1985), 77–88.

— 'Calvinism in France, 1559–1629', in Prestwich, M. (ed.), *International Calvinism 1541–1715* (Oxford, 1985), 71–108.

— 'Introduction', in Prestwich, M. (ed.), *International Calvinism 1541–1715* (Oxford, 1985).

Ritschl, D., 'Der Beitrag des Calvinismus für die Entwicklung des Menschenrechtsgedankens in Europa und Nordamerika', *Evangelische Theologie* 40 (1980), 333–45.

Rüsch, E. G., 'Eine private Bearbeitung der Institutio Calvins', *Theologische Zeitschrift* 24 (1968), 427–34.

Schmidt, A.-M., *Jean Calvin et la tradition calvinienne* (Paris, 1957).

Schweizer, A., *Die protestantischen Centraldogmen in ihrer Entwicklung innerhalb der reformierten Kirche* (2 vols: Zurich, 1854–6).

Skinner, Q., 'The Origins of the Calvinist Theory of Revolution', in Malament, B. C. (ed.), *After the Reformation* (Philadelphia, 1980), 309–30.

Speck, W. A., and Billington, L., 'Calvinism in Colonial North America, 1630–1715', in Prestwich, M. (ed.), *International Calvinism 1541–1715* (Oxford, 1985), 257–84.

Stauffer, R., 'Le Calvinisme et les universités', *BSHPF* 126 (1980), 27–51.

Torrance, J. B., 'Covenant or Contract? A Study of the Theological Background of Worship in Seventeenth-Century Scotland', *SJTh* 23 (1970), 51–76.

— 'The Covenant Concept in Scottish Theology and Politics and Its Legacy', *SJTh* 34 (1981), 225–43.

Vahle, H., 'Calvinismus und Demokratie im Spiegel der Forschung', *ARG* 66 (1982), 181–212.

Wallace, D. D., *Puritans and Predestination: Grace in English Protestant Theology, 1525–1695* (Chapel Hill, 1982).

Walzer, M., *Revolution of the Saints* (New York, 1970).

Weber, Max, *The Protestant Ethic and the Spirit of Capitalism* (London, 1930).

Yardeni, M., 'French Calvinist Political Thought, 1534–1715', in Prestwich, M. (ed.), *International Calvinism 1541–1715* (Oxford, 1985), 315–38.

Zaret, D., *The Heavenly Contract: Ideology and Organization in Pre-Revolutionary Puritanism* (Chicago, 1985).

Zeeden, E. W., *Die Entstehung der Konfessionen: Grundlagen und Formen der Konfessionsbildung im Zeitalter der Glaubenskampf* (Freiburg, 1967).

Zeller, W., *Theologie und Frömmigkeit: Gesammelte Aufsätze* (2 vols: Marburg, 1971–8).

Index